GLORIOUS FAILURE

ROBERT IVERMEE

Glorious Failure

The Forgotten History of French Imperialism in India

HURST & COMPANY, LONDON

First published in the United Kingdom in 2025 by
C. Hurst & Co. (Publishers) Ltd.,
New Wing, Somerset House, Strand, London, WC2R 1LA

A Cataloguing-in-Publication data record for this book
is available from the British Library.

ISBN: 9781805262954

Printed and bound in Great Britain by Bell & Bain Ltd, Glasgow

www.hurstpublishers.com

CONTENTS

LIST OF ILLUSTRATIONS

ACKNOWLEDGEMENTS

Research for this book was carried out in France, India and the United Kingdom. I am grateful to staff at the following institutions for their help and advice. In France: the Bibliothèque nationale de France, Paris; the Archives nationales, Paris; the Archives nationales d'outre-mer, Aix-en-Provence; the Archives diplomatiques du Ministère des Affaires étrangères, La Courneuve; the École française d'Extrême-Orient, Paris; the Bibliothèque universitaire des langues et civilisations, Paris; and the Musée de la Compagnie des Indes, Lorient. In India: the Institut français de Pondichéry, where I was hosted for a short stay; the École française d'Extrême-Orient, Pondicherry; and the Institut de Chandernagor (Indo-French Cultural Centre and Museum, Chandannagar). In the United Kingdom: the British Library, London; and SOAS University of London.

Colleagues at the Catholic University of Paris and Université Paris Cité are thanked for their support for the project, in particular Estelle Murail, John Dean, Ladan Niayesh and Stéphanie Prévost. The final chapters of the book were written during a stay as visiting scholar at Christ University, Bengaluru, for which special thanks are offered to Fr. Jose C. C. and Madhumati Deshpande. For their interest, encouragement and hospitality along the way, I should also mention Charles-Hubert de Brant, Rafaël Malangin, Sunam Mukherjee, Ramnath Reghunadhan, Meeuwis van Rijswijk, Priscilla Namrata Rozario, Anne Vallet and Anna Varghese. Michael Dwyer, Mei Jayne Yew, Lara Weisweiller-Wu, Kathleen May, Daisy Leitch,

Niamh Drennan and the rest of the team at Hurst have been a pleasure to work with, and the comments of the two anonymous reviewers of the manuscript were much appreciated. Sebastian Ballard must be thanked for producing the maps that accompany the text.

Glorious Failure would never have been written had I not met Jeanne Constans. Beyond reviewing the manuscript, she has challenged me to think much more about questions of identity, power and privilege which are vital to understanding not only the history of empire but the world today.

The work is dedicated to my parents, Sue and Fred Ivermee, who instilled a love of books in me from a young age and have always supported my projects. The football team that I support because of them has accustomed me to reflecting on failure.

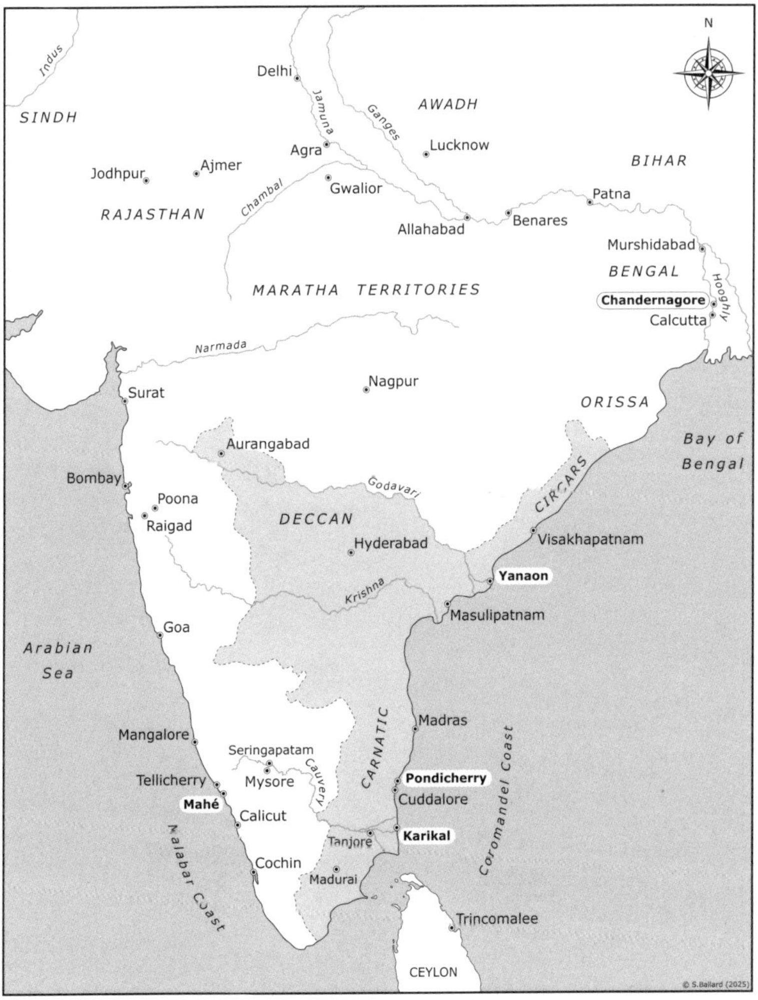

Map 1: Eighteenth-century India, showing the French colonies of Pondicherry, Karikal, Yanaon, Mahé and Chandernagore. The shaded area indicates French territories, territorial claims and areas of indirect control at the height of French imperial expansion (1750–54).

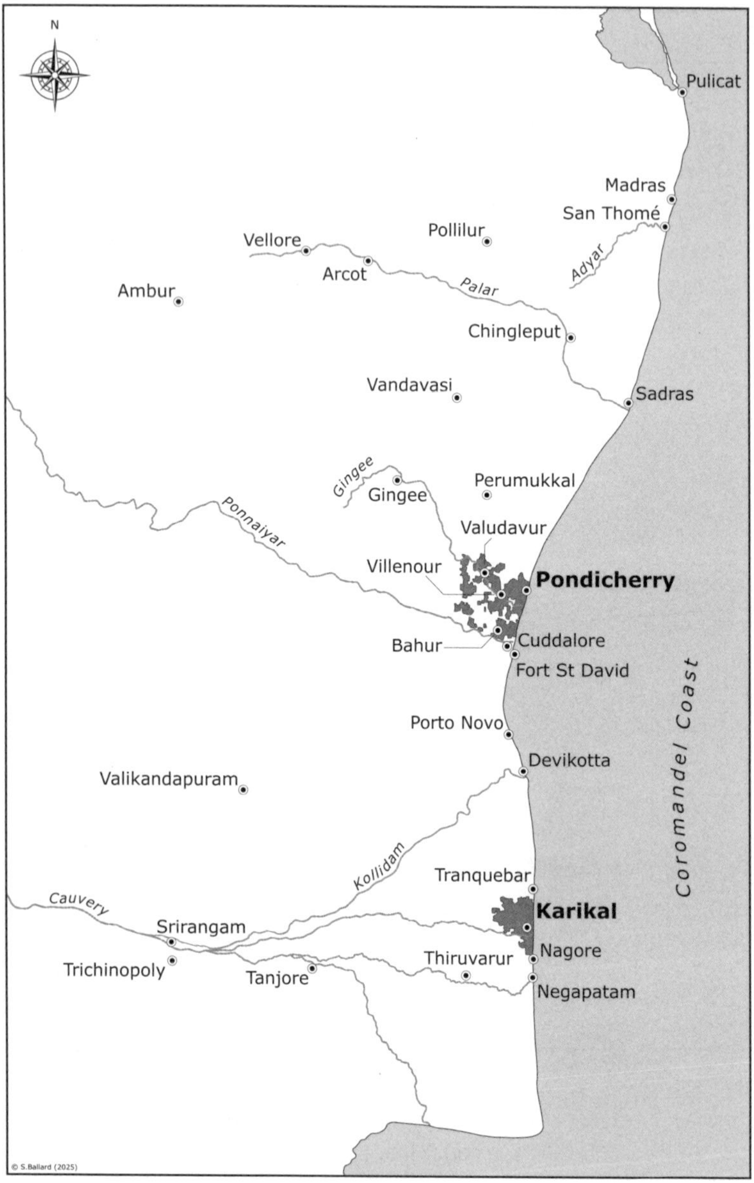

Map 2: The Carnatic and the Coromandel Coast. Pondicherry, Karikal and the surrounding marked territories were restored to France in 1816, after the Revolutionary and Napoleonic Wars, and only formally relinquished in 1962.

1

GLORIOUS FAILURE

At ten minutes to midnight, the prime minister in waiting of independent India takes to the podium in the nation's constituent assembly. Around the country, hundreds of thousands of people gather around radio sets to follow the historic moment. Millions more congregate in public squares and parks, where his speech will be relayed as part of joyous independence celebrations. In flawless, flowing French, he begins:

> Il y a bien longtemps, nous avons pris rendez-vous avec le destin. L'heure est venue d'honorer cet engagement. À minuit, quand le monde s'endormira, l'Inde s'éveillera à la vie et à la liberté.
>
> (Translation: 'Long years ago, we made a tryst with destiny, and now the time comes when we shall redeem our pledge. At the stroke of the midnight hour, when the world sleeps, India will awake to life and freedom.')[1]

The next morning, two hundred years of French rule over India is at an end. The blue, white and red tricolour of France is ceremoniously lowered from public buildings across the country and replaced by the saffron, white and green tricolour of India. The evacuation of French soldiers and civil servants begins, with much fanfare accompanying the departure of the first Europe-bound vessel from the great southern metropolis of Pondicherry. From the tiny enclaves of Calcutta, Madras and Bombay, the British look on, determined to maintain their presence on the subcontinent for as long as possible.

The scenario is counter-factual—reversing the positions of the French and British on the subcontinent at the moment of India's independence in 1947—but it is not far-fetched. For more than three hundred years, from the reign of Louis XIV to the post-war presidency of Charles de Gaulle, France maintained a colonial presence in India. During the first half of this period, from the premiership of Jean-Baptiste Colbert to the downfall of Napoleon, France was an aggressive imperial power on the subcontinent, attempting to extend its power, influence, territory and revenues through the threat and use of force. Through their East India company and state, the French established a far-reaching empire in India, only to see their dominant position undermined by conflict with local rulers, competition from other European nations and a series of strategic mistakes. Events during this period might well have turned out differently. If they had, France, rather than the United Kingdom, would likely have ruled India well into the twentieth century.

Far from being a great metropolis, Pondicherry today is a modest city of about twenty square kilometres and 350,000 people.[2] In the historic streets of its 'White Town', closest to the sea, the former French presence is visible at every turn. Stately public buildings like the *hôtel de ville* and the *chambre de commerce* have their function written across the doorway in the language of Molière. The grand, pink church of Notre Dame des Anges has a statue of Jeanne d'Arc in its garden, and the monument in the city park has echoes of the Arc de Triomphe. An arresting memorial to the soldiers of the 'French Indies' killed during the First World War is lit up in the blue, white and red of the *tricolore* after dark, attracting the attention of evening strollers. Colonial-era mansions line the streets, some hidden behind high walls. Many have been turned into boutique hotels with names like 'Hôtel de l'Orient' and 'Le Château', or trendy restaurants like 'Rendezvous'. A board on the seafront promenade welcomes visitors to 'The French Riviera of the East'.

In the city, there are alas few clues as to how Pondicherry became French or what happened next. The government museum includes a cannon, guns and swords, some period furniture, a vase from China and a palanquin, among the eclectic range of artefacts on display, but offers little explanation for the French presence. A short text in the corner of one room says only that France made Pondicherry 'a centre of trade' and a capital 'for all French territory in India'. No explanations accompany the street corner signs. The names that they display, like Rue François Martin, Rue Suffren and Rue de la Compagnie, remain shrouded in mystery. At the southern end of the promenade, on an oversized plinth, is the statue of a Marquis Dupleix, dressed in the waistcoat and jacket of an eighteenth-century notable. No details about the marquis are offered, however, not even the dates of his life or his first name. The inscription on the plinth states simply that the statue was erected in his memory in 1870 and moved to its current location in 1982. The rest must either have been forgotten or omitted.

Beyond Pondicherry, it is clear that a similar combination of forgetting and omission exists elsewhere concerning the history of French India. In France, discussions about colonialism and its legacies—when they take place at all—focus on North and Sub-Saharan Africa, with the Caribbean and Southeast Asia sometimes added on. While some awareness exists of French imperialism in the nineteenth and twentieth centuries—and perhaps of the early modern colonisation of North America—events in India are largely unknown. The Parisian descending at Dupleix metro station is no more likely than the Pondicherian walking past his statue to know who the marquis was. A similar incomprehension is probable on Avenue de Suffren, in the shadow of the Eiffel Tower, and Rue Suffren in the White Town. In India, meanwhile, colonialism is synonymous with the British and, to a lesser extent, with the Portuguese in Goa. French India rarely figures in the museums up and down the country dedicated to the nationalist movement and independence. No popular films have been produced depicting Indian heroes struggling against French rule.

Only, perhaps, within the world of academia is significant understanding of the history of French India to be found. In French universities and at the French Institute of Pondicherry—a research establishment financed and supervised by France—a small number of scholars continue to study France's historic presence in South Asia. Over the last two decades, they have been joined by a new generation of academics in the United Kingdom and the United States producing interesting and innovative studies of aspects of French colonialism in the region. For the most part, however, these studies, which remain few in number, have had a narrower thematic focus and concentrated on a shorter time period than this book. As hard as it is to believe, not a single English-language work charting the origins, development and ultimate failure of French imperialism in India from the late seventeenth to the early nineteenth century has been published for more than a century. It is this remarkable lacuna that the present work aims to fill.[3]

The book begins with the events leading up to the foundation of the French East India Company—the Compagnie des Indes—in 1664. Its establishment of a foothold in India is considered, alongside its early commercial operations. Attention then turns to the development of the French in India into a major territorial power, as substantial conquests led to the establishment of French rule over significant parts of the subcontinent, notably during the governorship of Dupleix (1742–54). By the early 1750s, France was the dominant European power on the subcontinent, with large territories in its possession across southern India and the east coast, and a zone of influence established as far north as the Deccan. Ten years later, however, this empire had collapsed in the face of internal weakness and hostility from both Indian powers and Great Britain. Right up until the downfall of Napoleon, French parties would attempt to win it back, enlisting powerful new ideas like *liberté* (freedom) and the rights of man in a new wave of imperialist ventures.

The focus of the book is the official French presence in India: agents of the first Compagnie des Indes on the subcontinent (1664–1714) and of its successor, the Compagnie perpétuelle des Indes (1719–70), plus representatives of the French state—civil and military—who were regularly dispatched from the *patrie* and who took over the government of France's colonies in India when the second company was wound up. Frenchmen in India in other capacities—including merchants, missionaries and mercenaries—are also considered, particularly their collaborations with French officials and their efforts to advance their country's interests, in which the boundaries between formal and informal French actors were often blurred. While events in India are the book's concern, the impact of decisions made elsewhere, not least by directors of the companies in Paris and government ministers in Versailles, is considered. The consequences for the French in India of events in other parts of the world—Europe, the Americas and elsewhere in the Indian Ocean—are examined. Underpinning the book is an understanding that, despite major disruptions—including the collapse of the companies, repeated wars and a revolution—France maintained a colonial presence and acted in an imperialist way on the subcontinent throughout the 150 years being studied. Though Pondicherry and the wider Coromandel Coast were the epicentre of that presence, French actions across India—from Bengal to the Malabar Coast—are considered.

Three major threads run through the narrative. The first is rivalry between France and other European powers in India, particularly the Dutch and British. The Compagnie des Indes arrived in India some fifty to sixty years after its Dutch and English counterparts—the Verenigde Oostindische Compagnie (VOC) and the East India Company (EIC)—and was therefore playing catch-up from the start. At first the rivalry was primarily commercial, but this is not to say that it was peaceful, nor that political ambitions did not also inform French actions. Shaped by the prevailing economic orthodoxy of mercantilism—according to which a greater volume of trade between India and Europe could only be won at the expense of others involved in that trade—the Compagnie's presence in the Indian Ocean was underpinned by the threat of force from the outset, with its ships armed and a small army permanently stationed in its territories.[4] After only six years in India, this force was used against a European rival on the subcontinent for the first time, following the 1672 declaration of war between France and the Dutch Republic in Europe. In total, France would spend exactly half of the 150 years between 1665 and 1814 at war with other European powers.[5] Where those powers included the Dutch or British, India—like other parts of the world subject to European imperialism—became a theatre of war in which armed trading companies fought alongside state navies and armies. The object of those wars was increasingly power and territory, not just commercial gain.[6]

The second thread is the French engagement with diverse Indian powers. At first the Compagnie des Indes operated on the subcontinent at least in part with the permission of the rulers concerned, whether the Mughal Emperor (in the case of Surat and Bengal) or local powers on the Malabar and Coromandel coasts. The colony of Pondicherry was founded at the invitation of the Muslim governor of nearby Cuddalore. However, as local power struggles intensified in southern India, the Compagnie began lending its army to its allies and waging war against their opponents. For its support, it was handsomely rewarded with gifts, payments and grants of land, and its development as a territorial power accelerated. Before long, the French were playing a leading rather than a supporting role in local conflicts, waging war to install sympathetic and even compliant rulers in power in Indian courts. The establishment of direct control over large swathes of territory, from which large land revenues were expected, was accompanied by forced regime changes, creating an even more extensive French empire of influence. The collapse of this fledgling empire in 1761 did not fundamentally change the French approach: in the decades that followed, France attempted to arm and assist its allies, like the kingdom of Mysore, in their conflicts against other local powers and the British, with a view to 'liberating' the subcontinent rule from British rule and—at least for some of the Frenchmen involved—re-establishing a territorial empire.

The third thread is life within the colonies of French India and the French impact on Indian society and culture. In Pondicherry and the other colonies, the French cohort was always outnumbered by a much larger population from diverse Indian backgrounds. Large numbers of non-French people therefore lived under Compagnie and later crown rule—and later still, after the Revolution, under the 'blessings' of French republican government. Significant mixing of the French and Indian populations existed, including intermarriage, while the French relied upon Indian intermediaries speaking local languages to organise their business and conduct diplomacy, as we will see in chapter 4. Nevertheless, distinctions of ethnicity, nationality, religion, class, caste, gender and language were deeply embedded and had a major impact on social standing and access to rights, with white, French-born, French-speaking, Catholic men from the aristocracy or nobility at the top of the colonial hierarchy. Even after many years of residence in India, most French people spoke Indian languages poorly, and had little understanding of local religions, cultures and traditions. Their ignorance was often accompanied by assumptions of superiority—a state of affairs worsened by the presence in French territories of Catholic missionaries intent on evangelising local people. Beyond this, the book draws attention to something almost entirely ignored in existing studies of French India: the possession of slaves in the French colonies, and French slave trading between India and other parts of the Indian Ocean—a key commercial activity for the Compagnie and private French merchants. The failure of the Revolution to dissolve the colonies' social and legal hierarchies is considered, exposing baldly the limits of French Enlightenment universalism beyond Europe.

In pursuing these threads, *Glorious Failure* insists on the imperialist nature of the French presence in India, going beyond the type of historical scholarship still present in Francophone academic circles that refers euphemistically (and often nostalgically) to the history of Franco-Indian 'relations' and the French 'adventure' on the subcontinent while avoiding the terms 'colonialism' and 'imperialism'.[7] The starting point for a new history of French India must be the correct designation of the phenomena at work. The terms 'colonial' and 'colonialism' are useful to denote aspects of the French presence in India, like the settlement of the French people who made Pondicherry and the other territories of French India their home. They may also be used to refer to the commerce that Frenchmen and other Europeans carried out—colonial trade. However, to describe France's attempts at conquest and territorial expansion in India, the term 'imperialism'—understood as the imposition and maintenance of a country's power or influence over foreign territories, primarily through force—is more applicable still. Whether through the medium of the *compagnies* or the direct action of the state, France was an imperialist power on the subcontinent—a reality that more and more scholars now recognise and make explicit.[8]

This imperialist approach was envisaged from the outset. As we will see in the next chapter, the articles of the Compagnie des Indes, signed off by Louis XIV, entitled it to carry arms and establish forts, to declare war on non-Christians and to conquer and occupy foreign lands. Governors of French India exploited these provisions to try to develop a territorial empire befitting, in their view, of the power and glory of France. Their ambitions were shared by many other Frenchmen on the ground—Compagnie agents and military officers, for example. Through the course of the eighteenth century, the support of the French crown and government for imperial expansion in India varied and wavered. The subcontinent was rarely France's foreign policy priority, and after the nation's catastrophic defeat in the Seven Years' War (1756–63), amid a surge in anti-colonial sentiment in France, the object of re-establishing an Indian empire was rhetorically disavowed. Compagnie directors periodically insisted that they were only interested in commerce. At vital moments, however, when the opportunity for territorial aggrandisement presented itself, statesmen in France *did* support the expansionist aspirations of their countrymen in India, discreetly sending weapons and money, for example, and, when circumstances in Europe allowed, dispatching the navy and army. As a rule, the expansionist policies of French leaders in India were only denounced in Paris and Versailles when their failure became clear.[9]

Through the course of this book, the consequences of French imperialism for India will become clear. They range from the immediate devastation wrought by war to recurring incidences of famine that forced local peoples to sell themselves and their children into slavery. As the strikingly different treatment of European and non-European prisoners of war in French captivity suggests—Indian soldiers in the service of the enemy risked being mutilated and executed—non-European lives and bodies were considered disposable.[10] Meanwhile, the economic costs for the subcontinent of a century and a half of imperialism cannot be ignored. When the Compagnie arrived in 1666, the wealth of India was legendary. By 1815, the subcontinent was well on its way to impoverishment—a reversal for which France was partly responsible. One important recent study of the decolonisation of French India suggests that present-day official and popular discourses about France's historic presence on the subcontinent, where they exist at all, contain a misleadingly positive view about French colonialism and its effects. France, it is suggested, is remembered as a 'good' coloniser, its influence positive or benign.[11] By highlighting the consequences of French imperialism for the subcontinent, *Glorious Failure* joins other recent scholarship contesting this misconception.[12]

The book's title should be explained, beginning with the emphasis on glory. All of the European trading companies operating in the Indian Ocean were supported by the states from which they issued. National governments accorded their respective companies a monopoly on their country's trade between Europe and Asia, helped to raise investment, granted their companies state-like powers and intervened to protect them where necessary.[13] In the case of France, however, the relationship between state and company was even closer still, as chapter 2 shows. Though the Compagnie des Indes was ostensibly modelled on the VOC, the initiative for its creation came from ministers of the crown, who, given the limited public enthusiasm for trade with the Indies, convinced French merchants and investors to get involved, rather than the other way round. Thereafter, the Compagnie's activities were closely controlled by the state through the influence of government ministers on Compagnie directors. The purpose of the Compagnie, from the beginning, was not just to make a profit but to enhance French power overseas as a part of Louis XIV's insatiable appetite for international expansion. The glory of the nation and of its monarchy were at stake.

What about the stress on failure? Recent years have witnessed a growing tendency among historians to focus on instances of failure in history, from military blunders to flawed technological innovations and, in the field of contemporary international history, the fiasco of American world leadership since 1945.[14] Putting to one side the genre of pseudo-inspirational writing about how every great success starts with a setback, this new emphasis should be welcomed. Earlier triumphalist versions of history—many of which are linked to the story of the nation-state (the *récit national*)—are corrected, and more interesting stories told. Focusing on failure in history challenges the implicit or explicit understanding, still common to much historical scholarship, of history as progress. Moreover, being attentive to failures in imperial history helps to expose imperialism for what it is—exploitative and violent—beyond the sanitised and airbrushed versions of empire usually recounted by imperial powers.

Some historians have warned against qualifying French efforts in India as a failure, pointing out, for example, the periods of commercial success that the Compagnies des Indes and private French traders enjoyed.[15] One note of caution suggests that it is because the French presence in India has been deemed a failure that it has been understudied.[16] Judged against the grand ambitions that they set themselves, and in comparison with their European rivals, there is no getting away from the fact that the French in India *did* fail, however. With the exception of a few years beginning in the late 1730s, French trade in India was consistently less voluminous and less profitable than that of the Dutch and then the British. After the short-lived period of major imperial expansion between 1735 and 1754, French political ambitions consistently met with defeat. The reasons for these failures—including the structural problems of the *compagnies*, the inconsistent support received from France, strategic errors and the superior resources of France's rivals—are considered in this book. It is precisely because of the failure of French imperialism on the subcontinent that it should be studied, I suggest. In describing that failure as glorious, the intention is not to suggest that French imperialism in India was praiseworthy, regardless of the outcome (quite the opposite). Rather, the term 'glorious failure' suggests a defeat that was ultimately emphatic, crushing and almost absolute, in which the vain pursuit of power and glory led to overstretch and collapse. To paraphrase one historian of eighteenth-century France, a fine line separated the pursuit of *gloire* from delusions of greatness and invincibility (the *folie de grandeur*).[17]

After the Seven Years' War, French actors were acutely aware of their failure in India. A further key concern of the book, taken up from chapter 7 onwards, is to consider how this failure was processed, interpreted and invested with new meanings after 1763. In response to the loss of their Indian empire, some Frenchmen insisted that their country had never wanted to be an imperial power anyway. While '*les Anglais*' (the English)—as the British were invariably denoted—were aggressive and imperialist, the French were peaceful, commercial and very respectful of India. Such revisionist thinking made a virtue of previous failures, presenting them as commendable or even glorious. In its most outlandish form, it depicted France as an anti-imperialist power committed to the protection of India from English aggression. In parallel, other French figures began to mourn the loss of their Indian empire, lamenting that a dominant position had been negligently surrendered. These regrets over a lost Indian empire ('*l'Inde perdue*') would take on a life of their own through exaggerations and embellishments glossing over the fact that French control over southern and central India was always precarious and incomplete, but they had a basis in fact.[18] In the later eighteenth century, French observers were forced to look on as the British established an empire in India in their place, copying many of their tactics.

As chapters 7, 8 and 9 show, these two seemingly contradictory narratives—that, on the one hand, France did not want an empire in India and was opposed to imperialism, and, on the other, that France had lost an empire in India—were both mobilised in the service of French imperialism after 1765. From the former narrative came the idea that France had a responsibility to rescue the people of India from oppressive English rule, and later, with the Revolution, that France should export the values of *liberté*, *égalité* and *fraternité* (liberty, equality and fraternity) to the subcontinent. The notion of glory was invested with new meanings linked to a supposed altruism or self-sacrifice as these plans were advanced. From the latter narrative, meanwhile, came the idea that France must recover its lost empire, or at least have its revenge on the English by expelling them from India. Around this final point, the two quite different narratives coalesced, and French and Indian interests were assumed to be the same: the English must be defeated. Thereafter, India might be returned to its 'rightful' local rulers or placed under the benign, enlightened government of the French. Despite—and increasingly because of—the rhetoric of liberty in late eighteenth-century France, the idea of a territorial empire in India was never entirely renounced. The territories of a new French India, it was claimed, would be administered 'justly' in the interests of the country's long-suffering people. Through its enlightened government of India, France would acquire 'everlasting glory'.[19]

Before we proceed, a few words about approach and terminology. The book is organised chronologically, but in parallel with its narration, it analyses and deconstructs, and in doing so sheds new light on causes and consequences. Existing assumptions are questioned and misconceptions exposed. The work is based on extensive archival research, relying on the records of the successive *compagnies*, the French government and the individuals involved, plus some contemporary English sources. Wherever possible, translations of sources in indigenous Indian languages have also been read. One outstanding record of events during the crucial years of imperial expansion and collapse is the long and detailed journal written by Ananda Ranga Pillai, Pondicherry's most high-profile Tamil resident and close confidant of Dupleix.[20] A large range of secondary sources have also been consulted, most focused on shorter periods or specific events within the scope of the book. Like any scholar writing about events over a long period, I am indebted to the authors of these works.

With one key exception—Jeanne Dupleix, the wife of Joseph François—there are no significant female characters in the work, an absence explained by the focus on the official French presence in India. (All those appointed to positions in the *compagnies* or to represent the French state were men.) The important and unusual public role played by Jeanne Dupleix at Pondicherry is briefly considered in chapters 5 and 6. Overwhelmingly, however, the book's protagonists are men. When the book recounts episodes of aggression, egoism and ignorance, we should remember that it is men exhibiting these traits. The imperialism on which the book focuses might be read as a form of male violence, though it remains for others to explore this theme in depth.

During the period under study, European nation-states were still in the process of formation. The geographical boundaries of France were in flux and its modern state apparatus under development. French was not widely spoken as a first language, with local dialects commonplace, and, at least until the final decades of the eighteenth century, French national identity was weak. Attachments to a particular region or religion were usually stronger than the feeling of being French.[21] When people born in France travelled to India, they brought with them those different identities. In India, as we have noted, they married local people or the mixed-race descendants of the Portuguese, who had been present on the Coromandel and Malabar coasts and in Bengal for much longer. The 'French' population in India was therefore much more mixed than the term suggests. Legally, French nationality was conferred through the male bloodline or, in rarer instances, through naturalisation, but after 1700 most French people in Pondicherry and the other Indian colonies were India-born and had never set foot in France.[22] Many felt stronger attachments to French India, or to the specific colony in which they lived, than to France itself. The label 'French' is used with all these caveats attached. Though the book is concerned with national rivalries, it recognises, furthermore, that close personal relations often existed between Europeans of different nationalities in India. French, Dutch and British figures socialised together and even collaborated in the launching of private trading ventures, with conflicts between the European nations sometimes treated as an inconvenience.[23]

Even more problematic is the category 'Indian', which meant nothing to the people born on the subcontinent during the period. While religious, ethnic, linguistic, dynastic, regional and caste identities did matter, to varying degrees, none of the protagonists in this book considered themselves Indian. As far as possible, more specific categories of identity like Mughal, Maratha or Tamil are used in this book. The term 'Indian' is used as a shorthand for people born on the subcontinent to non-European parents, wherever a more specific category does not apply. The designation 'Hindu', equally, was not used for self-identification during the period and is similarly deployed only where a more specific alternative like Brahmin does not fit. Part of the challenge for the historian of French India is to decipher what was meant by terms like '*noirs*', '*malabars*' or '*gentiles*', which are often used indiscriminately in primary sources.[24]

By recovering the largely forgotten history of French imperialism in India, *Glorious Failure* contributes to our wider understanding of European colonialism in South Asia. It shows, for example, that the establishment of British rule over the subcontinent was far from inevitable and reveals how later British strategies of conquest and revenue collection built on precedents set by France. Historians of the Portuguese, the Dutch and the British in the Indian Ocean will learn more about how their respective colonialisms were shaped by interactions with the French. The book will serve as a reminder of the importance of India to France's early expansion overseas, and allow those working on the second French colonial empire of the nineteenth and twentieth centuries—not least in Southeast Asia—to identify continuities with France's imperial past. For those interested in the larger phenomenon of empire, insights are offered into methods of formal and informal imperialism—from conquest and occupation to acts of regime change and resource extraction. The role in the practice of imperialism of different state and non-state actors, and of state-backed organisms like the French trading companies, is explored, along with the changing ideas and ideologies that sustained their efforts. A significant contribution is also made to our understanding of the history of South Asia, particularly in the parts of the book concerned with the major Indian powers of the eighteenth century, before the supremacy of the British and the final defeat of French imperial ambitions were confirmed.

2

THE PROMISE OF INDIA

On a chilly afternoon in February 1611, the town of Laval, a prosperous mercantile conurbation on the River Mayenne in northwest France, welcomed home a long-lost son. At first, little fanfare greeted his return. François Pyrard was still young, in his early thirties, but he looked much older, his frame stooped and his features worn by a decade of absence. Only as he climbed the winding steps of the medieval quarter towards his family home, carrying a single sack of belongings, did he begin to attract attention, followed by cries of recognition.

Ten years earlier, the merchants of Laval had collaborated with their peers in the nearby towns of Vitré and Saint-Malo to organise a trading expedition to the *Indes orientales* (East Indies), envisaged vaguely as the world east of the Cape of Good Hope. Two ships had set off together from Saint-Malo in May 1601, the *Croissant* and the *Corbin*, in the second of which Pyrard had found employment as a clerk.[1] The voyage started to go wrong almost from the start. Just nine or ten leagues out from the Brittany coast, the *Corbin*'s foremast broke. It was hastily repaired and the ships pushed on, passing the Canary Islands and following the coastline of western Africa southwards. In August the equator was crossed, but here the expedition's problems really began. Attempting to procure fresh water and other provisions from the Portuguese-held island of Annobón, off the coast of Equatorial Guinea, a quarrel broke out and the *Corbin*'s lieutenant was killed. The episode was a warning about the kind of reception that the French could expect in attempting to challenge Portuguese control of maritime trading routes between Asia, Africa and Europe.

As the ships got closer to the tip of Africa, shortages of supplies and sickness on board became critical, with scurvy rife. They passed the Cape of Good Hope in December, before a violent storm forced the expedition to find refuge on Madagascar, beyond the reach of the Portuguese. Three months were spent on the island gathering supplies from the local Malagasy population and undertaking repairs before the two ships set sail again, headed for India. At first, progress was encouraging, as favourable monsoon winds carried the ships across the western Indian Ocean towards the Indian peninsula. Before long, however, the *Corbin*—the smaller of the two vessels at just 200 tonnes—lost sight of its larger protector. Negotiating a passage through the Maldives archipelago, it struck a reef and was fatally damaged. Pyrard was one of just forty survivors who found themselves shipwrecked on the tiny Maldives island of Fuladú.

As uninvited guests in the kingdom of the Sultan of the Maldives, Pyrard and his surviving shipmates were imprisoned in the royal capital of Malé. Gradually he gained the Sultan's favour and, after acquiring a working knowledge of the local language, travelled around the archipelago as a royal adviser. Pyrard would spend a total of five years in the Sultan's service, treated well but prohibited from leaving, before obtaining his liberty in the most unexpected circumstances. In February 1607, the Maldives were attacked by the forces of the ruler of Chittagong, several thousand nautical miles away across the Bay of Bengal. The Sultan was slain and his palace pillaged. Mistaken for a Portuguese, Pyrard was stripped naked and almost killed before managing to convince his new captors that he issued from less belligerent, more likeable European stock. The Frenchman was offered a place on the ships returning to Bengal and granted his freedom on arrival.

More than six years after setting sail from France, Pyrard was now finally on Indian soil, albeit in a strange deltaic region beyond the eastern frontiers of the Mughal Empire, little known to other Europeans. After briefly exploring the country around Chittagong, he found passage on an Asian merchant vessel crossing the Bay of Bengal and skirting the Indian peninsula to arrive on the Malabar Coast. The small port of Muttungal, where he disembarked, lay in the territories of the Zamorin of Calicut, who over the preceding decades had been locked in an increasingly violent struggle to prevent the Portuguese stationed at Goa, to the north, and Cochin, to the south, from establishing control over his entire coastline. Pyrard journeyed on foot through the Zamorin's kingdom to his court at Calicut, where he was granted an interview with the ruler. He would spend the next eight months enjoying the hospitality on offer in the royal residence.

By early 1608, Pyrard had decided that it was time to return to France. In February that year he bid farewell to the Zamorin and headed for Cochin, hopeful of finding a ship returning to Europe. To enter Portuguese territories was a risk, however: authorities of the Estado da India, the Portuguese regime in the East, were often hostile towards other Europeans in the region. No sooner had Pyrard left Calicut than he was ambushed and shipped as a prisoner to Cochin. The Frenchman feared the worst, believing that he would be hung in the town square, a fate that had recently been suffered by several Dutchmen. The charges levelled against him were of being a spy and, even worse, a 'Lutherano' (Protestant).[2] After two months' imprisonment at Cochin, he was transported to Goa where, in the state-of-the-art Portuguese hospital, his deteriorating health began to recover. Pyrard was saved from another spell in prison by the intervention of a sympathetic Jesuit priest, but this time his freedom came at a cost: like many European prisoners of the Estado, he was forced into military service, travelling on Portuguese warships to Ceylon and Southeast Asia.

These expeditions complete, Pyrard secured an audience with the Viceroy of Goa and was unexpectedly granted permission to return to Europe. He left India for the final time in January 1610 but, like his passage out, his journey home would prove anything but straightforward. The ship on which he was travelling was damaged off the coast of Saint Helena in the southern Atlantic Ocean and diverted unexpectedly to Brazil, where the Portuguese had also extended their reach. From Salvador, a Flemish merchant vessel brought Pyrard back to Europe. Fulfilling a vow made when his circumstances looked most bleak, he set out directly from Lisbon on a pilgrimage to Santiago de Compostela to thank the Almighty for his safe return to the old continent, before finally returning to Laval.

Any hopes that the Frenchman may have had of a quiet retirement in his hometown would rapidly be dashed, however. To a monarchy waking up to the possibilities of enrichment through maritime trade, Pyrard's return was an opportunity not to be missed. Several years earlier, an account had been published of the voyage of the *Croissant*, which—unlike its partner, the *Corbin*—had made it successfully back to Europe loaded with a cargo of pepper and other spices from Sumatra.[3] Pyrard's experiences in the Indian Ocean were far more extensive, however. What was more, here was a Frenchman with first-hand experience of India itself. Summoned to Paris, he spent the summer and autumn of 1611 recounting his travels to counsellors of Louis XIII and responding to their questions. A first narrative of his adventures was published late that year, with an enlarged and substantially re-written second edition following in 1615.[4] Curiosity about India and the East extended to Parisian high society, where Pyrard acquired a degree of celebrity before his death in 1621.

Describing his travels, Pyrard was encouraged to provide as much information as possible about the geography, people and political regimes that he had encountered. After an extensive description of the Maldive kingdom, the narrative progressed to the Indian subcontinent. 'The most powerful king in all the Indies', Pyrard explained, was the Mughal Emperor, whose empire extended from the Arabian Sea to the Bay of Bengal across most of northern and central India. The emperor, he continued, had capitals at Delhi, Agra and Lahore and no less than 30,000 elephants.[5] In the south, meanwhile, the Zamorin of Calicut was 'one of the greatest and richest princes of India', with an army of 150,000 men.[6] His capital possessed some of the finest buildings imaginable, among them a sumptuous royal palace and a great temple. Systems for the collection of taxes and customs duties were described in detail. Law and order, meanwhile, were no problem: in the Zamorin's lands, Pyrard noted, 'everyone goes about in perfect safety'.[7] The European cliché of the uncivilised Indian was far from the mark, he added: 'I have never seen men of wit so fine and polished as are these Indians: they have nothing barbarous or savage about them, as we are apt to suppose.'[8]

The diverse populations that Pyrard had observed in India, each with their own particular social and religious practices, were briefly outlined in his text. On the Malabar Coast, he explained, the descendants of Arab Muslim traders lived side by side with prosperous Brahmin families and 'gentiles' (Hindus) of other castes. Marriages and religious festivals were celebrated with exuberance; bathing in the sacred tanks attached to local temples was an everyday practice. To a Frenchman who had grown up with the Wars of Religion and was familiar with the horrors of the Spanish and Portuguese Inquisitions, the degree of religious tolerance and open-mindedness in India was particularly striking. Hindus, Muslims, Christians, Jews and others lived peaceably together 'in the free exercise of their religions'.[9] Though himself a Muslim, the Mughal Emperor Jahangir was fascinated by Christianity and hosted Jesuit priests at his court.

Conscious of his audience—the French monarchy, aristocracy and wealthy bourgeoisie—Pyrard also gushed about the natural riches of India and the extensive possibilities for trade. The Bengal delta, he suggested, was 'healthy, temperate and wondrously fertile', its key exports including rice, fruit, sugar cane, cotton, silk and furniture—and slaves. 'One sees arriving there every day an infinite number of vessels from all parts of India for these provisions.'[10] Blessed with equal abundance was Malabar, 'the fairest and most agreeable [land] ever seen or even imagined'.[11] Coconuts, mangoes, pepper and precious stones could be found throughout the country; Calicut market was 'the most full of all traffic and commerce in the whole of India'.[12] Beyond the Indian peninsula, meanwhile, Ceylon was an 'earthly paradise' abundant in wood, fruits and especially cinnamon, the latter grown and traded in huge quantities by the Portuguese.[13] In an annex to his text, Pyrard listed and described the key spices, fruits and plants to be found and traded in South and Southeast Asia, along with the wild animals that might be encountered. The coconut, he promised, 'alone produces all commodities and things necessary for the life of man'.[14] The tiger, on the other hand, was 'a most ferocious and mischievous animal'.[15]

*

When the merchants of Laval, Vitré and Saint-Malo assembled at the turn of the seventeenth century and resolved to launch a trading expedition to the Indies, their decision was bold but not entirely without precedent in France. For centuries, spices from Asia—notably pepper, ginger, nutmeg and cinnamon—had arrived in Europe via Persia, Turkey and the Levant. Their use was largely medicinal; in France, they formed part of the famous concoctions created by the Faculty of Medicine at the University of Montpellier.[16] By the start of the sixteenth century, the search for a maritime route to the Indies was also on. In 1503 the merchants of Rouen organised a voyage that reportedly reached Madagascar, though no survivors lived to tell the tale. Twenty years later, a pair of brothers from Dieppe made it all the way to Sumatra, where they were noted attempting to buy pepper before disappearing without a trace. François I (r. 1515–47) and Henry III (r. 1574–89) issued declarations exhorting their subjects to undertake similar voyages before the *Croissant* and the *Corbin* were dispatched.[17]

Unfortunately for French maritime ambitions in the Indian Ocean, however, the Portuguese had got there first. In 1498, a decade after Portuguese mariners had first rounded the Cape of Good Hope, Vasco da Gama landed at Calicut, returning to Portugal the following year with a small quantity of spices. A second expedition to India followed the year after, and by 1504 a fortified trading post had been established at Cochin, despite the Zamorin of Calicut's opposition. Before the decade was over, Goa had also been possessed and the establishment of the Estado da India proclaimed. The setting up of trading posts on the Coromandel Coast in southeast India, within the Mughal Empire at Surat and in Bengal came soon after.[18] Meanwhile, the capture of Ormus in the Persian Gulf, Colombo on the island of Ceylon and Malacca in modern-day Malaysia signalled the Portuguese intention to dominate the Indian Ocean in its entirety. To claim and protect its trading routes, permits known as *cartaz* were issued by the Estado's authorities at Goa to Asian merchant vessels. Any vessel in the Indian Ocean not carrying a *cartaz* risked being seized or destroyed as the Portuguese exploited their maritime and military superiority to the full.

By the time that Pyrard arrived in India—a century after the Estado's founding—European challenges to Portuguese supremacy in the Indian Ocean had, however, begun to emerge. The first Dutch vessels in Asian waters dated to 1595, when four merchant ships reached the Indian peninsula before progressing to Sumatra. They returned successfully to Amsterdam in 1597, providing the confidence investors needed to inaugurate the VOC in 1602.[19] More regular voyages followed, inevitably provoking conflict with the Portuguese. In 1606 Malacca was besieged by VOC vessels and the Portuguese fleet destroyed. Two years later the Dutch blockaded Goa before forming an alliance with the King of Kandy to drive the Iberian power from Ceylon. Through a combination of force and diplomacy—for local rulers the Dutch presence was an attractive counterweight to Portuguese power—the VOC was in the ascendancy and the Estado in retreat. As these events unfolded, English vessels also appeared in the Indian Ocean. The inaugural voyage of the EIC in 1601 called at Madagascar, the Nicobar Islands, Acheh and Bantam, where a small trading post was established. The third voyage of the Company then spread its operations to India. Just as Pyrard was leaving Goa for Europe in January 1610, a fleet of English ships was arriving at Surat, where permission to start trading operations in the Mughal Empire was secured.[20]

Much to the delight of the royal ministers with whom he conversed after his return to France, Pyrard was an acute observer of these developments. Describing the Portuguese presence in India, the Frenchman noted that Cochin and Goa were magnificent towns in the European style, their palaces, forts, churches and monasteries equal to anything at home. Goa was a particularly 'wondrous sight', attracting merchants from around the Indian coast, Ceylon, the Persian Gulf, the east coast of Africa and Southeast Asia.[21] The *cartaz* system was described in detail, along with the punishments meted out to merchants of all nationalities who attempted to circumvent it. Huge carracks of up to 2,000 tonnes arrived annually from

Lisbon carrying silver, woollen cloth, arms and munitions, Pyrard recounted, their arrival the cause of much excitement among the residents of Goa. They returned to Portugal once the monsoon winds had changed, laden with spices, fine cloth and other goods to be sold lucratively in Europe.

Beneath the outward appearance of prosperity, however, the Estado was beset with problems and entering its final throes, Pyrard diagnosed. For one, corruption was endemic: Portuguese officials from the Viceroy downwards were more concerned with personal enrichment than with the interests of their nation. For all but a small minority of elites, life was violent and cruel; a strict racial hierarchy determined social status and access to justice, with white, European-born Portuguese on top. Religious persecution was rife, with the Inquisition more severe even than in Europe; on the flimsiest of pretexts, individuals were arrested and their property seized. Soldiers roamed the streets of Goa at night, robbing and killing indiscriminately. Pyrard was particularly critical of the 'decadence' of the Portuguese in the East; regardless of their social status in Europe, he remarked, 'after they have passed the Cape [they] give themselves titles of nobility' and refuse thereafter to do any work.[22] The entire Portuguese system, he continued, was dependent on the labour of slaves—men, women and children of African or Indian origin bought and sold 'like horses' in Goa and elsewhere.[23] Like the Spanish and Portuguese in the Americas, Pyrard noted, all Portuguese in India relied on slave labour. 'It would be impossible for the Spaniards and Portuguese to inhabit those lands and to make them worth the possession but for the energies and service of the slaves.'[24]

Adding to the sense of Portuguese decline, for Pyrard, was the mounting opposition of Asian rulers to their domination, coupled with the arrival of the Dutch and English in the Indian Ocean. The Zamorin of Calicut, Pyrard recorded, had successfully withstood Portuguese efforts to seize a number of smaller ports in his dominions. On Ceylon, a 'continual war' was being waged between Portuguese forces and those of the King of Kandy, the latter's guerrilla tactics in the island's thick forests and jungles draining the Estado's resources.[25] Pyrard recounted the siege of Malacca by Dutch ships and their subsequent blockade of Goa, plus the growing signs of an alliance between the Kandyan ruler and the VOC. Informed by his travels in Portuguese service in Southeast Asia he was able to describe the fall of the Spice Islands of Tidore and Ambon into Dutch possession. The Dutch and English were undoubtedly superior navigators to the Portuguese, Pyrard noted, the English in particular possessing a growing reputation as the 'kings' of the seas.[26]

When Pyrard's text was published in Paris, therefore, the overriding impression that it created was not simply of the riches to be won through commerce between Europe and the Indies but of the opportunity presented by the decline of Portuguese power in the region—an opportunity that the Dutch and English had already begun to seize. The book was a wake-up call. In 1616—the same year that a third European pretender to Portuguese supremacy, the Danish, arrived in India, installing themselves at Tranquebar on the Coromandel Coast—a new French initiative was launched: an association of merchants from Rouen, acting with royal approval, fitted out two ships that made it to Java, where Dutch hostility was encountered. A second expedition, this time with three ships, followed in 1619. Java was again reached and a healthy cargo of spices and sugarcane procured, but on leaving the island one of the ships foundered, with suspicions pointing towards the Dutch. The other two made it back to Normandy, their cargoes intact, but without the third, on which the most valuable goods had been placed, the venture was a financial defeat.[27]

More success had been enjoyed by early French expeditions to North America and the Caribbean, which over the next two decades would distract attention from Asia. In 1626 a company was founded for the colonisation of the island of Saint-Christophe in the West Indies. Its successor, the Compagnie des Îles d'Amérique, soon afterwards claimed French possession of other territories in the Antilles, laying the foundations for a lucrative sugar-producing colony on the island of Saint-Domingue. The Compagnie de la Nouvelle France was meanwhile expanding the borders of French territories in North America southwards and westwards from Quebec.[28]

In 1642, the same year that Montreal was claimed, investors were ready to try to break into Asian markets again. This time it was the merchants of Dieppe who led the way, petitioning the monarchy for permission to begin trading in the East. Cardinal Richelieu, first minister to Louis XIII, was conscious of the potential profits to be made and in 1642 a company was established with a twenty-year monopoly on French trade with the Indies.[29] To the detriment of nascent French ambitions in the Indian Ocean, however, Madagascar rather than India or Southeast Asia was the focus of the company's attentions. On Madagascar, a small French colony was established; a fort was built and, alongside an embryonic civil and military population, some of whom married local women, priests were sent out to convert the indigenous population. The unfamiliar climate and difficulties growing food meant that within a year one-third of the settlers had perished. The opposition of the Malagasy population to the French presence intensified as they began venturing into the interior of the country to find food, steal cattle and capture slaves—and by 1648, when a new governor, Étienne de Flacourt, was dispatched to restore order, it was clear that the colonisation and Christianisation of the island was failing. The brutal violence visited on the Malagasies by Flacourt's troops served only to intensify the conflict, which degenerated quickly into a state of all-out war ruinous to the company's finances and trade.[30]

Consequently, only a small number of Frenchmen followed Pyrard to India in the decades after his death. The accounts they wrote of their travels added to the sense that Pyrard had created in French minds of the exceptional but as-yet-unrealised promise of India.[31] Among the most conspicuous was Jean-Baptiste Tavernier, a Parisian jewel merchant who in 1638 set off across Syria and Persia for the subcontinent. From the port of Surat, Tavernier visited the Mughal city of Agra, where the construction of the Taj Mahal had just begun, before heading southwards to the site that interested him the most: the diamond mines of Golconda in the kingdom of the Qutb Shahs—a rival Muslim power struggling to retain control of the Deccan plateau in the face of Mughal expansion. Adopting Persian dress and fluent in the Persian language written and spoken by Indian elites, Tavernier purchased diamonds, rubies and other precious stones that would earn him a fortune on his return to Europe. Four more expeditions to India followed: as Tavernier's thirst for riches grew, his travels became increasingly ambitious, taking in Masulipatam and San Thomé on the eastern coast of India, plus the cities of Allahabad, Benares and Patna in the north. The account of these journeys that he eventually published was almost a guidebook to India—a prototype Lonely Planet or Routard—with detailed information about the regions through which he had travelled, including the attractions to visit, the routes to follow, the lodgings available and the quality of the water and wine.[32] Extensive advice was also offered about how to conduct trade, not least about the bribes that Mughal officials would demand and the often-unfavourable exchange rates to be expected. Tavernier's emphasis on diamonds and other precious stones contributed to the growing French sense of India as a kind of Eldorado—a place of unimaginable wealth and opportunities for enrichment—for those who knew how to overcome these hurdles.[33]

A second Frenchman following Tavernier on the overland route to India in the 1640s was François de La Boullaye-Le Gouz, an aristocrat of English descent dispatched by the French monarchy as a spy. Travelling under the pseudonym Ibrahim Bey, he too arrived at Surat, where, he observed, 'the English and Hollanders do all their commerce'.[34] La Boullaye-Le Gouz set about recording the details of this trade, including the main items imported and exported and the role of local intermediaries in helping the Dutch and English to negotiate commercial deals. On the whole, he noted, Europeans and other foreigners in the Mughal Empire were treated respectfully. Emperor Shah Jahan was clearly intelligent and appreciated the customs revenues derived from European trade. Restricting his travels to the western coast of India, La Boullaye-Le Gouz then sailed southwards to Goa, a city which, in his view, possessed 'the grandeur of Florence'.[35] En route, he was taken aback to witness the devastation to settlements along the coastline wrought by fighting between the Portuguese and the Dutch and English. The Portuguese-held island of Bombay, he remarked, was an empty shell, its houses and churches razed to the ground by the English. In La Boullaye-Le Gouz's estimation, some fifty to sixty Dutch vessels were present in the Indian Ocean; the English presence, though smaller, was growing. The Portuguese, he concluded, before returning to Europe via Arabia and Egypt, were no longer capable of expelling these rivals from India.

Until this point, French knowledge of the Mughal Emperor and his court had been acquired second-hand, mostly through the accounts of other European diplomats and missionaries who had secured audiences with the ruler. The emperor was a distant, semi-mythical figure, more legend than human. With the arrival of François Bernier on the subcontinent, this would change. A native of the Loire, Bernier had acquired medical training and spent time in Palestine, Syria and Egypt before arriving in India in late 1658. The timing was important. With Shah Jahan gravely ill, a succession struggle involving his four sons had begun. As Bernier made his way from Surat to Agra, following the path previously trodden by Tavernier, he encountered the eldest of the sons, Dara Shikoh, and joined his entourage as a physician. From this vantage point, he witnessed Dara's eventual defeat and the ascension of his younger brother Aurangzeb to the throne. Bernier was welcomed into the new emperor's court, where European medical knowledge was highly valued, and remained there for much of the next decade. As a royal doctor he accompanied Aurangzeb on his travels around the empire and gained unprecedented insider access to the Mughal regime.

Though his seizure of power had been cruel, involving the merciless killing of Dara and his other brothers, Bernier was in no doubt that Aurangzeb was a talented leader, 'endowed with a versatile and rare genius [...] a consummate statesman, and a great King.'[36] The resources of his empire, stretching from the Himalayas to the Deccan, were almost infinite. Its principal cities—Delhi, Agra and Lahore—were wonderous sights (though, naturally, not quite the equal of Paris, 'the finest, the richest, and altogether the first city in the world').[37] More than any European before him, Bernier had the opportunity to study the functioning of the Mughal polity. In letters sent back to France he explained how Mughal administration worked, outlining the system in place for the collection of revenues from the land—based on the fixed term award of land grants (*jagirs*) to those in Mughal service—and the degree of autonomy retained by local rulers. His conclusion was that the Empire was not as rich, strong or stable as it outwardly appeared; though its resources were immense, its income was unpredictable and its expenditure high. The collection of revenues from defaulting landholders and the threat of internal rebellion meant that a huge and expensive imperial army had to be maintained. The administration of justice was arbitrary and failed to protect the poor.

For all that, Bernier noted, the commercial possibilities for a well-organised European trading company were immense. Bernier outlined in detail the steps to be followed should the French wish to start trading operations in Mughal territories. Firstly, an embassy would need to be dispatched to Aurangzeb; court etiquette would need to be followed strictly, including the presentation of opulent gifts to the emperor, and a sum would need to be paid to secure permission to trade in the form of an imperial *firman*. Payments would then have to be made to the Mughal governor and other officials in cities like Surat, where trading posts were to be established. An eye would have to be kept on local political developments, to ensure that French interests were protected in the event of future upheavals. If French merchants were to export the riches of India to Europe, they would, of course, need to offer traders in India something attractive in return. The Dutch, Bernier noted, had enjoyed some success importing cloves, nutmeg and cinnamon to India from the Spice Islands and Ceylon; the English had begun importing woollen cloth from Europe, while demand also existed in India for imported horses, fruit, seashells, ivory, porcelain and pearls. To finance their purchases, however, the French would also need to import gold and silver bullion—the commodity that local traders and Mughal officials desired most. The large-scale export of spices, textiles and foodstuffs, for which India was renowned, might then begin.

*

In the early 1660s, as François Bernier was accompanying Emperor Aurangzeb on a royal tour of the Punjab and Kashmir, becoming in the process the first European known to have set foot in the fabled Himalayan valley, decisive French action would finally be taken to allow the promise of India to be realised. After the debacle of the

1642 company on Madagascar, France's relatively small banking and mercantile class, thinly spread across different cities and regions, had possessed neither the confidence nor the financial means to raise sustained investment for trade with India in the manner of its Dutch and English counterparts. The French state, meanwhile, had been too preoccupied with war and territorial gains in Europe and the pacification of its own rebellious population to commit time and resources to ambitious Indian Ocean schemes, however attractive they seemed.

A series of events in quick succession allowed for the end of this official inaction. In November 1659, the Treaty of the Pyrenees was signed, bringing to a close twenty-five years of conflict between the monarchies of France and Spain. Coming after the end of the Thirty Years' War, in which France had also been embroiled, it meant that peace in Europe had finally been obtained—at least for a short period of time. Sixteen months later, when his First Minister of State, Cardinal Mazarin, passed away, Louis XIV assumed personal control of his rule, adopting as a royal priority the expansion of the power and glory of France, not just in Europe but around the world.

Biographies of Louis XIV present the picture of a man obsessed by the pursuit of glory, whose ego and ambition propelled almost ceaseless efforts to extend the frontiers of his kingdom and expand his dynastic power over more than six decades of rule.[38] In the second half of the seventeenth century, as the principle of constitutional monarchy was taking hold in England, Louis XIV was proclaiming his divine right to rule. His personal emblem, the sun, projected his status as God's representative on earth and the giver of life to all things. His kingdom's already stretched finances were poured into epic vanity projects designed to reinforce his absolutist power, most strikingly the construction of the Palace of Versailles as his new royal residence and seat of government.

From his golden throne in the palace, Louis regarded with envy the territorial acquisitions and trade wealth of rival European powers—the Spanish, the Portuguese, the Dutch and the English—around the globe. If the Dutch Republic, a country of just 1.5 million people, or England, with just 4 million, was capable of overseas trade and expansion, why not France, whose population of 19 million dwarfed that of its rivals?[39] Why should the glory of France—and of the Bourbon dynasty—be confined to Europe? As spices, porcelain and Indian textiles, among other Asian products, found their way onto European markets via the ports of Amsterdam and London, the success of the Dutch and English East India companies was impossible to ignore.

Among Louis's ministers was one in particular who shared the regent's ambition to expand French power overseas. Jean-Baptiste Colbert, a native of Reims, had entered state service under Mazarin and risen to the position of Intendant of Finances. Fiscal reforms improving the public finances cemented his reputation in the eyes of the king and, after Mazarin's death, commerce, colonial expansion and the navy were added to his ministerial portfolio, making him the most powerful figure in Louis's government. Under Colbert's direction, state intervention to promote economic development was the order of the day. Tariffs were imposed to protect French producers and a council of commerce was founded to stimulate trade. Investment was poured into new roads, ports and canals—most impressively the Canal du Midi, connecting the Atlantic and the Mediterranean—and expenditure on the navy was increased thirtyfold.[40]

The economic orthodoxy underpinning these developments was known as mercantilism. Schooled in the mercantilist ideas then prevalent in northern Europe, Colbert considered the overall volume of trade and wealth in the world to be static, not something capable of indefinite growth. As such, a greater proportion of trade, and consequently of wealth, could only be obtained by one party to the detriment of others. It followed that the countries of Europe were locked in a competitive struggle for economic development; to enrich itself, France had no choice but to challenge and emerge victorious over its European rivals. Where success on the international stage had traditionally meant victories on the battlefield, competition between states would henceforth be economic, not just military. Economic progress was the continuation of interstate warfare by other means.[41]

Viewed from Paris, the principal obstacle to French economic progress was its overperforming northern neighbours. Colbert was convinced that France had to launch economic challenges to the Dutch Republic and England and considered that the Indian Ocean, as well as Europe, was a necessary theatre of competition. The success of Dutch trade in Asian waters was particularly vexing to the Frenchman. By 1664, the Dutch Republic was the dominant global trading power, with an estimated 600 ships in operation totalling more than 600,000 tonnes.[42] Ceylon had been prised from the Portuguese in the previous decade, while Cochin and a string of other possessions on the Malabar Coast were claimed between 1660 and 1663, and a trading post had been opened at Surat. The English were also established at Surat, and on the Coromandel Coast at Madras, and were beginning trading operations in Bengal.

For Colbert, the first step in the mounting of a French challenge to the Dutch and English in the Indian Ocean was imitation. Louis XIV's right-hand man envisaged the foundation of a French East India Company upon the Dutch and English model—a trading corporation financed by private investment that would advance the wealth and power of its nation while simultaneously delivering profits to shareholders. In May 1664, its articles were drawn up: the Compagnie des Indes orientales would hold a fifty-year monopoly on trade between France and the Indian Ocean. Alongside its commercial operations, the Compagnie would be entitled to carry arms and establish garrisons and forts; to declare war on non-Christians, engage in diplomacy and make treaties; and to administer justice and conquer and occupy foreign lands.[43]

Conscious that previous attempts to establish a company for trade with the Indies had failed to attract sufficient private investment, Colbert ensured that the Compagnie was granted generous concessions. The state, it was agreed, would advance one-fifth of all expenditure on ships and cargoes for its first three expeditions; losses suffered during the first ten years of its operation would be reimbursed from the public coffers. The Compagnie would moreover be exempt from the payment of duties on the construction of ships and some imports, and would pay half rates on others. Anybody might invest in the Compagnie, it was decreed, regardless of rank or status, including nobles, ecclesiastics and royal officials; those investing large sums would be recognised as members of the bourgeoisie (a legal category to which political and civil privileges were attached). Even foreigners might invest; the reward for a large investment would be the granting of French nationality. The Compagnie would be managed by a general assembly composed of representatives from Paris and nine provincial towns from which the most significant investment had been forthcoming.[44]

In August 1664, Louis XIV declared the Compagnie launched. The royal publicity accompanying this declaration left no doubt about what was at stake: the Compagnie, it was affirmed, was going to 'extend the power of the king' into the Indian Ocean, 'obtain for the kingdom the commerce of Asia and prevent the English and Dutch from profiting from it alone, as they have so far done [since the decline of the Portuguese].'[45] Enrichment and power, glory and the defeat of European rivals would go together. A new chapter was beginning, and Louis XIV's most glorious nation was about to start making up for lost time.

3

ESTABLISHING A FOOTHOLD

The first tasks for the Compagnie were to publicise its creation throughout France and attract investment. To this end, a celebrated writer of the Académie française, François Charpentier, was commissioned to write a pamphlet celebrating the Compagnie's foundation and encouraging Frenchmen to invest. 'The prosperity of a great kingdom is missing something when commerce does not thrive', Charpentier began, setting the scene. 'Among all the commerce in the world, there is none more rich or considerable than that of the East Indies', whose legendary riches included spices, cotton textiles and 'a thousand other commodities which the people, once accustomed, will find it impossible to part with.'[1] Cajoling his compatriots into action, he continued:

> Why should it be that the Portuguese, the Dutch, the English, the Danish reside in the East Indies, possessing there trading posts and fortresses, and that the French have neither one nor the other? What good is it to have such good ports, so many vessels, so many experienced sailors and soldiers? What good is it to be subjects of the number one monarch of the universe, if we do not have the courage to show ourselves in those places where the other nations have established themselves?[2]

The French, after all, were the most impressive people in the world, 'in whom merit, magnificence, natural goodness, civility, faith and high arts have chosen their home.'[3]

A description of the establishment of the Dutch, English and Danish East India Companies followed, and the extent of their commerce and possessions was outlined. If these other Europeans had mastered the maritime route to Asia, then the French certainly could, Charpentier asserted: 'It is certain that we have the best seamen that can be desired. Even the Dutch recruit Frenchmen to serve on their vessels.'[4] Slipping from exaggeration into outright falsehood, the development of Madagascar into a French colony and stopping post between Europe and India was then celebrated. There was no doubt, Charpentier claimed, that the colony might be transformed into a 'great establishment' where 'we will find no resistance'.[5] With France now at peace in Europe, the time was propitious for commerce. Where previous efforts to break into the Asia-Europe trade had failed, this one was sure of success: 'Is history not full of great enterprises that have only been achieved after more than one attempt?'[6] Reaching the end of his lengthy discourse, Charpentier sought to reassure the French nobility, accustomed to thinking of land as the only source of wealth, that commerce too was an 'honourable and certain means' of enrichment.[7] He finished with a eulogy to the king, followed by a rallying cry: 'It is on account of His Majesty's power and courage that we can be confident of the success of the enterprise. Unite therefore, generous Frenchmen, unite to open the glorious route [...] that will lead you to innumerable riches.'[8]

Charpentier's pamphlet was sent with a letter requesting investment to authorities in 119 cities and towns around France. Soon after that, agents were dispatched from Paris to sell the opportunity represented by the Compagnie and collect subscriptions in person. The merchants of Lyon and a handful of other cities responded enthusiastically, committing significant sums, but from across the country as a whole, subscriptions were received in a trickle rather than a flood. Many potential investors no doubt remembered the failure of Richelieu's company twenty years earlier. Despite the reassurances offered, members of the nobility struggled to conceive of trade as a noble pursuit and not an affront to their class. To challenge this reluctance, Colbert instructed his agents to apply pressure on possible subscribers with the message—a thinly-veiled threat—that royal favour depended on it.[9]

Six months after the subscription campaign had begun, a total of 3,500,000 livres had been promised to the Compagnie from private investors, along with 3,000,000 livres from the Crown—a long way from the target of 15,000,000 that Colbert believed would allow the French to compete on an equal footing with the Dutch.[10] Most of this sum had come from the aristocracy, the nobility and agents of the state, who found it hard to escape from Colbert's demands but had limited enthusiasm for the venture. Unlike in the Dutch Republic and England, not much organic interest existed in the Compagnie on the part of private investors and, except in Lyon and a few other cities with significant commercial pedigrees, there was little in the way of an entrepreneurial merchant class to drive the project forward. From the outset, the Compagnie was a state undertaking, the result of an '*impulsion étatique*' (state impetus)—a structural reality that would decisively shape its operations.[11]

To lay the groundwork for the Compagnie's arrival in India, a royal embassy was dispatched from Paris. François de La Boullaye-Le Gouz, whom we encountered in the previous chapter on an intelligence-gathering mission, was selected to head it. Once again, he journeyed across Persia to the subcontinent, this time continuing inland from Surat to reach Agra, where he secured an audience with Emperor Aurangzeb. Following Bernier's advice about the etiquette to be observed, La Boullaye-Le Gouz obtained permission from the emperor for France to trade in the Mughal Empire on payment of the same duties as the English and Dutch.[12] In parallel, preparations for the Compagnie's first maritime voyage got underway. Lorient, on the Atlantic coast of Brittany, was chosen as the Compagnie's port; warehouses and a shipyard were built. Work began on the construction of several light vessels and the 1,000-tonne *Soleil d'Orient*.[13]

Having inherited what was left of the French colony on Madagascar after two decades of violent struggle against the island's Malagasy population, the Compagnie's directors, assembled in Paris for the first time, were reluctant to abandon it altogether. In March

1665, four ships set sail for the island. The 520 people that they carried were supposed to breathe new life into the settlement.[14] Meanwhile, preparations for an inaugural voyage further into the Indian Ocean were ongoing. With in-house knowledge of navigation and trading routes in the East Indies limited, reliable information was vital. Agents were sent to Amsterdam and London to gather maps, reports and other useful data. In the Dutch Republic they went one better, meeting secretly with a former director-general of the Dutch company in Asia, François Caron. Raised in a French-speaking Protestant family in Brussels, Caron had served the VOC for more than three decades in Japan, Indonesia and Ceylon before being dismissed following a dispute about his private trading activities. Disgruntled, he was ripe for recruitment to the French cause. After extensive negotiations relating to his pay and conditions, he was naturalised as a French subject and appointed the first director-general of the Compagnie.

In the Compagnie's Paris office, Caron briefed the directors about how to profit from commerce in Asian waters. The rhythms of trade, he explained, were shaped by the annual cycle of the monsoons. In addition to import and export with Europe, establishing profitable trading routes between different sites in the Indian Ocean was essential—not least because it would reduce the amount of bullion required from France. Key commodities to be traded included ivory, gold and slaves from eastern Africa; cinnamon from Ceylon; and cloves and nutmeg from Indonesia—plus of course the riches that India had to offer. France, Caron suggested, would have no problem finding allies in the region, particularly from rulers like the King of Kandy who had suffered from Dutch aggression, just as the Dutch had earlier profited from local dislike of the Portuguese. A fortified headquarters should be established as the basis of the Compagnie's operations in the Indian Ocean, the apex of a network of *comptoirs* (trading posts).[15]

By March 1666, the time for talking was over. An impressive fleet of ten ships set off for the Indian Ocean with Caron onboard and in charge. Unfavourable winds and poor navigation south of the equator swept the fleet off course towards Brazil, where a six-month stay was required, before Madagascar was reached in March 1667.

The colony was found to be in a desperate state, with many of the settlers brought to the island two years previously already dead. With little land cultivated, food was in short supply, and disease had swept through the French population. Convinced that the Compagnie's fortunes would be made further east, Caron stayed on Madagascar just long enough to the lay the foundations for a modest trading post before setting sail again, leaving a few ships, a garrison of soldiers, several Compagnie agents and a few hundred new settlers behind.[16]

In the final months of 1667, the Indian peninsula was finally sighted. Caron's fleet advanced slowly up the western coast, stopping at several Malabar ports and alerting the Zamorin of Calicut to its presence. The Zamorin, whose predecessor François Pyrard had earlier befriended, was an ally to be made for the struggles against the Dutch to come. They then reached Surat, Caron's intended destination. As the most significant port of the Mughal Empire, the city was grander, richer and more cosmopolitan than anything the fleet had hitherto encountered. It was, recorded one bewildered Frenchman, 'a miniature Babylon' composed of 'men of almost every nation of the world, wearing their national costumes and speaking diverse languages.' It was also a hive of commercial activity: 'Merchandise is bought and sold continuously. The streets are always crowded with carts, elephants, camels, beasts of burden, coaches, horses, palanquins and other vehicles.'[17] The arrival of the French into this melting pot of different peoples is unlikely to have attracted much attention beyond the small Dutch and English communities in the city. The *firman* obtained from Aurangzeb granting the French trading permissions in his empire was presented to the Mughal governor of the city and a large townhouse was rented to serve as the Compagnie's lodgings and warehouse.

With operations at Surat beginning, the search for other trading posts got underway—'new establishments for the service and good of the Compagnie, the advancement of the nation, and the *gloire* of our monarch', as one French official put it.[18] François Bernier, who had just quit the service of Aurangzeb after a decade in the Mughal court, was convinced that the silk and cotton textiles of northern India should be the focus of the Compagnie's efforts and urged the establishment of a *comptoir* in Bengal.[19] Arachin Marcara, an Armenian employee of the Compagnie valued for his knowledge of Persian, was sent to establish trade at Masulipatam, halfway up the eastern coast of the peninsula in the kingdom of Golconda, where textiles were also the main attraction.[20] For Caron, however, informed by his decades in Dutch service, trade in spices rather than textiles offered the most promising prospects for the Compagnie. To launch the French into this trade, his attention was drawn towards the south of the peninsula.

While the political system and territorial limits of the Mughal Empire in northern and central India were understood at least in outline, southern India was a patchwork of different states and rulers enjoying far less political stability, with which Compagnie agents were now forced to contend. On the Deccan plateau, the sultanates of Golconda and Bijapur competed for territory, while trying to resist Mughal aggression and expanding south-eastwards to the Carnatic. Having broken free from the Sultanate of Bijapur, the Maratha Federation was on the rise from its base at Raigad in the western ghats. Further south, the kingdoms of Mysore, Madurai, Tanjore and Gingee were among those to have emerged from the break-up of the once dominant Vijayanagar Empire earlier in the century.[21] The Zamorin of Calicut, meanwhile, retained control of an important strip of the Malabar Coast. On Caron's instruction, Compagnie agents travelled to Rajapur, in Maratha territory, and Tellicherry, in the Zamorin's kingdom, to start procuring pepper and other spices.[22]

Not content with these developments, Caron then set his sights on Ceylon. Not only did the island possess spices in abundance, the director-general noted, it occupied a strategically important position at the crossroads of different Indian Ocean trade routes, making it the ideal centre for the Compagnie's operations. Were the French to help the King of Kandy to expel the Dutch from their strongholds of Colombo and Galle, Caron confidently predicted, the grateful monarch would allow them to establish a fortified base of their own. What better way to advance the Compagnie's interests and strike a blow against its Dutch rival?[23] Caron's colleagues on the subcontinent shared the view that such a strike was necessary. 'It will always be the policy of the Dutch to prevent our nation from establishing itself in the Indies', noted one in his diary, adding that even more than profit, what motivated the VOC was excluding the other European companies from Asian trade.[24]

In Europe, events were unfolding in such a way as to lend support to Caron's plans. Colbert had recently increased tariffs on goods entering France from the rest of Europe, provoking tensions with the Dutch Republic that were threatening to spill over into war. When the minister was informed of Caron's intentions regarding Ceylon, he backed them enthusiastically and convinced Louis XIV to send a naval expedition in support. A fleet of nine warships under the direction of seasoned military commander Jacob Blanquet de La Haye was dispatched in March 1670, the first French naval mission to Asia. Predictably, the fleet's first port of call in the Indian Ocean was Madagascar, where La Haye—who had awarded himself the preposterous title of 'Viceroy of the French East Indies'—embarked on an aggressive campaign against the Malagasy population.[25] 700 soldiers were marched into the interior of the country, where they sustained high casualties during several months of guerrilla warfare for which they were wholly unprepared.[26] This latest debacle complete, Madagascar was finally abandoned, the remaining colonists and their families shipped 500 or so nautical miles eastwards to settle on a small island identified as a better stopping post for ships bound for the Indies. The new colony was christened the Isle Bourbon (later Reunion Island), in homage to Louis XIV and his family.

La Haye's forces then headed for Surat, appearing at the mouth of the Tapti River on the approach to the city in October 1671. 'The arrival of such a powerful fleet struck terror all over the Indies', wrote Barthélemy Carré, a French missionary stationed there. 'Some were delighted; others were amazed that the French in so short a time since their appearance in India had been able to make such great plans and to assemble so powerful a fleet of warships.'[27] Carré was given to exaggeration, but the ships—among them three 500-tonne flûtes and the 1,000-tonne Man of War *Navarre*—were undoubtedly an impressive sight.[28] Aurangzeb was sufficiently concerned to send extra Mughal troops to protect the city.

In the event, he need not have worried. Not even the arrogant, puffed-up La Haye was reckless enough to start hostilities against the mighty Mughal Empire. (When the English were sufficiently foolhardy to declare war on the Mughals in the following decade, their forces, dwarfed by those of Aurangzeb, were chased out of Bengal and the EIC briefly banished from India.)[29] In January 1672 the fleet set off again, this time in the direction of its real target, Ceylon, with François Caron and reinforcements from Surat onboard. Its first port of call en route was Goa, where overtures were made to the much-diminished Portuguese about an anti-Dutch alliance. Authorities of the Estado agreed to provide La Haye with supplies and munitions but, to the commander's consternation, refused a formal alliance, arguing that they were bound to the same position of neutrality as their government in Europe, where Colbert's diplomatic efforts to gather the support of the Portuguese monarchy for a French attack on the Dutch Republic had also drawn a blank. A more positive response was received at Calicut, where the Zamorin agreed to side with the French and allow the development of their trading operations in his kingdom.

As the fleet progressed further southwards, passing Dutch-held Cochin without incident, La Haye was encouraged by the limited strength of Dutch maritime forces, which appeared thinly spread along the Malabar Coast. In late February, just off Cape Comorin, the peninsula's southern tip, a fleet of twelve Dutch ships was then sighted. La Haye favoured an attack: the Dutch vessels were numerous but poorly equipped and trapped between his fleet and the coastline, while the direction of the wind was favourable. Here was the coveted opportunity to strike a major blow against the VOC. Caron, however, urged caution: to his knowledge, war had not yet been declared between France and the Dutch Republic in Europe; until it was, a large-scale attack on the Dutch might be considered an unacceptable escalation of hostilities. After lengthy argument, La Haye deferred to Caron and the attack was postponed, the French fleet passing its Dutch counterpart without a shot being fired. When the failure of La Haye's mission in the Indies was later subjected to investigation, this episode was accorded the status of a vital opportunity missed. Caron's non-belligerent stance provoked accusations of pro-Dutch sympathies contributing to his recall to France before the year was out.[30]

On 22 March 1672, La Haye's fleet arrived on Ceylon, anchoring in the bay of Trincomalee on the island's eastern coast, far removed from the Dutch at Colombo and Galle. An embassy was sent across the mountains to agree an alliance with Rajah Sinha II, who was holed up in his capital, Kandy, in the interior of the country. In return for their assistance against the Dutch, the French expected formal recognition of their possession of Trincomalee. With the immediate term in mind, they also demanded provisions to feed their troops and labourers to help erect fortifications. The monarch's response was encouraging but, in the weeks that followed, no concrete support was forthcoming; mortality rates among the soldiers at Trincomalee grew steadily as food dwindled and disease spread. In mid-May, a reinforced Dutch fleet of fifteen ships appeared outside the bay. The French response was firm: Trincomalee was possessed with the permission of Rajah Sinha II; in the event of attack, it would be defended. This, however, was little more than bluster. After two months at Trincomalee, La Haye's forces were severely depleted, with hundreds of troops dead or dying. As Dutch soldiers began cutting off the few supplies that were making it through to the fleet overland, it was clear that the occupation had failed. Their safe passage negotiated, the French sailed out of Trincomalee at the beginning of July, their plans for a Ceylonese stronghold in tatters.

From Trincomalee, the closest stretch of Indian coastline was the Coromandel, eastwards of Cape Comorin. Vital supplies were procured from the Danish station at Tranquebar, where rumours of war in Europe circulated, before the French fleet headed northwards to drop anchor off San Thomé. The citadel of San Thomé, recognisable by its striking seafront basilica, had for more than a century been the principal Portuguese base on the Coromandel Coast. Ten years earlier, however, it had been captured by the kingdom of Golconda, with Dutch assistance, and the Portuguese expelled. To the French, reeling from their defeat at Trincomalee, the taking of the city was appealing: San Thomé was an important centre of the south Indian textile trade and, they reasoned, rightfully belonged in European hands. Moreover, it was poorly defended by a single garrison of the King of Golconda's troops. The caution exercised by La Haye since the arrival of his fleet in South Asia was now abandoned and in the course of a single morning, San Thomé was bombarded, stormed and captured. The victory, a first for French forces in India, went straight to the Viceroy's head: with appropriate reinforcements, he boasted, he would soon make Louis XIV 'master of both the Malabar and Coromandel coasts'.[31]

In fact, the capture of San Thomé, though a modest military success, had been a strategic mistake. For one thing, the kingdom of Golconda was the richest and most powerful state in southern India, its influence extending over large parts of the Deccan and Carnatic. When news of the fall of the city reached Golconda, 600 kilometres away, the dispatch of an army to retake it was inevitable. Secondly, the seizure of San Thomé was sure to antagonise the English, whose own base on the Coromandel Coast, Fort St George at Madras, was just 7 kilometres to the north. Until this point, the French had hoped that the English might be convinced to side with them against the more powerful Dutch in India. This was always a long shot: agents of the EIC had followed the efforts of the Compagnie to establish itself on the subcontinent with concern and were unlikely either to act in French interests or risk war with the Dutch. The capture of San Thomé confirmed the English in this position. Under the pretence of neutrality, they refused to sell the French arms and began covertly encouraging the King of Golconda to retake the city.[32]

In August 1672, as François Caron left India for France, his leadership and loyalty to the Compagnie in question, a huge Golconda force, estimated by one French observer to number 50,000, appeared outside San Thomé.[33] The superior French cannonry and hastily repaired land fortifications of the citadel were sufficient to repel the early Golconda attacks and before long, an attritional siege had set in. It would last no less than eight months before a ceasefire was negotiated and the Golconda army withdrew. Barthélemy Carré, who arrived at San Thomé just after the siege had been lifted, found the French forces in a very sorry state, though apparently their morale remained intact:

> There were wounded soldiers everywhere: some with sabre-cuts on their faces; some pierced in many places by lances, halberds, and javelins; others still had within their bodies the balls which

> hit them, and which no surgeon had been able to extract; while many had lost limbs through cannon shots, grenades, and other fire-arms. I was amazed to see that the misery and suffering of these brave Frenchmen, far from depressing them, had caused them only joy and satisfaction at having done their duty and upheld the glory and renown of their great King in this oriental country.[34]

As if his troops had not suffered enough, La Haye then decided to go on the offensive, his object to blockade the port of Masulipatam and demand payment from the King of Golconda, Abul Hasan Qutb Shah, for its release. However, the two vessels selected for this mission misjudged the approach to Masulipatam and overshot the port; the element of surprise crucial to La Haye's plan was lost and the French were forced to withdraw.[35]

While this misadventure was unfolding, an embassy had been dispatched to the Golconda court to negotiate a peace settlement. Representatives of Abul Hasan Qutb Shah had indicated that the monarch was willing to recognise French possession of San Thomé in return for a significant one-off payment, plus the reimbursing of expenses incurred during the eight-month siege of the city.[36] La Haye committed another major strategic error in refusing to entertain these demands, making a second siege inevitable. Without additional reinforcements from France or aid from the English—neither of which was forthcoming—the prospects of victory were close to zero. In September 1673, three months after the lifting of the first siege, the second began. Now that the fact of war between France and the Dutch Republic in Europe was well known to Europeans in Asia, the Dutch did not hesitate to support their Indian ally, blockading San Thomé from the sea while the Golconda army besieged it on land. In the early months of 1674, a series of French offensives to break through the siege were repelled. Daring sorties into the villages around San Thomé to seize food and other supplies served only to postpone the capitulation, which was confirmed in September of that year, as La Haye faced the desertion and possible munity of his unfed, unpaid troops.

In Europe, French forces had enjoyed stunning early success in their campaign against the Dutch Republic, advancing quickly through the Low Countries in the summer of 1672. Amsterdam had been saved only by the ingenious flooding of the surrounding countryside to bog down the French advance that autumn. The following year, Louis XIV's overstretched armies then suffered a set of serious reversals. Though France ultimately emerged victorious from the war, which rumbled on until 1678, most of its early gains against the Dutch Republic were lost.[37] In southern India, meanwhile, the triumphant Dutch razed San Thomé before leaving it in the possession of Golconda. Prisoners were exchanged between the European rivals and La Haye and his 500 surviving troops were ordered to return to Europe, with two ships made available for the purpose.[38] The first French naval expedition in the Indian Ocean had ended in humiliating defeat.

From the cloud of this defeat, however, emerged a most unlikely silver lining. During their struggles against the kingdom of Golconda, the French at San Thomé had appealed to other local rulers for political support and, as their situation worsened, for supplies of food and arms. Among these statesmen was Sher Khan Lodi, governor of the province of Cuddalore, a portion of the Carnatic ruled by the kingdom of Bijapur. Sher Khan responded favourably, granting the Compagnie permission to establish itself in a small coastal village in his territory: Pondicherry. The grant of Pondicherry must have seemed an irrelevance to La Haye and his soldiers as they left India for good, but just before their departure the remaining French civilians on the Coromandel Coast, a group of Compagnie agents and their families, totalling sixty, set off on foot for the village, trudging 150 kilometres southwards to make it their own.

*

At first glance, Pondicherry was an unlikely base for the Compagnie's commercial operations. Like many sites on the flat and marshy Coromandel Coast, it possessed no natural port; large ships were forced to anchor out at sea, their cargoes and passengers unloaded onto smaller vessels to be taken ashore. The countryside around the village was notoriously infertile, with foodstuffs imported from elsewhere in India. Extreme rainfall in August and September forced the pausing of all commercial activity for 5–6 weeks each year, while in other seasons water was in acutely short supply.

For the French party arriving in late 1674, however, the prospects of Pondicherry were not all bad. Here was a coastal site positioned neatly between the English and Dutch to the north, at Madras and Pulicat respectively, and the Danish at Tranquebar to the south—and a safe distance, at least 120 kilometres, from all of them. The River Gingee, which flowed south and west of the village, connected it with the interior of the country; its shallow waters were just about navigable for flat-bottomed boats and acted as a reasonable natural defence, as did the swamps and sand dunes to the north.[39] Beyond this, the key attraction was the local textile industry. Weavers at Pondicherry and in the surrounding villages were accustomed to producing cotton cloth in bulk, along with high-quality muslins spun from a finer thread. Earlier in the century, this production had attracted the Danish to the village, though they had long since departed when the French arrived.

Among the exiles arriving at Pondicherry from San Thomé was a Compagnie agent by the name of François Martin who would go on to assume the leadership of French efforts in India. The son of a grocery store owner in the famous Paris marketplace of Les Halles, Martin had joined the Compagnie on its creation, taking part in its inaugural voyage in 1665. After surviving Madagascar he had arrived in India with François Caron, working in the Compagnie's lodge at Surat before being dispatched on missions to Bandar Abbas, in the Persian Gulf, and Masulipatam, where he was stationed when the conflict with the kingdom of Golconda began. Escaping detention at Masulipatam, it was Martin who had negotiated the concession of Pondicherry from Sher Khan Lodi and who now took responsibility for the development of French operations there. His extensive memoirs are an excellent first-hand record of what followed.

Upon their arrival at Pondicherry, the exiles had crammed themselves into the house formerly belonging to the Danish in the village. Martin's immediate priority was the construction of new houses for the French settlement, plus a Compagnie lodge, and their protection, as far as possible, from outside aggression. In parallel, he attempted to restart the Compagnie's trade, which had ground to a halt during the war. However, the continued political upheaval in southern India could not be ignored. Most urgent was the outbreak of war between Sher Khan Lodi, the Compagnie's benefactor, and Nasir Muhammad, ruler of the kingdom of Gingee, whose capital of the same name was just a day's travel north-westwards from Pondicherry. The Marathas, meanwhile, were threatening to attack the kingdom of Bijapur and advance on Sher Khan's province.

Through Martin's clever diplomatic efforts, the dangerous situation that Sher Khan faced was turned to the French advantage. First, the governor of Cuddalore was loaned a sum of money to aid in his war effort against Gingee; in return, the Compagnie was granted permission to begin fortifying Pondicherry and maintain a small army in the fort. At Sher Khan's request, this force, consisting of just forty-two Frenchmen and sixty Indian soldiers, was put into action to help Sher Khan capture the nearby fort of Valadour—the first instance of French intervention in a conflict between two Indian rulers, and an episode that increased Sher Khan's debts to the Compagnie.[40]

In November 1676, peace was agreed between Sher Khan and Nasir Muhammad, but just six months later the Maratha threat materialised: Shivaji Bhosle concluded an agreement with the King of Golconda, paving the way for his capture of Bijapur and invasion of Sher Khan's territory. Once again, Martin advanced a large sum of money to help Sher Khan finance the defence of his province; when the governor was unable to repay this loan in cash, he accepted Martin's demand that Pondicherry be recognised as a French possession in perpetuity, with the revenues of a small territory around the town also awarded to the Compagnie.[41] Ultimately, the sums advanced to Sher Khan did little to improve his prospects against the Marathas; in July 1677, his forces capitulated without a fight and the governor fled. The Compagnie found its main ally in southern India dispossessed and powerless, and a Maratha attack on Pondicherry seemed likely. Martin, however, had learnt from La Haye's arrogant refusal, several years earlier, to negotiate with an Indian adversary of overwhelmingly superior strength, and entered into correspondence with the Maratha court. An embassy to Shivaji followed and despite the unimpressive gifts that it carried—'an old piece of gold and silk brocade', several other cloths and shawls, and a pair of double-shot rifles—met with success.[42] The Maratha leader acknowledged French possession of Pondicherry and gave permission for the French to trade in his territories in return for the recognition of his authority, a large one-off payment and a promise to remain neutral in any future conflicts.

The development of Pondicherry could now proceed with a degree of security. Work began on a small fort, within which the Compagnie's offices were based. Between the fort and the waterfront, houses for Compagnie employees and their families were constructed, transforming the village into an embryonic town. Weavers and other workers were attracted by the promise of low rent and protection from upheavals in the countryside; to the west of the fort, an Indian population, composed principally of local Tamils, began to grow. Alongside the Compagnie's main occupation—the production and export of textiles—a profitable side-line was developed in the import of corals from other Indian Ocean sites. In India, the corals were a prized commodity, used to make jewellery or ground down and added to medicine. A community of coral polishers grew up around the fort.[43]

The search for other *comptoirs* then resumed. During the preceding decade, a small French presence had been maintained at Surat. In 1681 Martin was instructed to visit it and journeyed there overland, from the southeast to the northwest of the subcontinent, taking in the kingdom of Golconda and other territories as he went. The Compagnie's operations at Surat were found to be in a worrying state, with trade stagnant and debts rising. Several attempts had been made to establish trade between Surat and the Persian Gulf, where silk, wool and wine were the main attractions, but little return had been seen on the investment in these routes. At Surat, Martin noted, it was easy to obtain credit from local moneylenders but much more difficult, in the face of competition from Dutch, English, Arab, Persian and other traders, to complete the commerce needed to repay it.[44]

En route to Surat, Martin had been received by the brother-in-law of King Abul Hasan Qutb Shah of Golconda, with whom diplomatic channels had been re-established following the fall of San Thomé. Permission was secured for the re-opening of a *comptoir* at

Masulipatam. The Compagnie's directors in Paris, however, were belatedly coming round to the idea, originally promoted by François Bernier, that Bengal was more deserving of its attention. The agent that they dispatched to Bengal in the 1670s confirmed that it was 'extremely fertile', adding that 'the best textiles are made there and cost very little'.[45] Permission was obtained from Aurangzeb to trade on the Hooghly River—the economic heartland of the region—first in the town of Hooghly, founded by the Portuguese in the previous century, and then in a dedicated Compagnie settlement. Chandernagore, a village just downriver from the Dutch station of Chinsurah, was selected and a brick warehouse was constructed with residential quarters for the Compagnie's employees. Though volumes of trade remained low in the early years, rice and other foodstuffs procured in Bengal and shipped from Chandernagore were vital to the feeding of Pondicherry as it grew.[46]

The establishment of trading routes between India and Southeast Asia was also appealing. In the late 1660s, before his attention turned to Ceylon, François Caron had undertaken an expedition to Bantam, a part of the Indonesian archipelago that he knew well from his years in Dutch service. A trading post had been established and remained in the Compagnie's possession, though little trade was completed before the ruler of Bantam was overthrown and the French kicked out in 1682.[47]

The attention of the Compagnie now turned to the kingdom of Siam, where King Ramathibodi III had granted the French permission to trade the previous year. Siam was of little interest to the French in its own right; its main produce, pepper, was inferior in quality to the pepper of south India. For the Compagnie, however, it was a potential gateway to the markets of China and Japan; in the years that followed the Compagnie's installation in the Siamese capital of Ayutthaya, the first voyages were undertaken to the Chinese ports of Tonkin and Canton and diplomatic relations were opened with the Chinese court.[48] French Jesuit missionaries harboured high hopes of converting Ramathibodi III and his family to Christianity and were an influential presence in the kingdom. From his new palace at Versailles, Louis XIV showed a particular interest in the Siam project, dispatching two royal embassies to his Asian counterpart.

In an unprecedented step, Ramathibodi III returned the gesture; the delegation that he sent aboard French ships returning to Europe caused a sensation when it arrived at Versailles in September 1686 carrying gifts of gold, tortoise shells, carpets, cannons and more than 1,500 pieces of fine porcelain.[49]

Notwithstanding its efforts to expand, however, the finances of the Compagnie were poor and deteriorating. In France, investors remained sceptical about the returns to be made; the Compagnie's reserves being long-since exhausted, each new voyage to the Indies required subscribers, who were less and less inclined to come forward. More critically, Louis XIV's interest in the riches and glory to be gained on the Indian subcontinent appeared to be waning. Despite Colbert's efforts, the crown had refused to reimburse the advances paid by the Compagnie to support La Haye's forces during their Indian campaign; for the remainder of Louis's long reign, conquest in Europe would take priority over enrichment in India. Consequently, Compagnie ships were dispatched inconsistently from Europe; in 1677 and 1678, not a single vessel left France for India.[50]

To make matters worse, Colbert and the Compagnie's directors stuck rigidly to the mercantilist belief that exports of bullion from France should be kept to an absolute minimum, ignoring the advice offered by Bernier and others that gold and silver were the imports most demanded on the subcontinent. Compagnie agents on the ground had their work cut out attempting to convince Indian merchants to accept French manufactured goods—among them lace, buttons, hats, wigs, mirrors, crystals and iron tools—in return for their coveted commodities. Martin was only too aware of this handicap to French trade: 'We have lost many opportunities to establish ourselves in the Indies because of the limited support sent from France', he lamented. 'The export of gold and silver from the kingdom, when it is employed in commerce, need not be disadvantageous.'[51]

In India, the Compagnie not only lacked funds to make purchases, but money was also required to facilitate commercial operations—paying local employees and intermediaries, bribing officials and paying duties, for example—and for the business of everyday life. The taking out of loans at high interest rates and regular defaults on repayments locked the Compagnie into cycles of debt in some *comptoirs*, particularly Surat, where the corruption of Mughal officials was particularly endemic and new taxes regularly imposed. Martin was convinced that if the Dutch, English and French worked together they could resist the governor of Surat's repeated demands for payment; he deplored the fact that his fellow Europeans preferred to negotiate alone, competing with each other in vain attempts to win Mughal favour.[52] The imposition of a new tax (the *jizya*) on the transactions of all non-Muslims in the Mughal Empire was almost the final straw for the Compagnie's operations at Surat. They dragged on limply until the end of the century, when the head of the *comptoir* was imprisoned and French commerce forbidden in the city because of unpaid debts.[53]

Given its limited means, the Compagnie's attempts to expand beyond India to the Persian Gulf and Southeast Asia in this period were, on balance, more an unhelpful dilution of its resources and efforts than an effective strategy. At Bandar Abbas, a trading post was maintained for eight years despite its agent being unable to undertake any commerce, on account of the lack of funds.[54] During the 1680s, no less than twenty-five voyages were undertaken to Siam, with little material return.[55] In 1688 a violent palace coup then saw Ramathibodi III deposed and executed and the French expelled from the Siamese kingdom—the most dramatic illustration of how local political developments could undo the Compagnie's efforts. A strategy more singularly focused on the export of textiles from India, centred on Pondicherry and Chandernagore, may have stood more chance of success, but here too developments in France were damaging the Compagnie's efforts. Concerned about Indian competition, representatives of the French textile industry had begun calling for protectionist measures and in 1686 secured the introduction of import duties on Indian cloth. Strict limits were soon after placed on the volume of textiles that the Compagnie was permitted to bring back to the *patrie* (homeland).[56]

Only a small number of ships therefore made the return journey from India to France each year; between 1679 and 1682, for example, just one vessel was dispatched home annually.[57] Those that did leave India were rarely fully charged—and there was no guarantee of them making it back to France safely. Within the Indian Ocean, timing was everything; the annual cycles of the northeast and southwest monsoons dictated when ships could set sail, with dates varying from Surat to Malabar to the Coromandel to Bengal. Vessels setting off too early or too late would invariably find themselves stranded. On the long voyage to and from Europe—a minimum of six months and often much longer—errors of navigation were commonplace, with sailing routes poorly understood. Ships were often dangerously dilapidated and ill-equipped for the return journey—another problem that Martin put down to the Compagnie's lack of resources in its *comptoirs*.[58] As such, only half of the vessels sent out to India in the years before 1700 made it back to France successfully, while the rest were lost to the sea, captured by hostile forces or abandoned.[59] When a ship was lost, its cargo also perished, with disastrous consequences for the Compagnie's finances; in 1681, for example, the *Soleil d'Orient* sank on its return from Siam to France with a large cargo valued at 600,000 livres.[60] Aboard ships on the Europe–India route, sickness and shortages of provisions meant that mortality rates were as high as 50%, a major drain on the Compagnie's human resources.[61]

Compounding these problems was the insistence of the Compagnie's directors in France on attempting to control its affairs some 8,000 kilometres away in Asia. While it was perhaps understandable that major decisions like the establishment of a new *comptoir* required the directors' approval, they also expected to determine details like which agents to send on particular trading missions. The result was that agents on the ground were unable to make decisions quickly, instead waiting months and even years for instructions from Paris. The desperately slow speed at which information travelled between Europe and India sometimes had farcical consequences: the directors, for example, not infrequently promoted or recalled an employee who was long since dead in India.[62] More damagingly, agents on the ground lacked knowledge vital to their roles, not least about the outbreak and progress of European conflicts. Rumour and misinformation were rife: during the occupation of San Thomé, for example, word spread in the

French camp that Louis XIV's army had captured Amsterdam, cuing wild, misplaced celebrations.[63]

After two decades in India, some Frenchmen remained convinced that their nation would take over from the Dutch as the subcontinent's pre-eminent European power, just as the Dutch had earlier superseded the Portuguese. The dislike felt by local populations for the Dutch offered grounds for optimism: the Dutch Empire, recorded François Martin, would soon fall apart because of the subjugation of people within it.[64] In their more realistic moments, however, agents of the Compagnie were also conscious of the Dutch and English East India Companies' superior strength and resources. 'The most insignificant of English and Dutch trading posts are better established and supported than the principal posts of your company', wrote the Pondicherry council to the Compagnie's directors when the patience of its members had run dry.[65] As time progressed, the growing success of English commerce was a particular source of consternation. From Pondicherry, Martin followed enviously the disembarking of fleets from England on the Coromandel: 'Four ships of the English Company arrived this month at Madras from Europe', he noted in July 1680. 'They came richly charged. In truth, over the past eight to ten years no other company has been able to organise its voyages and commerce so well.'[66] The superiority of English navigation particularly struck Barthélemy Carré: 'There is no other maritime nation that in general equals [the English] in the matter of navigation', he recorded, 'and if they are [even] more proud and haughty on sea than on land [...] they have some ground for it.'[67]

By 1682—the same year that French explorers in America arrived at the mouth of the Mississippi, laying claim to a territory christened Louisiana—the Compagnie's financial position was so bad that it began selling space on its vessels heading to India for the shipping of non-Compagnie goods as freight.[68] The following year, Colbert passed away, his grand plans for the Compagnie seemingly defeated. All hope was not lost, however. Taking over responsibility for the Compagnie from his father, Jean-Baptiste Antoine Colbert quickly raised sufficient capital to inject new life into its operations and stopped the carrying of non-Compagnie goods. No less than nine ships were sent out from France in 1687 and four in 1688.[69]

Unfortunately for the Compagnie's new investors, it was at precisely this moment that the political context in Europe and southern India deteriorated again.

*

Ten years on from the conclusion of France's last major expansionist campaign in Europe, Louis XIV—whose standing among European states had been damaged by the violent state-led persecution of French Protestants that followed his revocation of the Edict of Nantes—could not resist having another go. In September 1688 his armies crossed the Rhine at Strasbourg and occupied a string of German towns from Mainz down to the Swiss border to extend his dynastic and territorial claims over parts of the Holy Roman Empire. Emperor Leopold I and the states of the Empire determined to resist this aggression and, as dynastic loyalties realigned after the installation of William of Orange on the English throne, England, the Dutch Republic, Spain and Portugal sided with the Holy Roman Empire to form a Grand Alliance against France. The Nine Years' War was underway.

In India, Emperor Aurangzeb—who in his absolutism, his longevity, his divisive religious policies and his ceaseless desire to expand the frontiers of his empire shared many characteristics with Louis XIV—had meanwhile invaded the Deccan.[70] In September 1686, the Kingdom of Bijapur was defeated and the following year, after a brutal 9-month siege, Golconda fell to the Mughals. The kingdoms' respective dynasties, the Adil Shahis at Bijapur and the Qutb Shahis at Golconda, were extinguished. The other key target for Aurangzeb was the Marathas. For much of the previous decade, Mughal armies had attacked Maratha strongholds in the western ghats, homing in on their capital, Raigad. In February 1689, the new Maratha leader, Shivaji Bhosle's son Sambhaji, was captured; after refusing to bow to Aurangzeb, he was executed, sparking a succession struggle in the Maratha hierarchy from which Rajaram Bhosle, Shivaji's second son, emerged victorious. Not one to miss the chance of further conquest, Aurangzeb saw the division in the Maratha court as an opportunity and, just two weeks after Rajaram's coronation, encircled the new leader at Raigad, with the tacit support of the rival Maratha faction. Rajaram succeeded in fleeing, taking refuge 1,000 kilometres away in the fort of Gingee at the furthest extremity of the Maratha Empire.

From being a distant dynastic struggle, the Mughal-Maratha war had now arrived on the doorstep of the French at Pondicherry. In September 1690, Mughal forces under the direction of fearsome commander Zulfikar Khan laid siege to Gingee; Rajaram's army held their own and a stalemate set in. For François Martin, pondering the Compagnie's response to this upheaval, the situation was particularly delicate. News had reached Pondicherry the previous summer that France and the Dutch Republic were again at war. The Frenchman was aware that a Dutch embassy had made its way to Gingee and feared, not unreasonably, that it would pressure Rajaram for permission to capture Pondicherry. The intelligence leaking out from Gingee suggested to Martin that close aides of the Maratha leader had already granted their blessing for an attack.[71]

Martin's first response was to send a counter-embassy to Rajaram to argue that Pondicherry was rightfully theirs, as his father Shivaji had acknowledged. When this appeal fell on deaf ears, a loan of 6,000 pagodas was offered. To the cash-strapped Maratha leader, this was more persuasive: in return for the money, he signed a new *firman* promising support to the French in the event of Dutch aggression and granting the Compagnie the right to collect tax, customs and land revenues from Pondicherry until the loan was repaid in full. Martin suspected that, given Rajaram's perilous financial position and the whopping 18% rate of interest, it would never be repaid and noted with satisfaction that the Compagnie had in effect been re-awarded Pondicherry revenue collection rights in perpetuity.[72] Moreover, permission had been secured to strengthen Pondicherry's fortifications. In the months that followed, a new battery was constructed between the fort and the sea and extra cannons were installed. The garrison stationed in the fort was strengthened with the recruitment of more local troops.

Wishing to avoid throwing the Compagnie's lot in exclusively with the Marathas, Martin also sent agents to meet with Zulfikar Khan, whose army had remained in the vicinity of Gingee preparing a second siege. Through 1691 and 1692, after Rajaram's forces had gone on the offensive, fierce fighting between Mughal and Maratha troops spread through the Tamil countryside, coming within cannon-shot of Pondicherry in January 1692. Compagnie trade suffered as the local textile industry was disrupted by the pillaging and devastation of nearby villages. Martin could do little but attempt to placate both sides, sending gifts to the two leaders to ensure that Pondicherry was left untouched.

By the close of 1692, Rajaram again desperately needed to raise more cash. This time he approached the French camp, offering to sell the Compagnie the coastal fort of Devenapatnam, 30 kilometres south of Pondicherry, on high ground above Cuddalore, for the sum of 50,000 pagodas. The offer was attractive, but the Compagnie did not have the means.[73] A buyer was instead found in the English company, who took possession of Devenapatnam and renamed it Fort St David. The all-out purchase of Pondicherry was then offered to the French for a slightly more modest sum. Martin played for time, not confident that Rajaram would be alive long enough to make the purchase worthwhile—an opportunity on which the Dutch capitalised. In the summer of 1693, the VOC stepped in and offered 25,000 pagodas for the acquisition of Pondicherry, which Rajaram accepted. Not even a belated French offer to match this sum could convince him to change his mind.[74] The transaction complete, the Dutch had carte blanche to attack the town and eradicate the Compagnie from the Coromandel.

Until this point, direct Franco-Dutch hostilities in India related to the outbreak of the Nine Years' War had been all but avoided, though the conflict had spread to the French and English colonies in North America and the Caribbean. In September 1690, a squadron of six naval ships had arrived at Pondicherry from France; a brief skirmish ensued with the Dutch fleet anchored off Madras.[75] A second French squadron arrived at Surat in December 1692, but with just four ships, it too avoided being drawn into major hostilities. After the Dutch purchase of Pondicherry, however, this stand-off ended. In May 1693, as fierce fighting raged in the Low Countries, northern Italy and Catalonia, a powerful Dutch squadron of ten ships appeared off the Coromandel Coast from the VOC's Indian Ocean headquarters of Batavia (present-day Jakarta, Indonesia). As further reinforcements followed from Ceylon, the Dutch intention to attack Pondicherry was clear. Martin hastened to make sure that the town was ready: the fortifications were hurriedly finished, barricades were erected and houses in the line of fire from the fort were pulled down. All non-combatants were evacuated, among them Martin's wife and other Frenchwomen, who took refuge with the Danish at Tranquebar.

In August 1693, the Dutch fleet advanced to a position half a league southeast of Pondicherry. By this stage it was composed of nineteen large vessels and several smaller ones carrying an estimated 1,500 European and 15,000 Asian troops—the latter mostly Macassars from Indonesia and Sinhalese from Ceylon.[76] It was, in Martin's words, a veritable 'army at sea'.[77] The French, in contrast, had just 100 European combatants and 500 'country soldiers' at their disposal, among them 200 mercenaries from Rajasthan.[78]

In the final days of August, the Dutch troops disembarked to encircle Pondicherry on land. The bombardment of the town then started on 31 August. Two days later, the towers of the French fort were struck and on 5 September the fortifications were breached. In just a week, Pondicherry had fallen. During negotiations over the terms of the capitulation that followed, Martin attempted to secure free passage for all Compagnie employees to Bengal, so that French commercial operations could resume there. The VOC refused: instead, all French military and Compagnie personnel would have to leave India, except those who had married local women, who were permitted to withdraw to Cuddalore. Most soldiers and Compagnie employees were embarked on vessels for Ceylon and from there back to Europe. Martin and a few other high-ranking officials were taken to Batavia, however; the leader of Compagnie efforts at Pondicherry then travelled as a captive of the VOC to Sumatra and Malacca before being deposited in Bengal the following year. Reflecting ruefully on the capitulation, Martin laid the blame squarely on the lack of support received from Paris. 'Clearly, it was difficult for us to maintain ourselves any longer against a powerful European nation in the Indies and their local allies without receiving any assistance nor orders.'[79]

In the end, it was events in Europe that rescued Pondicherry for the Compagnie. In May 1697, the Treaty of Ryswick was signed, bringing to a close a conflict fought across several continents.[80] One of the articles of the treaty dictated the mutual restitution of places seized. Pondicherry was mentioned explicitly, with the stipulation that it should be returned to the French with its fortifications, strengthened by the VOC, intact. This was a significant victory for French negotiators, who had had the importance of Pondicherry impressed on them by Compagnie authorities.[81] Martin was now formally recognised as governor of all the Compagnie's establishments in India. He returned to the Coromandel from Bengal to find the Mughal-Maratha war also drawing to a close. In January 1698, the Mughals finally captured Gingee and forced the Marathas out of southeast India; the Carnatic region, including the Coromandel Coast, was consolidated into the Mughal Empire, with victorious commander Zulfikar Khan placed in charge. One of Martin's first acts after his return to Pondicherry was to send an embassy to the new Mughal governor. In return for a substantial bribe, French possession of Pondicherry and the surrounding villages, first granted to the Compagnie by Sher Khan Lodi, was confirmed.[82]

A rapid period of construction and development followed. In the European part of Pondicherry, closest to the seafront, a grand new residence was built for the governor, along with a hundred brick houses and shops. Weavers, artisans and merchants were attracted back to the non-European part, which, removed from the sea and slightly elevated, was laid out in a grid pattern with a large marketplace at its centre. Under the direction of M. de Nyon, a specialist engineer sent out from Paris, the fort was also upgraded. Its new pentagonal shape—based on the influential ideas of the Marquis de Vauban, who had revolutionised the design of fortifications in France—was the latest in military engineering. The first *fort Vauban* outside of Europe, it was christened Fort Louis and reinforced with the arrival of 200 troops from France. A strong defensive wall was also constructed around the town, encircling its European and non-European residents.[83]

In the summer of 1701, war was again triggered in Europe, this time as Louis XIV and Leopold I backed rival contenders to the Spanish throne after the death of the childless Charles II. The continued alliance of the Dutch Republic and England with the Holy Roman Empire meant that India was once more a possible theatre of war. Through a most fortuitous coup, however, the effectiveness of Pondicherry's new fortifications would not, in the end, be tested. In January 1705, as conflict in Indian waters appeared imminent, a French patrol seized a Dutch vessel, the *Golden Phoenix*, off the coast of Ceylon. On board was found the governor of the VOC's trading posts on the Coromandel Coast, Bernard Phronsen, who was taken to Pondicherry and imprisoned in Fort Louis. Through the negotiations that followed, François Martin secured a treaty of non-aggression between the French and Dutch on the Coromandel in return for the governor's release. Pondicherry was therefore spared a second Dutch attack and likely occupation in little over a decade.[84]

The following year, Martin, a veteran at the age of 72, passed away at Pondicherry. Over the previous forty years, he had played an influential role in the efforts of the Compagnie to establish itself in India, its fortunes inseparable from his. In his final moments, he could reflect on what had been achieved. Though little trading success had been enjoyed, and the position of the Compagnie's other *comptoirs* on the subcontinent remained perilous, a foothold in India had finally been secured. Pondicherry was the substantial, protected settlement and trading post that the French had so desperately sought.

4

LIFE AND DEBT

In the early months of 1707, just after François Martin's passing, the corridors of power in Paris and Versailles were a flurry of activity. The Compagnie was on its last legs, limping towards the end of its fifty-year monopoly on trade between Europe and Asia. With debts of 6.5 million livres, it was no longer able to raise funds for the repair of ships and dispatch of new vessels to the Indian Ocean.[1] Embroiled in the War of Spanish Succession, the Crown was also hugely indebted and unable to help. An association of merchants from the Breton port of Saint-Malo, backed by the wealthy financier Antoine Crozat, sought to profit from the Compagnie's demise. Following extensive negotiations with Compagnie directors and representatives of the Crown, they secured the right to dispatch vessels to the Persian Gulf and the Red Sea before taking over the Compagnie's monopoly on Indian Ocean trade in its entirety in 1712, in return for payment to the Compagnie of 10% of the value of sales.[2] The port and shipyards of Lorient, now surplus to the Compagnie's requirements, were leased to the navy.

With the Compagnie's commercial operations suspended, its trading posts at Surat and Masulipatam, which had never been profitable, were abandoned. The large unpaid debts left behind at Surat would tarnish the French reputation in the Mughal port city for decades to come, fatally undermining the efforts of the Saint-Malouin merchants to trade there. The settlements of Pondicherry and Chandernagore were retained, however, and for the French communities who had made them their home, the second decade of the eighteenth century was experienced more as continuity than rupture. Under François Martin, the Compagnie had already assumed responsibility for the administration of its small territorial possessions on the Coromandel Coast and in Bengal. With Europe-Asia trade now the preserve of the Saint-Malo association, colonial government became the Compagnie's raison d'être. Under the Compagnie's statutes, employees who had served for three years in the Indies were entitled to return to France; senior agents serving for eight years were promised titles of nobility when they got home.[3] In practice, however, requests to return to the *patrie* were rarely granted by the Compagnie's directors; additionally, the dangers of the voyage made many think twice about returning to Europe. As such, the French settlements in India were increasingly populated by Frenchmen who had spent most of their lives in the Indies, and by their children and grandchildren, who followed their elders into careers with the Compagnie or other livelihoods in India, and had never set foot in France. Pondicherry and Chandernagore ceased to be simple *comptoirs* and became veritable colonies to which stronger attachments were often felt than to France itself.

In spite of the Compagnie's demise as a commercial entity, Pondicherry continued to grow. By 1715 its European quarters—referred to in French records as the '*ville blanche*' (White Town)—extended along the seafront both north and south of Fort Louis. The non-European section—or '*ville noire*' (Black Town)—spilled over from the walled city into a new quarter south of the protective moat. According to the best available estimates, the population of the *ville blanche* numbered 1,000–2,000 and the *ville noire* as many as 50,000 at this juncture.[4]

The simple division of Pondicherry into 'white' and 'black'—European and non-European—parts masked a much more nuanced reality, however. For one, the French population was a mishmash of different occupations and social classes. Employed by the Compagnie were administrators, military personnel and others, in addition to whom the *ville blanche* welcomed private traders and settlers, including a smattering of Europeans of other nationalities, and Catholic priests of different denominations. Disputes between these constituencies were commonplace—not least, as we will see, in the exchanges between different religious orders and their dealings with Compagnie officials. The non-European population of Pondicherry was even more diverse, with differences of religion, ethnicity, caste, occupation and language concealed by the label 'black'. While a majority of the *ville noire*'s residents were Hindu, the city possessed a sizeable Muslim minority and a growing population of Christians. Caste identities ranged from the Brahmin at the top of the social scale to untouchables, who were confined to an enclosed 'village' within the *ville noire*, at the bottom. About one-third of the local population were weavers engaged in manufacturing textiles, while other notable occupations, which often overlapped with caste identities, included itinerant merchants, fishermen and carpenters. Tamil speakers from the countryside around Pondicherry predominated, though a bewildering variety of other linguistic and ethnic identities from across India and the Indian Ocean were also represented in the colony.[5]

In addition, the significant intermixing of Europeans and non-Europeans in Pondicherry calls into question the distinction between the colony's 'white' and 'black' populations and raises the question of what was meant by the label 'French'. Within the *ville noire* lived a significant number of Indo-Portuguese, referred to as '*topas*', the product of two centuries of relations on the Coromandel between men of Portuguese descent and local women.[6] By the early eighteenth century, a small number of French-born women had joined their husbands and fathers in India, among them the wife of François Martin, whose first name does not appear in records, and their daughter, Marie, who would go on to marry another Compagnie agent, M. Deslandes.[7] For most men in the *ville blanche*, however, particularly those of lower rank, the only option for marriage was a woman of Indian or Indo-Portuguese descent. Though marriages and other relationships between 'white' and 'black' were periodically condemned by the Compagnie and missionaries, they remained commonplace. The offspring of these relationships—referred to as '*métis*'—rendered increasingly meaningless the distinction between the two. In an attempt to demarcate between identities that were ever more blurred, new hierarchies were invented. Some French texts distinguished between the French born in France, those born in India to French parents and—the majority in the *ville blanche*—those born in India to parents of French and Indian or Indo-Portuguese descent.

The daily contact of Indian people with the French illustrates still further the difficulty of identifying two discrete populations.[8] Nowhere is this more evident than in the role played by local figures acting as middlemen or intermediaries between the French and Indian populations. Foremost among them were commercial brokers—labelled *courtiers*—charged with facilitating trade on behalf of the Compagnie (later the Saint-Malo association) and that of Europeans undertaking business on their private account. In the conduct of business in India, the *courtier* was essential: not only would he procure merchandise, negotiating with local merchants and placing orders with producers, but he was also an important source of credit, advancing funds for purchases.[9] If the *courtier* was often a figure of contempt or suspicion to the French, it was no doubt because of their dependence on him. Without a middleman, French merchants lacked an understanding of the local prices, exchange rates, weights and measures required to make purchases; the language skills needed to negotiate deals; and the reputation necessary to obtain credit directly from Indian traders.[10]

From Martin's time onwards, the Compagnie had taken to appointing a 'chief courtier' who worked closely with the governor and other French agents and supervised a network of intermediaries overseeing its operations on the ground. The organisation of the textile trade is illustrative. In May each year the chief courtier would convene the principal textile merchants of the region at Fort Louis. French demands were placed for the coming year and contracts were drawn up stipulating the quality and quantity of fabrics to be produced, the price and delivery date. Advances were paid to those with whom contracts had been concluded; through the remainder of the year, the chief courtier and his subordinates managed the relationship with each merchant and ensured that the contracts were fulfilled.[11] As the Compagnie's role grew to include the government of the colony, the position of chief courtier became even more important. The chief courtier was a vital source of information about what was going on within the Tamil community of Pondicherry and the wider region, and even managed relationships with Indian rulers.

Through the eighteenth century, the position of chief courtier was contested between two rival families, the Mudalis and the Pillais, who at different moments found themselves in or out of French favour. François Martin's trusted appointee, Tanappa Mudali, was the first of three generations of Mudalis to hold the office. Of the four or more Pillais to serve as chief courtier, meanwhile, Nayiniyappa Pillai (who served from 1708 to 1715) and Ananda Ranga Pillai (from 1746 to 1761) were the two most high-profile.[12] As chief courtiers, members of both the Mudali and Pillai clans collaborated closely with the governor, working in Fort Louis while residing in family mansions in the *ville noire*. Their jobs required them to move fluidly across Pondicherry's European-Indian divide, mediating between cultures and languages. Until the middle of the eighteenth century, Portuguese was the language used to bridge the gap between the Francophone population and speakers of Indian languages at Pondicherry, given the very small number of people proficient in, for example, both Tamil and French.

A second category of people who defy straightforward assignment to the 'white' or 'black' populations of Pondicherry were the slaves present in most households in the *ville blanche*. At Pondicherry, and indeed at Chandernagore, it was customary for Compagnie agents and other Frenchmen to keep slaves, who served in domestic roles, as cooks and housekeepers, for example. The Compagnie also possessed slaves of its own, who were often pressed into service as manual labourers on its ships and in its warehouses. At least half of the population of Pondicherry's *ville blanche* was in fact non-white and enslaved, while at Chandernagore, an estimated 1,500 slaves served a European population of just 500. One Compagnie official, Michel Fourmier, owned no fewer than 13 slaves.[13] The sale of individuals into slavery was commonplace on the Coromandel Coast each time incidences of famine rendered local populations desperate, while instances of kidnapping and forced enslavement are also on record.[14]

Slaves were brought to Pondicherry from the surrounding region to be sold at the colony's market. 'For a rupee', noted one French observer, 'one can have a slave who feeds and maintains himself and serves with complete fidelity.'[15] In the Bay of Bengal, meanwhile, the capture and traffic of slaves was a long-established practice, dating to pre-colonial times, from which the Portuguese, before the French, had sought to profit.[16] Most slaves in French possession at Pondicherry and Chandernagore were therefore of Indian or Arakanese (Burmese) origin. By 1715, however, some slaves had also been brought to India from Madagascar and the east and west coasts of Africa on Compagnie ships. As we will see, slave trafficking would soon become one of the principal French commercial activities and sources of profit in the Indian Ocean.

*

A thousand kilometres northwest of Pondicherry in the city of Ahmednagar, the year 1707 also witnessed the death of Aurangzeb, the last of the great Mughal emperors. Though the empire would survive in name for another 150 years, its break-up had begun. In the decades that followed, none of Aurangzeb's successors would come close to matching the longevity of his forty-nine-year reign. Instability at the imperial centre, as different dynastic factions fought for the throne, was coupled with disintegration at the margins, as a succession of Mughal provinces secured their de facto independence from the empire. They included the provinces of the Carnatic and Bengal, in which lay Pondicherry and Chandernagore respectively. Though both remained nominally part of the Mughal Empire, their governors increasingly ruled independently of the imperial centre—a transition secured, on account of the weakness of that centre, without the violent conflict that had characterised much of Aurangzeb's reign.

With Pondicherry and Chandernagore experiencing unusually long periods of peace, problems of survival for their inhabitants focused more on the challenges posed by their unforgiving natural environments and climates. Annual cycles of rain, extreme heat and wind dictated the rhythms of trade and everyday life. In the summer, wrote one French resident of Pondicherry, the sun was 'so violent that it burns and destroys the skin'.[17] When the hot winds arrived, added another, it was 'impossible to breath'.[18] In Bengal and on the Coromandel, cyclones were a regular occurrence. In their aftermath, the lakes around Pondicherry flooded the town, infesting it with snakes. Storms and earthquakes wreaked havoc, ruining entire settlements. Given the extremes of climate and limited understanding of disease transmission, it is not surprising that illness was rife. In French records the catch-all term '*peste*' (plague) was used to describe maladies including cholera, leprosy and smallpox. For the residents of Pondicherry and Chandernagore, meanwhile, India was experienced more as a land of scarcity than of abundance, contrary to the cliches peddled by early European visitors. On the Coromandel, in particular, food was regularly in short supply, with Pondicherry increasingly reliant on food imported from Bengal. Famine in the countryside was a frequent occurrence. After one particularly severe incidence, Francois Martin had earlier noted, 'villages that had accommodated 30–40,000 souls were now unpopulated. The countryside was covered with bones, while the houses and roads were full of dead bodies.'[19]

With Europe-Asia trade in the hands of the Saint-Malo association, which dispatched an average of three vessels per year to India from 1712, the Compagnie was reliant on other sources of revenue to cover the costs of maintaining its Indian colonies. A modest income was derived from the taxing of commercial transactions and the imposition of import duties on goods arriving at Pondicherry. Possession of a small territory around the city, meanwhile, allowed for the farming of tobacco and betel, a vital source of extra revenue.[20] The Pondicherry council—a group of seven, including the governor—was responsible not only for the government of French possessions in India but for the administration of justice in its territories. Cases involving at least one French party were to be decided in accordance with legal codes and rules operational in France, while a separate lower court known as the *chaudrie* attempted to apply local law and customs to disputes involving Indians only.[21] The fines and confiscations of property handed out by these courts—usually accompanied by imprisonment and severe corporal punishment—were another modest revenue stream.

For individuals in the French settlements, meanwhile, a key source of income was the private trade in which many participated, and which, for those with capital to invest, offered significant possibilities for enrichment. While trade between India and Europe was firmly the preserve of the Compagnie, and later the Saint-Malo association, much more ambiguity surrounded the right to trade between different sites in the Indian Ocean (the intra-Asian trade or, in contemporary French parlance, the *commerce d'Inde en Inde*). From the outset, the possibility of engaging in this trade, rather than the miserly salaries offered, had been a key motivation for joining the Compagnie and risking life and limb on a voyage to Asia. 'One goes to the East only to do business', announced one high-profile Frenchman in the most emphatic statement of this view.[22] The approach of the Compagnie directors vacillated from the prohibition of private trade, which was never extensively enforced, to tacit acceptance. Was it because of its employees' private commercial activities, which often took advantage of Compagnie resources—not least agents' time—that the Compagnie was unable to make a profit itself? Or could private and Compagnie business go hand-in-hand, with the incentive of personal enrichment creating opportunities for Compagnie trade and adding to its tax and customs revenue? Whichever way the wind was blowing in Paris, the practice of private trade at Pondicherry and Chandernagore was widespread. With increasing regularity, Compagnie officials and other Europeans invested jointly in the purchase of vessels and the launch of trading expeditions. Some were confined to the Indian coast, plying the route between Bengal and the Coromandel, for example, while others ventured to the Persian Gulf and Red Sea (for the purchase of coffee, wine, raw cotton and silver) or Southeast Asia and China (for spices, tea, silk and porcelain), which were then shipped back to India. As knowledge of trading routes grew, it was not unusual for profits of 20–40% to be made. By the 1720s, successful private traders stood to triple or quadruple their investments within the space of a few years.[23]

A constituency in the colony with an altogether different vocation, meanwhile, was the priesthood. In pre-revolutionary France,

Catholicism and the monarchy were inseparably intertwined. As a state-driven entity, the Compagnie des Indes therefore naturally had a religious dimension; its 1664 articles stipulated that in all colonial territories the Compagnie would maintain an ecclesiastical establishment and support the evangelisation of non-Christian peoples. Missionaries and other priests would be transported free of charge on Compagnie ships and lodged and fed in French settlements.[24] In this regard, the Compagnie took after the Portuguese regime in the East, the Estado da India, where commerce and Christianisation formed part of the same colonial project and the priesthood exercised an influential role. The approach was at odds with that of the major Protestant powers in the Indian Ocean, the Dutch and British, whose trading companies had declined any responsibility for the propagation of faith, fearing the disruptive influence of mission work on their business. In the Dutch and British settlements in the Indies, only skeletal church structures were maintained, their task being to look after the spiritual needs of their compatriots rather than to spread the faith.

Several years before the foundation of the Compagnie in 1664, an organisation dedicated to the propagation of Catholicism overseas—the Missions étrangères de Paris—had been established in France. With Louis XIV's encouragement its missionaries headed for the Indian Ocean; a small lodge was opened at Pondicherry and used primarily as a stopping post en route for Siam and China, the main focuses of missionary labours.[25] More significant to life at Pondicherry and Changernagore were the two rival Catholic orders that installed themselves in the French settlements almost immediately after the Compagnie had taken possession of them: the Capuchins and the Jesuits. In theory, a clear division of responsibilities separated one from the other: the Capuchins tended to the French and the wider European Catholic population of the two colonies, while the Jesuits were responsible for evangelisation and the development of a church of indigenous converts.[26] With this in mind, the Capuchins maintained a chapel in Fort Louis and a church, Notre Dame des Anges, in Pondicherry's *ville blanche*, while the Jesuits opened a church in the heart of the *ville noire*. This separation of roles did not, however, prevent the two orders from engaging in repeated and often acrimonious dispute.

From their headquarters in the *ville noire*, the Pondicherry Jesuits, a small band of five or so priests, followed in the footsteps of their Portuguese predecessors, who had been active in southern India since the mid-sixteenth century, in attempting to carry the faith to local populations in the Tamil countryside. With the aid of local converts, missions were established in towns and villages up to a week's travel from the colony, and further afield in Madurai and Mysore. The rudiments of the Catholic faith were translated into local languages and disseminated orally. For the Jesuits, mission activity was an often-thankless task. To avoid being attacked or robbed on unfamiliar roads in the interior of the country, the missionaries and their Indian catechists travelled at night, fearful of local hostility, 'which extends to the Holy Faith that we preach'.[27] The letters that they dispatched back to France complained regularly about the local population's lack of receptivity to the Word of God. Brahmins, in particular, fought fire with fire, advancing their own theological precepts and refusing to accept the superiority of Christian beliefs whenever the missionaries succeeded in engaging them in discussion. 'There is no people', noted one Jesuit at Pondicherry, 'more haughty, more obstinate against the Truth, nor more full of superstitions and the conceit of their nobility [...] They spare no pains to render us odious in the country.'[28]

Those people who did convert, it was added, faced the fierce hostility of their local communities, with violent reprisals and ostracisation often following. As such, the number of converts remained small and where conversions were secured, they usually had little to do with individuals seeing the light; within the official conversion figures relayed by the Jesuits to their superiors in Europe were all the local women who had married French men and the slaves possessed by French households, who were automatically baptised and given Christian names. Even then, the conversion figures were keenly contested. When, in 1720, the Jesuits claimed 15,000 conversions at Pondicherry, the reaction of the governing council was incredulous: 'Fifteen thousand Christians!' it exclaimed. 'An impressive sum. This number has been made up by those in whose interest it is that it is believed. We could in good conscience remove 12,500 from the total and the number remaining would still not entirely be likely.'[29]

What irked the Capuchins about Jesuit missionary activity was the willingness of the Society of Jesus to accept that converts to Christianity might retain customs and even beliefs linked to their earlier religious and caste identities. A pragmatic move on the part of the Jesuits struggling to win over local peoples—or looking to inflate conversion figures—this 'accommodation' was, for the Capuchins, an unacceptable dilution or rendering impure of the pristine Christian faith. In the Carnatic, as indeed elsewhere in south India where Portuguese and French Jesuits were active, Hindu converts to Christianity were permitted to continue celebrating local holy days; to add the ashes of dried cow dung, revered by Hindus, to the sacred oil used in baptisms and other ceremonies; and to wear amulets displaying figures of divinity, which to the Capuchins looked a lot like idols. After conversion, caste distinctions were also retained, with Jesuit churches containing separate sections for lower caste and untouchable converts to appease higher caste converts. Scandalised by these practices, the Capuchins appealed to the Pope, who in 1704 sent out a bishop from Rome to India to adjudicate. The Jesuit practices of accommodation—known as the 'Malabar Rites'—were decreed un-Christian and outlawed by the papacy, though the decree had little effect.[30]

Through their travels on the subcontinent and the studies that they undertook, some missionaries in the early eighteenth century acquired an understanding of Indian religions and society that went deeper than that of any other Frenchmen who had gone before them—for example François Pyrard or François Bernier, both of whom, in their seventeenth century writings, had attempted to explain Hindu religious practices and beliefs to the uninitiated in France. Jesuit father Jean Venance Bouchet studied the Hindu scriptures in the holy city of Madurai, writing to his superior to explain the trinity of Brahma (the creator), Vishnu (the preserver) and Shiva (the destroyer).[31] Father de la Lane at Pondicherry explained the principle of reincarnation, the 'transmigration of souls' from one being to the next in the Hindu tradition.[32] For the most part, however, these understandings remained superficial. With a few notable exceptions, the missionaries failed to master Indian languages, instead relying on the translations and explanations provided by local interlocutors.[33] Hindu beliefs and practices were studied not in and of themselves but in relation to Christianity, with an eye to assessing how far local peoples had to travel to become good Christians. Bouchet, for example, argued that because the gods of the Hindu pantheon were all manifestations of one Supreme Being, the transition to Christianity would come easily to Hindus with a little Jesuit help. Comparisons were drawn between descriptions of paradise, of floods and of Noah's Ark in the Old Testament and similar events in Hindu sacred tales. Hindu understandings of morality were read through a Christian lens. Generally speaking, noted one missionary, Hindus did not eat or drink to excess; they were 'very reserved as to women', respected their teachers, looked after the poor and cared well for their families.[34] In other words, they were ready to become good Christians, if only the remaining obstacles to their conversion could be overcome.

When the limits of their understanding were reached, however, some missionaries went in the other direction, emphasising what was strange and sensational in the local cultures that they encountered and contenting themselves with the performance of outrage. The lingam symbol of Shiva was interpreted as a phallus and dwelt upon extensively, along with the practice of sati—the immolation of widows on their husbands' funeral pyres.[35] Rather than deepening their understanding, certain missionary figures appeared to throw in the towel. 'Generally all the people of India worship some form of Deity', noted Father Martin from Madurai, 'but alas they are very far from the knowledge of the True God. Being worse blinded by their passions than by the Devil, they form to themselves monstrous notions of the Sovereign Being, and you cannot conceive on what vile creatures they lavish Divine Honours.'[36] 'In all directions there are temples of idolatry', despaired another observer. 'The people are to be pitied; and the Devil is very powerful among them, because he makes himself adored in so many places.'[37] Such descriptions offer weight to the conclusion later recorded by Ananda Ranga Pillai that most French men and women on the subcontinent, 'even those who had lived here for fifteen, twenty or thirty years, still appeared to be very stupid.'[38]

In general, agents of the Compagnie were supportive of the missionaries' endeavours. After the revocation of the Edict of Nantes, any remaining Protestants in Compagnie service had been forced out, with many finding employment in the Dutch and British companies in the Indies, their skills and experience appreciated by France's rivals. The Compagnie was therefore staffed exclusively by Catholics, many of whom shared the Jesuits' fervour for the advancement of the True Religion in the East and would have agreed with their periodic outbursts about the 'moral laxity' of the French lay population in India. François Martin was a devout believer who welcomed the Jesuit presence in Pondicherry, encouraged their construction of a school and hospital in the *ville noire*, and was on intimate terms with the mission's first leader, Father Tachard. For the Compagnie, missionaries were often a useful source of information about events beyond the walls of Pondicherry and, on occasion, were even used to relay messages and carry funds on the Compagnie's behalf.[39] The close link between French and Portuguese Jesuits in southern India served as an informal diplomatic channel between Pondicherry and Goa.

The differing priorities of the missionaries and the Compagnie meant, however, that a degree of tension between the two was inevitable. While, for the Jesuits, converting the heathen took precedence over all other imperatives, commerce, revenue generation and the maintenance of order were the Compagnie's main goals. Periodically, the frictions created by these different objectives flared into rancorous discord. Martin and his successor as governor, Pierre Dulivier, envisaged Pondicherry as a town that should be open to all, regardless of religious identity—an approach that they considered necessary for the development of the colony into a thriving commercial centre attracting merchants from across India and the Indian Ocean. A 1708 declaration issued by Dulivier stressed that all nationalities and religions could conduct commercial affairs in the French settlement.[40] The Jesuits, however, envisaged a colony where Christianity was superior, and would ultimately be the only religion in town. As such, they objected to the Pondicherry council allowing the presence of temples and mosques and the celebration of non-Christian festivals at Pondicherry. When these complaints fell on deaf ears they were forwarded to the Compagnie's directors in Paris and even to the King.

In the period up to 1715, three flashpoints stand out, highlighting the tensions between the diverging priorities of the Compagnie and the Jesuit mission at Pondicherry, and the response of the town's Hindu community, as its right to express its faith in the colonial public sphere was cast into doubt. In August 1702, when Hindu and Catholic religious festivals happened to fall on the same day, the Jesuits succeeded in securing from the Compagnie the prohibition of public Hindu celebrations in the town. In response, some 15,000 members of the local population, among them weavers on whom the Compagnie depended, threatened to quit the town, congregating at one of the city gates and demanding that it be opened. Panicked, the governing council lifted the prohibition.[41] The directors in Paris, pressured by the Pondicherry authorities and the Society of Jesus, soon after fudged a compromise: that, in future, Hindus would be authorised to celebrate festivals and conduct ceremonies relating to their 'false religion' only if their idols were carried at a distance from the principal arteries of the town.[42]

Three years later it was the proximity of a temple to their church in the *ville noire* that the Jesuits took umbrage at. From the grounds of the church, they protested, Hindu ceremonies could be heard. What was more, local converts feared passing the temple on their way to worship. When word leaked that the Pondicherry council was considering the mandatory relocation of the temple, a portion of the population again threatened to leave the town, and plans for a relocation order were scrapped.[43] The Jesuits, however, would not let the matter lie. In a petition to Louis XIV they argued that the Hindus of Pondicherry should be permitted the use of two temples only; all others should be barred shut and allowed to fall into disrepair. The Pondicherry council responded that such a move would provoke serious opposition, risking the 'complete ruin of this establishment', and the Jesuit claims were turned down.[44]

A similar exodus of the local population was threatened in February 1715 when, bowing to Jesuit pressure, Compagnie authorities at

Pondicherry attempted to prevent the Hindu celebration of the new moon on a Sunday. This time the protesting population of the *ville noire* made it clear that their intention was to relocate to Madras, where the British authorities were more accommodating of religious difference. The protestors included not only weavers essential to the Compagnie's operations but labourers responsible for loading and unloading vessels. At this moment, two ships of the Saint-Malo association were anchored at Pondicherry. The protestors held the trump card, knowing that without their labour it would be impossible to load the vessels and dispatch them to Europe before the monsoon winds changed. Once again, commercial interests ultimately won out over Jesuit complaints and, in the streets of the French colony, the new moon was celebrated boisterously.[45]

The Jesuits, however, were not prepared to take this defeat lying down and, before the dust had settled, turned their ire towards the Compagnie's chief courtier, Nayiniyappa Pillai, who was accused of organising the protests. In the weeks that followed, further accusations were added: that Nayiniyappa had publicly disrespected the missionaries and their faith by agitating to prevent conversions at Pondicherry and by distributing alms to those lower caste residents who had converted, traditionally the preserve of the Church.[46] Behind these accusations lay a refusal to accept that Nayiniyappa, the highest-ranking Indian in the Compagnie's service, had declined to convert to Christianity. From the moment of his appointment as chief courtier, back in 1708, the Jesuits had protested about the elevation of a Hindu to a position of such importance in the colony.[47] Now, their proselytising efforts having drawn a blank, they sniffed an opportunity to have him removed. 'Ask yourself, Monsieur, in the presence of God, if you can really keep any longer a Hindu in the position of chief broker?' wrote Father Tachard to the governor.[48]

At first, the Compagnie resisted calls for Nayiniyappa's removal, conscious that his value as a commercial agent and intermediary outweighed concerns about his faith. The Tamil's undoing, however, was the appointment of Guillaume André Hébert—an individual far more sympathetic to Jesuit interests—to replace Dulivier as governor. It is likely that the Society of Jesus, never far from the corridors of power in Louis XIV's France, had leant on the

Compagnie's directors in Paris to bring this change about.[49] Just after Hébert's swearing into office, Nayiniyappa was arrested. Charges of corruption and of the mistreatment of his subordinates were added to the accusations first levelled by the Jesuit mission, framed for the court as 'abuse of power' and 'incitement to sedition'. After a short trial heard by the Pondicherry council, Nayiniyappa was found guilty on all counts. His sentence was heavy: a public flogging and three years of imprisonment, plus the payment of reparations and a large fine. The flogging was carried out in front of Governor Hébert in the main square of the *ville noire*. Nayiniyappa's injuries were so severe that he never recovered, dying in prison two months later.

The condemning of Nayiniyappa represents one of the ugliest episodes in the early history of French colonial administration in India, the victory of bigotry and injustice over tolerance and the rule of law. In the condemned man's place, a member of the rival Mudali family, who themselves had converted to Christianity, was appointed chief courtier. Nayiniyappa's close associates and relatives were banished from the colony, the Pillai family disgraced. The guilty verdict was also motivated by greed: after his imprisonment, Nayiniyappa's possessions were seized and the records of his assets destroyed. Hébert, hugely indebted, profited from the auctioning of part of Nayiniyappa's property, and some of his belongings found their way directly into the possession of the governor and his allies.[50]

A degree of retrospective justice at least followed. The treatment of Nayiniyappa by Hébert and the Jesuits had outraged some observers at Pondicherry, among them members of the rival Capuchin order and merchants of the Saint-Malo association who had depended on the chief courtier's services. They protested to the Compagnie's directors and the Crown and, two years after Nayiniyappa's death, secured his posthumous pardon. The Pillai family returned to Pondicherry exonerated and, after travelling all the way to France to claim damages at Versailles, Nayiniyappa's son Guruvappa assumed his father's old position. Hébert was arrested and sent back to France, where he was found guilty of corruption and ordered to pay damages.

Before the Nayiniyappa Affair, a small number of dissenting French voices had questioned the sense of sending Catholic missions to the Indies. One merchant, Georges Roques, put his head above the parapet to note that the evangelisation of India was not a realistic prospect. Furthermore, the presence of missionaries in the Compagnie's territories was making commerce more difficult, preventing the establishment of the good relations on which all successful business depended.[51] Few others went that far, at least publicly, but in the aftermath of Nayiniyappa's posthumous rehabilitation the Compagnie recognised that the Jesuits had become too powerful and attempted to reassert control. A 1719 dispatch from Paris to Pondicherry requested Compagnie agents to ensure that missionaries stuck to religious matters and did not get mixed up in other affairs: 'You can let them know', it asserted, 'that if any of them do not conduct themselves as good and wise missionaries and give rise to discontent, you have orders to put them on the first Compagnie ships [back to France!]'[52] Declarations in the 1720s reiterated that all nationalities and religions were entitled to live freely at Pondicherry. For commercial reasons, if nothing else, the principle of religious tolerance—far from evident in France itself at this juncture—had gained ground.

*

In September 1715 the gangrenous Louis XIV, bed-bound for a month, passed away in the Palace of Versailles at the age of 76. During his unprecedentedly long reign, the geographical construction of France as we know it today had been completed, save for a few later additions like Lorraine, Savoy and Corsica. France had established itself as the dominant military power in Europe and boasted the largest population. The foundations had been laid for a colonial empire stretching from North America and the Caribbean to India and Southeast Asia. After five decades of almost incessant warfare—brought to a close only with the end of the War of Spanish Succession in 1714—the French state was bankrupt, however, with a fixed debt of 2.5 billion livres and a further 800 million owed in promises on future revenues.[53] 'The treasury is absolutely empty', noted the Duc de Noailles, head of the state financial council, a week after the king's death.[54] To make matters worse, the country's largely agrarian population was crippled by taxes. Almost a million had died during the severe winter of 1709–10, when famine ripped through the land.[55]

With Louis XIV's successor, his great grandson Louis XV, just five years of age, France entered a period of regency government, with Philippe d'Orléans—son of Louis XIV's younger brother Philippe I—in charge. At this point, a Scottish wizard also entered the fray. John Law, the offspring of an Edinburgh goldsmith, had enjoyed success as a gambler and financial speculator, gaining in the process an impressive understanding of systems of banking and finance in England, the Netherlands and different Italian states.[56] In 1705 he had published a treatise, *Money and Trade Considered*, confirming his reputation as an economist and monetary theorist. His renown extended to France, where he had first met d'Orléans in the late 1690s. Confronted with the state debt crisis, it was to Law that the Regent now turned.

Central to Law's economic thinking, outlined to the Duc d'Orléans in a detailed *mémoire* in the autumn of 1715, was the notion that an abundant supply of money was essential to the healthy functioning of an economy.[57] Money is to the economy what blood is to the body, he argued, its circulation essential to the health of the organism. The more money there is, the better the economy will function, to the general enrichment of all. In a country like France, without its own gold and silver mines, the logical strategy to follow was therefore the replacement of gold and silver currency with paper bills, which would allow for the amount of money in the economy to be increased and the debts of the French state to be repaid. 'Money is not the value for which goods are exchanged, but the value by which they are exchanged', the Scotsman stressed.[58] Why not, therefore, end the dependence of the economy on bullion?

To put theory into action, Law lobbied for the creation of a French national bank comparable to the Bank of England, founded some twenty years earlier. Its role, he explained, would be to receive tax revenues, finance investment in the economy, keep interest rates low and pay off the national debt. As a first step, he established a private bank, the capital of which was one-quarter bullion and three-quarters paper bills. Once the hesitation of members of the Regent's council had been overcome, the bank was nationalised, with the state acting as guarantor of the value of the paper currency. As Law had envisaged, the collection of tax revenues and managing of the state debt were added to the bank's remit.[59]

Law then turned to his other big idea for the creation of national wealth: overseas trade. What the Scotsman envisaged, specifically, was the bringing together of the existing French companies for maritime trade to form a single organisation capable of dominating world commerce. The profits derived by its shareholders, he promised, would be reinvested in France, stimulating growth and contributing to the repayment of the state debt. In August 1717 a new trading company for the exploitation of French colonies in the Americas, the Compagnie d'Occident, was inaugurated, its capital provided by Law's bank. The monopolies on overseas tobacco farming and French participation in the Atlantic slave trade were withdrawn from their previous holders and granted to the new organisation. Eighteen months later, the Compagnie d'Occident was fused with the Compagnie des Indes orientales and the remaining other companies responsible for portions of French trade in the Atlantic, the Pacific and the South Seas, to form the mega-company that Law had imagined. Renamed the 'Compagnie perpétuelle des Indes', it held a monopoly on French global maritime trade from which only northern Europe, the Levant and the Lesser Antilles were excluded.[60] Its object was to deliver both riches and *gloire* to the nation.[61]

The final step in Law's grand plan was to merge the bank into the Compagnie. In February 1720 this took place; the Compagnie took on the bank's monetary and fiscal responsibilities, exercising a critical influence on the domestic economy and national debt as well as on overseas trade.[62] After nominally converting to Catholicism, Law was named controller-general of finances. The vast operation over which he presided was referred to simply as the *système*. At first the public response to Law's innovations was positive. Investors hastened to obtain his paper bank notes and purchase shares in the Compagnie and, before long, the rush became a frenzy: speculators from across France flocked to Rue Quincampoix in Paris to invest, hoping to get rich quick; the Compagnie's share price sky-rocketed and more and more bank notes were printed to meet the rising demand. By spring 1720, paper notes to the value of 3 billion livres had been issued for gold reserves of just 500 million.[63] Law was referred to as an '*enchanteur*' (wizard) for his ability to conjure money out of nothing.[64]

Unfortunately for the Scot, the boom was too good to last. By the time of his appointment as controller-general of finances, Law was aware that a dangerous gap was opening up between the real economy in France and its colonies, which was stagnant, and the parallel economy of financial speculation that he had created. As investors hurried to purchase shares in the Compagnie, gripped by 'Louisiana fever', Louisiana itself was starving. Moreover, inflation had set in as the paper notes began to circulate through the country. Law responded with a forced devaluation of the bills, first by 20% and then by 50%, the effect of which was to shatter confidence in the new monetary medium.[65] A new rush followed, this time to convert paper currency into bullion or invest it in secure assets like land. A string of arbitrary measures was attempted to restore confidence in the bank notes, like the prohibition of purchases in silver above a certain threshold, but the bubble had burst. The offices of the Compagnie, freshly installed on Rue Vivienne in the shadow of the Palais-Royal, were besieged and Law's coach was attacked, as the amount of capital in the *système* tumbled from 4.1 billion livres to 411 million in the space of six months.[66] The wizard's spell was broken: before 1720 was over, Law was removed from office and expelled from France.

For the French at Pondicherry and Chandernagore, whose information about these developments was patchy and consistently out of date, what mattered most was that the Compagnie perpétuelle des Indes was salvaged from the wreckage of the *système*. After Law's banishment it was separated from the national bank and stripped of its domestic functions but survived as a commercial entity oriented towards overseas trade, with the support of d'Orléans and a group of powerful financiers who had been critical of Law's schemes, among them Antoine Crozat and others who had earlier invested in the Saint-Malo association. The port of Lorient was reclaimed and three vessels were dispatched to Pondicherry; they returned to France in

December 1721 with goods fetching an impressive 6 million livres at auction in Nantes.[67] In the first few years of its operation, the new Compagnie also launched trading expeditions to Senegal, Louisiana, the Caribbean and elsewhere, but, with limited means to exploit these routes, the results were mixed. Gradually, the Compagnie's less profitable monopolies were renounced, while Louisiana was handed back to the Crown. The Compagnie, henceforth, would concentrate on the Indian Ocean and trade between Asia and Europe, continuing where Colbert's Compagnie and the Saint-Malo association had left off.

Through the remainder of the 1720s, at least three to four vessels were dispatched annually from France to Pondicherry. The colony continued to grow, striding towards a population of some 100,000 in 1735.[68] Signs of prosperity began to emerge, like new two-storey brick mansions in the *ville blanche*, paved roads and a canal for irrigation. The priority for the new governor, Pierre Lenoir, was the revival of trade. Soon after his appointment, a lodge was re-opened at Masulipatam. A further trading post was then established at Yanaon, near the mouth of the Godavari River, where most of the textiles sold at Masulipatam were produced. In Bengal, the Compagnie's operations were also expanding. *Comptoirs* subsidiary to Chandernagore were opened at Qasimbazaar, the centre of the Bengali silk trade, and Patna, further north on the Ganges, where saltpetre and opium were the main attractions. A decisive step was also taken towards the re-launch of commercial operations on the Malabar Coast. In April 1721 permission was secured from the rajah of Vatakara, a small coastal territory north of Calicut, for the establishment of a *comptoir* to profit from the local pepper trade. At Mahé, where the river of the same name entered the Arabian Sea, a modest French fort was constructed. To the British, stationed just ten kilometres to the north at Tellicherry, this was an alarming development. In a rehearsal of Anglo-French hostilities to come in the following decades, the rajah of Vatakara was persuaded by the British to turn against the Compagnie. A fleet of five French ships was dispatched from Pondicherry to Mahé to protect, successfully, the new French base against this attempted expulsion.[69]

To finance its purchases in India, the Compagnie's main export from Europe was bullion. By the 1720s the authorities in France, no doubt influenced by Law's teachings, were slightly less wedded to the idea, predominant since Colbert's time, that exporting gold and silver from the metropolis was a drain of wealth to be avoided. The directors of the new Compagnie recognised better than those of the old that bullion was required for the purchase of textiles, for example, though some reliance on local credit remained. Alongside bullion, copper, iron and lead were shipped out from Europe to be sold on the subcontinent.[70] The remaining space on outward-bound Compagnie vessels was taken up with provisions for the colonies—not least alcohol. Each year, the unloading of French wine and spirits at Pondicherry was a moment cherished by the colonial population. The governing council demanded an annual supply of 10,000 bottles of Bordeaux, 20,000 bottles of *eau de vie* and 20,000 bottles of madeira to keep the colony refreshed![71]

Heading in the opposite direction, from India to Europe, the staples of the Compagnie's import trade were white cotton textiles and muslins, which had escaped the strict protectionist controls placed on the entry of coloured textiles into France, plus a smaller volume of raw textiles. Pepper, cinnamon, cardamon and other spices were also shipped from the subcontinent, along with sugar and saltpetre.[72] As the confidence of the new Compagnie grew, trading posts were established elsewhere in the Indian Ocean. Coffee was purchased at Mocha in the Red Sea, while wine and carpets were acquired at Bandar Abbas and Bassorah in the Persian Gulf. Expeditions were launched to the port of Canton in China, where tea and porcelain were bought. The return of these products to France was met with enthusiasm, as domestic tastes diversified. A steady growth in the overall volume of the Compagnie's Europe-Asia trade resulted, though as once-exotic fabrics and foodstuffs became more commonplace in the *patrie*, prices and therefore profit margins began to fall.[73]

Alongside these commercial activities, the Compagnie was a major actor in another booming Indian Ocean trade to which our attention must now turn: slave trafficking. For too long, the role played by France and other European powers in the purchase, possession and sale of enslaved peoples in Asian waters has been effaced from the historical record. While the horrors of the transatlantic slave trade are widely (though still, no doubt, insufficiently) recognised in Europe today, European slave trafficking in the Indian Ocean has escaped sustained scholarly or popular attention.[74] The ways in which European colonial projects in India were supported by, and in turn supported, Atlantic and Indian Ocean slave trafficking have been largely overlooked. Europeans did not invent the institution of slavery east of the Cape of Good Hope, nor did they ever monopolise the commerce in enslaved peoples. Arab, Persian and Swahili slavers exploited trading routes in the western Indian Ocean from before the arrival of the Portuguese in Asian waters right through until the nineteenth century, while long-standing slave trading routes linked Bengal and the east coast of India with modern-day Myanmar and Southeast Asia—examples reminding us that slave-trading in the Indian Ocean took place across diverse and multidirectional networks.[75] After their installation in the Indian Ocean, however, Europeans took over the exploitation of many existing slave trade routes and developed new routes of their own, dramatically increasing the overall volume of the trafficking of enslaved peoples.

First were the Portuguese. Some two decades before the first slave voyage from Portugal to Brazil in 1526, vessels of the Estado had begun shipping slaves from Mozambique to the Portuguese settlements in India and Southeast Asia, a traffic involving 'great numbers' of Mozambican slaves by the end of the sixteenth century.[76] Goa, François Pyrard had observed, was the site of a vast market for the purchase of African (and Indian) slaves, on whose labours the functioning of the colony depended.[77] With increasing regularity, slaves were also exported from India, often towards Malacca and the other possessions of the Estado in Southeast Asia.[78] Meanwhile, Portuguese freebooters captured and sold significant numbers of people from the Bengal delta and the Arakanese coast. The participation of the Portuguese at Hooghly in this trade provoked their expulsion from Bengal by the forces of the Mughal Empire in 1632.[79] In a revealing example of the way in which slave trading routes connected the Indian Ocean, the Atlantic and the Pacific, tens of thousands of enslaved peoples of South and Southeast

Asian descent were transported to Spanish-ruled Mexico and the Philippines during the period of union between the Spanish and Portuguese crowns (1580–1640).[80]

When the Dutch succeeded the Portuguese as the dominant European power in the Indian Ocean, they also took over the mantle of the region's largest slave traffickers. The VOC transported African and Asian slaves to work in its warehouses, on its plantations and on the construction of its infrastructure in the Indies. Some 4,000 African slaves were used to build the fortress of Colombo, for example—a small proportion of the more than 65,000 slaves believed to have been in Dutch possession at this time.[81] While Africans were sold on the Indian subcontinent, enslaved Indians were shipped further east, from both the Malabar and Coromandel coasts. An estimated 15,000 Indian slaves reached Batavia between 1618 and 1680; in total, approximately 100,000 enslaved Indians were removed from the subcontinent on Dutch ships during the seventeenth century, with Ceylon, Java, Malacca, Mauritius and the Cape Colony the other major destinations.[82] As Mughal opposition to the Dutch export of slaves became more pronounced, the VOC then gradually turned to Southeast Asia for the supply of most of its slaves.

In England, the early voyages of slave ships across the Atlantic, which began in 1562, were given a royal stamp of approval after the Civil War with the foundation of the Royal African Company, which transported almost 150,000 enslaved Africans to the Americas between 1672 and the 1720s.[83] Concurrently, the EIC was engaged in the shipping of slaves across the Indian Ocean and in the exploitation of slave labour. Slaves were transported from Madagascar, Mozambique and the Comoro Islands to the Company's posts in Southeast Asia, with a smaller number taken to Madras and Bombay, which were more often sites for the purchase of Indian-born slaves for shipping eastwards. Compared to the transatlantic slave trade, the numbers involved in the EIC's slave trafficking were far fewer, but the practice of slave trafficking was systematic, nonetheless. With increasing regularity, orders were placed by agents at Bantam and later Benkulen, the EIC's main trading posts in the Indonesian archipelago, for the shipping of African and Asian slaves to meet the labour demand arising principally from its trade in pepper.[84]

Significant historical precedent thus existed for French slave trafficking in the Indian Ocean, which would explode in the eighteenth century. According to a long-standing legal principle—the '*principe du sol libre*' (freedom principle)—enslaved people setting foot in France automatically became free.[85] Records of the application of this principle, which was reaffirmed by Louis XIV, date at least to the fifteenth century. As French maritime trade expanded, however, so did the possession and trade of slaves. By the middle of the seventeenth century, the sight of enslaved people from north and sub-Saharan Africa, Turkey and the Levant working and moving about in chains in the port cities of Marseille and Toulon was commonplace. Most were employed rowing galleys, loading and unloading ships and staffing the royal arsenals.[86] When the Compagnie des Indes orientales was founded in 1664, its articles authorised the possession and trade of slaves.[87] Evidently, no attempt to limit the institution of slavery comparable to the freedom principle would apply to French colonial possessions in the Indies. As we have seen, influential early actors in the Compagnie, like François Caron, envisaged slave trading as a major business opportunity from the outset. The decision of the Compagnie's directors to revive plans for a colony on Madagascar was informed in no small way by this thinking, building on attempts to enslave the Malagasy population dating to the 1640s. Colbert's infamous *Code Noir*, published in 1685, then confirmed that the institution of slavery was a vital part of the French colonial endeavour, providing it with a firm legal foundation and linking it closely with race, wherever French colonies were established.[88] In the *Code*, '*noir*' (black) was a catch-all term for non-white peoples the world over, including Africa and India. Just a year before it was published, François Bernier, now back in France after his decade at the Mughal court, had published a treatise considered by many to be the first modern classification of humans into distinct races.[89] The theoretical and legal foundations for the use of racial difference to justify colonial exploitation and slavery were being laid.

That the *Code Noir* was published in 1685 was strategic, not arbitrary. By this point, the French colonies in North America and the Caribbean were faced with acute labour shortages, as very few French men and women crossed the Atlantic voluntarily to settle in the New World. (Life was so agreeable in France, noted one patriotic observer, that why would anybody want to leave?)[90] A first attempt to launch France into the transatlantic slave trade had been made in 1673 with the foundation of the Compagnie de Sénégal. This was followed, in the year that the *Code* appeared, by the establishment of the Compagnie de Guinée. Trading posts dedicated to the purchase of slaves were established on the west coast of Africa from the mouth of the Senegal River down to Bissau. Such was the demand for slave labour that private French merchants were also permitted to ply the transatlantic routes, and by 1715 an estimated 77,000 enslaved Africans had been shipped to French territories in the Americas.[91] The main source of Antoine Crozat's wealth was slaving: first he directed the Compagnie de Guinée before securing the exclusive right to supply slaves to the Spanish colonies in the New World. The extraordinary profits that he made from this commerce, when not reinvested in new colonial ventures like the Saint-Malo association and the Compagnie perpétuelle, were deployed in the construction of some of Paris' most iconic buildings, among them two spectacular *hôtels* (mansions) on the Place Vendôme—one of which today houses the Ritz—and the Palais de l'Élysée, now of course the official residence of the President of the French Republic.[92]

After its foundation in 1719, the Compagnie perpétuelle inherited the transatlantic slave trading rights that had previously belonged to the companies that it had swallowed. Expeditions were dispatched to the coast of Senegal and Guinea to purchase enslaved Africans and ship them to Saint-Domingue and Louisiana. For the directors of the new Compagnie, many of whom had previous experience of the trade, trafficking slaves was considered a quick way to turn a profit to be reinvested in other commercial ventures.[93] A cut was also taken from the profits of private French slave merchants permitted to continue their transatlantic operations. From 1725, as the Compagnie turned its attention away from the Atlantic towards the Indian Ocean, the licensing of private slavers operating between Africa and the Americas remained an important source of revenue.

In the Indian Ocean, the failure of Colbert's Compagnie to colonise Madagascar and enslave Malagasies was followed, as we have seen, by the installation of a small French community on the Isle Bourbon, where the institution of slavery would be embedded. By the turn of the eighteenth century, slaves were being imported to the island from Madagascar, Mozambique and the western coast of Africa, primarily to work as agricultural labourers cultivating rice, corn, vegetables and spices.[94] When the cultivation of coffee on the island then began in 1715, slave labour was even more in demand. That same year, France laid claim to the Isle Bourbon's larger neighbour, Mauritius, which had recently been abandoned by the Dutch. Re-christened the Isle de France, it too was rapidly populated with slaves. Most were imported on Compagnie ships and remained the legal possession of the Compagnie, which put them to work in its warehouses and stores, employed them as soldiers and relied upon them for the construction of the harbour, shipyards and fort of Port Louis.[95] As in the Americas, efforts to colonise the Isle de France suffered from limited French enthusiasm for emigration, coupled with high mortality rates. Slaves were therefore also leased by the Compagnie to the colonial population to work on the land and reproduce.

In a number of important ways, the development of French colonialism in India benefitted from the French trafficking and trading of slaves in both the Atlantic and Indian Oceans. While some of these have already been touched upon, they merit restatement to challenge the omission of slave trading from almost all existing works on the French in India. For one, slaving helped to finance commercial ventures in India, whether of Colbert's Compagnie, the Saint-Malo association or the Compagnie perpétuelle. As French involvement in the transatlantic slave trade grew, the Americas were an increasingly important source of bullion, which was received in large part from the sale of slaves. A portion of this bullion found its way to the French colonies in India, allowing their critical shortages of gold and silver, needed for trade on the subcontinent, to be partially addressed.[96] Private French trade in the Indian Ocean was also frequently financed through profits derived from slave trading, which constituted a significant part of the private trade undertaken.[97]

Beyond these financial connections, French efforts in India benefitted greatly from the colonisation of the Isle Bourbon and the Isle de France—known collectively as the Mascarenes—which, as we have seen, was reliant on slave labour. By the 1730s Port Louis had become a vital stopping post for ships voyaging between France and India and a military and communication hub of major strategic importance for France in the Indian Ocean. In a more direct connection still, some enslaved Africans were brought to India on Compagnie ships, though exact figures are unknown.[98] Before long, slaves would be forced to make up the numbers in the military reinforcements sent from the Isle de France to India, as we shall see in the chapters that follow.

Meanwhile, the French presence in India supported the expansion of slave trafficking in ways that demand more extensive analysis. Among the key items exchanged for slaves on the African coastline and Madagascar were textiles and cowries (a shell recognised in many parts of the Indian Ocean as a form of currency) acquired in India. Profits made by French traders in India were not infrequently reinvested in slave trading ventures. Furthermore, India was also a source of slave labour; from the subcontinent, slaves were exported to the Mascarenes on French ships with increasing regularity. At Pondicherry and Chandernagore, it was earlier noted, the French possession of slaves was commonplace. Slaves could be acquired cheaply through pre-existent trafficking networks in the Tamil countryside or directly from desperate families when serious incidences of famine struck. François Martin considered slave trading an activity 'unworthy' of the Compagnie but during his governorship slaves were nevertheless exported from India to the Isle Bourbon on French ships.[99] By 1708, two years after his death, there were eighty-five Indian slaves in French possession on the island, just over 30% of its small but growing slave population.[100] Twenty-seven years later, in 1735, the two Mascarene colonies together possessed a slave population of more than 7,000, some four-fifths of the islands' total population. Though the majority were of African or Malagasy origin, approximately 1,000 hailed from India—a number inflated by the succession of severe famines that had struck southern India from 1728, forcing individuals to sell themselves or family members into bondage.[101] Records of the Pondicherry council confirm that the

Compagnie was directly responsible for a portion of this trafficking, with slaves exported on its ships.[102] In French minds, Indian slaves were usually considered more trustworthy and intelligent than their African and Malagasy counterparts and thus capable of more than just manual labour.

In the decade up to 1735, the growth in the French export of slaves from India to the Mascarenes was also encouraged by the decision of the Compagnie to formally relinquish its control over intra-Asian trade, instead officially permitting its employees and private French merchants to trade within the Indian Ocean. The trade in slaves, like that in all other commodities, would henceforth be liberalised. During this period, slaves were usually trafficked on ships that also carried other merchandise. As numbers grew, dedicated slaving expeditions from India to the Masacarenes were then organised, the earliest of which appears to date to February 1729, when *La Sirène* left Pondicherry with 300 slaves.[103] For each slave sold between private parties in its territories, the Compagnie levied a tax of 5%.[104]

Without any testimonies from enslaved people in France's nascent Indian Ocean empire, understanding their lived experiences is impossible. Contained within the *Code Noir* were a set of provisions—considered by many to be progressive at the time—that attempted to establish certain minimum rights for enslaved people, among them the right to be fed, housed and clothed.[105] On the Mascarenes, regulations were passed that supplemented the *Code*, dictating more generous food rations, for example, and empowering slaves to bring complaints to the Compagnie.[106] It would be naïve, however, to think that these provisions were widely respected. Though a small proportion of slaves on the Isle de France were trained in specific crafts and even paid a small wage, life for the vast majority must have been mercilessly hard. Back-breaking physical labour, sexual exploitation and chronic shortages of food were endured, forcing many into rebellions and desertions for which the punishments, if caught, were brutal. (The penalties prescribed in the *Code*, which after all was primarily concerned with protecting the interests of French slave owners, were anything but humane.)[107] Any restraint that slave owners exercised was no doubt motivated more by economic calculation than humanity: according to one estimate, a slave imported to the Isle de France had to remain alive for at least three years for the costs of his purchase and shipping to be covered and a profit made.[108]

Most slaves owned by the French at Pondicherry and Chandernagore had been spared the gruelling and frequently life-threatening experience of being shipped up to thousands of nautical miles from their place of origin. With relatively little land cultivation to take care of, they typically worked in domestic roles or in the service of the Compagnie, as noted above. The idea common to older historiography that this form of servitude was less exploitative and inhumane than slavery in other parts of the world—often founded on a gendered assumption that domestic work was easier—cannot, however, be sustained.[109] Moreover, the fact that slaves in French households were nominally converted to Christianity and awarded Christian names tells us almost nothing about how they were really treated.[110] 'There is nobody in the world more unfortunate and miserable than the slaves of Pondicherry', wrote one unusually candid Frenchman.[111]

The possession and trafficking of slaves was a fundamental part of French colonialism in India—a reality that no account of the French presence on the subcontinent in the eighteenth century can any longer ignore. The growth of French slave trafficking in the era of the Compagnie perpétuelle was one of the pillars, indeed, on which the imminent expansion of French power in India was constructed.

5

IMPERIAL EXPANSION

By 1735, the Compagnie's commercial operations were flourishing, with increased investment in France rewarded by a higher volume of imports and sales, as European demand for Indian Ocean commodities rose. Among them were cotton cloth and muslins from the Coromandel, raw silk from Bengal and pepper from the Malabar Coast—plus coffee from the Mascarenes and tea and porcelain from China. The intra-Asian trade was also booming, with Compagnie and privately chartered vessels regularly setting off from Pondicherry and Chandernagore for the Persian Gulf, the Red Sea and the Mascarenes, Southeast Asia, China and Manila. Over the preceding two decades, major conflict between the European powers had been avoided. The Coromandel and Bengal had enjoyed relative political stability under the rule of Muslim dynasties—the Nawayaths and the Nasiris—operating largely independently of the Mughal structures of authority in which they were theoretically embedded. Governors from François Martin onwards had avoided conflict with Indian powers, prioritising commerce and the government of the French colonies.

During the two decades that followed, this would change dramatically. First, the political stability of southern India collapsed, as conflict erupted between the Nawayaths and a host of local powers in the Carnatic. Second, war between France and its European rivals returned and was projected onto the global stage, with huge repercussions in India. The focus of the French on the subcontinent shifted, as conflict with Indian powers and the British replaced the imperative of peace. Commerce was relegated to an afterthought, as territorial acquisition and the extension of political influence became the priority. In part the motivation remained profit—the acquisition of territory meant the right to collect revenues—but imperial expansion was first and foremost about the pursuit of power and glory for the French crown, the Compagnie and the individuals involved, and those individuals' personal enrichment. On the initiative of authorities in Pondicherry, the Compagnie acted as an aggressive imperial power using military force, hawkish diplomacy and forced regime change towards its own ends.

From the outset, the French presence in the Indian Ocean was underpinned by the use or threat of military action, as we have seen. Before 1715, this had primarily been directed at the Dutch on the subcontinent and their local allies. Alliances with some Indian rulers had been concluded and modest territories obtained around Pondicherry. The successive Compagnies des Indes had never been entirely peaceful entities, nor had they turned down the opportunity to take control of land. The direction taken after 1735 nevertheless marked a significant departure, turning the Compagnie into a very different animal. By the early 1750s, French rule or influence had been established over most of southern India; the Compagnie was, at least in principle, in possession of the eastern side of the Indian peninsula from Masulipatam to Cape Comorin, including the Carnatic, and had installed a compliant ruler in the Deccan. French armies populated with European and Indian troops enforced the Compagnie's authority, suppressing internal and external rivals and trying to extract revenue.

The development of the Compagnie into an imperial power largely took place during the governorship of Joseph François Dupleix (1742–54), on whom our attention must focus. Under Dupleix's direction, imperial expansion took place at a dizzying speed, through conquest, diplomacy and regime change—all underpinned by military power and a growing sense of French civilisational superiority. Even before Dupleix took centre stage, however, the nature of the French presence in India was beginning to change. It is therefore with his predecessor, Pierre Benoît Dumas (1735–41), that we begin.

*

First, an explanation of the increasingly unstable political context that Dumas was confronted with on his arrival at Pondicherry from the Mascarenes, where his term as governor of the Isle de France and the Isle Bourbon had just come to an end. The Carnatic, we have noted, remained nominally a part of the Mughal Empire. Its *nawab* (governor) was answerable to the *nizam* (ruler) of the Deccan, who was in turn subordinate to the Mughal Emperor. From 1724, under the rule of Asaf Jah I, a former general of Emperor Aurangzeb, the de facto independence of the Deccan from the Mughal Empire had, however, been secured. Links between the Deccan and the Carnatic had also been practically severed, with Nawab Saadatullah Khan developing an efficient, independent administration over the Carnatic from his capital of Arcot. In 1732, after more than two decades of rule, the *nawab* passed away, leaving the throne to his nephew, Dost Ali Khan, whose control of the Carnatic was never as secure. In comparison with the north, where Mughal structures of authority had been deeply entrenched for almost two centuries, alternative local powers—mostly Hindu rajahs and feudal chiefs—had survived in the Carnatic through the periods of rule by Mughal governors and Saadatullah Khan.[1] Sensing Dost Ali Khan's weakness, some now resisted the new *nawab*, refusing to recognise his authority and revenue demands. Dost Ali's response was to dispatch his son-in-law Chanda Sahib to bring the rajahs of Tanjore, Madurai and Trichinopoly into line, resulting in a succession of bloody and inconclusive military campaigns. Chanda Sahib was eventually installed as governor of Trichinopoly, but a host of new enemies had been made.

The Pondicherry council had cultivated good relations with Saadatullah Khan during the final years of his reign, with one of the *nawab*'s favoured officials, Imam Sahib, acting as an intermediary between Pondicherry and Arcot.[2] Chanda Sahib, meanwhile, had been received warmly at Pondicherry in 1733, before his first campaign against Tanjore got underway. Just after taking office, Dumas was able to put these strong relations with the Nawayath dynasty to good effect. One of the main costs eating into French profits from trade on the Coromandel was the need to transform gold and silver shipped out from France into local currencies in the *nawab*'s mint, an expensive operation on which transaction rates of 6–8% were usually paid. In return for a substantial one-off payment, Dost Ali Khan conceded to the Compagnie the right to mint pagodas in gold and rupees in silver at Pondicherry. Not only were the costs of using the *nawab*'s mint saved, but a new source of revenue had been tapped, with merchants from up and down the Coromandel henceforth heading to Pondicherry for their supply of coins.[3]

In parallel with the construction of the mint, work began at Pondicherry on a grand new government house looking over the central square of the fort. A new hospital was constructed, in part to cater for the colony's growing body of troops. Just several hundred European soldiers were stationed at Pondicherry at this juncture, but early in Dumas's governorship the organised recruitment of Indians—mostly Tamil and Malayalam speakers—to the Compagnie's military ranks began. A small army of local recruits was trained and equipped in the European fashion. In an indication of French belligerence to come, it was pressed into action in the autumn of 1736 in a punitive expedition against the governor of Mocha who, in the view of the Pondicherry council, was deliberately disrupting the Compagnie's coffee trade in the Red Sea. The expedition was a success, the governor conceding to the French demand to reduce taxes on the export of coffee to a modest 2.5%.[4]

Buoyed by this victory, it was not long before Dumas was tempted into military intervention in the Carnatic, where tensions had continued to rise after the death of the rajah of Tanjore, the Maratha Tukkoji Bhonsle, in 1736. As the succession struggle intensified, and the throne passed quickly from one contender to the next, Shahji Bhonsle, who claimed to be Tukkoji's son, appealed to Dumas for support and a deal was struck: in return for military backing to secure his throne, Shahji would grant the Compagnie the coastal trading station of Karikal, some 130 kilometres south of Pondicherry, along with five surrounding villages considered valuable for the provision of cloth.[5] As it turned out, Shahji didn't need French help. Having secured his throne before the Compagnie's force arrived to help him, he tried to renege on the agreement, refusing to relinquish Karikal. For Dumas, this was an unacceptable breach of trust. When negotiation failed, the governor reached out to Chanda Sahib at Trichinopoly, whose forces captured Karikal in February 1739 before advancing on Tanjore and deposing Shahji. Karikal was handed over to the French, consummating the budding alliance between the Compagnie and the Nawayath dynasty. A new trading base on the Coromandel had been secured, along with land expected to deliver an annual revenue of 100,000 livres.[6]

As would soon become clear, however, the capture of Karikal had destabilised an already volatile political situation further. In early 1740, responding to an appeal from the new rajah of Tanjore, Pratap Singh Bhonsle, a huge Maratha army under Raghuji Bhonsle, head of the powerful kingdom of Nagpur, entered the Carnatic. At Ambur, west of Vellore, it confronted the forces of Nawab Dost Ali Khan, who was killed in battle. Arcot was then captured, though not before the families of the deceased *nawab* and of Chanda Sahib had managed to escape. Safdar Ali Khan, Dost Ali's son, now demanded that the families be allowed to take refuge in Pondicherry, presenting Dumas and his council with a dilemma: to not support Safdar Ali would destroy the Compagnie's alliance with the Nawayaths; agreeing would place it on the wrong side of the Marathas and make Pondicherry a likely target of attack. After deliberation, the council agreed that Safdar Ali's request could not be refused, and the gates of Pondicherry were opened to the royal refugees from Arcot.[7]

As expected, a Maratha advance towards Pondicherry resulted. The surrounding countryside was devastated and the Dutch trading house at Porto Novo, 50 kilometres to the south, was ransacked. A demonstration of Maratha military strength was staged within view of Pondicherry, followed by a request for tribute, which Dumas refused, confident that the city could withhold a terrestrial attack unaccompanied by a blockade at sea. An agreement between Safdar Ali and Raghuji Bhonsle was then reached, the Maratha leader agreeing to call off hostilities and recognise Dost Ali's son as *nawab* in return for the payment of 10 million rupees.[8] The threat to Pondicherry had been paid off by the Compagnie's new protector. Before Raghuji Bhonsle's forces withdrew from the Carnatic, however, there was a setback. While Safdar Ali had shown himself willing to compromise with the Marathas, Chanda Sahib was not. After the death of his father-in-law Dost Ali, he had continued to fight, before retreating to Trichinopoly in the face of the Maratha army's overwhelming strength. In March 1741 Trichinopoly was captured. Chanda Sahib's life was spared by his promise to pay a ransom; taken prisoner, he was transported across India to the Maratha stronghold of Satara in the western ghats. The peace in the Carnatic was nothing more than a temporary pause in hostilities. Meanwhile, Dumas departed for France and Dupleix arrived at Pondicherry to take his place.

*

Born in northern France at Landrecies, Joseph François Dupleix was destined for a career in the Indies from a young age. Issuing from the emergent bourgeoise, his father François had invested in the Saint-Malo association of merchants and John Law's speculative schemes before becoming one of the directors of the new Compagnie. While François's first son, Charles-Claude-Ange, followed his father into the Compagnie administration in Paris, Joseph François was sent to a Jesuit convent before being dispatched on a first voyage to the Indian Ocean at the age of 18, serving with the Saint-Malouins. Five years later, his father's influence secured him employment with the Compagnie and a seat on the Pondicherry council, the cue for Dupleix to pack his bags for a long residence in India.[9]

In Pondicherry, the appointment of such a young and inexperienced officer to the governing council could not fail to irritate his new colleagues. Shortly after his arrival, Dupleix was induced to accept a post at a lower grade and demonstrate his worth through action before getting his feet under the council table. The 25-year-old accepted the challenge. In the autumn of 1722, he led an expedition against the local governor of Porto Novo, who was accused of mistreating one of the Compagnie's allies. The following year he represented the Compagnie at Madras before being selected for a voyage to Canton, China, where the Compagnie hoped to expand its commercial operations. To contemporaries, Dupleix's talents as a merchant were quickly evident. In parallel with his tasks for the Compagnie, he launched himself into private trade, investing the small sum that he had brought with him to Pondicherry in trading ventures to Surat, Bengal, Manila and Mocha. The returns on these investments were impressive; between 1725 and 1730 Dupleix was able to purchase a mansion in Pondicherry, along with a plot of land on the Isle Bourbon and a plantation on the Isle de France, the latter co-owned with a close friend and fellow employee of the Compagnie, Jacques Vincent.[10]

When the position of director of the Compagnie's operations in Bengal fell vacant in 1730, Dupleix was the obvious candidate to fill it. He arrived at Chandernagore the following year to find a colony, dating to 1688, that was finally showing signs of prosperity. The town extended for a kilometre along the right bank of the Hooghly River, up and downriver of Fort d'Orléans, the Compagnie's headquarters.[11] For Dupleix, the prospects of the Compagnie in Bengal were more promising even than those on the Coromandel, with the export of cotton, silk, muslins, saltpetre, opium, rice, sugar and indigo potentially lucrative. Within a couple of years of Dupleix's arrival, the number of ships leaving Chandernagore for Europe, via Pondicherry, had doubled from two to four. Operations to transport opium and saltpetre downriver from Patna to Chandernagore were intensifying, and the volume of silk purchased at Qasimbazaar, near Murshidabad, was on the rise.[12] The Compagnie's prospects were further improved when, a couple of years after Dumas's similar success on the Coromandel, Dupleix secured permission from the *nawab* of Bengal, Shuja ud-Din Muhammad Khan, to establish a mint and coin money in the French colony.

Meanwhile, directing the Compagnie's operations in Bengal also provided Dupleix with excellent new opportunities to expand his private trading initiatives. No sooner had he arrived in Chandernagore than the Frenchman was cajoling his compatriots and other Europeans in Bengal to invest in trading ventures which, over time, became increasingly ambitious: expeditions to Burma, the Malabar Coast and the Maldives were followed by voyages to the Red Sea, the Persian Gulf and Manila. When ships returned safely, large profits were reaped, but the risks were also high: one-third of ocean-bound vessels setting sail from Chandernagore did not make it back to Bengal; with each lost vessel, potentially ruinous financial losses were incurred.[13] With Dupleix both the highest-ranking Compagnie official at Chandernagore and the colony's most prolific merchant, the lines between official and private business were blurred. Though profits were of course pocketed by Dupleix and the other individual investors involved, commerce was often carried out in the Compagnie's name to secure access to markets, while the Compagnie's ships were regularly used to transport private goods. Later, as we shall see, a failure to separate Compagnie and private accounts would in part prove Dupleix's undoing. In the short term, however, while the Compagnie's operations were expanding and its profits growing, a blind eye was turned to these practices.

After a decade at Chandernagore, with the colony flourishing, Dupleix's ascension to the position of governor of all French establishments in India was completed. His success in Bengal was impossible for the Compagnie's directors to ignore, particularly with his brother Charles-Claude-Ange, who had succeeded their father François on the board, singing his praises. Dupleix's commercial acumen, intelligence and sense of duty were particularly valued in Paris.

Those who had been following his career closely, however, should also have had grounds for concern as the new governor arrived in Pondicherry, his landing marked by the firing of twenty-one cannons. Even more so than his peers, among whom in-fighting was common, Dupleix had shown himself to be cantankerous, clashing especially with Dumas's predecessor as governor, Pierre Lenoir. At Chandernagore, Dupleix had come very close to establishing his independent command, ignoring almost entirely the orders sent to him from Pondicherry. With those that he considered inferior—just about everybody—Dupleix was haughty and impatient, his ambitions frequently spilling over into vanity and arrogance and revealing a lack of empathy or understanding of other people. When a difficulty was encountered, for example a financial loss, he was liable to become enraged, and he was quick to bear a grudge and claim victimhood.[14] In 1735, when Dumas was appointed governor, Dupleix had threatened to quit the Compagnie and return to France, feeling slighted at being overlooked for the top job. Questions had also been raised about his honesty; after his return from China in 1725, he had even been suspended from Compagnie service, pending an investigation into claims that he had scammed a colleague at Canton.

Dupleix was not wholly ignorant of the civilisations of the Indian subcontinent that, for some twenty years, had been his home. On the Coromandel and in Bengal he visited Hindu temples and admired their art. A music lover, he also learnt to play the vina. On the whole, however, his interest in India was limited; he rarely travelled far beyond the French colonies and did not acquire a working knowledge of Tamil, Bengali or Persian—the languages that would have most usefully served for commerce and diplomacy. Instead, Dupleix's correspondence reveals a xenophobic strain that grew the longer he remained on the subcontinent, despite his close relationships with some people of Indian birth. For Dupleix, all non-Europeans were '*noirs*' (blacks), the distinction between different linguistic, ethnic and religious groups only sometimes being made. They were, Dupleix claimed, dishonest by nature, greedy and without honour. 'All the blacks are rogues', he recorded at Chandernagore, before adding: 'There is nothing more deceitful than all these Asiatic nations [...] Moors [Muslims] and Gentiles [Hindus] alike are as concerned for their master's grandeur as for their own honour—that is to say, not the least in the world. Money and nothing else is their god.'[15] Tamils, Dupleix would occasionally remark, were more trustworthy than other '*noirs*', but were no match for Europeans in manliness. 'The Tamils eat the diet of an animal', Dupleix noted, 'because what is there except their vegetables and curry? It is not the food of a man.'[16]

From almost the beginning of his time at Chandernagore, meanwhile, Dupleix advocated military action to advance the Compagnie's interests. In Bengal, he lamented, the greatest obstacle to profitable trade was the repeated demands for payments and presents made by Nawab Shuja ud-Din and his officers. When these demands were not met, goods were liable to be seized and the passage of ships on the Hooghly blocked. Dupleix was convinced that the best means of curtailing the demands was military force and requested to Pondicherry and Paris that reinforcements be sent to Chandernagore to build up the meagre army of 100–200 soldiers at his disposal.[17] The invasion of the Mughal Empire by Nadir Shah of Persia and his easy capture of Delhi in 1739—reportedly accompanied by the slaughter of 100,000 people—then confirmed to Dupleix that the Compagnie should adopt a more muscular approach in its dealings with Indian courts: 'The present revolution is a certain proof of the little fear that these miserable Muslims should inspire in us', Dupleix wrote. 'It shows how weak we have been in suffering them so patiently [...] For too long they have been spitting in our face with impunity.'[18]

In return for his support of Safdar Ali Khan in the Carnatic, Dumas had, just before leaving for France, been awarded, for himself and all French governors in India thereafter, the Mughal title of *mansadbar*—an appellation which, though largely symbolic, recognised that the French were no longer guests in India but a part of the Mughal system, a first among the European powers on the subcontinent.[19] From the moment of his installation as governor, Dupleix set great store by this title, despite the contempt with which he spoke of Emperor Muhammad Shah and his officials. The arrival at Pondicherry of the edict from Delhi confirming the title was marked with a spectacular ceremony just after Dupleix had taken office. Two long columns of elephants proceeded through the streets, followed by fifty palanquins, the most impressive of which carried the governor. A flag decorated with his Mughal insignia was carried into the fort and raised to the sound of kettle drums. From this moment onwards, Dupleix never left home without a banner displaying his insignia and an entourage of guards dressed in the Mughal fashion. On the rare occasions that he ventured far from Pondicherry, he did so in a horse-drawn coach accompanied by a procession of at least 100 horsemen and three elephants.[20] In part these ceremonies may have been strategic, a deliberate show designed to enhance French prestige and authority in the Carnatic. It is hard to resist the conclusion, however, that the honours bestowed by Muhammad Shah went to Dupleix's head. As his sense of self-importance ballooned, Dupleix renamed a village just north of Pondicherry, in which his country residence was located, after himself ('Dupleixpettai'), threatening fines for anyone caught using the old name instead.[21]

Within the Pondicherry council, Dupleix's style of government was top-down. The governor was not big on listening to what other members of the council had to say, preferring to command than to consult. Beyond the council, however, Dupleix relied heavily upon two close confidants who would play influential roles in events to come. The first was the Tamil Ananda Ranga Pillai, nephew of Nayiniyappa Pillai, whom we encountered in the previous chapter. Born in 1709, Ananda was too young to remember much about the trial and death of his uncle but, after Nayiniyappa's posthumous rehabilitation and the installation of his son Guruvappa as chief courtier, he entered the Compagnie's service aged 16, rising quickly to become its commercial agent at Porto Novo. Two years later, when Guruvappa passed away, he assumed responsibility for the family's commercial affairs and greatly expanded them: a network of warehouses and shops was established throughout the Coromandel, principally for the textile trade, and the right to farm betel and tobacco was purchased from the Compagnie. Vessels were chartered to trade with Persia, China and the Philippines.[22] By the age of 32, when Dupleix returned to Pondicherry as governor, Ananda was one of the colony's wealthiest residents, his extensive knowledge and list of contacts vital to the Compagnie's operations. Only in 1746 was he formally appointed chief courtier, but from the beginning of Dupleix's governorship he played a central role: Dupleix relied upon Ananda, who was fluent in Tamil, Persian and French, to organise the Compagnie's commerce with the Tamil community and conduct diplomacy with Indian courts. Through their daily morning meetings, Dupleix was kept informed of goings-on in the Carnatic and beyond. What is more, Ananda had the excellent idea of keeping a journal. Covering in detail a period of twenty-five years, it is an outstanding, intimate record of Dupleix's time as governor and the travails that followed.

The second key figure at Dupleix's side, an even more consistent presence, was his wife Jeanne (née Albert de Castro). Born in

Pondicherry, her mother an Indo-Portuguese Christian and her father a French surgeon, Jeanne married Dupleix after her first husband, Dupleix's friend Jacques Vincent, had passed away in 1737, while all three were at Chandernagore.[23] Because of her rare status as a woman of public prominence, a number of stories have accumulated about Jeanne over the years. Some see her as more powerful than Dupleix, controlling the decisions that he made and leading him astray. Others accuse her of corruption and religious intolerance, citing her supposed attempts to extract money from wealthy Hindu merchants at Pondicherry as evidence.[24] Beneath these layers of myth, several important facts can be established. As a Tamil and Portuguese speaker, Jeanne regularly served as her husband's translator. She communicated with prominent women in Indian courts, thereby playing an important diplomatic role. Through friends, acquaintances and family members on the Coromandel—among them her daughter Marie-Rose, who married an Englishman at Madras—she was able to acquire information important to the Compagnie. She also involved herself in money-making, as records of some commercial contracts and landholdings in her name testify.[25] For an individual jealous of Jeanne's proximity to Dupleix and convinced that women had no place in public affairs, there was plenty of scope for embellishment: the origins of most fabrications about Jeanne can be traced to Ananda and his journal, the volumes of which contain repeated references to Jeanne's inappropriate public prominence and malicious influence on the governor.[26]

As Dupleix settled into his new office in Fort Louis, he was right to identify 'storm clouds gathering on all sides'.[27] After Chanda Sahib's capture the previous year, the incursions of the Nagpur Marathas into the Carnatic had continued. Now secure on the throne of Tanjore, Pratap Singh Bhonsle eyed the recovery of Karikal from the French. Meanwhile the Nawayath dynasty was destroying itself with in-fighting. In November 1742 Safdar Ali Khan was murdered by his brother-in-law, Murtaza Ali of Vellore, who lasted just a month on the throne before fleeing Arcot, replaced as *nawab* by Safdar Ali's son, Saadatullah Khan II.

Dupleix's initial response to this disorder was to strengthen Pondicherry's fortifications. Despite the shortage of funds at his disposal, wholesale improvements were commissioned. 'I am going to devote myself', he noted, 'to putting this town in a position to defend itself.'[28] To this end, the recruitment of Indian soldiers (sepoys) was also accelerated and the army at Dupleix's disposal was divided into battalions, each trained and commanded by a French officer. A small force was dispatched to Karikal to protect it against Tanjore. Informed of events at Arcot, Dupleix also opened correspondence with the imprisoned Chanda Sahib and in early 1743 offered a loan to this ally of the Compagnie, whose family remained at Pondicherry, to help secure his release through the payment of the ransom that the Marathas demanded.[29] In this offer we see the first indication of a method that would become central to French imperial expansion over the next decade: the installation of sympathetic, even compliant, rulers in Indian courts. Dupleix envisaged that after his release, Chanda Sahib—who professed to the governor his Francophilia, even dropping in the name of one or two French writers—would return to the Carnatic and claim the nawabship.

Unfortunately for Dupleix, the *nizam* of Deccan Asaf Jah I, had other ideas. In the spring of 1743, he arrived in the Carnatic at the head of a huge army, estimated by Ananda to include 70,000 horses, its advance 'as though the sea was rising and flooding the land'.[30] Arcot was taken, the countryside 'utterly laid [to] waste' and a new *nawab* nominated: Anwar ud-Din Khan, a trusted lieutenant of the *nizam*.[31] After years of abstention from affairs in the Carnatic, Asaf Jah had belatedly decided to exercise his right, in the Mughal system, to determine the province's *nawab*. For Dupleix, the *nizam*'s intervention was difficult to accept, and he ramped up his efforts to secure Chanda Sahib's release. The subject was raised with the Pondicherry council and a further loan to Chanda Sahib, this time of 100,000 rupees, was agreed. To justify his actions, Dupleix argued that the nawabship of the Carnatic had become a hereditary office and that Chanda Sahib was the most illustrious remaining representative of the dynasty, the Nawayaths, to which it rightly belonged. Clearly, however, his support for Chanda Sahib was primarily about the advancement of French interests. 'It is desirable that Chanda Sahib, the brother-in-law of Safdar Ali Khan, become *nawab*', explained Dupleix to the Compagnie's directors. 'We would find in him a degree of protection quite unlike that offered by the other newcomers who have no aim but to fill their coffers and who owe us no particular obligation.'[32]

As Dupleix outlined these intentions, the deterioration of relations with the British became the focus of his concerns. After 1700, the volume of Dutch trade in India had stagnated. Though the VOC retained trading posts on the Coromandel at Sadras and Negapatam, on the Malabar Coast at Cochin, and in Bengal at Chinsurah, India was not its priority; Ceylon, Batavia, Malacca and Japan were more important sources of revenue. The main commercial competitors to the Compagnie in India were therefore the British. On the Coromandel, Madras was growing rapidly, while Fort St David, overlooking Cuddalore, was a strategic asset, its fortifications strengthened in 1725. In northeast India, the EIC's commercial operations were expanding, with the growth of Calcutta outstripping that of Chandernagore and British and French agents competing for merchandise at Patna and Qasimbazaar. On the western coast, the city of Bombay was on the rise, while Tellicherry rivalled Mahé for the Malabar pepper trade.

Over the past thirty years, relations between the British and French in India had generally been good, with exceptions—like the conflict played out over Mahé in 1725 or a British attempt to block the passage of French ships on the Hooghly in 1731—contained and short-lived. The directors of the two companies recognised that peace was good for trade and even collaborated on occasion to prevent other Europeans, like the Austrian-backed Ostend Company, from challenging their trade. French and British investors in India participated jointly in private trading initiatives—some of the expeditions organised by Dupleix at Chandernagore included British capital from Calcutta—while social relations were often warm. On the Coromandel and in Bengal, French and British governors attended dinners and balls organised by their opposite number, often staying for a few days. Marriages between Europeans of different nationalities were not uncommon, as the example of Jeanne Dupleix's daughter Marie-Rose shows us.[33]

Undeniably, however, the commercial competition between the two companies was intensifying. In 1736, one EIC report described the French as 'our most dangerous rivals'. The following year, the directors of the British company added: 'The most particular intelligence procurable concerning those powerful competitors, the French, and their commerce, must annually be communicated to us.'[34] Between 1738 and 1741 the Compagnie's investment in trade matched that of the EIC for the first time; the two companies were direct competitors not just in the trade between India and Europe, but also on routes connecting the subcontinent with the Persian Gulf, Southeast Asia and Manila.[35] In 1739, renewed tensions on the Malabar Coast were provoked by the attempt of local chieftains, incited by the British, to prevent French agents from accessing the areas of the countryside most bountiful in pepper. In response, a fleet was dispatched from the Isle de France under the command of Bertrand-François Mahé de la Bourdonnais, Dumas's successor as governor of the Mascarenes, on whose watch Port Louis on the Isle de France was developing into a major naval and commercial station built on the back of slave labour and enriched by slave trafficking.[36] Fifteen years earlier, when Mahé had first been threatened by the British, La Bourdonnais had led one of the columns that relieved it. Now he returned to the site of his former glory with a force of 600 European soldiers and 400 sepoys. Two key hilltop positions were seized and the local opposition was broken, an action for which La Bourdonnais received royal honours.[37]

In Europe, relations between France and Great Britain were worsening, the diplomatic situation on the continent tense after the outbreak of war between Britain and Spain in the Caribbean over the traffic of contraband goods. When the Habsburg Emperor Charles VI then died in October 1740, sparking a succession struggle, the descent into a general European war began. At Versailles, the Anglophile Cardinal Fleury found his desire for peace increasingly contested. From the Isle de France, La Bourdonnais, fuelled by his Mahé success, appealed to the French court for permission to launch a large pre-emptive strike against the British in Asian waters.[38] On Rue Vivienne, however, the directors continued to favour peace, worrying about the impact of war on the Compagnie's bottom line.

In late 1742, they proposed a treaty of neutrality in the Indian Ocean to their counterparts in London. In parallel, Dupleix was instructed to seek an accord with the British authorities on the Coromandel, which he did so earnestly, writing to Governor Nicholas Morse to propose neutrality and hosting the governor's subordinate, John Hinde, at Pondicherry. At this point, Dupleix appears to have genuinely wished to avoid conflict with the British, to protect the Compagnie's trade and his own commercial interests.

In both London and on the Coromandel, the British response was non-committal: Morse stuck to the line that he was not authorised to agree a treaty without his directors' approval, while the directors played for time in the knowledge that a squadron of the Royal Navy was being prepared for India. In May 1744, just after Louis XV and his uncle, Philip V of Spain, had agreed to declare war on Britain, the squadron departed. It arrived in Indian waters before the end of the year and immediately began disrupting French shipping: a vessel returning from Manila with a cargo of 400,000 rupees was captured in January 1745, followed by three Compagnie ships returning from China the following month. Vessels from Surat, Basra and Mocha suffered the same fate and by the summer of 1745 French trade was almost entirely suffocated.[39] Dupleix now realised that the British had no intention of agreeing to neutrality in the Indian Ocean and appealed to Anwar ud-Din for protection. The *nawab* responded with a letter to the authorities at Madras directing the two European nations to live in peace both on land and at sea, but the seizure of French ships continued. Pondicherry, wrote Dupleix, was in a 'wretched state' and its very survival threatened.[40] Without the dispatch of a naval force capable of opposing the English, he warned the directors, 'the Compagnie will be able to consider its establishments in India lost.'[41]

Some biographers suggest that the surprise of British hostility at this juncture had a major psychological impact on Dupleix, who interpreted the seizure of French ships as a personal affront and breach of trust. Thereafter, they add, Dupleix was driven by a hatred of the British, whom he had previously considered almost as friends.[42] Ananda describes Dupleix at this moment as 'irritated' and 'anxious'.[43] Privately he began to speak of a desire to 'root the English from this land', as his conception of an Anglo-French struggle for survival in India took shape.[44] With the British dominant at sea, the most realistic chance for a counter-offensive was on land. A march on Fort St David was considered, but Dupleix had his eyes on a bigger prize: Madras. If the city was captured, he reasoned, the British presence on the Coromandel would suffer a serious blow. Moreover, Madras was surprisingly vulnerable, its fortifications incomplete and just a couple of hundred EIC troops in place to defend it, according to the reports reaching Dupleix from a Portuguese priest at San Thomé, with whom Jeanne was in contact.[45] In September 1745, Anwar ud-Din was invited to Pondicherry. A meeting was held in the *nawab*'s camp, just outside the city walls, and Dupleix secured Anwar ud-Din's permission to attack Madras in retaliation for the British aggression at sea—or at least he thought he did.

With authorities in France now also realising that there would be no neutrality accord in the Indian Ocean, La Bourdonnais was given the green light to return to India. A fleet of nine ships—five sent out from Europe plus four already in the Mascarenes—was prepared. 700 slaves from the Isle de France and the Isle Bourbon were rented from their owners and added to the army of 2,700 at his disposal.[46] In July 1746, off the coast of Negapatam, a first engagement took place with the British squadron that for the previous eighteenth months had controlled the coastline uncontested. Both fleets sustained high casualties, but after two days of fighting it was clear that the British had come off worse. The British squadron withdrew to Bengal, leaving the French in control of the Coromandel.

After the celebrations marking the arrival of La Bourdonnais and his fleet at Pondicherry had calmed down, Dupleix and the commander set about preparing the attack on Madras. It was launched in September, as soon as favourable winds allowed. Under La Bourdonnais's command, 1,200 troops were landed south of the city to encircle it from the west while it was bombarded simultaneously from the sea. As anticipated, the British defence was insufficient; after three days of heavy bombardment, Madras fell. For Ananda, the surrender of the city was the fault of Governor Morse, 'a worthless fellow' who was 'destitute of courage and fortitude'.[47] Its capture, meanwhile, was confirmation of Dupleix's talents: 'God has favoured him with unswerving resolution.'[48] Compliments flooded in from the courts of southern India as word of the French exploit spread.

A bitter disagreement was almost immediately to flare up between Dupleix and La Bourdonnais about what to do next, however. The pair had clashed from the moment of La Bourdonnais's arrival at Pondicherry, the commander taking umbrage at Dupleix's lack of deference towards him.[49] Now it emerged that before the capitulation of Madras, La Bourdonnais had acted alone to agree terms with the British: the commander would restore the city to them in return for the payment of 500,000 pagodas upfront and a further 600,000 in Europe.[50] On hearing this news, Dupleix was filled with 'an anger and vexation' that 'cannot be adequately described.'[51] The governor's plan had been to raze the city and force its merchant population to relocate to Pondicherry, thereby striking a serious, long-term blow against the EIC. He implored La Bourdonnais to renege on the agreement, arguing that 'we must not be satisfied with simply an immediate advantage, we must think of the future.'[52] La Bourdonnais refused to budge, arguing that destroying the British settlement would be dishonourable. 'Madras is not a French colony', he insisted, 'but a conquest that I have just made; nobody therefore has the right to govern it but me.'[53] Dupleix was certain that La Bourdonnais had been bribed; reports circulated that he had received 100,000 pagodas in gold and diamonds from the British to return the city and guarantee its integrity. 'The ransom that you intend to exact for the town of Madras is only a momentary advantage', he wrote to the commander, 'and a very dubious one at that.'[54]

Realising that La Bourdonnais would not be swayed, Dupleix also wrote to the King and to the Compagnie in France accusing him of treason: 'La Bourdonnais is acting contrary to the honour of the nation and the interests of the Company, and in a way which compromises the king's majesty.'[55] An unexpected turn then put Dupleix back in control of events. At the start of October the Coromandel was visited by a cyclone that wreaked havoc on La Bourdonnais's fleet: one ship was lost and two others saved only by the dropping of the cannons overboard. La Bourdonnais had little choice but to return to the Isle de France, where his fleet could be repaired. He left behind 1,200 soldiers which, added to the 2,000 already at Pondicherry, amounted to an impressive army at Dupleix's disposal.[56] Soon after his return to the Isle de France, La Bourdonnais was deposed as governor and sent back to Europe, where he spent three years imprisoned in the Bastille, while Dupleix's accusations against him were investigated. He was cleared of the charge of treason and released just a few months before his death in November 1753, his health broken by the imprisonment.

With La Bourdonnais out of the picture, Dupleix could do with Madras what he liked. The pre-surrender agreement was declared void and all Brits expelled. Morse was taken prisoner and made to suffer a humiliating public arrival at Pondicherry. The pillage and destruction of Madras then ensued, with the prosperous suburb of Mylapore, where many local traders had warehouses, particularly suffering, as Dupleix's wish to force the relocation of Indian and Armenian merchants to Pondicherry was carried out. Large bribes and oaths of allegiance to the King of France were demanded of those who wished to stay on in the city. Following events from Fort St David, where most Brits had taken refuge, the EIC's council protested that 'the Proceedings of the French [...] have in General been so Cruel and Inhumane that they seem rather to imitate a Persecution than a War.'[57]

Anwar ud-Din now resolved to intervene, the *nawab* denying that he had ever given the French permission to take Madras. In late October, his son Mahfuz Khan arrived outside the city with an army of 10,000. French field guns succeeded in protecting it and a sortie towards San Thomé pushed Mahfuz Khan's forces back to the banks of the Gingee River, a few kilometres to the south, where, despite their huge numerical superiority, they were routed. Beyond the preservation of Madras by the Compagnie, the significance of this event was severalfold. The norms of diplomacy between Anwar ud-Din and the French—including their recognition of the *nawab*'s authority—had been ruptured and a new tone of aggression entered Dupleix's correspondence with him. When three French envoys at the *nawab*'s court were prevented from leaving it, Dupleix threatened to order the massacre of the Muslim residents of Madras and Pondicherry, including members of Anwar ud-Din's family, unless the detainees were returned safely. 'We shall shed their blood until it flows like a river', he menaced the *nawab*.[58] Dupleix's resolve to replace Anwar ud-Din with a more amenable *nawab* was meanwhile strengthened. 'They can count on the fact that I will do all I can to support the first rival who comes to take control of the government of the province', he recorded. 'I am master, when I want, to support whoever I decide it is best to.'[59]

More significantly still, the rout of Mahfuz Khan's forces confirmed what Dupleix and other Frenchmen had for a long time suspected: that a disciplined army with European and Indian troops trained and equipped in the European fashion was capable of defeating Indian enemies greatly superior in number. Not only could European field guns fire rapidly to defeat a charging cavalry, but infantry armed with European muskets and bayonets were much more effective than their Indian counterparts.[60] After Adyar, Dupleix boasted that all of south India might soon be subdued, adding that it was his desire that 'the fame of the French should reach the Court of Delhi.'[61] On this second point, his wish would soon come true. When Emperor Muhammad Shah was informed of the French success, Dupleix's *mansadbar* ranking was raised. Congratulations were also received from Asaf Jah and Raghuji Bhonsle; in Indian courts, Dupleix and his army were henceforth to be taken seriously, and even feared. Ananda flattered Dupleix by repeating the popular Tamil songs reportedly sung in praise of the governor.

To complete the defeat of the British on the Coromandel, the final step required was the capture of Fort St David. The intelligence received by Ananda suggested that its fortifications were also in a poor state, but the fort's position on high ground above Cuddalore gave its defenders a natural advantage.[62] In December 1746, the French force camped outside the fort was caught off guard by a joint army of the British and Mahfuz Khan, whose causes were now aligned, and a retreat to Pondicherry was ordered. Three months later, a second attempt on the fort was made, this time commanded by the highly capable Swiss mercenary Paradis. For the British, the situation was desperate. Five months had passed since the fall of Madras and still no reinforcements had appeared. Just a day after the siege had begun, however, relief arrived in the form of a new

British squadron from Europe. Paradis abandoned the offensive and returned to Pondicherry to prepare its defence.

With the arrival of the new squadron, followed by reinforcements from Calcutta and Bombay, the numerical superiority of French forces against their British counterparts was eroded and an uneasy stalemate set in. The threat of an attack on Pondicherry, which was blockaded from the sea, prevented a further attempt on Fort St David from being made in the immediate future, though Madras remained in French hands. To tip the military balance in its favour again, Versailles committed to the dispatch of another squadron to India in the autumn of 1747 and London followed suit. The British squadron, which arrived on the Coromandel in July 1748, was the more impressive; combined with the previous year's fleet, France's rivals now had an unprecedented thirty-nine vessels at their disposal and more than 4,000 European troops, plus 2,000 sepoys. Dupleix, in contrast, had just 1,800 European soldiers and 3,000 Indians.[63] Knowing that a British attack on Pondicherry was coming, the governor commissioned one final attempt on Fort St David. When its failure became clear, he launched into the preparations for a long defence of the colony.

'God knows what fear reigns in the town; man can neither measure nor describe it', wrote Ananda as the British encircled Pondicherry from land and sea.[64] Among the residents fleeing in terror were the families of Dost Ali Khan and Chanda Sahib, eight years on from their flight from Arcot. Tensions erupted in the streets when Dupleix ordered the demolition of the town's most sacred temple, the Vedapuri Iswaran Koil, to ensure a clear line of fire from the fort. When the siege began in August, the early signs were not good. Paradis was killed during a sortie and a unit of Anwar ud-Din's cavalry arrived to support the British. Ananda complained that Dupleix was 'confused' and 'alarmed', the first indication that he was beginning to doubt the governor.[65] No British breakthrough came, however, and after fifty-seven days, as the monsoon rain began and disease spread through the ranks of the besiegers, the assault was called off. Pondicherry had been stocked with food and other provisions to hold out for twice that long.[66]

Despite his status as a civilian governor, the credit for the successful defence of Pondicherry went to Dupleix. At the feast celebrating the lifting of the siege, a poem was read in his honour. Representatives of the merchant community visited the governor to thank him for saving the town and Ananda forgot all his earlier reservations, gushing that Dupleix was 'destined to win great glory, which will shine throughout the whole country.'[67] When news of the defence reached Europe, the directors of the Compagnie declared themselves 'very satisfied' with their governor, and the rank of *chevalier* (knight) was awarded to him by Louis XV.[68] Dupleix had never been one to reject praise but was at least gracious enough to acknowledge the contribution of God to the successful outcome. The Almighty, he suggested to his brother, had chosen 'to work through me for the conclusion of an affair that will forever be celebrated in India and maybe in Europe, if things are accorded their correct value.'[69] From this moment onwards, Dupleix was convinced that divine providence was on his side—and, even more alarmingly, that God had selected him to ensure the Divine Will was implemented on earth. The glory of the King and Compagnie—and of course his personal glory—were henceforth inseparable from the glory of God.

*

In the same month that the siege of Pondicherry was called off—October 1748—the signing of the Treaty of Aix-la-Chapelle brought an end to the War of Austrian Succession. Under its terms, the possessions of France and Great Britain in Europe, India and the Americas were restored to their pre-war owners; Louisbourg, on the coast of Canada, was returned to France, while Louis XV gave up French gains in Europe and committed to the restitution of Madras to the British. Dupleix was ordered by the directors in Paris to restart the Compagnie's commerce, which had been brought to a standstill by the conflict. After a lengthy delay to allow the dismantlement of its fortifications to be completed, the keys of Madras were handed back to the British council on the Coromandel. The French marched ceremoniously out of the city through its southern gate, towards Pondicherry, as the British entered from the north.

There was no getting away from the fact, however, that the peace concluded in Europe had left feelings of dissatisfaction and antipathy on both sides. Dupleix resented giving up Madras, which he feared would permit the EIC to recover its commercial strength; he was aware too that Nawab Anwar ud-Din would likely remain their ally.[70] Emboldened by his success and the recognition that had followed, the governor wanted to press home the French advantage and bring more glory on the Compagnie and himself. The British, meanwhile, were smarting from the destruction of Madras and out for revenge. In the immediate term their anger was directed towards those residents of the colony who were suspected of siding with the French, among them several wealthy Indian merchants and Catholic priests, who were subject to reprisals. The British council, which remained at Fort St David while the reconstruction of Madras got underway, then took a leaf out of the French book by concluding an alliance with the exiled former ruler of Tanjore, Shahji Bhonsle, whom Chanda Sahib had deposed in 1739. In return for military assistance to help Shahji attempt to recover his throne, the Company was granted the port of Devikotta at the mouth of the Kollidam River, in an area valuable for its production of cloth. Watching this development, Dupleix's mood soured further and his mind turned to the possibility of more military action against Indian powers. 'Experience of this country has made us know that it would often be more expedient to impose our will not only on the Tanjoreans but upon all Asiatics in general, but our present situation does not yet permit us to use consistently this violent remedy.'[71]

Two events in quick succession then all but confirmed that hostilities would resume. First, Asaf Jah I passed away at the age of 77 after an impressive twenty-four years in power in the Deccan. Almost in parallel, Chanda Sahib was released from his imprisonment with the Marathas at the end of almost seven years in captivity. The obvious successor to Asaf Jah as *nizam* was his son, Nasir Jang, whose support for Anwar ud-Din in the Carnatic was beyond question. In the months that followed the *nizam*'s death, however, one of Nasir Jang's nephews, Muzaffar Jang, staked a claim for the throne and in his favour was able to produce a *firman* from Ahmad Shah Bahadur, the new Mughal Emperor in Delhi. Sensing an opportunity,

Chanda Sahib approached Muzaffar Jang and an alliance was formed between the pair: the former would support the latter's campaign to be recognised as *nizam* of the Deccan in return for his installation as *nawab* of the Carnatic. The causes of Muzaffar Jang and Chanda Sahib, in the Deccan and the Carnatic respectively, were henceforth aligned.

What made the new allies confident of success was the support that they could count on from the French. Over the preceding two years, while the conflict with the British and Anwar ud-Din was ongoing, Dupleix had continued his efforts to secure Chanda Sahib's release, negotiating with the Maratha leader Raghuji Bhonsle to lower the ransom demanded to 200,000 rupees and agreeing to act as the guarantor of its payment.[72] 'We are most anxious for him [Chanda Sahib] to get control of the Carnatic', Dupleix wrote in explanation of this action, 'since he is truly the friend of the nation'.[73] In February 1749, Chanda Sahib now liberated, the terms of an alliance were secretly agreed by the governor: funds would be advanced by the Compagnie and a corps of European and Indian troops under a French commander lent to Chanda Sahib and Muzaffar Jang to support their joint invasion of the Carnatic. In addition to the repayment of the sums advanced, the Compagnie would in exchange be granted territories on the banks of the Gingee River at Villenour, just west of Pondicherry, which would add an estimated 50,000 rupees per year to its revenues from land.[74] The Pondicherry council agreed that Chanda Sahib would be helped 'until he be installed in peaceful possession of his government.'[75]

The theatre of war now shifted from the Coromandel into the rock-strewn, dry landscape of the interior of the Carnatic. In the summer of 1749, the joint army of Muzaffar Jang and Chanda Sahib, a force of 12,000, invaded the province. A Compagnie corps of 400 European soldiers and 2,000 sepoys set out from Pondicherry to join them and, at Ambur, the forces of Anwar ud-Din were engaged.[76] After two hours of battle, the *nawab*'s army ceded; a massacre at close quarters followed and Anwar ud-Din was killed. Four days later the victorious army entered Arcot; Muzaffar Jang assumed the role of *nizam* to name Chanda Sahib as *nawab*. From here they proceeded to Pondicherry, where the arrival of Chanda Sahib was greeted with the ceremony that a newly crowned *nawab* might expect. For its contribution to the success, the Compagnie was rewarded far in excess of what it had been promised. Besides the territories at Villenour, land in the district of Bahur, not far from Fort St David, was made over to the French in perpetuity, along with the busy port of Masulipatam and a large area around it with annual revenues of 800,000 rupees.[77] Dupleix, Ananda, Jeanne and the commander of the Compagnie corps, Louis Hubert de Combault d'Auteuil, received money and land grants (*jagirs*) in their names, and the spoils of war—cannons, elephants, camels, jewellery and rupees from Anwar ud-Din's camp—were divided out among the victors.

The conflict, however, was far from over. While Anwar ud-Din's eldest son, Mahfuz Khan, had been captured at Ambur, his second son, Muhammad Ali, had managed to escape. From the safety of Trichinopoly, he now appealed to Nasir Jang for assistance. Chanda Sahib, it was clear, would only be secure as *nawab* if Muhammad Ali was eliminated. Moreover, the campaign to install Muzaffar Jang as *nizam* had only just started.

Outwardly, the British had accepted the appointment of Chanda Sahib as *nawab*, even inviting him to Fort St David to celebrate the occasion. In truth, they had little choice; just 800 European soldiers remained at their disposal from the reinforcements sent out during the war.[78] After Ambur, however, the British council was in no doubt about the threat to their interests that Dupleix and his Indian allies represented and discreetly opened negotiations with Nasir Jang about a joint response. A force of 700 sepoys and thirty Europeans was sent to support Muhammad Ali at Trichinopoly and San Thomé was occupied, the presence so close to Madras of a small Portuguese settlement with pro-French sympathies being considered intolerable.[79] Antonio Noronha, the priest in contact with Jeanne, was arrested. Observing these developments, Dupleix was incensed, doubling down on his argument that the nawabship belonged legitimately to Chanda Sahib's dynasty, the Nawayaths. The English, he railed, were supporting Muhammad Ali because of 'their shameless thirst for [his] money'.[80]

The governor was meanwhile urging Chanda Sahib to move quickly and decisively against Muhammad Ali at Trichinopoly, without success. First, Chanda Sahib delayed his departure, preferring to sit out the month of October at Pondicherry. When he did finally set off with his army, accompanied again by the Compagnie corps under Combault d'Auteuil, he insisted on first heading for Tanjore to collect tribute from Pratap Singh Bhonsle. The winter of 1749–50 was wasted in an unsuccessful siege of the rajah's capital that ruined the surrounding countryside, placed a strain on Chanda Sahib's finances and cost significant casualties in French ranks.

This delay would prove critical. In March 1750, Nasir Jang entered the Carnatic at the head of an army of as many as 300,000 men.[81] For Dupleix, it was not too late to negotiate: despite the size of his army, Nasir Jang was fearful of the French; if Dupleix dropped his support for Muzaffar Jang, peace between the *nizam* and the Compagnie might be agreed. Dupleix, however, was determined to push on with his aggressive forward policy. Nasir Jang, he insisted, was a 'drunken fool', his commanders 'the greatest cowards in the world, and our bombs and grenades terrify them indescribably. We must take advantage of their timidity.'[82] The governor insisted to Chanda Sahib and Muzaffar Jang that under no circumstances should they negotiate with the *nizam* and urged them to confront him straight away. 'We are giving you all necessary help, so what is there for you to do? If you refuse to attack him, you will dishonour me, your ally. Till now I have got nothing but glory, so go forth and fight, and all will happen as God wills. Put your trust in Him and attack.'[83]

On this occasion, however, His plans were out of line with Dupleix's. On 3 April, 20 kilometres inland from Pondicherry at Valudavur, Muzaffar Jang was captured by his uncle during the first engagement between the rival armies. The *nizam* now insisted that Dupleix abandon his support for Chanda Sahib as a precondition for peace. When the governor refused, forces were dispatched to seize the French trading posts at Masulipatam and Yanaon. Muhammad Ali ventured out from Trichinopoly accompanied by his British contingent to open up another front against the French. The Compagnie army continued to deliver, however. Masulipatam and Yanaon were quickly recovered by troops sent out from Pondicherry, the forces of the *nizam* were pushed back to Arcot and Muhammad Ali's troops were defeated at Tiruviti, with Chanda Sahib's rival shot in the leg and wounded. The supposedly impenetrable fort of Gingee was then captured during the monsoon.

In parallel, Dupleix was trying to engineer Muzaffar Jang's escape. In May 1750, the governor had entered into contact with a group of disaffected Pathan commanders in the court of Nasir Jang who favoured the installation of Muzaffar Jang as *nizam*. The priority was to extract Muzaffar Jang before his uncle ordered his execution. To this end, Dupleix sent 2,000 rupees to serve as bribes and ordered the stationing of agents, camels and boats along a planned escape route from the *nizam*'s camp back to Pondicherry. When Nasir Jang then retreated to Arcot, Muzaffar Jang was imprisoned in the fort. A second *romanesque* (far-fetched and adventurous) escape plot ensued involving an attempt to bore a hole in his cell wall.

What happened next merits close attention. As heavy rain delayed military movements in early December, a further round of negotiations between Dupleix and Nasir Jang took place through the *nizam*'s envoys. On 16 December, 20 kilometres north of Gingee, the *nizam*'s camp was then attacked by the Compagnie's troops. Before the attack was over, one of the Pathan commanders in Nasir Jang's ranks, Abdul Nabi Khan, shot the *nizam*, while another stabbed him. His head was severed from his body and placed at the feet of Muzaffar Jang, who was released from captivity and declared *nizam*. Nasir Jang's treasury was then seized, his brothers imprisoned and his army broken up.[84] It is impossible to be sure that Dupleix was implicated in the killing of Nasir Jang, not least—though this itself is highly suspicious—because a crucial four month period either side of the murder is missing from Ananda's diary. Some historians have suggested that just before the attack on the *nizam*'s camp, a peace agreement had been reached by Dupleix and Nasir Jang, with the latter agreeing to recognise Chanda Sahib as *nawab* of the Carnatic and confirm the territorial awards of Chanda Sahib and Muzaffar Jang to the Compagnie.[85] Even if such an agreement had been reached, however, there is no guarantee that Dupleix intended to stick to it. Over the preceding six months, the governor had been in regular contact with the Pathan rebels in Nasir Jang's court. The murder of the *nizam* satisfied their interests and allowed Dupleix's policy of regime change to be extended from the Carnatic to the Deccan, ensuring that in both territories rulers suited to French interests were in power.[86]

When news reached Pondicherry that Nasir Jang was dead, Chanda Sahib reportedly forgot all decorum and ran through the streets to the fort to embrace Dupleix. Ten days later Muzaffar Jang made his triumphal entry into Pondicherry. Wild celebrations followed, after which the new *nizam* distributed the contents of his uncle's treasury—some twenty chests of jewels and 12 million rupees in coin—among the victors. An estimated 2 million rupees went to Dupleix and the Compagnie and a further 400,000 rupees was shared out among the French troops. Dupleix and his commanders received more *jagirs* in their name, with that of Valudavur, which went to the governor, promising annual revenues of 150,000 rupees to him personally.[87] 'The treasury was opened for the gratification of the French', wrote one soldier present. 'The officers each received sixty thousand rupees. Never had we seen so much gold at Pondicherry.'[88]

Taking on a ceremonial role usually reserved for the Mughal Emperor, Dupleix then symbolically confirmed Muzaffar Jang as *nizam* by presenting him with six ornate axe-knives representing the six provinces of the Deccan.[89] Muzaffar Jang confirmed the Compagnie's possession of Masulipatam and added new lands around Gingee and Madras to its growing list of territories. In a departure from Mughal precedent, the *nizam* then took the unusual step of naming Dupleix as his deputy, with responsibility for all southern India below the River Krishna, which crossed the subcontinent from west to east to arrive in the Bay of Bengal near Masulipatam.[90] The powers attached to this title were not fully defined but included the nomination of the *nawab* of the Carnatic and the collection of the province's revenues at Pondicherry rather than Arcot. In the days that followed, Dupleix confirmed Chanda Sahib as *nawab*, but the Frenchman was now formally his superior, with control of his purse and the option of removing him in the future. Dupleix's rank of *mansadbar* was also raised (again); henceforth he had right to keep 7,000 horses and be escorted by twelve elephants. The prestigious Mughal symbol of the fish was added to his personal flag.[91]

In the months that followed, Dupleix moved into the new government house, now almost finished after more than decade of construction. It was, he must have thought, a residence fit for a deputy *nizam*, with its imposing two storeys, its ionic-columned façade and a large portico decorated with the Compagnie's arms. From a ground floor of gleaming marble halls, a magnificent staircase led up to the meeting room of the Pondicherry council, the governor's office and rooms, and a large terrasse overlooking the sea. Dupleix christened the building his very own '*palais des Indes*' (Palace of the Indies).[92] As Ananda's flattery reached new heights—'Your fame will shine like the sun in every country washed by the ocean'—the governor began to consider his place in history.[93] Commemorative medals were commissioned depicting the most glorious moments of the campaign that had just finished—the capture of Gingee, the possession of Masulipatam and the coronation of Muzaffar Jang.[94] On the site of Nasir Jang's death, a celebratory column was erected around which, Dupleix envisaged, a new town would be built. Its name would be 'Dupleix Fatehabad' (The City of Dupleix's Victory).

*

The celebrations at Pondicherry complete, it was time for Muzaffar Jang to return to the Deccan and make sure that his authority was recognised there. Hyderabad, the capital of the *nizam*'s dominions, had to be gained and the court of Nasir Jang pacified before any rivals to succeed the deceased *nizam* could stake their claim. The intentions of Muzaffar Jang's cousin Ghazi ud-Din Khan, the eldest son of Asaf Jah I, were particularly to be feared, but he was away in Delhi. Muzaffar Jang needed to get to Hyderabad and announce himself as *nizam* before Ghazi ud-Din could return. To help secure his position and ensure French influence on his side, it was agreed that he would be accompanied to the Deccan by a Compagnie army of 300 Europeans and 1,800 sepoys led by Charles Joseph Patissier de Bussy, a 32-year-old commander who had served in India since 1742 and distinguished himself with the capture of Gingee the previous year.[95] 'Work towards the objective I so much desire—namely that all the world may see that our nation has limitless capacities when she is in earnest about any undertaking. You are in a position to make her name glorious forever', Dupleix instructed Bussy.[96]

Things got off to a very bad start, however. Just a few weeks into their long march northwards, as they left the plains of the Coromandel behind and entered a mountain pass, Muzaffar's column was attacked by the same group of Pathan chieftains who had plotted against Nasir Jang. It appears that the new *nizam* had failed to honour promises made to the Pathans before Nasir Jang's death. A defence was mounted but for Muzaffar Jang it was too late; the *nizam* was struck in the head with a spear and killed. For the French, this was potentially disastrous. The figure that they had struggled to install as *nizam* had lasted only two months in the role, and not even made it to his capital. Bussy, whose knowledge of Persian and understanding of Mughal customs far exceeded that of Dupleix, now showed, however, that his military capacities were matched by a talent for diplomacy. Insisting that the march towards Hyderabad continue, he nominated Salabat Jang, one of the captured brothers of Nasir Jang, as *nizam*. The situation was even turned to French advantage, with new concessions extracted from the *nizam*-elect: extra villages around Masulipatam were granted to the Compagnie, along with cash payments supposedly for military expenses, and gifts for Bussy and his officers. Bussy reported to Dupleix: 'The treasures of Golconda [Hyderabad] will be given to us on our arrival, if you desire it. I believe that the nation can derive great advantages from this revolution [...] There will never be a better occasion to extend the glory of the French name and ensure the good of the Compagnie.'[97] Dupleix was full of praise for the initiative that Bussy had shown in replacing Muzaffar Jang, responding that 'the way in which you have acted has added enormously to the glory which the nation has gained from this happy enterprise.'[98]

Two months later Hyderabad was reached and Salabat Jang declared *nizam*. The treasury was emptied and a *diwan* (first minister) supportive of French interests, the Brahmin Ramdas Pant, was installed at the *nizam*'s side. In return for further payments, Bussy then agreed to continue with Salabat Jang to Aurangabad, 500 kilometres to the northwest and the second most important city in the *nizam*'s dominions. The aim, in Dupleix's words, was 'to conserve the possessions of the Compagnie, to increase them even.'[99] When Aurangabad was reached in June, the good news was received that, in Delhi, Emperor Ahmad Shah Bahadur had approved Salabat Jang's nomination as *nizam*. This was the occasion for a further round of rewards for the Compagnie, which was granted the territories of Arcot, Trichinopoly and Madurai, free of tribute, in return for continued French support. In other words, the entire Carnatic was handed over to the Compagnie—a concession beyond what even Dupleix and Bussy had dared to imagine. 'Nothing is more glorious for the reign of our monarch', noted Dupleix, who instructed Bussy to send an envoy to Delhi so that the grants might be rubber stamped by the emperor.[100] Salabat Jang, Bussy responded, is 'nothing but your slave [...] All of the Deccan belongs to you and you are free to appoint whoever you want there.'[101]

Dupleix now began to think even bigger, firing off an astonishing succession of ideas to expand French influence still further. In Bengal, Nawab Alivardi Khan had proven a very effective ruler, capable of holding the influence of the French and British in check. Why not, Dupleix asked, demand Ahmad Shah Bahadur to add Bengal to Salabat Jang's jurisdiction and have Bussy invade the province to depose Alivardi? To Bussy, the governor wrote: 'You alone are strong enough to become master of the country which is ripe for this invasion because of the tyranny of the present government.'[102] The occupation of the Circars—a large area of exceptionally fertile land on the coast north of the Carnatic, including Masulipatam and Yanaon—was also envisaged, before the governor's attention turned to western India. Surat might be captured with Maratha support and the British finally driven from Tellicherry to cement the Compagnie's dominance on the Malabar Coast. In the south, the kingdom of Tanjore, sworn enemies of the French, might finally be extinguished.

Dupleix no longer hesitated to describe his aim as 'the French domination of India' and was not content to stop there.[103] In line with the method of military-backed regime change to install compliant rulers that had proven effective in the Carnatic and the Deccan, a plan was formed to help the recently imprisoned Sultan of the Maldives, Muhammad Imad ud-Din III, recover his throne. In parallel, an envoy was sent to Burma to negotiate with leaders of the Mon people, who were locked in a struggle with the Burmese, and a French invasion of the Irrawaddy Delta was envisaged.[104] Unfortunately for the glory-hungry governor, however, it wasn't long before French control in the Carnatic began to unravel.

6

IMPERIAL COLLAPSE

Surveying the scene in the Carnatic in January 1751, just after Bussy's departure for Hyderabad with Muzaffar Jang, Dupleix was no doubt aware, despite his ever-growing ambitions, that his appointment as deputy *nizam*—a move theoretically confirming French authority over the entire province—belied a more complex reality. The Compagnie and its *nawab*, Chanda Sahib, were in a strong position in the north and centre of the province, where the capital of Arcot and the stronghold of Gingee were in their possession. In the south, however, it was a different story. At Tanjore, Rajah Pratap Singh Bhonsle was determined to resist Chanda Sahib and the French. Muhammad Ali, meanwhile, had returned to nearby Trichinopoly after the murder of Nasir Jang. From here he appealed to the British for help to win back the nawabship snatched from his father, Anwar ud-Din, some eighteen months earlier.

Ever since the outbreak of hostilities between France and Great Britain in 1744, the British on the Coromandel had allied with opponents of the French, notably Anwar ud-Din and Muhammad Ali, offering them military support. Given the small troop numbers at their disposal, coupled with doubts about how far Dupleix was really willing to push his strategy of aggression, this assistance had been modest: just thirty European soldiers were included in the contingent sent to support Muhammad Ali in 1749, as we have seen. With the murder of Nasir Jang, however, the remaining British doubts about Dupleix's intentions were blown away and a firm resolve to stand up to the French took hold. Thomas Saunders, the new British governor at Fort St David, was convinced that if Dupleix was not stopped, the days of the Company on the Coromandel were limited. Dupleix's argument that Chanda Sahib was the province's legitimate ruler was dismissed with the observation that force, rather than legitimacy, was what ultimately mattered in the Carnatic. Chanda Sahib, he asserted, was nothing more than a 'screen for French ambitions'.[1] Stringer Lawrence, commander of the British troops, agreed: 'To leave the Carnatic to Chanda Sahib would be to leave it in the hands of the French, who make use of Chanda Sahib for their own ends', he noted.[2] Later, in his memoirs, Lawrence added that Muhammad Ali, rather than Chanda Sahib, was the province's legitimate ruler, because his father Anwar ud-Din had been appointed to the role by Asaf Jah, an argument often repeated in British ranks. 'It was necessary to put a stop to the progress of the French', he explained, 'whether in justice to assist the lawful prince against the rebels, or as an act of self-defence, and to prevent an increase of power in an oppressive neighbour that must, at last, have proved our ruin.'[3]

Ahead of the new round of hostilities, Dupleix had every reason to be confident. Even with over 2,000 soldiers tied up in the Deccan expedition, French troop numbers were superior: while both Dupleix and Saunders had about 2,000 sepoys at their disposal, the Compagnie had roughly double the number of Europeans (1,500 to 750).[4] Moreover, the reputation of the French military was superior: Indian courts 'tremble at the mere mention of our army', noted Ananda.[5] Following the escalation of British efforts to stand up to the French from Pondicherry, the Compagnie's chief courtier was unconcerned: 'Just as even a worm will raise its head and dance when it sees the cobra dancing, so the English, their hearts burning with jealousy of the French, have themselves attempted to conquer their enemies and get possession of territory. But who can get what he wants by the mere force of desire? He alone succeeds whose destiny it is and whose hand is marked with the line of victory.'[6]

When fighting resumed in March 1751, the early engagements suggested that this confidence was well-founded. At Valikandapuram, on the route from Pondicherry to Trichinopoly, the army of Chanda Sahib and the Compagnie secured an important victory, forcing the British to flee. 'Never have the English been so disgraced! It is marvellous that they can still show their faces anywhere', gloated Dupleix.[7] At this point, however, the relationship between the governor and Chanda Sahib began to sour. Dupleix, it will be recalled, already had reservations about the *nawab*'s decision-making in military matters, which had surfaced when he opted to besiege Tanjore en route for Trichinopoly in late 1749. Now the governor questioned why the British had been permitted to retreat from Valikandapuram to Muhammad Ali's Trichinopoly refuge, seventy kilometres to the south, without a decisive blow being struck against them. Chanda Sahib, Dupleix complained, was 'unfit to command' and 'of the same character as all the Muslims, who are the most wretched creatures and the biggest cowards.'[8] To make matters worse, the funds available to Chanda Sahib were drying up and his debts mounting. This Dupleix attributed to the fact that the *nawab* was 'not in possession of the country'.[9] Since taking office, Chanda Sahib had failed to have his authority recognised and collect revenues from the province's Hindu landowners, the governor suggested. His support among them had dwindled through mismanagement, as he reneged on promises of titles and land grants made to influential local parties.

Dupleix gave serious consideration to removing Chanda Sahib and naming himself *nawab*—suggesting that he could ship Chanda Sahib off to Mecca if he resisted— but was dissuaded from this course by Bussy, who urged caution while Salabat Jang's reign in the Deccan was in its infancy. Instead, the governor resorted to trying to control the *nawab* as closely as possible, sending him two to three letters a day with instructions relating to revenue collection and the conduct of the military campaign. Henceforth Dupleix took important decisions without consulting Chanda Sahib and contacted some of the province's largest landowners directly to demand contributions, threatening to seize their land if they didn't pay. When the results produced by these efforts were disappointing, the governor started ploughing his own money into the financing of the war. For his part, Chanda Sahib complained that the Compagnie had not delivered all the loans that it had promised him and objected that the Europeans in his camp were costing a lot and achieving very little—particularly Commander Combault d'Auteuil, to whom the *nawab* passed on the blame for the British escape to Trichinopoly.

The siege of Trichinopoly by the army of Chanda Sahib and Combault d'Auteuil began in July 1751 with these recriminations ongoing and the French commander threatening to resign his post. After six weeks of deadlock, with Muhammad Ali and his British contingent holed up in the fort, an audacious diversion was staged: an attack from Madras on Chanda Sahib's capital of Arcot by a small expeditionary force under Robert Clive. Thanks to Jeanne's contacts in Madras, which by this point had been sufficiently rebuilt to permit the British to return, Dupleix knew that the attack was coming, but could not act quickly enough to prevent it. Arcot was poorly defended and fell without much resistance—a major setback for the French and a humiliation for Chanda Sahib. Dupleix's response was to divert a small force from Trichinopoly to retake the town and to commission the freelance Muslim commander Mir Azam to join it with 2,000 cavalrymen.[10] The British, however, went one better, negotiating an alliance with the Maratha mercenary Morari Rao, who was no stranger to the Carnatic, having already fought against Chanda Sahib on behalf of Pratap Singh Bhonsle and, more recently, in the service of Nasir Jang. A force of 6,000 Maratha cavalrymen arrived at Arcot in November 1751 to prevent the French from recapturing it, driving them westwards towards Vellore.[11] Caught as they tried to cross a river pursued by the British and the Marathas, the French forces suffered heavy losses and were expelled from the north of the province.

On being informed of this, Dupleix was 'so angry [...] that even I fear to stand before him', recorded Ananda, and worse was to follow.[12] In February 1752, British reinforcements arrived from Bengal. The following month, two companies of infantry landed on the Coromandel from Europe. The rajah of Tanjore, Pratap Singh Bhonsle, now threw all his weight behind the British, followed by Krishnaraja Wadiyar II of Mysore, who had earlier been alarmed to find his kingdom—falling as it did below the River Krishna—theoretically rendered part of Dupleix's jurisdiction. For the first time, Ananda began to have doubts about how the war would end, noting in his journal that 'the English have determined to fight to the end, and even spend the Company's money on continuing the war if Muhammad Ali Khan can find no more. They have fought so hard that they are certain not to give way now but will fight harder than ever.'[13]

All hinged on Trichinopoly, where the siege of Muhammad Ali and his British troops had been maintained by Chanda Sahib and the French through the winter of 1751–52, even as Arcot and the northern Carnatic were lost. One of the two British infantry companies freshly arrived from Europe set off immediately to relieve the city, where supplies were running low and a capitulation likely without reinforcements. After months of threatening to abandon Chanda Sahib, Combault d'Auteuil had been taken ill and was replaced as commander of the French troops by the inexperienced Jacques Law.[14] When the British company, under Stringer Lawrence, was sighted approaching, accompanied by an army of the rajah of Tanjore, Law ordered his forces to withdraw to Srirangam, a holy island in the River Cauvery just north of Trichinopoly. Law was not confident of taking on the reinforced British, despite overall numerical parity and the larger number of European troops under his command.

Realising that disaster was looming, Dupleix rushed Combault d'Auteuil from his sickbed and dispatched him from Pondicherry with an extra company of French troops, but their passage southwards towards Srirangam was blocked by the British army under Clive that had previously driven the French out of Arcot and, at Valikandapuram, Combault d'Auteuil was forced to surrender. Lawrence and his Indian allies—Muhammad Ali and Pratap Singh Bhonsle—now had free rein to encircle Srirangam, turning the tables on the army of Chanda Sahib and the Compagnie, which for nine months had laid siege to Trichinopoly but was now besieged. With few provisions to feed his troops, the situation was desperate for Law. Some food and funds were extracted from the island's sacred Sri Ranganatha Swamy

Temple with the threat that it would otherwise be destroyed, but after two months the game was up and Law surrendered.

As part of the terms of capitulation, Law tried to secure a promise from Lawrence of Chanda Sahib's safety. Not confident that this could be guaranteed, the *nawab* then attempted to escape Srirangam disguised as a fakir, but was recognised and captured. Ominously, it was to Tanjore, where ever since his invasion in 1733 he had been detested, that Chanda Sahib was taken as prisoner. Two days later he was beheaded.

*

When Dupleix was told about Law's surrender and the death of Chanda Sahib he was 'so overcome that he could neither go to church nor eat his dinner.'[15] Over the space of nine months, the governor's Carnatic strategy had almost completely unravelled. Of the possessions gained by the Compagnie over the previous four years of conflict, only the fort of Gingee remained. With the soldiers who had surrendered at Srirangam taken into British custody, the strength of French forces had meanwhile been seriously depleted. In the months before the surrender, Dupleix and Saunders had exchanged letters about the terms of a possible peace: Dupleix had hinted at his willingness to recognise Muhammad Ali as ruler of Trichinopoly if Chanda Sahib was recognised as *nawab* of the Carnatic in return.[16] After Srirangam, however, the British held the trump cards and would refuse, in future negotiations, to consider the agreement of peace on terms which Dupleix found acceptable. On its way from Arcot to intercept Combault d'Auteuil's company at Valikandapuram, Clive's army had stopped off near Gingee to raze the foundations of Dupleix Fatehabad and to bury the Frenchman's victory column, a fitting metaphor for the fate that the governor's Carnatic aspirations was now suffering.[17]

Consistent with one of his long-standing character traits—a tendency to feel wronged that strongly resembled paranoia—Dupleix appears at this juncture to have truly convinced himself that the British were the real aggressors in the Carnatic and he and his compatriots their victims. From Pondicherry he dispatched a long and incoherent letter to Saunders in which he tried to justify his conduct since the beginning of the hostilities, concluding after almost 100 pages of rambling self-vindication:

> You have made all your efforts to have our establishments destroyed; you and your predecessors have incited the troubles and ravages of this province; you maintain Muhammad Ali, who is himself a traitor, in his rebellion [...] The misery of the people does not affect you, on the contrary you seek to increase it and you concern yourself only with the means to this end. You are no longer affected by the considerable loss of men that these troubles have occasioned England; you forget the commerce and standing of your nation [...] How many pretexts have you and your predecessors made use of to justify, to your superiors, your conduct towards us and the princes of India? [...] All of Europe must be informed of what you and your predecessors have resorted to.[18]

The argument that Muhammad Ali was an illegitimate candidate for the nawabship and the British support of him self-interested were not new in Dupleix's thought, but as the conflict turned against the French they were repeated and exaggerated, until the British attained an almost pantomime villain-like status. 'The most fundamental customs and the mutual respect which nations owe to one another have not stopped the English [...] who hold nothing sacred which stands in the way of their ambitions', wrote Dupleix.[19] 'The sight of gold and silver usually has an enormous influence on this nation; they will sacrifice everything to get it.'[20]

With the British governor unmoved by Dupleix's protestations, French hopes rested on events in the Deccan. Once the position of Salabat Jang was secured, his army and the French contingent under Bussy could return to the Carnatic, where their intervention might be decisive. Bussy, however, had his work cut out in the Deccan, struggling against a host of opponents to the new *nizam* both within and beyond his court. In April 1751, before Salabat and Bussy had even completed their triumphal march to Aurangabad to announce Salabat's ascension to the throne, supporters of the *nizam*'s eldest brother, Ghazi ud-Din, had induced *peshwa* Balaji Rao to invade the province and occupy Hyderabad. On the advice of Bussy, who was concerned about the invader's strength, the Maratha leader was paid off and the occupation averted, but the peace was only temporary. Through the summer of 1751, Bussy focused on growing and training the army at his disposal, which combined the European soldiers and sepoys from Pondicherry with troops provided by the *nizam*, among them a growing number of Muslim commanders instructed in European military techniques.[21] By the autumn, the army was sufficiently strong for a counter-offensive against the Marathas to be launched. After a month's march into Maratha territories, Balaji Rao's camp was attacked and overrun during an eclipse, while the *peshwa* and his soldiers were occupied with their devotions. Bussy and Salabat then advanced to within a day's march of the Maratha capital of Poona before food shortages, exacerbated by the Maratha's scorched earth tactics, forced them to turn around. A favourable peace treaty followed in which Balaji Rao recognised Salabat's authority and agreed, at least on paper, to respect the territorial integrity of his dominions.[22] Updated on these developments by Bussy's letters, Dupleix was delighted: 'Whoever would have thought that a handful of Frenchmen could carry steel and fire into the heart of the Mahratta [sic] country?' he asked joyfully. 'The glory of the king and nation are at their highest point.'[23]

Not for the first time, however, the celebrations proved premature. In April 1752, Salabat's *diwan* Ramdas Pant, who controlled domestic affairs while the *nizam* was on campaign, was assassinated at court by opponents who considered him, with justification, an agent of the French. Worse still, news reached the *nizam*'s court that Ghazi ud-Din had set off from Delhi, his long-anticipated return to the Deccan underway. Bussy now scrambled to ensure that Balaji Rao would keep his word and not enter the pending civil war in the Deccan on Ghazi ud-Din's side. To no avail. When Ghazi ud-Din's army entered the northern Deccan in September 1752, the *peshwa*'s forces re-invaded the kingdom from the west, and the Nagpur Maratha ruler Raghuji Bhonsle was also recruited to Ghazi ud-Din's side. The coalition aligned against Salabat Jang and the French was now a serious cause for alarm. Bussy and the *nizam* fell back on Hyderabad, from where the Frenchman urgently appealed to Dupleix for assistance. A further retreat to Masulipatam or Pondicherry was then envisaged.

Only another convenient murder prevented this ignominious flight from being necessary. One month after his return, while stationed at Aurangabad preparing to march southwards, Ghazi ud-Din was poisoned by a member of his family and his remaining two brothers imprisoned. The coalition against Salabat broke up and a new peace treaty, the second in as many years, was concluded between Balaji Rao and the *nizam*. For Dupleix, the killing of Ghazi ud-Din was 'without doubt the most joyful event that we could hope for' and another sign that divine providence was on the French side.[24] 'It would be hard not to see in this the Hand of God', he wrote to Bussy, 'and I am sure that it was to Him that you offered thanks when you heard of the death of Salabat J.'s rival.'[25]

Bussy, truth be told, was thinking more about a holiday. After two years of almost constant turmoil at Salabat Jang's side, the Frenchman was exhausted and pleaded to Dupleix to be recalled. Though the immediate threats had been seen off, he had little hope left of securing Salabat's position for long: the *nizam*, he lamented, had lost the support of most of his court and army and would soon be bankrupt—a state of affairs that many at Hyderabad blamed, not unreasonably given the payments repeatedly demanded by Bussy and his officers, on the French presence. Suffering from fever and dysentery, Bussy was finally granted leave and withdrew to Masulipatam, leaving one of his officers, Goupil, in charge at Hyderabad. With his departure, the French influence on the *nizam* began to wane.

Dupleix now faced a decision about how much to report back to the directors in Paris about events in the Carnatic and the Deccan and the setbacks suffered. As a rule, his approach since becoming governor had been to say as little as possible in advance of new military and diplomatic initiatives, instead presenting the directors with the *faits accomplis.* Where explanation was necessary, Dupleix stressed that the use of force was small-scale and defensive in nature, in the face of English aggression, and argued that it was essential to protect the Compagnie's commerce, which the governor knew was the directors' priority. He repeated that in both the Carnatic and the

Deccan, the Compagnie was supporting the provinces' legitimate rulers and promised that hostilities would soon be over, with France and its allies victorious.

The directors, as we have seen, had urged on Dupleix the resumption of peaceful commerce after the Treaty of Aix-la-Chapelle was signed in October 1748. When Dupleix presented the installation of Chanda Sahib as *nawab* as not only legitimate but necessary to protect that commerce, his explanation was accepted. The governor was even congratulated for having bestowed on the Compagnie 'glory that will forever render the French name respected in the East'.[26] Some concern was soon after expressed about Nasir Jang's advance on the Carnatic, but the death of the *nizam* and the installation of Muzaffar Jang provided reassurance to the directors that peace was around the corner. A first sign that the directors were worried about Dupleix's intentions followed, however, when they got wind that Bussy and his army had accompanied Salabat Jang to the Deccan. 'It is not in the interests of the Compagnie to engage in wars in the interior of India', the directors stressed, nor its object 'to become a territorial power, except to form new establishments the utility of which is well recognised, and the measures for obtaining them discussed and agreed on with the Compagnie [i.e. with the directors].' A solid and lasting peace, Dupleix was instructed, was 'the sole aim that you should pursue'.[27]

In Versailles, the attitude of ministers of the crown to Dupleix's actions was broadly similar to that of the directors. The governor was praised for bringing glory upon the nation in southern India and was elevated to the rank of marquis before concerns were expressed, as the expansion of the Compagnie's power on the subcontinent began to cause diplomatic ripples in Europe. In the government, pacifist and Anglophile figures were in the ascendancy and avoiding another conflict with the British was the priority. The king's *commissaire* (commissioner), Étienne de Silhouette, cautioned Dupleix in late 1751 to 'apply yourself and your attention to deliver the fruits of peace to the Compagnie, and to increase its commerce with friendly alliances.'[28] The following year, as it became clear that this instruction had been ignored, he reiterated:

> Here [in France] we prefer peace to conquests, and the success of those conquests does not change the fact that we desire a situation less spectacular but quieter and more favourable to commerce [...] We are beginning to fear possessions that could engage the nation in wars with the princes of India. We desire not to be mixed up and to play no part in such affairs [...] We don't want to be a political power in India; we just want a few establishments to support and protect commerce: no more victories, no more conquests, just a lot of merchandise and an increase in dividends.[29]

Dupleix's initial reaction after the surrender of Law and the death of Chanda Sahib in June 1752 was to say nothing to the directors. The defeat was not reported by the governor until October. By the time that his letter reached France, the events at Trichinopoly and Srirangam had already been published in the *London Gazette*, copies of which had found their way across the Channel to Paris.[30] Here was confirmation for the directors that Dupleix was delaying or withholding information from them. The fact of serious conflict with the British and of significant military and financial losses could no longer be denied. New dispatches to India followed in which the directors repeated that they desired peace not war, commerce not territorial acquisitions. Dupleix's schemes to invade Tanjore and Burma were denounced.[31] The governor would not, however, give up the fight, suggesting that peace with the British at this juncture would be 'dishonourable' and 'shameful' and adding that in India war was necessary for business, as the examples of the Dutch and Portuguese had shown.[32] 'I realize perfectly that a commercial company should never make war', he responded, 'but how many exceptions to this rule there have been!'[33] Dupleix insisted that he was acting for 'the glory of the King, that of the nation, and the benefit of the Compagnie' and even requested the directors to support him with more money.[34] When this request was turned down, he invested more of his personal funds into the financing of the military campaigns.

For a full two years after the surrender at Srirangam, Dupleix persevered with the conflict in the Carnatic. With the size of his army much reduced, the governor resorted to 'send[ing] soldiers, sepoys and horsemen to create disturbances' in the countryside, ruining cultivation to prevent Muhammad Ali and the British from collecting revenues as they advanced northwards towards Gingee.[35] Through a series of intelligent diplomatic manoeuvres, French prospects were then improved. First, Dupleix reached out to the Portuguese viceroy at Goa, envisaging an alliance of the Catholic powers against the Protestant British.[36] The Maratha leader Morari Rao was then convinced to switch to the French side in return for 125,000 rupees per month, before a division between Muhammad Ali and the Kingdom of Mysore was exploited. The support of Mysore ruler Krishnaraja Wadiyar II, it emerged, had been obtained by the British the previous year in return for a promise that Muhammad Ali would cede Trichinopoly to Mysore, which he had no intention of doing. Dupleix capitalised on the acrimony that this deception generated by promising military support to Mysore for the capture of Trichinopoly, in exchange for which Krishnaraja Wadiyar offered significant financing to the Compagnie. In reality, the rajah had little choice: the Compagnie's offer of an alliance was accompanied by a threat that, should it be declined, Salabat Jang would invade his kingdom to extract tribute.[37]

While Mysore mobilised for an attack on Trichinopoly, Dupleix made one last attempt to revive the Nawayath dynasty and install a puppet *nawab* in the Carnatic. Murtaza Ali, the local governor of Vellore, had kept a low profile since murdering his brother-in-law Safdar Ali Khan and making a bid for the nawabship back in 1742. Eleven years on, Dupleix invited him to Pondicherry and offered him the title of *nawab* if he agreed to fight on the Compagnie's side and prevent the impressive Vellore fort falling to the British. Murtaza appears to have accepted the nomination and committed to an alliance, but over the months that followed he proved far more difficult to control than Dupleix had anticipated, taking the Compagnie's artillery without a second thought but refusing to accept the presence of French soldiers at Vellore. None of his own troops were contributed to the French campaign in the Carnatic as it rumbled on through 1753.

In May, the Mysore army arrived outside Trichinopoly, accompanied by a French contingent, and a new siege of Muhammad Ali's stronghold began. When no quick breakthrough came, Dupleix dispatched reinforcements, but still the offensive failed. With funds running low and casualties rising, the governor's frustrations mounted: 'Is it then decided, once and for all, that two Frenchmen are needed to defeat one Englishman?' he lambasted his new commander, Jacques Maissin.[38] Trichinopoly was once again proving the rock on which French ambitions foundered, with 400 Europeans killed, wounded or captured by September. As the siege dragged on into the winter, the Compagnie's new allies began to slip away. Morari Rao was paid off by the British and Murtaza Ali reached an agreement with them. Krishnaraja Wadiyar, meanwhile, was unsurprisingly struggling to keep up with the extortionate payments to the Compagnie to which he had been forced to commit. In December, a rumour swept through Pondicherry that Trichinopoly had fallen, before being proven false the following day. 'For two years the Governor has never looked so happy as he did yesterday, or so sad as he does today', noted Ananda, who added that a sense of resignation was beginning to affect Dupleix.[39] Not only had he distributed alms to the poor, a very unusual act for the governor, for whom '30 pagodas is a great thing', but for three days, he had 'never been angry, and neither kicked, beaten nor abused anyone', an equally uncommon occurrence.[40]

Aware that his chances of victory were slipping away, Dupleix now focused on developing a further justification for his actions as governor. In a lengthy *mémoire* intended to be read in Paris and Versailles, the governor argued not simply that war was necessary to protect commerce, in the manner of his earlier dispatches, but that commerce would never be consistently profitable for France in India unless accompanied by territorial acquisition. The argument hinged on the question of bullion. To finance its purchases in the Indian Ocean, the Compagnie had, ever since its foundation, exported gold and silver from France, Dupleix reminded his readers. This drain was widely believed to have a negative impact on French national wealth: 'it is a long-established maxim', noted the governor, 'that the more bullion there is in a state, the more it flourishes.'[41] The acquisition of land in India provided the Compagnie with a 'fixed and certain' source of income through revenue collection; the more land the Compagnie held, the less it would need to export bullion from Europe, and the greater the profit to the nation.[42]

Dupleix's *mémoire* was skilfully argued but not, as most historians suggest, an explanation of the governor's real motivation for warfare and territorial acquisition over the preceding decade.[43] Rather, it was an intelligent retrospective justification for the policies that he had pursued, designed carefully to exploit long-standing metropolitan concerns about the impact of the export of bullion on national wealth. The extraction of revenue from land was dependent on cultivation and collection that was almost impossible while conflict continued and the countryside was devastated—and yet Dupleix continued to reject the opportunities for peace that came his way. Representatives sent by Muhammad Ali to discuss terms were dismissed from Pondicherry empty-handed, and in January 1754, when Dupleix and Saunders agreed to send delegates for talks in the neutral Dutch station of Sadras, Dupleix refused to make a single compromise, insisting on the recognition of his right to govern the entirety of southern India below the Krishna, as originally bestowed on him by Muzaffar Jang. It is likely that Dupleix dispatched the delegates only to convince authorities in France that he sought peace, knowing full well that Saunders would not accept his terms.[44] In his view, the Compagnie was locked in a struggle until the end: 'There is no longer any middle path', he wrote. 'This province must either belong to them or to us. We must make up our minds as to which suits us best.'[45] The imperative was not to secure peace but to 're-establish the glory of the French name'.[46]

The Deccan, rather than the Carnatic, offered the best prospects for doing this. In June 1753, Dupleix convinced Bussy to return to Hyderabad and continue the work that he had started, cementing French influence on Salabat Jang. He arrived to find the *nizam*'s new *diwan* Sayyid Lashkar Khan overtly hostile to his return and required all his diplomatic ability to win over other members of court before removing the *diwan* from office. Bussy was now more powerful than ever at Salabat Jang's side, effectively reducing the *nizam* to his subordinate, but the problems of paying troops and securing a consistent flow of revenue for the Compagnie remained. To remedy this, the Frenchman hatched a plan to secure, in the form of a *jagir*, the districts of Chicacole, Rajahmundry, Eluru and Guntur on the east coast of the *nizam*'s dominions, a large part of the area collectively known as the Circars.[47] Combined with the territories already in French possession in this part of India—notably Masulipatam and Yanaon—the award would give the Compagnie absolute control of a long strip of coast north of Madras, including the fertile delta lands of the Godavari and Krishna, with potentially huge annual revenues. 'What glory you have won for yourself, and how much the nation owes you for having re-established our reputation', wrote Dupleix to Bussy, once Salabat Jang had acquiesced to this grant.[48] 'Not only are you an intrepid soldier, but at the same time a consummate diplomat.'[49]

Before any revenue could be collected, however, events on the ground spiralled out of control, with the governor of the Circars, Jafar Ali Khan, resolving to resist the handing over of his territories to the French and enlisting Raghuji Bhonsle to his cause. In April 1754, Salabat Jang and Bussy marched on Nagpur to force the Maratha leader to abstain from the conflict, but as soon as the *nizam*'s army departed, 15,000 Maratha cavalrymen were dispatched to the Circars to resist the French.[50] After several months of fighting, Jafar Ali's opposition was crushed but the conflict prevented revenues collected in the summer of 1754 from meeting the sums expected and covering the Compagnie's military costs. The best that Bussy could achieve was to extract promises from the principal landowners about the revenues to be collected the year after.

This episode reveals perhaps better than any other why, despite the expansion of its territory and influence, the Compagnie found itself in such a financial mess in India by the end of Dupleix's time in charge. For a decade, commerce had stalled. The acquisition of land that had replaced it came with expectations of revenue collection that were very rarely met; the military-backed extraction of revenue from lands devastated by war consistently underdelivered. In his correspondence with the directors, Dupleix stressed that where losses had been suffered, he had covered them through his own personal fortune.[51] It would later become clear, however, that significant funds had also been taken from the Compagnie's accounts to finance military campaigns without the knowledge or permission of the directors. According to the best available estimates, the costs of Dupleix's wars were covered to the tune of 38 million livres by the different Indian courts involved, 21 million by the Compagnie and 7 million by the governor himself—though the latter sum was mostly the reinvestment of profits derived by Dupleix from the conflicts, in the form of payments from Muzaffar Jang and other rulers, plus the spoils of war that he and other Compagnie officials had pocketed.[52] From 1752, as these sources of income dried up and the costs of war mounted, the governor, like the Compagnie, then became indebted, borrowing from moneylenders at Pondicherry and counting on future land revenues that never came. 'The receipts are not even a quarter of the expenditure which has been daily increasing', noted Ananda as the debts worsened.[53]

Within Fort Louis, as Dupleix obsessed over the details of the interior of his *palais des Indes*, showing off to Ananda the green velvet and lace curtains that had just arrived from France, along with four statues representing the virtues of truth, justice, commerce and wisdom, he must surely have known that the end was fast approaching. Over the preceding months, a number of Frenchmen had broken ranks and criticised the governor to the directors: one member of the Pondicherry council accused him of plunging the colony into poverty with his warmongering, while the head of the Compagnie in Bengal, Georges Duval de Leyrit, urged the directors to choose between the recall of Dupleix and many more years of conflict.[54] Ananda was even in contact with Rue Vivienne above Dupleix's head, arguing that the governor was no longer fit to govern, not least because of the supposedly excessive influence of his wife on the Compagnie's affairs.[55] With the extent of the Compagnie's financial problems becoming clearer, its shareholders exerted pressure on the directors to act. Silhouette was also out of patience, arguing, in reference to Bussy's schemes, that 'the idea of dictating the law to all of the Deccan with just a handful of Frenchmen is crazy' and repeating that the Compagnie 'should not be a military power in India, it should limit itself to commerce.'[56]

With this idea ringing in their ears, Compagnie representatives were sent to London to conclude peace terms with their British counterparts. To secure peace, the Compagnie distanced itself from the actions of its governor at Pondicherry and proposed to give up the territories that it had acquired since 1749, except for Masulipatam, the commercial value of which was clear. The Compagnie's chief negotiator, Pierre Delaître, was prepared to accept the relinquishing of Dupleix's title of deputy *nizam* and even indicated a willingness to recognise Muhammad Ali as *nawab*. For the British, however, there were two sticking points preventing a treaty from being signed: why, they asked, should Masulipatam be permitted to remain in French hands if Dupleix's approach had been disavowed? And how could peace be guaranteed while Dupleix remained in post? Saunders was adamant that any peace agreement should include Dupleix's recall and said so to his superiors. The EIC's representatives at the negotiating table indicated that Dupleix's continued presence on the Coromandel would 'present obstacles and will perhaps prevent us from reaching a definitive agreement', adding that 'he shows towards our nation, we don't know why, a hatred that prevents him from concluding any affair with us with cold blood.'[57]

The decision to recall Dupleix, for some time under consideration, was therefore confirmed. On the board in Paris, a majority of directors concurred that peace would be impossible if the governor remained in post. The faction supporting Dupleix at all costs had lost influence after the death of his brother Charles-Claude-Ange some three years earlier. Charles Godeheu, once a friend and protégé of Dupleix from their time together at Chandernagore, was selected for the mission. The instructions that he was given, to be opened only once his ship had passed the Cape of Good Hope, were to replace Dupleix and send him back to France; to investigate the financial state of the Compagnie's settlements in India; and to agree peace terms with the British council at Madras, if talks in London had not reached a successful conclusion. More detailed instructions dictated what should be done if Dupleix resisted recall, including the detention of the governor and the arrest of Jeanne to make sure that she could not help him escape.

On 2 August 1754, Godeheu landed at Pondicherry after a voyage of seven months.[58] That afternoon he informed Dupleix of his recall, news which the governor took calmly and shared with his council before the week was out. Godeheu then set about the other actions with which he had been tasked, agreeing a three-month ceasefire with Saunders that brought the fighting in the southern Carnatic to a halt. 500 British soldiers were released from Pondicherry as part of an exchange of prisoners between the belligerents.[59] Scrutinising Dupleix's accounts, Godeheu attempted to separate the deposed governor's personal finances from those of the Compagnie, an almost impossible task that raised tensions between the pair. Dupleix argued that the Compagnie owed him 7 million livres as a result of advances made to support its operations; Godeheu responded that Dupleix had acted above his position to pursue wars in direct contravention of the directors' orders and accused him of concealing the extent of losses to the Compagnie that those wars had occasioned.[60]

After two months of preparation and delay, Dupleix could postpone his departure no longer. To the firing of cannon, he bid farewell to Ananda, unaware that the chief courtier had agitated for this moment, and boarded the *Duc d'Orléans*, accompanied by Jeanne and her family, their twenty-two servants and twelve slaves. The property embarked with Dupleix confirms that despite mounting personal debts, the deposed governor had lived like a Mughal sovereign to the end: 194 cases were taken aboard the *Duc d'Orléans* and a second ship, containing almost 3 million livres in bullion, plus ornaments, jewellery and precious stones. Two camels, two donkeys, a horse, five monkeys, a goat, eight cats and twelve cages of birds completed the ships' loads; of Dupleix's collection of animals, only his twelve elephants were left behind.[61] With the sailing of the *Duc d'Orléans*, more than thirty years in India—and almost thirteen as governor of Pondicherry—were brought to an end. 'Such is the fate of the man who seeks his own will without the fear of God', concluded Ananda, rejecting the notion that Dupleix and the Almighty were one and the same. 'He has eaten the fruit of his actions.'[62]

Looking back on Dupleix's time as governor, some historians suggest that the expansion of the Compagnie's power and territory was not his intention. They propose that the development of a veritable empire during his governorship, combining territories ruled directly by the Compagnie with others under its informal control, was the result not of design but of fortune or chance—'a succession of circumstances that could not have been foreseen'.[63] Dupleix, others maintain, was nothing more than a mercenary, selling the services of his army to the highest bidder and collecting the rewards, which, it quickly became clear, were more lucrative than those to be expected from commerce.[64] In this view, Chanda Sahib and Muzaffar Jang were the key protagonists on the French side, rather than Dupleix, who had no aspirations to extend his power. When more power did inadvertently come his way, he did not want it, as his decisions to name Chanda Sahib and Murtaza Ali Khan to the Carnatic nawabship show.

Such a line of arguments cannot be upheld. Dupleix, we have seen, was disposed towards the use of military power to advance the French position in India from as early as his time in Bengal. By 1744, just a couple of years into his governorship at Pondicherry, his policy of regime change was in place; the governor targeted the release of Chanda Sahib and his installation as *nawab* to promote the Compagnie's interests. The outbreak of war with the British shifted Dupleix's priorities towards the defeat of France's European rival, but in this conflict he did not hesitate to use military force against Nawab Anwar ud-Din, breaking decisively with the norms of diplomacy and deference that had previously governed relations between the European powers and Indian authorities. As noted, the conflict confirmed to Dupleix the military superiority of the French over much larger Indian armies, providing the governor with the confidence required to embark on a military-led campaign of imperial expansion after peace with the British had officially been obtained in 1748. The capture of Madras and the successful defence of Pondicherry during the war appeared to show that there was little to be feared from British forces on the Coromandel.

The conclusion of the alliance with Chanda Sahib and Muzaffar Jang in early 1749, followed by their joint invasion of the Carnatic, then allowed for Dupleix's policy of regime change to be enacted, first in the Carnatic and the following year in the Deccan. From the beginning, Dupleix attempted to control Chanda Sahib and Muzaffar Jang closely, dictating their diplomatic, military and revenue collection efforts. The decision that Bussy would accompany Muzaffar Jang and then Salabat Jang to the Deccan was as much about guaranteeing French influence over the new *nizams* as it was about securing their position. Over time, Dupleix's frustrations at his inability to completely control Chanda Sahib rose and he considered taking on the nawabship himself, but there were a number of good reasons for not doing this that had nothing to do with Dupleix not wanting power. First, Chanda Sahib was a source of enrichment for Dupleix and the Compagnie; the *nawab* owed large sums to the governor that would only be recuperated if he stayed in power.[65] More importantly, the continued presence of Chanda Sahib as *nawab*—like that of Salabat Jang as *nizam*—conveniently masked the growth of French power. As the influence of Dupleix and Bussy in the Carnatic and Deccan grew, the power of Chanda Sahib and Salabat Jang was undermined, but the pretence of the rulers' sovereignty concealed to other Indian courts, to the British and to authorities in France the extent of the Compagnie's power and territory—or, in other words, how far the French in India had become an imperial power.[66]

Much of the old and recent misunderstanding of Dupleix's imperialist aspirations appears to stem from the misconception that only the imposition of direct French rule over new territories can be considered imperialist in nature. It should, however, be clear that removing hostile or non-compliant rulers and installing others in their place before trying to establish indirect rule through the control of those new rulers were also imperialist activities. They were accompanied by the direct acquisition of more and more territories and revenue-collecting rights by the Compagnie and its officers. After his appointment as deputy *nizam*, Dupleix attempted to organise the direct remittance of the revenues of the Carnatic to Pondicherry, cutting out the *nawab* entirely. In private, as we have seen, the governor confessed that his object was the French 'domination' of India; he developed plans for the extension of the Compagnie's power across the subcontinent.[67] The foundation of these plans—like that of French imperial expansion in the Carnatic and the Deccan—was the use of force against non-European rulers considered unable to withstand French military prowess.

We have noted that the arguments made by Dupleix to justify the policies that he pursued—that war was necessary to protect the Compagnie's commerce and the acquisition of land required to make sure that commerce was profitable—were partial and insufficient. How then can his bid to secure a French empire in India be explained? The incentive of personal enrichment cannot be overlooked. Through the deals struck with Chanda Sahib, Muzaffar Jang and Salabat Jang and the victories won, Dupleix and his principal officers became wealthy beyond their wildest dreams, securing *jagirs* with high annual incomes, along with gifts and presents from Indian courts and the immediate spoils of war.[68] Directives from France clamping down on the acceptance of *jagirs* and presents were ignored, as Compagnie employees from Dupleix downwards scrambled to line their pockets. The wills written by Frenchmen at Pondicherry in the early 1750s, filled with references to jewels, pearls and large cash sums, testify to the heady enrichment that imperial expansion had delivered.[69]

More important to Dupleix, however, was the pursuit of power and glory—as his readiness to gamble his personal fortune on further war and conquest confirms. In part, this was about the power and glory of King and country. Within the context of war among the European powers, Dupleix was a firm patriot, strongly anti-English from 1744, and no doubt believed that he was acting 'for the glory of the King [and] that of the nation'.[70] To a far greater extent, however, Dupleix was motivated by the aggrandisement of his personal power and glory, his already significant ego inflated by his early successes and the honours and marks of respect that had followed. As we have seen, Dupleix was convinced that God was on his side and acting through him. He was also obsessed with his place in history. Even as his fledgling empire fell apart in the final two years of his reign, he revived plans to build a monument to himself, this time in Pondicherry.

We should close with a summary of why Dupleix failed. Here too historians have been quick to accept the explanations that the governor himself offered, during or after the event, among them the lack of support for his policies offered by the Compagnie and the French crown; the inferior quality of reinforcements sent from Europe, compared with those of the British; and shortages of money.[71] No doubt there is some truth in these assertions: at no point during Dupleix's governorship was India one of the crown's priorities; Madras, for example, was handed back to the British in the Treaty of Aix-la-Chapelle with little understanding of its value. These disadvantages were compounded, however, by mistakes that Dupleix himself made. The maintaining of Bussy in the Deccan was a classic example of imperial overstretch, depriving the Compagnie of its best commander and of more than 2,000 soldiers whose presence on the Carnatic would surely have proven decisive as the conflict continued. Refusing to compromise during negotiations with Muhammad Ali and the British was another strategic error; Dupleix had decided that it was all or nothing in the Carnatic long before his rivals came round to a similar view. After the success of the Compagnie's campaign against Anwar ud-Din, meanwhile, Dupleix's sense of French military superiority was exaggerated; the capacity of other Indian powers, particularly the Marathas, was consistently underestimated.

The defects in Dupleix's character pre-disposed him towards these mistakes—and of course meant that he was never likely to recognise them. In his recent work on the rise of the EIC, William Dalrymple suggests that Robert Clive—who above all else was responsible for the establishment of British rule in India after Dupleix's departure and would later be elevated in Britain to the status of national hero—was in fact a dangerous 'sociopath', 'intermittently mentally unstable'.[72] It is time that Dupleix was subject to a similar reassessment. In India, the Frenchman displayed an obsession with his own importance that might well be considered megalomania.[73] Alongside the belief that God was working through him, it manifested itself in a conviction of his moral and intellectual superiority that made it impossible for him to collaborate with most other people, including his countrymen, without belittling them or otherwise descending into rancour. During his long term as governor, Dupleix clashed with almost all his colleagues; Bussy is a very rare example of a peer whom he held in esteem and did not regularly fight with. Unable to place confidence in others, the governor tried to micromanage, issuing instructions and reprimands to his commanders on the ground that were often counterproductive.

Coupled with Dupleix's desire for power and control was a paranoia that became increasingly evident as setbacks were suffered. The governor was convinced that the British on the Coromandel sought the elimination of the Compagnie years before the Madras council thought in such terms. Dupleix's conception of a Franco-British struggle for survival in India bore little resemblance to the British position, which was essentially concerned with commercial supremacy and defensive military action during his governorship. What other historians have described as Dupleix's 'optimism' about French victory as the conflict in the Carnatic turned against him would be better understood as delusion or the inability of the governor to accept his own fallibility and that of his plans, which made compromise with his opponents impossible.[74] As the defeats accumulated, Dupleix sounded more and more unhinged, directing blame and vitriol towards Chanda Sahib, the Compagnie's commanders and officers, and the directors in Paris. The *mémoires* that he wrote for the directors justifying his policies and requesting further support contained arguments that many would have found convincing. They were undermined, however, by their accusatory tone and the personal attacks that they contained.[75]

The final word on Dupleix should be left to Louis Barthélemy, the first member of the Pondicherry council to denounce the governor, seeing through his professed intentions and retrospective justifications with a clarity that has escaped most subsequent observers. In a dispatch back to Paris ultimately influential in the decision to recall Dupleix, Barthélemy wrote:

> It is not difficult to discern the motives of the war in course. Even the least clear-sighted will judge that they have no other basis than an insatiable greed for riches, an excessive ambition without limits, and a ridiculous vanity to eternalise his name. The enterprise has succeeded beyond the hopes of their initiator: fifty or sixty millions, without exaggeration, have entered into his coffers, but, it seems, even that is not sufficient to extinguish

> the thirst for gold that he possesses. The honours that he has received and those that he hopes to yet receive will only satisfy a part of his vanity [...] As far as immortality is concerned, he can certainly boast to have obtained it in this country.[76]

*

The irony that would go a long way towards sealing the fate of French ambitions in India was that the Compagnie resolved to seek peace just as the British determined that their interests would be best served by war. Dupleix was recalled with his conception of a Franco-British struggle for survival in India on the verge of becoming a reality. In the years that followed Dupleix's departure, his ambition of a European power ruling over large parts of the subcontinent was realised, but that power was Great Britain.

To understand why, we should consider the context beyond India. In Europe, the possibility of an alliance between France and a historic enemy, the Austrian Habsburgs, was causing diplomatic waves and pushing Britain to conclude an alliance with Frederick the Great of Prussia. Once again, France and Britain were lining up on opposing sides in the event of a general European conflict. In North America, meanwhile, tensions between the two powers were erupting into fighting in the French colony of Acadia on the northeast seaboard and, further south, along the Ohio River, as British forces tried to prevent the construction of French forts guarding access to the fertile valley. With their maritime superiority beyond doubt, the British were again giving in to the temptation to harass French ships, this time in the Atlantic, disrupting the lucrative French sugar trade. Before long, France was threatening to retaliate with an attack on Hanover, whose prince-elector was of course George II of Great Britain.[77]

In December 1754, two months after Dupleix's departure and just a few days before their three-month ceasefire came to an end, Godeheu and Saunders concluded a peace treaty for ratification in Paris and London. The governors agreed to renounce possession of all territories gained in southern India since the Treaty of Aix-la-Chapelle, with the exception of the Circars, which were to be divided equally between them. In the Indian Ocean, neutrality between the two powers would be observed and both would abstain from interference in the politics of the Carnatic.[78] When copies of the provisional treaty reached Paris and London in the summer of 1755, the directors of both companies indicated their willingness to ratify it, with the resumption of commerce their priority, but the British government had other ideas. It was only a matter of time before the two countries were again at war, they reasoned, and, when war was declared, the British navy would undoubtedly have the upper hand. What good was a commitment to neutrality in the Indian Ocean when French naval forces were inferior and France had already reined in its expansionist policies with the recall of Dupleix?[79] These geopolitical considerations took precedence over the companies' commercial interests, and the ratification of the treaty was delayed in London, without ever being refused outright.

The Deccan had been omitted from the terms of the provisional treaty, allowing Bussy to return to the court of Salabat Jang after his unsuccessful attempts to collect revenue in the Circars. Now the British began to worry about what the commander was up to, fearing that while the menace of Dupleix had been removed from the south, Bussy was 'every day enlarging the valuable and extensive possessions which the French held in the north.'[80] Particular concern was caused by the interception at sea of a top-secret letter from Bussy to the French government in which the commander requested permission to march to Delhi and form an alliance with the Mughal Emperor against the Marathas, in return for which, he promised, large payments and new territorial awards would follow.[81] The chances of the French government approving Bussy's project were next to none, but for the British this was the *casus belli* needed to prepare pre-emptive action. Six British warships were at this moment on their way to India with 700 troops on board. Their commanders arrived at Madras to find the provisional treaty in place and, no longer needed on the Coromandel, set about planning a march on the Deccan to eliminate the threat posed by Bussy. The hopes that Dupleix had harboured of establishing French influence in Burma were squashed with the dispatch of a small British force to occupy the port of Syriam and with the capture and killing of the French envoy the Sieur de Bruno by the Burmese.[82]

As the plans to move against Bussy were being finalised at Madras, however, news reached the Coromandel of a disturbance in northeast India demanding British attention, and the freshly arrived British troops and warships were hastily diverted to Bengal. Throughout the sixteen years of his rule, the *nawab* of Bengal, Alivardi Khan, had kept a tight rein on the European trading companies in his territories, imposing strict regimes of taxation and prohibiting the companies from using force against each other. Alivardi followed events in the Carnatic and Deccan closely and had even threatened the seizure of the Compagnie's property in Bengal after the murder of Nasir Jang in 1750.[83] In April 1756, however, the *nawab* passed away to be succeeded by his grandson, Siraj ud-Daula—the cue for major upheaval in the province. As some readers will no doubt be aware, Siraj very soon took umbrage with the British, who, with one eye on the coming conflict with France, had taken it upon themselves to strengthen the fortifications of their Bengal base, Fort William at Calcutta, without first seeking his permission. After several warnings were ignored, the new *nawab* responded by attacking the fort with 30,000 troops. Just a single British garrison was in place to defend it; on the fourth day of the attack, the British capitulated and fled.

'Instead of the Revolution with which we thought the country was menaced at the death of the old Nawab, everything appears to be quiet', the Chandernagore council reported just after Siraj's assumption of power.[84] A couple of weeks later, however, the *nawab* approached representatives of the Compagnie to request its support in his offensive against the British, offering to grant the Compagnie all of the EIC's privileges in the province, including possession of Calcutta, in return. The offer was generous but the director of French operations in Bengal, Pierre Mathieu Renault de St Germain, felt compelled to reject it. No direct attack on the British could be countenanced, he reasoned, before the two countries were officially at war again. There was no guarantee that Calcutta could be held, particularly with a fleet of British warships now in Indian waters. Moreover—and most significantly—could Siraj be trusted? The new *nawab* was renowned among all Europeans in Bengal for his cruelty, his character 'reputed to be one of the worst ever known'.[85] After the expulsion of the British, was it not probable that the French would be next? 'We cannot take too much precaution against the resentment he may feel towards us and which must be expected from a man so violent', noted the Chandernagore council, despite Siraj's professions of friendship.[86]

The residents of Chandernagore therefore stood by and watched from across the river as Siraj's huge army marched down the left bank of the Hooghly from the *nawab*'s capital of Murshidabad to Calcutta to launch its attack. Once the British settlement had fallen, a contribution of 340,000 rupees was made to the *nawab* to make sure that Chandernagore did not also fall victim to this 'most terrible revolution'.[87] For the next six months, the French were the predominant European presence in Bengal—with just small Dutch and Danish stations on the Hooghly to keep them company—but this situation was not exploited to the Compagnie's advantage, with fear of Siraj remaining the overwhelming sentiment. The *nawab* 'knows no laws except those of his own wishes [and] spares no one', wrote one observer; 'there is everything to be feared from this prince in the future', added another.[88] Instead of preparing for the war with the British to come, residents of Chandernagore entertained hopes 'that the European nations may form a league to repress the insolence of this prince'.[89] Even Renault de St Germain confessed that his 'strong detestation of the tyranny of the Nawab, and of the excesses which he was committing against Europeans, made me long for the arrival of the English in the Ganges to take vengeance for them.'[90]

At the start of December, the director got his wish: the British warships arrived at the mouth of the Hooghly with 1,000 sepoys added to their European contingent and began preparing to retake Calcutta. A few days later news reached Bengal that France and Britain were officially at war. Surely now the reservations about Siraj would be put to one side and an alliance agreed with the *nawab* against the British? Jean Law de Lauriston, head of the Compagnie's trading post at Qasimbazaar and its representative at Siraj's court, argued for such an alliance, but once again Renault de St Germain refused to commit, citing with some justification the very small number of troops—360 Europeans and 170 sepoys—that he had at his disposal.[91] The director instead approached the commander-in-chief of the British forces on the Hooghly, none other than Robert Clive, about a pact of non-aggression which he hoped might be observed in Bengal even with the two countries at war.

What followed once had a canonical status in the annals of the EIC. On 2 January 1757, Calcutta was recaptured by British troops. After a bruising encounter just outside the city at the start of February, Siraj then demanded peace, committing to the restoration of trading rights and the payment of extensive damages to the British. The opportunity for the French to join forces with the *nawab* against their European rival was lost. Ignoring the non-aggression pact still on the table, the British then resolved to capture Chandernagore, citing Siraj's offer to hand over their trading privileges to the Compagnie and the unsubstantiated claims that French gunpowder had been used in the attack on Calcutta as proof that the French had colluded with the *nawab* from the beginning.[92] Beyond these flimsy pretexts, the capture of Chandernagore was too good an opportunity for the British to let slip. Informed by his experiences in the Carnatic, Clive could not resist striking a major blow against his familiar foes and, with British military superiority over Siraj now clear, cared little what the *nawab* thought.[93]

In March, three of the British warships made their way up the Hooghly past a barricade of ships hastily scuttled to block the route. Two arrived in a position to bombard Chandernagore, and the colony surrendered after a couple of hours of cannonading. Renault de St Germain and the other members of his council were detained and taken to Calcutta, while the Compagnie's soldiers and sailors were shipped off to Madras and the civilian population of Chandernagore forced to take refuge in the other European colonies on the river. It was, wrote Renault de St Germain, a 'sad catastrophe [...] the whole colony is dispersed.'[94] With the Seven Years' War in its infancy, it was also a major strategic loss: French prestige in India had been dealt a severe blow and for the remainder of the conflict, Pondicherry and the Compagnie's other Indian territories were deprived of the imports of food from Bengal on which they usually depended.

Clive now targeted Jean Law de Lauriston and the small group of about sixty Frenchmen who remained with him at Qasimbazaar, further upriver near Murshidabad, demanding that Siraj send troops from his capital to detain them. Law de Lauriston was considered a dangerous influence on the *nawab* who might yet convince him to restart hostilities against the British, a concern strengthened when the *nawab* refused to apprehend the Frenchmen. Instead, he permitted them to slip away from Qasimbazaar in the direction of Bihar, providing them with money and passports. Just outside Murshidabad they were joined by forty compatriots who had escaped capture at Chandernagore, forming with the services of sixty sepoys a small band to keep the flame of French ambitions in northeast India alight. In the weeks that followed, Law de Lauriston led them to Rajmahal and from there to Patna, evading the British division sent in pursuit.[95]

Uncertainty about Siraj's next moves—the *nawab* was rumoured to have appealed to Bussy for-large scale French military intervention in Bengal—then contributed to the British decision to remove him from power. In developments strongly reminiscent of Dupleix's regime change initiatives, an agreement was reached with disaffected members of Siraj's court about his deposal and the installation of nobleman Mir Jafar in his place. As relations between Siraj and the British deteriorated, their respective armies met at Plassey in June; the *nawab* was defeated after Mir Jafar and other leading generals switched to the British side. Siraj attempted to flee but was captured, returned to Murshidabad and executed, and Mir Jafar was confirmed on the throne. As with the assassination of Nasir Jang and the installation of Muzaffar Jang in his place, a European-backed court coup rather than a military victory had proven decisive. For their participation in the coup, Clive and his British colleagues were handsomely rewarded by the new *nawab*, like Dupleix and other Frenchmen in the south. In return for the military backing that Mir Jafar was offered, Clive would later be awarded a *jagir* and the rank of *mansadbar*, continuing where Dupleix had left off. Before long, the commander-in-chief was referring to the British as rulers of Bengal and the *nawab* as merely their puppet.[96]

The French fightback, were it to materialise, would therefore have to begin elsewhere on the subcontinent. As the British moved northwards to retake Calcutta, Bussy and his army, now numbering

4,500, had been on their way back to the Circars from Hyderabad to collect the revenues promised during their previous expedition there.[97] For the commander, the idea of neutrality between the French and British in India was a 'chimera'.[98] On hearing that war had been declared, therefore, Bussy immediately dispossessed the British of their small trading posts on the coast before capturing the principal British settlement of Visakhapatnam in June 1757, no small measure of comfort three months on from the fall of Chandernagore. Following these events from Pondicherry, Ananda was certainly reassured, noting that they corresponded with the predictions of the astrologers that he regularly consulted. 'The Shastras say that the English will lose all their factories in India; what is happening now confirms it', he recorded. 'The English forts and ports are falling into French hands, and all may rest assured that all places, from England in Europe to Madras and Fort St David in India, will pass into French hands. I am sure that this will happen.'[99]

More good news was to follow with the arrival at Pondicherry in September of a squadron of ten vessels carrying 1,000 soldiers of the regular French army, followed seven months later by a further 1,000 men and a detachment of the royal artillery, plus enslaved soldiers from the Mascarenes. Fighting in the Carnatic had resumed even before France and Britain were known to be again at war, with the French encroaching on Muhammad Ali's territories and the British launching expeditions to raise revenue in Madurai and Vellore. The Compagnie had then responded to the loss of Chandernagore with another unsuccessful attempt to take Trichinopoly. The arrival of such significant reinforcements, however, now tipped the military balance on the Coromandel decisively in French favour, particularly with the British committed in Bengal. France had a total European force of 3,000 to deploy compared to 1,000 on the British side in a conflict that was henceforth between two nations, rather than two companies, with royal rather than company armies playing the leading roles.[100]

Arriving with the second set of reinforcements was a new leader for the French army, Thomas Arthur de Lally-Tollendal, a general of Irish Jacobite ancestry who had served with distinction in Europe during the War of Austrian Succession.[101] Since 1752,

Lally had projected himself as the right man to secure French possessions in India. With war now declared, the crown was won round to his arguments, but not without some reservations: the new lieutenant-general of the French forces in India was ignorant of the subcontinent's geography, climate and political context and unlikely to want to learn from those Frenchmen who knew it better. From the outset, Louis XV's minister of war, the Comte d'Argenson, predicted that Lally would clash with the Compagnie's authorities at Pondicherry, his rancorous character likely to cause a 'civil war'.[102] His reservations were dismissed, and Lally was dispatched with instructions to drive out the English from India and consolidate French possessions, without—and here the recent experience of Dupleix remained foremost in ministers' minds—getting involved in Indian politics or acquiring territory in the interior. Command of the French navy in Indian waters was meanwhile given to the Comte d'Aché, the head of the squadron on which Lally arrived.

For Lally, the capture of Fort St David was the first target. Just a day after his arrival, 700 troops were assembled to march southwards towards the British fort. Locals of all castes were forced to carry military equipment; villages were plundered and cattle, carts and boats seized, provoking resentment. In parallel, d'Aché's squadron engaged the British off Cuddalore in the first of three key naval battles on the Coromandel. The French fared worst, with 500 casualties compared to 118 on the British side, but after the firing was concluded both squadrons were forced to return to their bases—Pondicherry and Madras—leaving the path clear for Fort St David to be besieged from the land.[103] Lally's troops made hard work of what followed, failing to make their new numerical superiority count for more than a week. The lieutenant-general hid himself in his tent with a loaded pistol at his side, threatening to shoot anyone who dared to disturb him and, in a telling indication of the little value placed on non-European lives, ordered that all sepoys serving with the British be shot on sight.[104] After a week, however, the breakthrough came and Fort St David was captured. In the months that followed it was systematically dismantled—'a lasting reproach of wanton barbarity to the French' in the view of one British observer.[105]

Momentum and numbers were on the side of Lally, who, with the capture of Fort St David, had succeeded where Dupleix had three times failed. An immediate advance on Madras—the last British stronghold on the coast—was now a possibility, but Lally decided to wait until a more decisive naval engagement with the British had taken place, convinced that Fort St George, which had been impressively rebuilt over the preceding decade, would only be captured once the squadron defending it had been taken out of the picture. Moreover, the lieutenant-general was confronted with the more pressing issue of finding money to pay his soldiers and purchase provisions. The 2 million livres with which he had arrived from France had mostly been used up paying off the Compagnie's debts, leaving little for military operations, a state of affairs which Lally blamed on the Pondicherry council, launching into acrimonious disagreement with Georges Duval de Leyrit, who had succeeded Godeheu as governor.[106] Despite the encouraging start to Lally's military operations, the seeds of future problems were sown. Lally belittled the Compagnie's 'business of pepper and ginger' and declared himself proud to know little about it, 'not being a spice merchant'.[107] Leyrit responded by forcing the lieutenant-general and his troops to camp outside the walls of Pondicherry and supplying them with the bare minimum of provisions.

A potential source of money was of course an alliance with one or more Indian courts—overtures were made to Lally from Salabat Jang about a renewed partnership between the *nizam* and the French—but Lally was adamant, in line with the instructions that he had received, that his role was to defeat the British, not to get involved in Indian affairs. Writing to Bussy, he dismissed the commander's long efforts in the Deccan, insisting that:

> The King and the Compagnie sent me to India to chase out the English. It is with the English that we are at war, all other interests are foreign to me. It matters little that a younger brother and his elder brother dispute the Deccan or that such and such rajah disputes such and such nawabship. When I have finished exterminating the English from this coast, I will be ready to undertake, without leaving my office and with little

> expense, operations much more effective than those which have up until now cost the king so many subjects and the Compagnie so many rupees.[108]

Lally may have had a point, but it was undermined by what he did next. As his shortage of funds became critical the lieutenant-general was persuaded by Père Lavaur, a Jesuit priest at Pondicherry and former confidant of Dupleix, to march southwards to collect revenues promised by Pratap Singh Bhonsle of Tanjore to Chanda Sahib some eight years earlier. The pretext for this campaign was weak and its execution bungled from the start. First, Lally and his 1,600 hungry and unpaid troops headed for Karikal in search of provisions. When few were found they plundered the Tanjorean port of Nagore before advancing into the interior, raiding the villages on their route. At Thiruvarur a sacred temple was ransacked in a fruitless search for treasure. Lally then ordered the execution of six Brahmins accused of being spies. The punishment was intended to strike fear into the local population but instead rallied them against their aggressors; vital food supplies were withheld as word of the atrocity spread.[109]

When Lally and his army arrived outside Tanjore in early July, a million rupees were demanded. The rajah refused, replying that his debts had been to Chanda Sahib and not to the French, at which point the lieutenant-general threatened to take him prisoner and ship him off to the Isle de France as a slave. An attack was now unavoidable if the expedition was to be a success, but Lally had neglected to bring any heavy artillery with him, and his soldiers were short on ammunition. An attempt to scale the city walls was ordered and after a week of fierce fighting a small breach was made, but news then reached Lally of a British threat to Karikal and a withdrawal was hurriedly announced. The expedition had been a fiasco, costing 600 lives in the French ranks with nothing to show for them.[110] Ill-discipline had been rampant, with European soldiers 'going through the streets, stabbing people, throwing stones at them, [and] troubling women.'[111] Lally too painted a dismal picture, describing himself during the withdrawal, as his troops were picked off by the Tanjoreans, as 'without victuals, money, or munitions, barefoot and half-naked, worn out with fatigue and in despair at having been engaged in so wild an adventure.'[112]

The British threat to Karikal turned out to be a false alarm—the Tanjore expedition had been abandoned for nothing—but while the expedition was in progress, a second major naval battle had taken place, this time off Negapatam. Again, French casualties were high; d'Aché's squadron was so badly damaged that he insisted on withdrawing to the Isle de France for repairs, despite the protestations of Lally and the Pondicherry council. The lieutenant-general could console himself with the knowledge that the British squadron would also soon leave the Coromandel to avoid the dangerous winter monsoon that annually struck the southeast of the peninsula, not to return from Bombay until February. A four-month window presented itself for Madras to be taken while it was deprived of any naval support.

To fund the attack on Madras, Lally and members of the governing council dug into their own pockets. Contributions were demanded from the merchants of Pondicherry and a million livres arrived from France via the Mascarenes. In preparation for the offensive, Arcot was reclaimed and the lands south and west of Madras occupied by French troops. In a decision with far-reaching consequences, Bussy and most of his troops were also recalled from the Deccan. Though the commander's military talents would no doubt be helpful during the attack, if properly exploited, French influence at Hyderabad was again diminished, this time, as we shall see, never to be recovered.

The advance on Madras began at the start of November but was slowed by heavy rain and flooding.[113] Only on 12 December were the outskirts of the city reached. The suburbs, populated by local merchants, were occupied without resistance and plundered, in scenes reminiscent of the previous occupation under Dupleix. A further important delay was then suffered while Lally waited for the siege equipment to arrive; it was not until 2 January 1759 that the bombardment could begin. Lally had command of a total of 8,000 crown and Compagnie troops, of whom half were European, but his army remained hindered by shortages of arms and ammunition. The British garrison in Fort St George was roughly half that size but had sufficient munitions and reserves of food to withstand at least three months of siege.[114] Knowing that the British squadron would return at the end of February, Lally did not have that long and committed to a major offensive. In the first week of February, following weeks of attritional exchanges, a small breach was opened in the fort wall but the approach to it was too well protected by British guns to be entered. Ananda recorded:

> Madras was plundered, the fort was blown to pieces, the houses within it demolished by shells and levelled with the ground, the walls destroyed and beaten into the ditch, and the attack was so severe that those outside could see those inside the fort, and those within see those without, and yet, despite this fierce attack, the fort was not taken.[115]

Significant British reinforcements then arrived from the small fort of Chingleput, 60 kilometres to the south, which Lally's troops had neglected to capture before the siege began. They occupied Saint Thomas Mount, on the edge of the city, and disrupted French supplies, forcing Lally to divert a third of his troops into an unsuccessful attempt to claim the hilltop position. By the third week of February, as word spread that the British squadron was approaching, it was clear that the siege had failed. Bussy and his officers sacked it off before Lally's order to withdraw was confirmed, and a disorderly retreat to Pondicherry followed.

Unfortunately, the news from north India was not much better. In Bengal, the British suspected *nawab* Mir Jafar, like his predecessor Siraj ud-Daula, of trying to solicit French intervention; Mir Jafar might well have seen the arrival of Lally and his army on the Coromandel as the beginning of his liberation from British supervision. This, however, had not prevented the British from consolidating their position in his territories. After British forces accompanied the *nawab* on revenue collection campaigns into Bihar in the first half of 1758, the EIC was granted large territories north and south of Calcutta and was fast becoming a major territorial power in its own right. Law de Lauriston, meanwhile, was travelling from one court to the next with his band of soldiers, trying to rally support for an offensive against the British. From Patna he had headed to Allahabad before calling on Shuja ud-Daula, *nawab* of the kingdom of Awadh, in his capital, Lucknow. The next stop was Delhi. Law de Lauriston arrived there to find the Mughal capital under the control of the Marathas, with the ageing emperor Alamgir II a 'phantom king' unable to act independently of his occupiers.[116] At this point, the Frenchman began to despair. Money was running out and no response had been received to his requests for help from either Bussy or Leyrit. Moreover, the Indian rulers with whom he had spoken seemed unconcerned about the fate of Bengal and appeared to find it difficult to tell the French and British apart. The only encouragement came from an audience with the emperor's son, the crown prince Ali Gauhar, who was unable to act in the short term, with the Marathas watching his movements closely, but who offered Law de Lauriston 11,000 rupees and a promise of future collaboration.

By September 1758, the British were sufficiently confident in their control of Bengal that, on Clive's insistence, half of their forces in the province—500 Europeans and 2,000 sepoys, out of a total of 5,000—were reassigned southwards.[117] Their first port of call was the Circars, where they could count on the support of local chieftain Ananda Raz, who shared their enthusiasm for seeing the French sent packing. From Visakhapatnam, where Raz received them, the British advanced southwards towards Rajahmundry. The modest French force left in the region under the Marquis de Conflans marched out to meet them at Chendurthi, where the British secured a 'most complete victory [...] for the enemy lost their whole camp, baggage, ammunition, and all their artillery.'[118] Rajahmundry was then captured as Conflans and his troops fled to Masulipatam, 150 kilometres to the south. In April 1759, just a couple of months after the siege of Madras had been called off, Conflans surrendered, as Masulipatam and Yanaon also fell to the British. The award of the Circars to the Compagnie by Salabat Jang was now nothing more than a dead letter—and soon the letter would be torn up. Realising which way the wind was blowing, the *nizam* called time on eight years of collaboration with the French and signed a treaty handing over control of the Circars and their revenues to the British, in return for a British promise not to support any rival pretenders to the Deccan throne. Had Bussy remained at Hyderabad, the conclusion of this treaty would have been prevented. Lally's recall of the commander had been ordered at just the wrong time.[119]

For close to a decade, the alliances with Muzaffar Jang and Salabat Jang had gained the Compagnie prestige and influence. The speed with which Salabat Jang rushed to conclude an agreement with the British at this juncture reminds us, however, that the French position in the Deccan had ultimately been fragile and beset with structural problems. For one, French influence on the *nizam* was reliant on the presence of Bussy; each time the commander left the *nizam*'s court, the Compagnie's position was undermined. Even Bussy's control of the *nizam* was at times precarious, as the number of opponents at court trying to dislodge the Frenchman shows. More than anything else, it was the military power at Bussy's disposal and his army's reputation that mattered, as he himself acknowledged, noting that it was best to deal with 'Asiatics [...] in making them feel not that we are their friend but that we will be their enemy.'[120] Dupleix had concurred, writing to Bussy that the treaties and awards secured from the *nizam*s were 'worth nothing unless supported by a certain amount of force'.[121] Maintaining a large army in the Deccan was expensive, however, and after Bussy and his troops had emptied the Hyderabad and Aurangabad treasuries in 1751, Salabat Jang teetered on the edge of bankruptcy.

Meanwhile the other benefits that Dupleix and Bussy had envisaged from the expansion of French influence into the Deccan had only partially materialised by the time the Compagnie was finally expelled. Certainly, the possession of huge swathes of territory, most notably the Circars, had, on paper, been secured. As we have seen, however, the Compagnie struggled to translate these grants into a regular income, relying on the expensive and ineffective extraction of revenue by its armies. French influence in the Deccan was supposed to reinforce the Compagnie's control of the Carnatic, with Muzaffar Jang's appointment of Chanda Sahib as *nawab* and of Dupleix as deputy *nizam* bestowing legitimacy on the governor's Carnatic strategy, while the intervention of the *nizam*'s army to support the Compagnie's efforts in the Carnatic was potentially decisive. In practice, however, the British had refused to accept Muzaffar Jang's appointments, arguing that he himself was an illegitimate ruler installed and propped up by the French, or simply ignoring these claims. At no point, meanwhile, had the forces of Salabat Jang returned to the Carnatic to support French efforts after 1751; Bussy and the *nizam* were far too occupied with upheavals in the Deccan to intervene against Muhammad Ali and the British. Ultimately, therefore, the alliance with Salabat Jang diverted vital French military resources away from the Carnatic, rather than adding to them.

The Carnatic was now the only prize that the French had left to fight for, and the prospects there were beginning to look bleak. In September 1759, one year on from his departure for the Mascarenes, d'Aché and his squadron returned to Indian waters with food, money and munitions. On the final approach to Pondicherry, the British squadron engaged them: 880 were killed on the French side and d'Aché himself was injured.[122] The vessels that had survived deposited their supplies at Pondicherry before again withdrawing to the Isle de France, this time for good. Thenceforth, the British were uncontested in their control of the coast. Adding to the sense of gloom was the news that d'Aché brought with him about setbacks in other theatres of war. In Canada, notably, Louisbourg had once again fallen to the British.

With the siege of Madras abandoned and d'Aché's squadron so badly hit, the shortage of funds that had handicapped Lally from the outset now became acute. To remedy this, the lieutenant-governor targeted Pondicherry's population, resorting to increasingly oppressive measures to convince the town's residents to part with their gold and silver. Compagnie officials were targeted and local merchants imprisoned. The wealthiest began secretly transferring their goods to other towns on the Coromandel; shops closed as more and more residents quit Pondicherry, often on the pretence of going on pilgrimage.[123] When Lally threatened to execute three wealthy locals who refused to make financial contributions, a wave of protest spread around the town. Fearing a popular uprising, the lieutenant-general responded by ordering the seizure of all weapons in Indian possession.[124] Bands of French soldiers went from house to house plundering what they could find, despite the objections of the Pondicherry council. 'The town is in a panic and the people are in great distress. What affair can prosper with money got by thus torturing people?' protested one Tamil petition.[125] In response to the fact that there was little bullion left, parchment rupees were then officially recognised as currency.

Lally now belatedly came round to the idea that some Indian allies might be a good idea. One possibility was Chanda Sahib's son, Raza Sahib, who remained at Pondicherry with other members of the deceased *nawab*'s family. As the Pondicherry council pointed out, however, Raza Sahib had few funds at his disposal and was unlikely to be much help.[126] More promising was the prospect of an alliance with Basalat Jang, one of the younger brothers of Salabat Jang, who sought for himself a position of power. Bussy was tasked to negotiate with him and appears to have envisaged supporting Basalat to become *nawab* of the Carnatic before the negotiations were undermined by an event beyond the Frenchman's control. In October, the main body of French officers and troops remaining in the Carnatic mutinied, aware that d'Aché's squadron had come and gone yet still they were unpaid, their wages a year in arrears. 50,000 rupees were hurriedly found and the mutineers granted full amnesty, but on learning of the mutiny, Basalat called off the proposed alliance. The only help that could be secured was the hiring of 2,000 Maratha cavalry under Morari Rao, to be paid on a month-by-month basis.[127]

The support of the Marathas was required almost immediately. In November, the British army, emboldened by the arrival of a new regiment from Europe, advanced on the fort of Vandavasi, roughly equidistant from Madras and Pondicherry in the interior of the country, and captured it with ease from the French defenders. A counterattack was organised in which Lally and Morari Rao joined forces, leading to the largest land battle of the entire conflict in the Carnatic and a defeat that would prove decisive. In January 1760, as they assembled to retake Vandavasi, the French army was surrounded and attacked. 450 were killed on the French side and 150 taken prisoner, among them Bussy, whose horse was shot from under him, as the counterattack collapsed.[128] In the weeks that followed, the French forces were driven out of the northern Carnatic. Karikal then fell to the British in April after a combined attack from land and sea. One final attempt to ally with an Indian ruler was then made.

In the summer of 1760, General Haidar Ali, who had effectively claimed control of the throne of Mysore from Krishnaraja Wadiyar II earlier that year, visited Pondicherry after promising 2,000 cavalry and 3,000 infantry to the French. The red carpet was rolled out to welcome him and a ball held in his honour, but the proposed assistance did not materialise. After a month's stay, the Mysore ruler departed, leaving Pondicherry to its fate.[129]

As the British army closed in, Lally intensified his efforts to extract contributions from the town's population, his powers reinforced by a royal decree elevating his authority above that of the Pondicherry council.[130] A list was drawn up of the 150 wealthiest residents and an expected contribution assigned to each. Those who failed to pay were imprisoned in the dungeon of the fort, among them members of Ananda's family. Ordinary artisans and tradesmen were also targeted: even the barber, noted Ananda, was forced to pay 200 rupees.[131] 'Today', Ananda recorded, 'Europeans, Tamils and all the townspeople have given up hope and are in despair. Men's anxiety is indescribable and they are white with fear.'[132] Continuing his reign of terror, Lally ordered the mutilation and killing of a Brahmin accused of passing information to the British. This, according to Ananda, was the first ever instance of a Brahmin being executed at Pondicherry and confirmed that the town was 'destined to ruin'.[133]

By September, Pondicherry was surrounded on land and at sea. The town's fortifications were strong and well-equipped with cannon, but for the British it was sufficient to maintain the blockade and wait. With food already in short supply, the town would sooner rather than later be forced to surrender or starve. The British navy therefore resolved to continue the blockade through the winter, risking whatever damage the monsoon might wreak on its ships. Lally now ordered the civilian population to leave the town, so that the remaining food supplies could be reserved for the army, but this achieved little but to delay the inevitable. In November, with French troops already weakened by hunger and disease, the bombardment of the town began. A brief glimmer of hope arrived in the first week of January 1761 when a cyclone disrupted the blockade, sinking several ships and drowning 1,000 men, but within a few days it was reimposed, and the starvation of Pondicherry continued.[134] On 12

January, Ananda passed away, aged 52. A few years earlier, ill health had forced him to step aside as chief courtier, and four months before his passing he had stopped making entries in his diary. His death, hastened by the siege, was another indication that the end of an era was fast approaching. Three days later, Pondicherry surrendered. Lally was imprisoned, to be shipped in captivity to England.

Simultaneously, French hopes of recovery in northern India were extinguished. In the spring of 1760, Jean Law de Lauriston's efforts to form an alliance to reclaim Bihar and Bengal from the British had finally borne fruit. After fleeing the Marathas at Delhi, Ali Gauhar had summoned the Frenchman to his court near Allahabad, where an offensive against the British was agreed. Law de Lauriston's troops entered the crown prince's service and Law de Lauriston himself was appointed master of his artillery. Before the offensive got underway, news reached Ali Gauhar that his father had been murdered in Delhi. The crown prince was declared Emperor Shah Alam II and the coming military action was elevated to the status of an imperial campaign to re-establish the authority of the Mughal Empire in northeast India. The epicentre of the fighting was Patna. In April, the forces of Shah Alam and Law de Lauriston engaged the British army just outside the principal city of Bihar and won an encouraging victory; Patna was besieged and Shah Alam's troops were on the ramparts before British reinforcements arrived to drive them back. Instead of retreating, Shah Alam then made an audacious bid to advance towards the Bengali capital, Murshidabad. The British had seen enough and in October replaced the bankrupt *nawab* Mir Jafar with his son-in-law Mir Qasim, who it was felt would make a better fist of defending the province. Shah Alam's advance was halted on the banks of the Damodar River, just a hundred or so kilometres from Murshidabad, by a joint army of the British and Mir Qasim, who forced the emperor to retreat to Hilsa, just south of Patna. Here, on 15 January 1761, the same day that Pondicherry capitulated, Law de Lauriston was encircled and captured, his last stand against the British at an end.[135] The following month, a small British force from Tellicherry captured Mahé with the minimum of fuss. Each and every one of the Compagnie's territories on the subcontinent had now fallen to its European rival. The collapse of the French empire in India was complete.

At Pondicherry, the British commanders who had captured the town were inclined to spare it from destruction but the EIC's authorities on the Coromandel had other ideas. In their view, the recent fate suffered by Madras and Fort St David under French occupation was 'sufficient, by the Laws of Retaliation, to justify the utter demolition of Pondicherry.'[136] Residents were given three months to pack up their affairs and leave, before the town was razed. Among the buildings destroyed was the government house, which, even more than Dupleix's 'City of Victory', stands out as a metaphor for the rise and fall of French imperial ambitions on the subcontinent. Begun during the governorship of Dumas, it had of course been completed under Dupleix and elevated fleetingly to the status of a *palais des Indes*, the high command and symbolic centrepiece of France's Indian empire. Nine years on, the British had blown it up, with the rest of Pondicherry, and all that remained were the ruins.

7

REANIMATION

Elsewhere in the Indian Ocean, the course of the Seven Years' War had been more favourable to Louis XV's nation. British trading posts on the western coast of Sumatra had been captured, along with the EIC's base at Gombroon in the Persian Gulf, and French ships had briefly established control over the Malacca Strait. In North America, however, early French successes were short-lived. The fall of Louisbourg in July 1758 was followed by the surrender of French fortresses along the Ohio River and the British capture of Quebec and Montreal. In Europe, meanwhile, Franco-Austrian attempts to defeat Prussia and reclaim Silesia for the Habsburgs had been an expensive and bloody failure. Globally, the picture improved when Spain entered the conflict on the French side in 1762, but the Spanish navy was no match for that of the British, whose capture of Havana and Manila from the Spanish Empire forced France and her allies to enter peace talks.[1]

The treaty that followed in February 1763 was a severe blow to French colonial ambitions. In North America, almost all territories in French possession before the conflict were ceded to Great Britain, including Ohio, Acadia, and Louisiana east of the Mississippi River. (The rest of Louisiana was then given by France to Spain to compensate the latter for its loss of Florida to the British.) A couple of insignificant islands off the coast of Newfoundland, retained for the purposes of fishing, were all that remained of the once-vast territory of New France. Less damaging peace terms were extracted in relation to the Caribbean, where Saint-Domingue, Martinique and Guadeloupe were returned to the *patrie*, though British possession of Dominica, St Vincent, Tobago and Grenada was conceded. Across the Atlantic, meanwhile, Senegal was also lost, except for the slave-trading island of Gorée. With respect to India, military failure and the capitulations that had followed meant that all French territorial claims subsequent to the previous peace of 1748 had to be relinquished. The surrender of all of Dupleix's territorial gains was rubber-stamped, with the Compagnie reduced to the possession of Pondicherry, Chandernagore, Mahé, Karikal and Yanaon. Moreover, France was forced to recognise the sovereignty of Muhammad Ali over the Carnatic and that of Salabat Jang over the Deccan. The re-fortification of Chandernagore and the presence of French soldiers in the town was forbidden.[2]

The reception of the Treaty of Paris in the metropolis exposed deep divisions in educated French society over the country's colonial endeavours. For some, the treaty was a humiliation and an affront to the glory of the nation. Relief over the preservation of control over at least some lucrative sugar-producing colonies in the Caribbean was outweighed by regret over the demise of New France and outrage that Louisiana had been given up. Criticism was directed towards the monarchy and its key institutions—the army, the navy and the state administration—whose weakness and incompetence the war appeared to have unmasked.[3] The fate of the French empire in India raised less concern than that of France's interests in the Atlantic, yet for some who were personally invested in the outcome the treaty was a nadir. After his return to France in 1755, Dupleix had installed himself in a mansion on Rue des Capucines, just a few minutes' walk away from the headquarters of the Compagnie perpétuelle des Indes. From here, he continued his campaign to defend his actions as governor at Pondicherry, launching into bitter disputes with former colleagues like Jacques Law and Charles Godeheu, whom he considered to have wronged him, and with the Compagnie directors, whom he held responsible for his debts.[4] On learning of the terms of

1763 peace, he believed himself vindicated, writing to Godeheu that 'it is to my recall from India that my country, which has always been dear to me, to the glory of which I devoted my youth, my possessions and my funds, and which I made respected and enriched, owes all its misfortunes in Asia [...] You are the primary cause of its defeat.'[5] The statement can be read as a final testament; later that year Dupleix passed away, bankrupt and embittered.[6]

Others, however, greeted the treaty with indifference or even relief, a response that requires more explanation. As we have seen, the French nobility and bourgeoisie had always had reservations about colonial trade, as testified by the difficulties raising investment, concerns about the export of bullion, and the introduction of tariffs on textile imports. By 1750 these reservations had found an intellectual home in an increasingly powerful school of economic thought—*physiocratie*—emphasising that agriculture and land cultivation were the basis of national wealth. For the physiocrats, international trade contributed little to economic development and was even a negative influence, draining resources and distracting attention from the domestic economy. The plantation colonies of the Caribbean were pardoned, because at least the sugar trade was profitable for the nation, but commerce with India was condemned: not only did the expenses outweigh the profits; the import of spices, silks and other 'luxury' goods weakened the moral character of the French, while the climate of India had a degenerating effect on Frenchmen and other Europeans who spent time there.[7] After the defeat of 1763, the physiocrats were emboldened and their ideas adopted by a growing number of writers. Trade with India had been 'ruinous' for France, wrote Voltaire—himself an investor in the Compagnie perpétuelle—in his *Précis du siècle de Louis XV*. 'Ultimately there remained for the French in this part of the world only the regret of having spent, over more than forty years, immense sums to maintain a company that never made the least profit, that never paid anything to its shareholders and creditors.'[8]

As awareness of the devastation wrought by the Seven Years' War around the world grew in France, attention was also drawn to the morality of the European presence on other continents. Why, it was asked, had commerce given way to colonisation? Was war between

France and other European countries an inevitable consequence of commercial competition overseas? Philosophers of the French Enlightenment—the *philosophes*—now turned their attentions to European colonial expansion in the Indian Ocean, with Dupleix's actions in India particularly subject to criticism. Displaying a reasonable understanding of events over the previous two decades, Voltaire argued that Dupleix's regime changes in the Carnatic and the Deccan and his attempts to establish a French empire in India were morally unjustifiable because their basis was expansion through warfare. To finance his wars, which were ultimately about the vain pursuit of power and glory, Dupleix had pillaged the riches of India and misappropriated Compagnie funds intended for peaceful commerce. Once 'the happiest in the world', the peoples of India had been plunged into misery.[9] The decision to recall Dupleix and renounce the Compagnie's Indian territories was therefore to be applauded.

While some people moved to defend Dupleix against these charges, arguing for example that subsequent events had proved his conception of a Franco-British struggle for survival in India correct, one figure that most observers were happy to see condemned was Lally-Tollendal. Critics of French colonialism and war-making argued that he was guilty of arbitrary and excessive violence, citing his terrorising of the civilian population of Pondicherry and the execution of the Thiruvarur Brahmins among his crimes. For defenders of French ambitions, meanwhile, his catastrophic military leadership amounted to a 'betrayal of the interests of the King, the state and the Compagnie des Indes'.[10] Shipped back to Europe by the British, Lally was arrested and imprisoned in the Bastille, where he would spend almost two years awaiting charges. In the highly mediatised trial that followed, he was found guilty of treason and beheaded.[11]

Against this tumultuous backdrop, the experienced Jean Law de Lauriston was appointed governor of the French colonies in India and travelled back out from France to receive possession of them from the British. After the handover of Karikal, he proceeded to Pondicherry, where the scale of the reconstruction required appeared to shock him. 'Never have I seen destruction as complete as that of

Pondicherry', he recorded. 'It is horrifying. All the fortifications have been ruined by mines. All the houses have been razed.'[12] Painstakingly, the streets were cleared of rubble and rebuilding began, with new houses constructed on the foundations of the old. The planning of new fortifications got underway. At Chandernagore, where Law de Lauriston travelled next, it was a similar story, with the colony's fort and its most important buildings in ruins. The French population of the colony remained in refuge in the Dutch and Danish settlements on the Hooghly, while the local population had dispersed.

Alongside reconstruction, then, the priorities in each colony were to induce people to return and restart trade. On the first front, some success was enjoyed. Within three years the population of Pondicherry had regrown to approximately 60,000 Indians and 1,000 Europeans, with the rebuilding of the town proceeding apace.[13] The resumption of the Compagnie's trade was handicapped, however, by shortages of funds. With little money arriving from France and the Compagnie's land revenues now so limited, Law de Lauriston encouraged residents of the colony to invest in trading ventures and resorted to borrowing from British bankers in Madras. Trading posts were re-opened at Masulipatam, Surat, Patna and Dacca, and the establishment of a *comptoir* in Southeast Asia was considered. This, Law de Lauriston envisaged—repeating well-worn arguments—would allow the Compagnie to profit from the region's spice trade, reducing its reliance on bullion from Europe.[14]

In France, however, demands for a more radical change were growing. With debts of over 60 million livres, the Compagnie was in dire financial straits.[15] Its directors argued that more autonomy from the state was required to raise investment and free the Compagnie from political interference, effectively remaking it in the image of its more successful British counterpart. For others, however, among them physiocrat economists and powerful merchants in port cities like Saint-Malo and Nantes, the Compagnie's monopoly on French trade in the Indian Ocean was the problem. Not only was the principle of monopoly objectionable, they argued, prioritising entrenched privileges and hierarchies over the common good, but in practice, the Compagnie's monopoly had been a commercial and financial disaster. After several years of polarising debate, these arguments carried the day.[16] The Compagnie saw its monopoly privileges suspended in 1769 and was wound up the following year, with its land and assets transferred to the Crown. Employees in India, from Law de Lauriston downwards, were stripped of their commercial duties and became servants of the monarchy devoted to the administration of what were henceforth royal colonies. The small Compagnie army that had returned to Pondicherry with Law de Lauriston—then composed of 600 Europeans and the same number of sepoys—became a royal regiment.[17]

Historians suggest that the overall impact of this change was a revival of French commercial activity in the Indian Ocean, as merchants from Le Havre, Saint-Malo, Nantes, Bordeaux and Marseille entered the trade. The organisation of private trading voyages took time, however—to raise investment, purchase goods to sell in India and obtain the all-important *passeport* (passport) from the government—and in the years immediately following the suspension of the Compagnie's monopoly, Pondicherry and the other colonies continued to languish. The situation was 'deplorable', wrote Law de Lauriston, with commerce all but at a standstill and basic provisions lacking.[18] To make matters worse, it now seemed to Law de Lauriston and his compatriots that they were entirely at the mercy of the British. The French may have been forced to recognise the sovereignty of Muhammad Ali in the Carnatic but, in their view, it was the British who were really in charge of province, closely controlling the *nawab*. Muhammad Ali, lamented one observer, is 'less the sovereign of this country than the slave of the English'.[19] Law de Lauriston concurred, adding that the English would 'profit from their superiority to erect a thousand barriers in our way. They are the masters of the country. Muhammad Ali Khan is no more than a phantom whom they make act as they please.'[20]

In northern India, the situation was more alarming still. Here, the war between the British and the Mughal Emperor Shah Alam II and his allies had concluded in 1765 with the concession to the EIC of revenue-collecting rights over the provinces of Bengal, Bihar and Orissa. Successive *nawab*s were maintained on the throne at Murshidabad but, even more so than in the Carnatic, it was clear that power really lay in British hands. Shah Alam was himself living under British supervision at Allahabad, pacified by the promise that when an opportunity presented itself, the EIC would help him retake Delhi from the Afghan invaders who had captured it.[21] Frenchmen living at Chandernagore complained that the British were getting rich beyond imagination through their collection of revenues in the three provinces, while acting despotically to monopolise trade. Their own trade, they objected, was being impeded, with merchants and agents threatened and local weavers prevented from working for them. French ships, meanwhile, were regularly stopped and searched on the Hooghly and new duties were arbitrarily imposed. The trade in saltpetre was entirely in British hands, and procuring regular supplies of silk from Qasimbazaar, cotton from Dacca and opium from Patna was proving impossible.[22]

Law de Lauriston's choice as governor of Chandernagore was a Bengal veteran, Jean-Baptiste Chevalier, whose indignation at the way his compatriots were being treated knew no limits. Impeding French trade was 'contrary to all policies and to all laws of natural justice', he objected to the British authorities at Calcutta, before insisting that French commercial rights dating to before 1757 be recognised.[23] A temporary improvement in relations with Calcutta saw the ban on the presence of French soldiers at Chandernagore relaxed, with permission secured for the maintenance of a small force in the colony to maintain law and order. When Chevalier ordered the digging of a ditch around the town, however, the Calcutta council objected and dispatched soldiers to fill it in. Chevalier claimed that the ditch was needed for drainage, but for the British it was an attempt to fortify the colony, in contravention of the Treaty of Paris. When a French vessel on the Hooghly was then fired upon from the British fort of Budge Budge, Chevalier erupted: 'Our ships are attacked by arms, our flag is insulted on all the Ganges, torn into pieces and trampled upon. *Voilà* the horrible excesses that the English no longer fear to carry out in the name of the *nawab*, which they adopt as a veil for their tyranny and violence.'[24] 'We are reduced to the most humiliating state of slavery', he added, while the English act with 'impunity'.[25]

Confronted by this English 'despotism', Law de Lauriston appealed for diplomatic intervention in Europe to ensure that French trading rights in India were respected. Without this, he argued, his country would soon be forced to abandon the subcontinent altogether.[26] In parallel, both he and Chevalier began to envisage a new war against the British that would avenge the defeat of 1763 and restore France to a position of strength. Law de Lauriston suggested that his country should act unconcerned by the loss of its Indian empire while discreetly preparing to win it back. Investment in the navy was essential, including the build-up of ships and men on the Isle de France. In India, the fortifications of Pondicherry, Karikal, Mahé and Yanaon had to be rebuilt, sepoys recruited and trained and new alliances formed. At Pondicherry, a peacetime standing army of 2,000 Europeans and 2,000 sepoys was required. When the time to strike arrived, it would be supported by expeditionary forces from Europe and the Mascarenes.[27] Chevalier, for his part, was not prepared to wait and argued for the immediate dispatch of 5,000 European troops to invade Bengal and capture Calcutta.[28]

Interestingly, both Law de Lauriston and Chevalier justified their plans for a new war against the English by arguing that the people of India required help to liberate themselves from oppressive English rule. This was not entirely new. As early as 1758, Frenchmen in Bengal were claiming that the population of the province regretted the fall of Chandernagore and the establishment of English dominance that had followed, suggesting that 'all the Moors and Indians sigh for our re-establishment'.[29] Law de Lauriston framed his attempts to form an anti-British coalition with Shah Alam, Siraj ud-Daula and others in the years that followed as a war of liberation.[30] After 1765, he adopted this rhetoric again, suggesting that once his countrymen had expelled the English from India, they would return the country to its legitimate rulers. Chevalier carried this rhetoric to a new level, justifying his plan for an invasion of northeast India with the grand claim that:

> There is not a soul in Bengal who would not contribute with all his heart to facilitate, through our channel, the total expulsion of the English nation. All the people from the biggest to the smallest are tired of their yoke and can no longer bear it; they are only waiting for a favourable occasion to give vent to their

> sentiments, and it is in the French alone that they place all their confidence for their deliverance.[31]

For Chevalier, both the people of India and Frenchmen in the country were victims of English tyranny. Accordingly, the causes of exacting French revenge and of liberating India from English rule were united, and only through French action could the latter be achieved. France therefore had a duty to liberate India, while also restoring its own national pride. So strong was the 'hatred' of Indian princes for the English, Chevalier believed, that a French invasion of Bengal was sure to succeed. 'There is not a single one of them', he argued, 'who is not ready to employ his forces and his money in our favour as soon as they see us declare war.'[32] Once Bengal had been freed from the English, the rest of India would follow; given its financial importance to the EIC, Bengal was the trunk of the English tree of tyranny, and Madras and Bombay the branches.

Five years on from the Treaty of Paris, such ideas found an increasingly receptive audience in France when they made their way back there. By this time, the reality of British domination in Bengal and on the Coromandel was clear, and understandings of what had happened in India over the preceding decades were rapidly being revised. Ever since the War of Austrian Succession, the English had sought to conquer India, argued the Abbé Roubaud in 1768. After realising this design in Bengal, they were deriving unimaginable profits. A re-evaluation of Dupleix's actions followed, with the former governor now presented as a great statesman and diplomat who had understood perfectly how to advance his country's interests in India. After all, what had the English done subsequently but copy him, employing a combination of force and diplomacy to establish their control over vast territories while pretending that others were sovereign? 'The English', concluded Roubaud, 'have embraced the system of M. Dupleix: what they have done in Bengal, M. Dupleix had already done on the Coromandel.'[33] The difference was simply that English protagonists on the subcontinent had been supported by their company's directors and government to carry these policies to their conclusion, while Dupleix had been let down by the Compagnie and the crown. If Dupleix had not been recalled, France would now rule over India!

Perhaps more surprisingly, a similar revisionism was also taking place among those previously critical of the French presence in India. It was now inevitable, noted Voltaire in a new essay on the subject, that England 'will dominate India like it dominates America'.[34] Though Dupleix had been overzealous and some of his actions misguided, he had at least attempted to prevent this outcome. The *Histoire philosophique et politique des établissemens et du commerce des Européens dans les deux Indes* (1770), a large collaborative work counting the Abbé Raynal and Denis Diderot among its principal authors, is usually considered the most influential anti-colonial text of its day, with sections on each of the European powers and their maritime empires.[35] Its overall contention was that the expansion of European trade and influence around the world was morally and legally unjustifiable because it was based on military conquest and oppression. With respect to India, however, its criticisms were largely directed towards the English, whose thirst for riches was considered insatiable. In Bengal, it was recorded, the English now possessed 'absolute power under the modest title of revenue collector', deploying force to monopolise trade and extract as much revenue as possible.[36] The EIC, it was concluded, was 'abusing to such an extent the unjust right that it has acquired through victory [...] that the *philosophes* must wish its ruin.'[37] The French, in contrast, were absolved of blame for their actions in India. Dupleix, it was contended, had 'made up for his faults with great qualities' and, when power came his way, had skilfully integrated the Mughal system, reconciling Indian powers to the Compagnie's authority.[38] The preservation of French rule over the Carnatic would undoubtedly have been better for the people of the province than the English ascendancy that followed.

Some commentators insisted that, moving forward, the French in India should restrict their role to peaceful commerce. Across a broad political spectrum, however, support was forming for a new war against Great Britain. If *revanche* (revenge) was not an acceptable justification, liberating India from the 'yoke' of the English was. *Gloire* would be found not just in the accumulation of power and riches for France but in delivering a subject people from their servitude. 'In India, no people of Europe have been fairer, gentler, more ingratiating, more ready to accommodate themselves to local customs, more warmly welcomed in the courts, more liked and more esteemed by the peoples and the princes, more understanding of the state and politics of the country, than the French', wrote the Abbé Roubaud.[39] The English, in contrast, were 'less liked than feared, and less feared than hated'.[40] When the next conflict began, France could therefore count on Indians' support. The authors of the *Histoire philosophique et politique* concurred. France, they suggested, might put itself at the head of a 'universal league' against the English, working with the dispossessed princes of the country.[41] The result would be a new revolution in India, after which the English would find themselves, like the French after the late war, 'without possessions, revenues or commerce'.[42]

Such an idea chimed well with the plans of France's chief minister, Étienne-François de Choiseul, a diplomat-turned-statesman who had entered Louis XV's government in 1758, accumulating responsibilities for foreign affairs, the navy, the colonies and war. No sooner was the ink dry on the Treaty of Paris than Choiseul had started to plan for a new conflict against Great Britain to recover France's power and honour. England, he believed, was the nation's 'sworn enemy [...] centuries more will pass before it is possible to establish a lasting peace with this state, which aims for supremacy in the four corners of the world.'[43] First, though, France's economic and military power needed to be rebuilt. To this end, the resumption of trade in the Americas, the Caribbean and the Indian Ocean was encouraged, and a major reorganisation and professionalisation of the army took place. More significantly, huge investments were made in the navy, doubling the number of vessels to 63 battleships and 31 frigates within a few years. During the late war, Choiseul noted, the superior capacity of the British navy had been decisive; challenging their global domination must start with contesting their control of the seas.[44]

In Choiseul's view, undermining English dominance in North America was essential to redressing the European balance of power. 'Only a revolution in America will weaken England to the point where she is no longer to be feared in Europe', he contended.[45] When the new war began, no fewer than twenty-four battalions should be sent across the Atlantic to bring this revolution about. This, however, did not mean that India was forgotten. Covertly, Choiseul began planning an invasion of the subcontinent ('Operation Hindustan') to be launched from the Mascarenes where, from 1766, the build-up of ships, soldiers, ammunition and artillery began. An attack on the English bases in India, Choiseul reasoned, would divert the enemy's resources and attention from the American and European theatres of war. With Royal Navy ships lured away from the Channel, the British Isles might even be invaded.[46]

Before we consider the fate of these plans, a word about the intentions of the French authorities with respect to India at this juncture. Noting that, for Choiseul, a new campaign against the British on the subcontinent was just one part of a wider Franco-British struggle for supremacy, in which events in Europe and America would ultimately be decisive, some historians have concluded that French ambitions in India after 1763 were ultimately 'non-imperialistic'.[47] Taking at face value the rhetoric of liberation adopted by many French writers and statesmen at the time, they suggest that France's aims in India were limited to dislodging the EIC from its ascendant position on the subcontinent, liberating the people of India and restoring the conditions for peaceful trade. After defeating the British, reads one influential study, France wanted to return the country to its legitimate rulers—'restor[ing] freedom and liberty on the Indian soil'—and would thereafter 'confine its presence in India uniquely to peaceful commercial pursuits'.[48]

Such interpretations are alarming for a number of reasons. First, it should go without saying that for one European power to use the Indian subcontinent as the stage for a war intended to strike a blow against another is an imperialist act, even where that war is also supposedly in the interests of local powers and peoples. As we will see, France continued to act in an imperialist way in India after 1763, from the continued administration of land to the clandestine arming of local powers and the dispatch of its own army and navy. Moreover, while it is true that for Versailles, India was rarely a foreign policy priority, the possibility of imperial expansion on the subcontinent was never entirely abandoned. As will become clear, at vital moments over the following decades, when occasions for new territorial acquisitions in India arose, French leaders in Europe, the Mascarenes and India tried to capitalise on them. The re-establishment of a territorial empire was meanwhile a powerful motivation behind the actions of many Frenchmen on the ground in India.

To understand the imperialist motivations that continued to inform French actions in India after 1763, it is important to appreciate the distinction between words and deeds. *Revanche*—exacting revenge—and *libération*—freeing India from English oppression—were two key ideas around which public and political support for a new war against Great Britain could be mobilised in France. In the metropolis, the strong current of anti-colonial thought made arguments for the winning back of a French Indian empire a difficult sell to many. Around the discourses of *revanche* and *libération*, in contrast, different factions were able to unite. Moreover, discourses of liberation that presented French and Indian interests as aligned—or even, in some instances, claimed that France would fight disinterestedly against the English solely for the benefit of oppressed Indians—were considered the most useful language to be used in forming alliances with Indian powers. Documents penned by French officials stressed repeatedly that Indian leaders '*must be persuaded* that France has no project of conquest in India', or words to that effect.[49]

An ambiguity, meanwhile, was present in discourses about liberating India from the outset. While, for most contributors to these discourses, liberation meant the return to power in different parts of India of rulers whose autonomy had been undermined by the English, a minority of Frenchmen suggested that following a war of liberation, English despotism might be replaced by the good and generous government of the French. From this seed, new arguments for the revival of a French Empire in India would grow, employing notions of freedom and justice that had earlier been used to criticise French imperialism in the region.

*

While the build-up of forces on the Isle de France continued, Law de Lauriston and Chevalier focused on the forming and strengthening of alliances. In the Carnatic, Muhammad Ali was considered too firmly under British supervision to be influenced, but hopes were entertained that the three most significant powers of central and southern India—Hyderabad, the Marathas and Mysore—might be brought within an anti-British coalition.

Much had changed since the fall of Pondicherry in 1761. In the Deccan, Nizam Ali Khan had seized control, imprisoning and later executing his older brother, Salabat Jang. French influence at Hyderabad was now close to non-existent. Some hope was offered, however, by the presence of a contingent of 600 French soldiers in the service of one of Salabat's other brothers, Basalat Jang, who had been banished to the *circar* of Guntur by the new *nizam*. Through the Savoyard leader of these troops, Henri François Pierre Charles de Motz Lallée, Law de Lauriston established contact with Basalat and hoped that he in turn might influence the *nizam*.[50] Over the decades that followed, the growing cohort of French and Savoyard mercenaries in the service of different Indian courts—mostly soldiers left over from the Carnatic Wars—were a significant resource for the French authorities to draw upon.

At Poona, meanwhile, a new *peshwa*, Madhav Rao I, had been installed. From his capital in the western ghats, he was sovereign over a confederation of territories stretching up the western coast from Canara to Gujarat and inland across Rajasthan and Berar all the way to Orissa, on the eastern coast, bordering Bengal and the Circars. Though the Marathas had suffered a serious military defeat at the hands of the Afghans at Panipat, north of Delhi, in 1761, and the Mughal capital was no longer in their hands, the Maratha Empire appeared 'formidable' to Law de Lauriston.[51] Moreover, further conflict between the Marathas and the English was very likely, he reasoned, given their respective territorial ambitions. 'An alliance with the Marathas appears to me the most valuable for all of operations', he recorded, and began making overtures to Poona.[52]

In Mysore, the years following Haidar Ali's 1760 visit to Pondicherry had seen the upstart general consolidate his hold over the kingdom, imprisoning Krishnaraja Wadiyar II and shifting the seat of power 15 kilometres north to the fortress of Seringapatam, on an island in the Cauvery River. Through a series of conquests, the frontiers of the kingdom had been expanded towards the Arabian Sea, swallowing the territories of the Zamorin of Calicut and encircling the French settlement of Mahé, and it seemed unlikely that Haidar Ali was going to stop there. Ever since 1753, when Dupleix had sent French reinforcements to assist Mysore in the capture of Trichinopoly, Haidar, then a talented but little-known cavalry commander in the Mysore ranks, had been impressed by European military technology and techniques, carefully studying French weaponry and methods of siege warfare. After the fall of Pondicherry, he then welcomed into his army a contingent of 300 French hussars, followed by other French mercenaries, who participated in his wars of expansion on the Malabar Coast.[53]

In many respects, Mysore was a more natural ally for France than the Marathas. For one, Haidar appeared far keener on an alliance than his Maratha counterpart Madhav Rao. Alongside the presence of the hussars, the Mysore ruler sought to inaugurate European-style artillery and infantry units in his army, for which further collaboration with the French would be invaluable. After seizing the port of Mangalore, he also invested in the creation of a small navy, which by 1766 consisted of two warships and forty-seven smaller vessels.[54] The launch of a state-led maritime trading company followed, as Haidar, who revealed himself an intelligent and perceptive statesman, attempted to modernise his kingdom along European lines. In addition, Haidar refused to accept Muhammad Ali's legitimacy as *nawab* of the Carnatic, rendering further conflict between Mysore and the British inevitable. The betrayal experienced a decade earlier, when Muhammad Ali had reneged on his promise to grant Trichinopoly to Mysore, lived on in Haidar's memory, while the long, poorly defended border that the Carnatic shared with Mysore made it ripe for invasion.[55]

More problematic for French interests was that Haidar's expansionist aims also threatened the territories of Nizam Ali and Madhav Rao, making the formation of a grand alliance against Muhammad Ali and the British a remote possibility. From 1761, a series of offensives had been launched by Nizam Ali against the Marathas, whose territories surrounded his dominions on three sides. In 1766, however, the belligerents agreed to peace to focus their efforts on combatting Mysore's expansion. Before the year was out, the *nizam* then signed a new treaty with the British confirming the EIC's possession of four of the five *circars* in return for an annual tribute and the provision of military support.[56] Rather than a coalition against the EIC, what had taken shape was an alliance of the British, Muhammad Ali, the Marathas and Hyderabad against Mysore. A British military detachment was sent to Hyderabad in anticipation of the coming war.

Haidar Ali now dispatched a series of secret letters to Pondicherry requesting French support in the imminent conflict, but did not receive the response that he expected. In Law de Lauriston's view, Haidar was not to be trusted: if he attacked the Carnatic, what guarantee was there that Pondicherry would be saved? Moreover, a war against all the other powers could not be risked, particularly when the governor had so few troops at his disposal and the refortification of Pondicherry was incomplete. While assuring Haidar Ali of his friendship, Law de Lauriston therefore fell back on the argument that the Treaty of Paris prevented France from getting involved in his 'quarrel' with the English, leaving the Mysore ruler on his own.[57]

Over the months that followed, Haidar proved that he was more than equal to the challenge. First, he succeeded in buying off the Marathas, removing the most serious threat from the coalition confronting him. When the joint army of Nizam Ali and the British then invaded Mysore territories in April 1767, its advance was halted near Bangalore and the *nizam* convinced to make peace. The path was now clear for a Mysore invasion of the Carnatic. In August, a force of 50,000 crossed over the range of hills separating the two territories and descended onto the Carnatic plains. While the EIC's Madras army marched out to meet it, Haidar's son Tipu led a cavalry unit into the suburbs of the British city, burning houses, pillaging goods and terrorising the inhabitants. The following year, a British counter-offensive from Bombay put Haidar on the defensive and shifted the main theatre of the conflict to the Malabar Coast, but, by December, Mysore forces were back in the Carnatic and closing in on Madras, leaving a trail of destruction in their wake. Haidar's army was just 8 kilometres from Madras when the British, panicked, sued for peace in March 1769.[58]

9–12. People of the Coromandel Coast whose lives and livelihoods were shaped by the French presence: weavers, manual labourers ('coolies'), servants ('peons') and soldiers in French service ('sepoys'). Lithographs from Jean-Jacques Chabrélie (ed.), *L'Inde française* (Paris: Chabrélie, 1827).

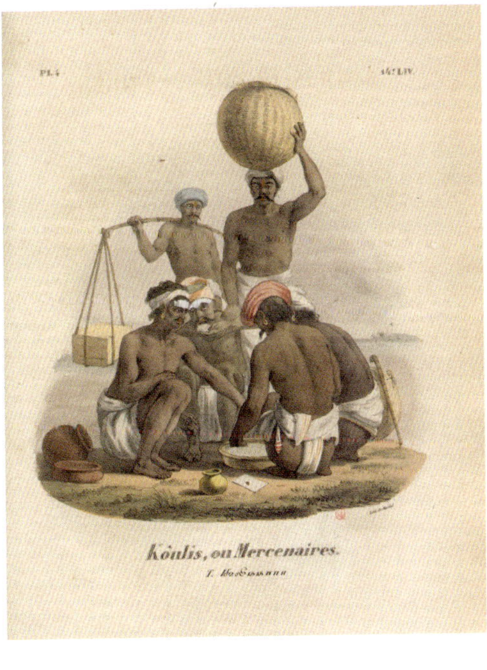

PL. 6. 6e LIV.

Peons.

PL. 6. 7e LIV.

Cipayes.

13. Ships off the Coromandel Coast near Pondicherry. Lithograph from Jean-Jacques Chabrélie (ed.), *L'Inde française* (Paris: Chabrélie, 1827).

M.r JEAN LAW CON.er DU ROY EN TOUS CES CON.ls CONTROLEUR
GNÁL DES FINANCES en 1720.

14. John Law. As controller general of finances at Versailles, he was responsible for the launch of the Compagnie perpétuelle des Indes in 1719. Leonardus Schenk, 1720.

15. Joseph François Dupleix, governor of French India from 1742 to 1754, and the main architect of France's imperial expansion on the subcontinent. Antoine Louis François Sergent, c. 1786.

16. Ananda Ranga Pillai, chief *courtier* under Dupleix. His journal is a vital source of information about events in Pondicherry and wider southern India from 1736 to 1761. Unknown artist, c. 1760.

BERTRAND-FRANÇOIS MAHÉ DE LA BOURDONNAIS,
Chevalier des Ordres militaires de St. Louis, et de Christ,
Capitaine de frégate dans la Marine de France, Capitaine
de vaisseau dans celle du Roi de Portugal, Gouverneur des
Isles de France et de Bourbon, Président des Conseils
supérieurs établis dans ces deux Isles, et Commandant
Général des vaisseaux de la Compagnie des Indes,
né à St. Malo en 1699; mort à Paris le 10 9.bre 1753.

17. Bertrand-François Mahé de La Bourdonnais, governor of the Mascarenes (1735–47) and the commander responsible for capturing Madras from the British in 1746. After a drawing by Jean-Claude Naigeon, 1789.

18. Muzaffar Jang, an ally of the French who was declared *nizam* of Hyderabad in December 1750. Despite French protection, he was assassinated just two months later. Unknown artist and date.

19. Dupleix's *palais des Indes* (Palace of the Indies), inaugurated in 1751 and destroyed a decade later after the British capture of Pondicherry. Champia de Fontbrun, 1755.

20. Pondicherry from the sea, with the grand warehouses of the Compagnie des Indes lining the seafront. Unknown artist, c. 1755.

21. French and British troops facing off in the Carnatic. The event depicted on the wall-hanging is likely the 1760–61 siege of Pondicherry. Unknown artist, c. 1762.

22. Étienne-François de Choiseul. Chief minister in Versailles, he planned an invasion of India as part of a new global conflict against Great Britain after 1763. Jean-Baptiste-André Gautier-Dagoty, c. 1760.

23. Charles Gravier de Vergennes, Foreign Minister during the American War of Independence. When peace talks with the British began, Vergennes attempted to negotiate substantial territorial concessions in India. Charles Clément Bervic, 1780.

24. Maratha *peshwa* Madhav Rao I, with whom French authorities at Pondicherry signed an agreement for military collaboration in 1771. The agreement was never ratified in Versailles. Bhoj Raj, 1763.

25. Nana Fadnavis. As chief minister in the Maratha court at Poona, he sought French involvement in a grand alliance against the British. John Thomas Seton, 1778.

26. Shuja ud-Daula, *nawab* of Awadh. He maintained a corps of 400 French troops in his service and viewed the French as a potential counterweight to the British in north India after 1765. Tilly Kettle, 1772.

LE COLONEL GENTIL.

27. Jean-Baptiste-Joseph Gentil, who spent fifteen years at the court of Shuja ud-Daula and commanded the French corps in the *nawab*'s service. Unknown artist, 1822.

72
HYDER ALLY.
Commandant et Chef des Mahrattes.
A la tête de son Armée contre les Anglais dans les
Grandes Indes.
le Beau Sculp
A Paris chez Esnauts et Rapilly, rue St. Jacques à la Ville de Coutances.

28. Haidar Ali, ruler of Mysore from 1760 to 1782 and a French ally. In this contemporary illustration, he is mistakenly referred to as the leader of the Marathas. Pierre Adrien Le Beau, c. 1781, after a drawing by J. Leister in 1776.

29. The Battle of Pollilur (1780), when the Mysore army inflicted a crushing defeat on the British. This detail from a 20-metre-long mural in Tipu Sultan's summer palace in Seringapatam shows French artillery (top) supporting the Mysore advance. Unknown artist, c. 1785.

30. Pierre André de Suffren, the commander of French naval forces on the Coromandel, meeting Haidar Ali in July 1782 to discuss the terms of military collaboration. Jean-Baptiste Morret, 1789.

31. Noblemen of the court of Nizam Ali of Hyderabad, escorted by infantry (left) in European-style uniforms. Nizam Ali employed French troops in his ranks before finally deciding to side with the British. Venkatchellum, c. 1790.

32. Michel Joachim Marie Raymond, the patriotic commander of a large force of sepoys in the service of Nizam Ali between 1785 and 1798. Unknown artist, c. 1929.

33. Mughal Emperor Shah Alam II. His blinding at the hands of the Rohillas in 1788 marked the end of French attempts to revive the Mughal Empire. Khairullah Musawir, c. 1800.

34. Tipu Sultan, son of Haidar Ali and ruler of Mysore from 1782 to 1799. Tipu tried repeatedly to secure more substantial French support for his campaigns against the British. Unknown artist, c. 1790.

35. Napoleon in Egypt. France's invasion and occupation of Egypt, Palestine and Syria (1798–1801) was intended as the precursor to an advance on India. Jean-Léon Gérôme, c. 1863.

36. The statue of Joseph François Dupleix installed in Pondicherry in 1870 on ornamental pillars plundered from a temple in Gingee during the Carnatic Wars. Unknown photographer, c. 1930.

The First Anglo-Mysore War—a name later accorded to the conflict by British historians—was not strictly 'the first war that the Europeans finished demanding peace from the Indians', as one French participant, Maistre de La Tour, put it, but it no doubt signalled that the gap between European and Indian military capacities was narrowing, as Mysore and other Indian courts adopted weapons based on European designs and drilled their troops in the European fashion.[59] When Haidar's army invaded the Carnatic, the British were taken aback to find that his soldiers were armed with rifles 'based on the latest French designs' and that his artillery was superior to their own.[60] British suspicion naturally fell on the French, with authorities at Pondicherry and Versailles accused of supplying Mysore with officers and arms.

As far as Versailles was concerned, the accusation was not entirely false, but also credited the French government with a speed of thought and action that was lacking. Choiseul and his colleagues had been aware since 1766 that a conflict between the British and Mysore was likely. For almost two years after the conflict began, they deliberated, before finally resolving to send a handful of 'officers of merit' to the court of Haidar Ali 'with the highest possible secrecy'. Their task was to expand the size and capacity of French forces in Haidar's service and make sure that the Mysore ruler was on their side 'in the event of war between France and England'.[61] The covert mission was led by Colonel Hügel, who knew Haidar Ali personally, having served for five years in the contingent of French hussars at Mysore before returning to France. To avoid detection by the British, Hügel and his officers sailed to India on a private vessel which landed at Goa in late 1770, some eighteen months after the First Anglo-Mysore War had finished. (The news of the peace, wrote one of the officers, 'disturbed all our projects!')[62] As such, the Frenchmen who had served in Haidar Ali's ranks during the conflict were mercenaries rather than agents of France, though some no doubt had patriotic motivations. With their help, Haidar had begun the manufacture of French-style rifles in workshops in his kingdom.

Turning to northern India, the obvious candidates with whom alliances might be cultivated were the rulers defeated by the British in 1764–65. Alongside the exiled Mughal Emperor, Shah Alam, they included Mir Qasim, who had been granted and then stripped of the nawabship of Bengal by the EIC, and the *nawab* of Awadh, Shuja ud-Daula. Further afield, the Maratha ruler of Berar and Cuttack, Janoji Bhonsle, and his counterpart at Gwalior, Mahadaji Sindhia, could be counted on to object to British expansion and to seek the recovery of the power lost in 1761 when Delhi had been surrendered to the Afghans.

Determined to bring plans for a new war against the British to fruition, Jean-Baptiste Chevalier first solicited Mir Qasim, who had fled to upper India in 1764. Before long, the governor of Chandernagore was reporting to Versailles that the former *nawab* had 80,000 troops at his disposal and wished only to add 2,000 Frenchmen to his army before retaking Bengal by force.[63] To cement this fledging alliance, an agent, M. Visage, was dispatched from Chandernagore to meet Mir Qasim at Gohad, south of Agra. En route, he called on Janoji Bhonsle at Nagpur and secured a promise from the Maratha leader to support Mir Qasim's invasion. According to Chevalier, Janoji himself wanted to add 800 Frenchmen to his army, along with French arms and artillery, for which he would pay.[64]

With Shah Alam under British supervision at Allahabad, it was all but impossible for the French to establish a direct connection with the emperor. In Shuja ud-Daula's capital, Lucknow, however, it was a different story. After 1765, the *nawab* of Awadh had retained in his service a corps of 400 French troops led by Jean-Baptiste-Joseph Gentil, who had served both Mir Qasim and Shuja ud-Daula during the late war and represented the latter during the peace negotiations with the British that followed.[65] Gentil was an honoured member of Shuja ud-Daula's entourage and ideally placed to convince him of the merits of a new campaign against the British, outlined in correspondence from Chevalier. According to the governor, Shuja ud-Daula was won over. The *nawab*, he reported, desired the expulsion of the English from Bengal and had promised to 'provide troops and money in the event of a [new] war'.[66] In preparation for the conflict, it was added, he too desired to purchase fusils, cannons, bombs and bullets manufactured in France. Chevalier tended to exaggerate and his reports to Versailles from Chandernagore cannot be considered a wholly accurate description of Shuja ud-Daula's intentions, nor those of Mir Qasim and Janoji Bhonsle. To ministers in France, Chevalier stressed that the initiative for a new conflict against the English was coming from the different Indian courts, whereas in reality he himself was the prime agitator. Nevertheless, Shuja ud-Daula appears to have at least entertained the possibility of an alliance with France and even wrote secretly to Choiseul professing his friendship.[67]

By 1770, Choiseul's plans for a war of *revanche* against the British appeared to be coming to a head. The reconstruction of the French navy was almost complete and, in a first expansionist act in Europe since the Treaty of Paris, Corsica was conquered by French troops. As many as 8,000 soldiers were now amassed on the Isle de France in preparation for an invasion of India, and the groundwork for alliances with Indian powers had been laid.[68] The British, for their part, were worried, noting that it was clearly the French intention 'to strike some important blow in India'.[69] The price of EIC shares fell as fears of an invasion grew, and at Calcutta the defences of Fort William were hurriedly strengthened. Units of the company's army were recalled from campaigns further north to protect the city.

Events elsewhere in the world conspired to provide the *casus belli*. In the summer of 1770, France's ally Spain squared off with Britain over the Falkland Islands, and war seemed certain. However, the international alliances on which Choiseul was counting, notably with the Ottoman Empire, failed to materialise. Louis XV began to have reservations about a new conflict and chose to dismiss his hawkish first minister. A de-escalation followed, as the European powers rowed back from the edge of war.

*

For the next four years, with pacifist factions in the ascendancy at Versailles, Law de Lauriston and Chevalier could count on little support from France for their aspirations to challenge the British ascendancy in India. The new colonial minister, the Marquis de Boynes, cautioned them against doing anything that might provoke war. A period of financial retrenchment followed in which the already meagre funds allocated to Pondicherry and the other French Indian territories were reduced still further.

Any encouragement that might have been found after these setbacks came from the signs that covert collaboration with Mysore was finally concretising. In February 1771, Hügel and his officers made it to Seringapatam after a dangerous march up through the tiger-infested jungles of the western ghats.[70] Here, an agreement with Haidar Ali was concluded: 700 French infantrymen and 300 cavalrymen would enter into Mysore service, and 20,000 guns and 90 cannons would be supplied from France. The shipment would be secretly landed at Mangalore and paid for by Haidar's agents at Pondicherry. Meanwhile, Hügel and his officers would immediately enter Haidar's army. Commercial collaboration was also discussed and agreed in principle: 'I would be charmed to have free commerce between your nation and mine', recorded Haidar. 'The French vessels that come to my ports will be regarded and helped like my own subjects, and I hope for the same assistance for my vessels at the Isle de France and the Isle Bourbon.'[71]

The first conflict into which Hügel and his officers were pressed was a new Mysore campaign against the Marathas. From the account penned by one of the officers of this campaign, the picture emerges of a countryside ravaged by war, in which food was in short supply and Haidar's hungry army regularly attacked by bands of Maratha cavalry.[72] After a year of inconclusive fighting, a truce was agreed, but not before Hügel had been killed in battle. One of his officers, Colonel Russel, stepped forward to take command of French efforts at Seringapatam and focused on military recruitment and training. By mid-1773 the corps of hussars in Haidar's service numbered 600. French commanders and artillerymen had begun integrating with the regular army, which grew to 15,000 cavalry and 10,000 infantry and increasingly resembled a European force in its weapons, uniforms, organisation, and tactics.[73] A cantonment for French soldiers was created on the edge of the city, labelled the 'French Rocks', and the foundry used to fabricate weapons and gunpower was expanded.

To minimise the risk of a British reaction to these developments, Law de Lauriston disseminated the rumour that his compatriots at Mysore were a band of impoverished adventurers with no relation to the French authorities.[74] Direct contact with Russel was avoided, though a discreet line of communication was maintained between

Pondicherry and the French at Seringapatam through Russel's brother, who lived on the Coromandel, and official diplomatic correspondence between Law de Lauriston and Haidar continued.[75] Other Frenchmen quietly slipped away from Pondicherry towards Haidar's capital, among them a highly reputed military engineer, Le Goux de Flaix, who oversaw the remodelling of Seringapatam's fortifications along Vaubanesque lines and the construction of a string of other *forts Vauban* around the kingdom.[76] French advisers aided Haidar in the planning of military campaigns, the design of new ships for his navy and the reform of his land revenue system to abolish *jagirs* in favour of European-style revenue collection. So impressive were these developments, in Russel's view, that he worried that Haidar Ali was becoming too strong. Should the Mysore ruler ever turn against the French, he reasoned, his power would be unassailable.[77]

Haidar, however, was not satisfied. Of the 20,000 guns promised from France, only a quarter arrived over the years that followed, prompting the Mysore leader to protest to Russel that the terms of their treaty had not been fulfilled.[78] Repeated requests for more muskets, cannons and cannonballs followed. 'I ask you to send all those that you can from Pondicherry at a fair price and to dispatch the rest from Europe', he insisted.[79] In 1773 the forces of Muhammad Ali and the British invaded the kingdom of Tanjore, a nakedly aggressive move on the part of Madras designed to secure new sources of revenue. With so few soldiers at his disposal and ministers in France insisting on peace, Law de Lauriston and his colleagues at Pondicherry were unable to react—a state of affairs that Haidar found difficult to accept. 'Why is the King of France not sending troops to this country?' he asked Russel, who struggled to reassure him of the value of their alliance.[80]

Unfortunately for Russel and his compatriots, a second incident even more damaging to relations with Mysore swiftly followed. With Picot de la Motte on leave, the governorship of Mahé had temporarily been entrusted to the inexperienced Pierre-Antoine Duprat, who decided to make a name for himself. In December 1773, without consulting Law de Lauriston, Duprat concluded a treaty with the Zamorin of Calicut promising French support for the restoration of his kingdom, which Haidar Ali had subsumed into his own. A hundred soldiers and three pieces of cannon were landed at Calicut from Mahé to support the Zamorin's cause.[81] When Haidar Ali responded by dispatching an overwhelmingly superior force to surround the city, the Zamorin fled and Duprat was forced to back down, but the contrition that Haidar expected to accompany this submission was not forthcoming. Instead, Duprat wrote menacingly to Haidar suggesting that France could at any moment raise any army sufficient to put him in his place and insisted that the French possessed monopoly rights on the Calicut pepper trade, referring back to agreements made with the Zamorin in the 1720s. If Haidar and his subjects wanted to partake in the trade, duties would have to be paid to Mahé![82]

Duprat's thinking and actions were of course wholly at odds with his country's established policy towards Mysore. The acting governor was dismissed and recalled to France, while Law de Lauriston scrambled to reassure Haidar that their alliance remained intact. The Mysore ruler was eventually placated, but in Law de Lauriston's view, lasting damage had been done. 'What could he [Haidar Ali] think of a nation that after a thousand professions of friendship, after so many repeated promises to provide him men, arms and munitions and to act in concert with him, sends a commander who starts by insulting him and by trying to dictate to him the law?'[83] Law de Lauriston feared that the episode might even have encouraged a rapprochement between Haidar and the British, who might resolve to put their animosity aside and divide southern India between them. 'Why do you want me to be the enemy of the English?' he imagined Haidar asking. 'If you don't have any forces to give me, leave me to make the decisions, without obliging me to provoke the only nation that I should fear and of which the friendship might be advantageous.'[84] Law de Lauriston's internal monologue glossed over Haidar Ali's animosity towards Muhammad Ali and other major obstacles to reconciliation between Mysore and the British. For this reason, however, it is all the more revealing of his anxieties about France's position in India, born ultimately from a realisation of powerlessness.

Duprat, for his part, would later publish a *mémoire* attempting to justify his actions at Mahé, notable because of the rhetoric of liberation that it employed. In his account, Haidar Ali was depicted as a tyrant who had acted despotically to seize control of Calicut. The Zamorin, in contrast, was an 'unfortunate prince who requested the protection of France'.[85] In going to his aid, Duprat argued, he had wanted nothing more than the 'the glory of rescuing the oppressed'.[86] With this set of contentions, designed to win favour among readers in France susceptible to appeals to *liberté*, the double standard inherent in French discourses of liberation was inadvertently laid bare: while English 'tyranny' in India was consistently condemned, allies of France like Mysore that also conquered and annexed territories were given a free pass. In other words, the French commitment to *libération* was far from absolute, and often merely rhetorical, with realpolitik and *revanche* far more important guides to French actions on the subcontinent.

If anything was going to make Haidar Ali consider a rapprochement with the British, it was probably the signs coming from further north that a treaty between France and the Marathas might be on the cards. In upper India, a 'revolution' had just taken place: out of patience with the British, whose promises to help him recover his throne had proven empty, Shah Alam had concluded an alliance with Maratha leader Mahadaji Sindhia and been reinstalled as emperor at Delhi after Maratha forces had expelled the Afghan occupiers from the city.[87] From Chandernagore, Chevalier followed these developments with glee, noting that the English would soon have a 'ruinous' war with the Marathas on their hands, and rushed to offer French support to the new partners.[88] An emissary, Lionel du Jarday, was sent to Delhi disguised as a Muslim merchant to meet with Shah Alam and Mahadaji Sindhia. In late 1772, he concluded an agreement with the Maratha leader, who ultimately controlled the emperor: France would supply troops to help consolidate Mughal-Maratha control over upper India; once this pacification was complete, the allies would march on Bengal to expel the English, while a separate French force invaded the province from the coast.[89]

Notably, the supreme authority of the Maratha confederation, *peshwa* Madhav Rao I, was also beginning to show interest in an alliance with the French—no doubt provoked by the growing military strength of Mysore—after years of indifference to the diplomatic overtures coming from Pondicherry. Representatives of the *peshwa* visited the French colony to request the supply of men and weapons from France, particularly artillery, in return for payment in cash and territory.[90] There now seemed the very real possibility of French alliances with the Marathas in both northern and southern India. Law de Lauriston, who had consistently pressed for collaboration with the Marathas, was delighted, noting that 'this Maratha nation is unquestionably the most powerful in India [...] and the only one whom the English respect.'[91] Chevalier agreed, recording that the Marathas were the 'most formidable power in Hindustan' and a Franco-Maratha alliance the prospect that the English most feared.[92]

The problem was that the treaties concluded with Mahadaji Sindhia and Madhav Rao required ratification at Versailles, and that without the dispatch of large numbers of troops from France they would be nothing but dead letters. For the operations in north India, Chevalier wanted a force of 5,000 Frenchmen, while Madhav Rao expected 10,000.[93] To put it bluntly, there was not a hope in hell of ministers in Versailles accepting these requests, wary as they were of provoking the British—and indeed of angering Haidar Ali, who remained their favoured ally. The untimely death of Madhav Rao, who had contracted tuberculosis, then threw another large spanner in the works. A succession struggle followed that removed the French alliance from the agenda at Poona and forced Sindhia to return to the Maratha capital, undermining his influence at Delhi.

To deliver his ambitious plans, the only other resource on which Chevalier could now try to call were compatriots serving as mercenaries in the courts of north India. Beyond Gentil, who was more an advisor and diplomat at Shuja ud-Daula's court than a mere soldier of fortune, there was one outstanding candidate, a Breton called René Madec, 'celebrated throughout the empire for his vigorous actions and courage'.[94] Madec had arrived in India as a sailor of the Compagnie before jumping ship to join the French army fighting in the Carnatic during the Seven Years' War. Captured after the fall of Pondicherry, he had then accepted service in the British army over imprisonment at Madras, seeing action in Bengal and Bihar before deserting with 200 other French soldiers in 1763. Here began his long career as a mercenary in north India. With the help of Gentil, he entered the service of Shuja ud-Daula and was injured fighting against the British in October 1764. The terms of peace between the *nawab* and the EIC the following year forced Shuja ud-Daula to get rid of most of his French troops; Madec found employment with the Rohillas, followed by the Jats, two local powers from the lands around Delhi seeking to profit from the Mughal Empire's decline. In Jat service, his power and reputation grew rapidly; by the early 1770s he had under his command a large army that had more than proved its worth in the region's power struggles. Madec lived on a large estate near the Jat capital of Bharatpur and had amassed a fortune of 600,000 rupees.[95]

Chevalier believed that Madec was 'in the position to render great services one day, because of the esteem with which he is held in the country'.[96] After Shah Alam's return to Delhi, he considered that that day had come and wrote to Madec urging him to enter the emperor's service, taking his soldiers with him. Over the course of several letters, Chevalier revealed the full extent of his plans: Shah Alam was to be secured in his position as emperor, with the territories of upper India forced to submit to his authority and sources of revenue secured. The forces of the emperor were then to be prepared for a campaign to retake Bengal.

To convince Madec to follow him, Chevalier appealed skilfully to the Breton's pride and patriotism, arguing that the acquisition of riches was nothing compared to the glory of serving one's country, and renown in India incomparable to eminence in France:

> You have, I'm told, a large number of well-disciplined troops under your command. You are brave and capable of commanding them. The princes of India seek your help, and it's them that you can serve. The circumstances offer you an opportunity to immortalise your name and render it forever memorable in the country of your birth. In your position, with what facility you will be able to effect a revolution capable of elevating your nation from the languid state that it finds itself in in India today [...] What satisfaction and what glory for you, if you could succeed in

> returning to your nation its reputation and its splendour, which for a long time it held but which is in tatters since the loss of Pondicherry.[97]

Madec was at first reluctant, suggesting that quitting the Jats for Shah Alam might put his family and fortune at risk, but after Chevalier dangled before him the prospect of honours from the court of France and implied misleadingly that a new war with the British was imminent, he was won over.[98] The 'sorry state of his nation in Bengal', he later recorded, convinced him to 'sacrifice everything' to prepare the 'revolution' that Chevalier had planned.[99] 'Were it not for my zeal to serve my King and my love for my country, I would take the more reasonable choice of retiring to France with my fortune.'[100]

Madec was right to fear that abandoning the Jats would be complicated. Attempting to leave the kingdom, he found his route blocked and was shot in the arm in the ensuing skirmish. Nevertheless, twelve days later he was entering Delhi, where Shah Alam offered him a welcome 'fit for a monarch'.[101] The Breton had his work cut out leading campaigns to restore the emperor's authority in the heartlands of Hindustan. To help him, he was awarded a large grant of land south of Agra, between the Jamuna and Chambal rivers, from which revenue was derived to pay troops. His forces were gradually expanded to number 4,000 infantrymen and 2,500 cavalrymen, to Chevalier's delight.[102]

Chevalier and Madec now began to plan in greater detail the campaign to liberate Bengal that was to follow. The governor of Chandernagore continued to frame this campaign as a virtuous struggle to liberate India from English oppression, but his plans for the conduct of the war showed no regard for the wellbeing of the province's people. Writing to Madec, he suggested that there was 'a sure means of conquering Bengal—to defeat the enemy without fighting them'—and elaborated:

> For that we need a well-commanded cavalry corps that, through a campaign of destruction, puts a stop to all manufacturing and farming of the land, while avoiding engagement with the enemy. This will spread famine across the land, ruin all commerce, and

> destroy all revenues. The English, once weakened thus, will be forced to demand peace, and to accept it on our terms, because they will find themselves unable to fight a war, given the lack of funds to pay their troops. The troops, finding themselves without pay, will not hesitate to abandon them, especially the sepoys, who will be prepared to defect to us when we make them a better offer.[103]

Madec concurred and put even more emphasis on the need for a total war targeting soldiers and civilians indiscriminately:

> My plan is to target the English establishments on both sides of the Ganges, and to take all that they possess from Allahabad to Patna. While the forces of the king attack from the bottom of the river, I will devastate them in the upper parts, and will leave no corner of Bengal untouched by destruction. I have cavalry, and they have very little cavalry. I will direct to follow after me a world of bandits and plunderers who will make a desert of this beautiful country of Bengal, burning the countryside, destroying the crops, seizing the flocks of animals, and committing all sorts of military executions. During this time, my regular troops will extract contributions from the towns, which are always keen to avoid being pillaged. This type of war will deprive the English, for several years, of the fabulous revenues that they derive from this immense country; and, not being able to afford to preserve their control, the misery and hunger will chase them from one of the most fertile and opulent regions of the earth.[104]

The moral reprehensibility of these plans—formulated just a couple of years after an estimated 10 million Bengalis had been killed in a famine exacerbated by British revenue-collecting practices in the province—need hardly be pointed out.[105]

With Shah Alam short of cash, the key question for Madec was how the campaign would be financed, but here too a cunning plan was taking shape: Madec and a second Frenchman who arrived in Delhi at this time, the Comte de Modave, convinced the emperor to cede to France the province of Tatta, on the coast of Sindh. In Tatta, the French would extract revenues and maintain a large army that, when the time was right, would unite with Mughal forces to retake Bengal.[106] To minimise the risk of his letters being intercepted en route for Chandernagore, Madec wrote directly to Versailles to outline the plan. Shah Alam, he recorded, had proposed the concession of Tatta because he was fed up of seeing 'a handful of English without courage or discipline dictate the law in a most imperious manner over a considerable proportion of Hindustan.'[107] The advantage of the province was that it was far from any British possessions on the subcontinent—and its occupation thus unlikely to antagonise them. Moreover, the land was fertile and untouched by 'the long succession of wars that the [Mughal] Empire has suffered these last thirty years'.[108] The land revenues extracted would be more than sufficient to cover the expenses of maintaining an army, so the occupation of Tatta would cost the government nothing.

When Chevalier was informed of the plan, he backed it without hesitation and wrote immediately to Versailles asking (once more) for the dispatch of troops, plus equipment to arm locally recruited sepoys. A force of 3,000 Europeans and 12,000 Indians was estimated sufficient to bring Tatta under French control.[109] Again, however, no response was received, with ministers in France continuing to reject a forward policy. Instead, Chevalier and his compatriots were forced to look on as British control over northern India was strengthened, first when the EIC resolved to stop paying tribute to Shah Alam, and then when it launched into the conquest of Rohilkhand with Shuja ud-Daula, who decided, in the final years of his life, that it was more advantageous to work with rather than against the British. When the *nawab* of Awadh passed away in January 1775, his kingdom moved definitively into the sphere of influence of the EIC. His son, Asaf ud-Daula, bowed to British pressure to expel the remaining Frenchmen from his service, among them Gentil, bringing the colonel's fifteen years at Lucknow to an end.[110]

Chevalier now despaired that 'all of India is on the verge of falling prey to the English'.[111] This sentiment was shared by Modave, who cautioned:

> Of the Mughal Empire, there now exists only the corpse; and the soul that should animate this body is an empty shadow,

> without credit and without influence [...] The English watch this situation closely in the hope of profiting from it, because the spirit of greed is as active in them as the mania for conquests [...] I have no doubt that the constant troubles that weaken the force of the Empire appear to them a means to take control of it bit by bit [...] Soon they will be masters of the Ganges from Allahabad to the sea.[112]

Attempting to shake ministers at Versailles from their inactivity, Madec meanwhile warned that time was running out 'to prevent the English from continuing their conquests. They are becoming very powerful, and soon it will be difficult to defeat them.'[113]

Little did Chevalier and Madec know that events on the other side of the world, in far-away North America, would soon set up the showdown with the British that they craved.

8

RECKONING

On 19 April 1775, as Chevalier and Madec waited impatiently for a response from Versailles, Patriot militiamen in Lexington, Massachusetts emerged from the Buckman Tavern to find a British force advancing towards them from across the village green. Shots were exchanged, eight of the Patriots were killed and one British regular took a bullet in the thigh. A decade of rising discontent over British taxation and neglect in North America—most iconically expressed by the emptying of 342 chests of tea into the harbour at nearby Boston—had turned violent, and the American War of Independence was underway.

Two months later, 20-year-old Louis XVI was installed on the French throne after his grandfather, Louis XV, had succumbed to smallpox. At Versailles, a changing of the guard was enacted, with a new government established under the Comte de Maurepas. The appointment of Charles Gravier de Vergennes as Foreign Minister and Antoine de Sartine as Minister of the Navy and Colonies signalled a return to the policies of Choiseul, with preparation for a new war against Great Britain once again the order of the day. 'England is the natural enemy of France', Vergennes proclaimed. 'It is our duty then to seize every possible opportunity to reduce the power and greatness of England.'[1]

With their country's navy not yet the equal of its British counterpart, Vergennes and Sartine needed to tread carefully. Events in America were certainly too great an opportunity to pass up, however, and while state resources were poured into rearmament and shipbuilding, covert support for the Patriots got underway. First, arms, gunpowder and other provisions were shipped across the Atlantic through fake companies like Roderigue Hortalez and Co., which operated out of Lisbon. Volunteers like the Marquis de Lafayette were then encouraged to join the American cause, taking advantage of grants of leave from military service, and French ports were made over to pro-Patriot privateers.[2] The secret arming of opponents of the British had, of course, been trialled over the preceding decade with Mysore, and as support for American independence grew in France, the same rhetoric of liberation seen in relation to India was deployed. 'All of the facts, all of the events testify to the despotism and the tyranny of Great Britain', declared the noble playwright and politician Pierre Beaumarchais, one of the instigators of the Roderigue Hortalez and Co. scheme. 'For a century, England has aimed at nothing less than to dominate on all the seas and put Europe and the world in chains.'[3]

The respective positions of the French and British in India now began to receive far more attention in government, as momentum gathered for a new war against the old foe. Informed by estimations made in Bengal, Vergennes and Sartine speculated about just how much revenue the British derived annually from their control of the province, concluding that domination in northeast India was the financial foundation of British supremacy the world over. Undermining this supremacy, it followed, required action on the subcontinent.[4] The astronomical figures mentioned in these conversations seemed to confirm that British rule in India was fundamentally exploitative, adding weight to the notion that the country needed liberating. The EIC gained 'immense sums' from its Indian territories, noted one observer. 'Everyone knows that these riches are not the fruits of legitimate industry, but of the yoke that it imposes on the sovereigns and people of these vast and fertile countries.'[5] The great famine of 1770–71 was evoked as proof that the British had conquered Bengal solely to increase their revenues, with disastrous consequences. During the famine, it was contended, officials of the EIC were confronted with a choice between revenue collection and the lives of millions of people, and had chosen the former.[6]

In the coming conflict, therefore, Versailles was convinced that it was on the side of freedom: in India as in America, challenging British domination would be a fight for liberty over despotism. 'The princes of Asia, the Emperor himself, suffer impatiently the yoke of the English', wrote the retired Marquis de Bussy, advising the government. 'They wait for an occasion to break free from their chains and put themselves back in possession of their riches and authority.'[7] 'From the moment of our first success we will see all of the Indian princes break free from their chains and show themselves ready to cooperate with us to ruin their oppressor', added another.[8] Most official memoranda produced at Versailles insisted that, just as the Patriots in America would be helped to secure their freedom, the aim of a new war in India would be to defeat the English and return the country to its rightful rulers. From the outset, however, some officials had other ideas and a degree of mission creep was present. If the war was prosecuted successfully, noted the head of the India office at Versailles, M. Badouin, 'the king of France will be able to dictate the law to all of India'.[9] Without land, the French presence in India would never be profitable, another mentioned, restoring one of Dupleix's old arguments for the acquisition of territory. Once the English were defeated, France should therefore 'conserve the possession of the territories that it wishes to retain in this part of Asia'.[10] Bussy agreed, suggesting that France should retain a proportion of its coming conquests in India to support itself after the war.[11]

A first concrete step to preparing the new conflict in India was the recall of Law de Lauriston and his replacement as governor of Pondicherry by Guillaume Léonard de Bellecombe, a royal and military man who had received the Ordre de Saint-Louis for his service in America during the Seven Years' War. His arrival at Pondicherry with two men-of-war was meant to signal to Indian courts that France was serious in its intention to challenge the British.[12] There remained, however, a huge discrepancy in the forces that the two European nations had at their disposal. In Bengal, Bellecombe estimated, the British army comprised 9,000 Europeans and 60,000 sepoys; in the Carnatic, they had 3,000 Europeans and 20,000 sepoys; and at Bombay, 2,000 Europeans and 15,000 sepoys. The French, in contrast, had just 700 European soldiers and 950 sepoys spread across their Indian bases![13] To improve this situation, an amnesty was declared for those soldiers who had deserted to take service in Indian courts, and an attempt was made to induce the deserters back.[14] At Pondicherry, efforts were made to recruit more sepoys and the reconstruction of the fortifications—paused under Law de Lauriston for lack of funds—restarted.

As far as alliances were concerned, Bellecombe was ordered to prioritise the relationship with Mysore. Haidar Ali, he was instructed, was a 'precious and necessary' ally who 'will be a great help for us in the removal of the English from the Coromandel and Malabar coasts'.[15] Indeed, England was the 'natural enemy' of Mysore just as much as of France.[16] Other potential allies were not to be discarded, however: good relations were to be cultivated with Nizam Ali at Hyderabad and his brother Basalat Jang at Guntur, and a diplomatic channel to be opened with Muhammad Ali in the Carnatic, if possible. The prospects for an alliance with Shah Alam were to be investigated, and fresh overtures made to Asaf ud-Daula at Lucknow.

Acting on these instructions, Bellecombe dispatched an envoy, M. de Coutaneceau, to Haidar Ali's court. Reassurances were offered that the weapons promised to the Mysore ruler by the French government would materialise.[17] A second envoy, M. Gardé, was sent to Hyderabad disguised as a private merchant to warn Nizam Ali about the pending war and convince him to side with France.[18] At the same time, the Comte de Modave made his way from Delhi to Guntur, where the terms of an alliance with Basalat Jang were provisionally fixed. The French troops in Basalat's service under the Savoyard Lallée were an important potential resource in the coming conflict.

Developments at Poona meanwhile forced Versailles to at last give serious consideration to collaboration with the Marathas. Ever since the death of Madhav Rao in November 1772, the Maratha court had been in turmoil: Madhav's younger brother and successor Narayan had lasted just nine months on the throne before being murdered by his uncle, Raghunath, who in turn managed only eight months in power. In the summer of 1773, the opposition faction at Poona, led by influential minister Nana Fadnavis, seized control with the support of Mahadaji Sindhia and the other influential Maratha chieftains of the north. Narayan's posthumously born infant son—crowned Madhav Rao II—was installed as *peshwa*, with Nana in control of the government. Raghunath survived this deposal, however, and in March 1775 concluded a treaty with the British authorities at Bombay, who promised to help him recover his throne in return for territorial concessions on the west coast. The campaign that followed was short-lived; after a few months of inconclusive fighting in Gujarat, the Bombay army withdrew. Significantly, however, the alliance between Raghunath and the British sufficiently alarmed Nana Fadnavis that he began to consider an alliance with France and contacted Pondicherry.[19]

Informed of these developments, Versailles decided to seize the initiative by dispatching an ambassador to Poona. Its choice was Joseph Alexis Pallebot de Saint-Lubin, a well-connected veteran of India who managed to convince Sartine that he was an expert on Maratha affairs.[20] He landed at Chaul, just south of Bombay, on a vessel carrying 15,000 muskets destined for Poona, plus secret letters from Louis XVI to the infant *peshwa* and from Sartine to Nana Fadnavis. For Bellecombe, Saint-Lubin was a liar and schemer who could not be counted on to represent French interests at Poona, but over the months that followed he stuck closely to the script agreed by Versailles, concluding a treaty that matched almost verbatim what the French government had envisaged.[21] When war with Great Britain was declared, 2,500 French soldiers would be sent to Poona to fight alongside Maratha forces and 25,000 Maratha cavalry would be on hand to help France. When the conflict was over, Chaul would be handed over to the French, who would be guaranteed freedom of trade in Maratha territories.[22] The British followed these developments with alarm and stepped up their efforts to undermine the influence of Nana Fadnavis, rallying support at Poona for Raghunath's return to power.

In parallel, the proposed occupation of the province of Tatta now received serious attention in Versailles for the first time. One confidential government document noted the 'inappreciable advantages' that might be derived from the scheme.[23] To Chevalier's delight, a reconnaissance mission was approved to travel up the Indus, taking observations about the river's navigability, the surrounding land and existing fortifications.[24] In late 1777, François Emmanuel Dehaies de Montigny, a major in the navy, was then sent to India to conclude arrangements with Shah Alam. Regrettably for French interests, by the time that Montigny arrived in upper India, René Madec had quit the emperor's service, disillusioned with the French government's apparent lack of interest in his plans.[25] Montigny remained at Agra trying to keep the French alliance with Shah Alam alive, but the Tatta project was shelved, only to be revived a few years later when plans for the dispatch of a French expeditionary force to India were under discussion.

News then reached India that the imminent war between France and Britain was formally underway. In America, the British had suffered a damaging defeat by French-armed Patriots at Saratoga in October 1777, a surprise that convinced Versailles that it could now side openly with the American independence cause. A treaty of alliance with the Patriots was concluded in February 1778, followed in March by the declaration of war on Great Britain. A fleet under the Comte d'Estaing set sail for America in April. No corresponding fleet was sent to India, however, with French forces considered insufficient by Versailles for a campaign in India alongside fighting in America and Europe. Pondicherry and the other French territories were therefore exposed to the overwhelming military superiority of the British on the subcontinent, with just a small squadron of five ships already in Indian waters to support their very modest ground troops.

On learning that the war had begun, Bellecombe appealed urgently to different Indian courts to come to France's aid, but with the exception of Haidar Ali, who instructed local chieftains on the Malabar Coast to prevent the British advancing on Mahé, his appeals went unanswered. Unfortified Chandernagore surrendered first; Chevalier went on the run but was captured in Orissa three weeks later and deported to Europe.[26] Karikal was then evacuated and Yanaon seized, leaving Pondicherry the only remaining territory on the eastern coast in French hands. The siege of the town began in August, pitting an offensive force of almost 20,000 against 1,500 troops and a set of unfinished fortifications on the French side.[27] When the squadron aiding the defence of Pondicherry sustained damage and withdrew to the Isle de France, the die was cast. After holding out for seventy-seven days, Pondicherry capitulated. The unsuccessful defence of the town had cost the lives of approximately half of those involved.

Unlike in the Seven Years' War, however, the surrender of Pondicherry and the other colonies this time signalled the beginning of a conflict rather than its end. Versailles had not had its final say on events in India, while a powerful coalition of Indian interests was finally forming against the British, led by Nana Fadnavis. In the summer of 1778, British efforts to influence the course of politics at Poona had seen the Maratha chief minister briefly sidelined and Saint-Lubin expelled from court. Just days before Pondicherry fell in October, a new agreement had then been struck between the EIC and Raghunath Rao in which the British again committed to install Raghunath as *peshwa*. Article 15 of the agreement stated that once Raghunath was in power 'no manner of intercourse or connection shall be maintained between the Maratha Government and the French nation'—confirmation that concern about a French-Maratha alliance was one of the main motivations behind the continued British intrigues in Poona.[28] The campaign that followed was a disaster for the EIC, with its army surrounded and forced to surrender by hostile Maratha forces in the western ghats. By the terms of the surrender, signed in January 1779, the EIC handed over Raghunath and gave up the territories around Bombay that it had acquired over the preceding years from the want-to-be *peshwa*.[29]

Nana Fadnavis, whose talents as a statesman would earn him the designation 'the Maratha Machiavelli', now reached out to Haidar Ali to secure Maratha-Mysore collaboration against the British. Clearly, the Maratha chief minister anticipated further hostilities against this 'intolerably belligerent' nation.[30] Two British missteps in the opening months of 1779 ensured that Haidar Ali's response was positive.

First, the Bombay administration dispatched an army through his kingdom to seize Mahé, despite Haidar's warning that this would be considered an act of aggression. The town was taken from the French in March. The Madras council then concluded a treaty with Basalat Jang that saw the *circar* of Guntur rented to the EIC, and the body of French troops under Lallée expelled from Basalat's service, in exchange for British military protection. To Haidar, this too was a sign that the British were spoiling for another war.[31] What is more, the conclusion of a treaty with Basalat Jang without so much as a word to Hyderabad was a major affront to Basalat's brother, Nizam Ali, who put aside his differences with the Marathas and Mysore to join the new alliance. Lallée and his troops were welcomed into the *nizam*'s service.[32]

In a matter of months, aided by a series of British blunders, Nana Fadnavis had succeeded where for fifteen years Law de Lauriston, Bellecombe and ministers at Versailles had failed: he had assembled a grand alliance of the three most powerful kingdoms in central and southern India—Mysore, Hyderabad and the Marathas—against the British. Plans were sketched out for coordinated attacks on Bombay from Poona, on the Circars from Hyderabad, and on the Carnatic from Seringapatam and Bangalore. Realising what an immense opportunity had opened up for his country, Montigny now quit the court of Shah Alam and rushed southwards to assure Nizam Ali and Nana Fadnavis that France was on the allies' side. A large expeditionary force would soon be dispatched from Europe, he promised.[33] The problem was that it wouldn't. Instead of devoting resources to India, Versailles doubled down on its focus on the European and American theatres of war, building up resources at Brest for an invasion of England and sending a new expedition of 6,000 soldiers across the Atlantic.[34] A squadron of four ships was all that could be spared for the Indian Ocean, with the limited aim of protecting the Mascarenes and disrupting British shipping.

The involvement of Hyderabad in the grand alliance proved fleeting. Within a couple of months, the treaty signed between Madras and Basalat Jang had been disowned by the British authorities at Calcutta, to whom Madras and Bombay were answerable, and Nizam Ali conciliated. Lallée's contingent was forced out of Hyderabad and entered Haidar Ali's ranks, with the Savoyard succeeding Russel as the leader of the French forces at Mysore. The conflict between the British and the Marathas restarted, however, with armies dispatched from Bengal on ambitious overland campaigns to attack Gwalior, Mahadaji Sindhia's seat of power, and Poona. Meanwhile the commencement of hostilities between Mysore and the British was imminent. Buoyed by the arrival of Lallée and his troops, Haidar Ali sent a force to recapture Mahé and besiege the nearby British fort of Tellicherry. In July 1780, thirteen years on from his first invasion of Muhammad Ali's territories, he then entered the Carnatic with a formidable-looking army of about 90,000 men, among whom were at least 30,000 infantry trained in the French fashion, backed by French artillery.[35]

A string of victories followed, with the French in Haidar's army amazed to find the Carnatic so poorly defended.[36] The country was laid to waste and Muhammad Ali's capital, Arcot, surrounded. As in 1767, Haidar's son Tipu led a cavalry raid into the well-to-do suburbs of Madras. In late August, British reinforcements set out from Madras to stop Haider's advance; near the village of Pollilur, 70 kilometres to the west, they were surrounded and annihilated. Pollilur was one of the most damaging defeats in the history of the EIC and signalled the 'virtual annihilation of the Madras army', with 3,000 soldiers killed and 500 taken prisoner, among them almost all the British officers.[37] 'The heat was so violent and the crowd so great', wrote one of the Frenchmen involved, that 'the enemy could neither advance nor retreat. The Europeans, who were nearly the only people that faced us, were all killed, wounded or made prisoners. There is not in India an example of a similar defeat.'[38] Weighing up the wider significance of Pollilur, Maistre de La Tour reflected: 'The English are engaged in a most ruinous war. With the help of the French, it may be hoped that Haidar Ali takes possession of the whole of the Carnatic.'[39]

*

The spectacular 20-metre-long mural of the Battle of Pollilur that was later commissioned for the royal palace at Seringapatam by Haidar Ali's son Tipu confirms that for the Mysore rulers, Pollilur was a particularly glorious moment in their struggle against the British domination of south India. It depicts the Mysore army closing in on its trapped British counterpart from the left and right, with Haidar commanding from his horse. Lallée looks on through a telescope from behind the frontline, his artillery pointed at the British troops, as the massacre begins. If, for Haidar and Tipu, Pollilur was a source of great pride, for French observers further afield it was the Indian equivalent of Saratoga three years earlier in America—an emphatic victory for France's allies, convincing those observers that the British could be defeated, leading to more decisive military intervention.

The first moves were taken by François de Souillac, governor of the Mascarenes and, with all French territories in India under British occupation, the closest French authority to the subcontinent. In October 1780, one month after Pollilur, he dispatched a fleet of six warships to the Coromandel from the Isle de France with a regiment onboard. In parallel, he entered into correspondence with Haidar Ali about the terms of joint action in the Carnatic. For the British, the situation was serious. Madras was defended by just 500 troops, while the remains of the British army in the interior were being driven back towards the coast. In January 1781, the fleet appeared off the coast of Cuddalore. If the soldiers that it carried were landed, the British would again be encircled and surely forced to surrender. To Haidar's great frustration, however, the commander of the fleet, Thomas D'Orves, insisted that his troops remain on board until the negotiations between Souillac and Haidar had produced a formal treaty.[40] The British slipped away to fight another day, soon to be strengthened by the arrival of significant reinforcements from Bengal.

At Versailles, the Ministry of the Navy and Colonies was meanwhile taken over by renowned military commander Charles Eugène Gabriel de La Croix, the Marquis de Castries, who was tasked with preparing a large naval and terrestrial campaign in the Indies. Now back in Paris, Chevalier pleaded with Castries to focus on capturing Bengal and put the plan to occupy Tatta before the minister. The former governor of Chandernagore even proposed to lead the expeditionary force himself.[41] These suggestions were dismissed. Though Bengal was undoubtedly the most valuable

British asset in India, it was also the hardest to conquer. The idea of marching an army 2,000 kilometres across north India from Tatta to Bengal, in alliance with Shah Alam, was 'a chimera and a fairy tale'.[42] The campaign would therefore take place in southern India, but where would its focus lie? Fresh from his recent stay at Poona, Montigny argued for the capture of Bombay and the dispelling of the British from the Malabar Coast, in collaboration with the Marathas, after which attention could be turned to the Carnatic.[43] For others, however—among them Haidar's former general Russel—the Mysore alliance had to be prioritised and the extermination of the British from the Coromandel completed first.[44]

While the assembling of a grand expeditionary force began in France, a new squadron of five warships was dispatched from Brest in March 1781, under the celebrated naval commander Pierre André de Suffren, who had just returned from action in the Atlantic.[45] Suffren's first task was to stop the Cape of Good Hope from falling into British hands. With lightning speed, he caught up with the British fleet that had set out for southern Africa a week before his own and incapacitated it with a surprise attack at Cape Verde; the Cape of Good Hope was secure in the possession of the Netherlands, France's allies. On the Isle de France, six more warships and nine troop-carrying vessels were then added to Suffren's fleet, which was soon ready to proceed to India.

Travelling with Suffren as far as the Mascarenes was Montigny, who had been ordered back to Poona to keep the Marathas on side. From there he boarded a smaller vessel bound for Goa, where, in October 1781, he crossed paths with Zain-ul-Abedin, an envoy of the Marathas sent by Nana Fadnavis to travel in the opposite direction to the Isle de France and secure concrete French assistance in their ongoing fight against the British.[46] Nana's previous appeals to Souillac for the dispatch of 2,000 French troops to Poona had gone unanswered by the governor, whose priority was the Carnatic, and in the absence of French help, the Anglo-Maratha War was turning in the EIC's favour. Sindhia's capital, Gwalior, had been captured, along with the strongholds of Ahmedabad and Bassein, and the Maratha general had been forced to accept a truce after suffering a heavy defeat at Sivpur. When Montigny arrived at Poona in November, he found the British trying to secure peace by promising Nana Fadnavis a share of any conquests made against Mysore. The Frenchman scrambled to prevent this détente but struggled to disabuse the Maratha leader of the impression that France was prioritising its alliance with Haidar Ali over its professed friendship with him—an impression strengthened when Suffren's squadron arrived in Indian waters and headed immediately for the Coromandel.[47]

The first engagement between Suffren's squadron and the British took place off the coast of Madras on 17 February. After a three-hour combat, the nine vessels defending the British city came off worst and were saved only by a turn in the weather and the arrival of nightfall. Suffren then proceeded southwards to Porto Novo, where 2,000 troops were landed. Their general, Pierre Duchemin, set about concluding the agreement with Haidar Ali that Souillac had initiated, with the help of André Piveron de Morlat, an agent sent by Souillac to represent French interests at Haidar's court.[48] The drawn-out negotiations that followed merit careful consideration, revealing as they are of both French intentions and Haidar's frustrations at this juncture. Souillac's plan was to secure Haidar's acceptance that, once the British had been driven from the Carnatic, France would retain control of all British territories in the province, plus an additional large area of land capable of yielding a colossal 20 million rupees of revenue per year.[49] Though the governor of the Mascarenes was later rebuked by Versailles for this request, it confirms that the acquisition of territory remained a part of French thinking as the conflict unfolded. Haidar, for his part, agreed to add 6,000 sepoys and 4,000 cavalry to the force under Duchemin's command and to contribute 100,000 rupees per month for its upkeep.[50] He refused, however, to pay more, remarking that he did not know that 'whites eat more than blacks'.[51]

Behind the disagreement over money lay conflicting ideas about whose war was being fought and which party in the France-Mysore relationship was ultimately helping the other. In their negotiations with Haidar, Souillac and Duchemin employed the habitual rhetoric of liberation to suggest that France was sending troops to India uniquely to enable Mysore and other powers to free themselves from British domination. It was natural, therefore, that the costs of the conflict be borne by those powers. Haidar was too smart to fall for such an argument, knowing full well that a successful war was as much in France's interest as his own. Moreover, he pointed out, his kingdom was in a much stronger position to realise this design than the French, who so far had done little more than talk about expelling the British.[52] With great deftness, Haidar even began to reverse the rhetoric of liberation, presenting himself as the protector of France's interests in India, his main concern to 'punish and destroy' its enemies.[53]

Putting these differences on hold, Haidar and Duchemin began joint action in the Carnatic. As Suffren again engaged the British Navy, this time off the eastern coast of Ceylon, their combined terrestrial forces captured Cuddalore, followed by the fort of Perumukkal. Suffren and his squadron returned from Ceylonese waters to target Negapatam, which had been seized by the British from the Dutch when the war began, and a third major naval battle took place. Its outcome was inconclusive, and British control of Negapatam was retained, but Suffren's reputation as a naval commander continued to grow. For the first time since the 1740s, France was mounting a serious challenge to British control of the seas.[54]

In July, Suffren then landed at Cuddalore and went to meet Haidar in his camp, just north of the town. Here the full extent of the Mysore ruler's frustrations with his European allies became clear. For almost two years, he pointed out, his kingdom had fought against the British without significant assistance from France. A small French force was now supporting his efforts, but its commander refused to listen to his orders; Duchemin's failure to follow the capture of Perumukkal with an attack on Vandavasi was cited as evidence. The supply of weapons and ammunitions from France had been inconsistent and failed to match the agreed quantities. Moreover—and most seriously—the large expeditionary force promised at the beginning of the conflict had still not arrived in the Carnatic. Without it, his army risked becoming overstretched; its presence was also needed on the Malabar Coast to defend Mysore against the British counter-offensive that had just been launched there.[55] To ram home his irritation, Haidar read out a letter that he had received from the commander-in-chief of the British forces in India, Eyre

Coote, and challenged Suffren to disprove him. The French, Coote had written, were 'a careless nation, without character, that never honours commitments or keeps promises, when they are opposed to its interests.'[56]

On the conduct of Duchemin, Suffren could offer little reassurance to Haidar, pointing out that he had no authority over the army. As far as the expeditionary force was concerned, however, there was good news to be shared with the Mysore ruler: following a decisive victory for France and the Patriots at Yorktown, Virginia, the previous October, the war in North America appeared to be won. A month after this victory, Louis XVI had signed off on the departure of the expeditionary force for India. It had set sail in December and had just made it to the Isle de France. What is more, the leader of this force was the Marquis de Bussy, whose fame was reportedly known throughout India for his exploits during the time of Dupleix.[57] Thirty years on from his march to Hyderabad to install Salabat Jang as *nizam* of the Deccan, and after almost twenty years back in France, Bussy was returning to India at the behest of his government, an ageing boxer coming out of retirement for one more fight.

A few days after Suffren's audience with Haidar Ali, an envoy, M. de Launay, arrived at his camp from the Isle de France to present the Mysore ruler with a portrait of Louis XVI and to confirm that the expeditionary force had indeed made it to the Mascarenes. The Coromandel, it was promised, would be its next stop. What de Launay didn't share, however, was that a serious outbreak of scurvy had spread through the ranks of the force during its voyage from Europe; on arrival at the Isle de France, half of the 6,000 soldiers at Bussy's disposal were hospitalised, including sixty-two officers, plus Bussy himself.[58] The stopover on the Isle was clearly going to last months rather than weeks. Though it was tempting to blame bad luck, the outbreak was more the result of negligent planning—a combination of overcrowded ships, limited medical personnel, inadequate clothing and poor food, not least rotting bread that had already crossed the Atlantic twice.[59]

Over the next few months, the conflict in southern India therefore dragged on without a major breakthrough being made. Suffren captured the Ceylonese port of Trincomalee from the British and then withdrew his squadron to Achin, northern Sumatra, to avoid another confrontation with the recently reinforced British navy before Bussy's forces arrived. Haidar, meanwhile, resumed the siege of Vellore, which had stubbornly resisted capture over the preceding two years. The effects of the war were now being felt across the Carnatic, with famine setting in and neither side spared from blame by French observers. 'The unfortunate town of Pondicherry has once again been the victim of the last appearance of the English', wrote one resident. 'All of the surrounding area has been ravaged, the population pillaged, and numerous inhabitants already reduced to very small provisions of rice have seen most of their stocks taken.'[60] 'Haidar Ali Khan has ravaged all the province of the Carnatic from Pullicat to Negapatam', wrote another. 'He took the families that could be useful to him and had them transported to his country. The small number of cultivators who remain do not have the heart to work the land.' At both Madras and Pondicherry, this second author added, the population was starving. In the British-occupied French colony, 'the paths are littered with dead bodies and all have died of hunger. It is horrifying.'[61]

By mid-December, Bussy and his army were finally in sufficient shape to proceed to India. Their illness-induced stay on the Isle de France had lasted a very costly six months. Haidar, however, would not live to see their arrival. In that same month, aged 62, he died of an abscess on the neck which the French surgeons summoned to his camp were unable to remove in time. The death was kept quiet while Haidar's son, Tipu, returned from military action on the Malabar Coast to be confirmed as his successor. According to the late-eighteenth century historian Michaud, Haidar's final instructions to Tipu were to use French help to defeat the 'all-powerful' English, without which their resources and army would eventually overwhelm the kingdom.[62] As Bussy approached the Coromandel, however, it was unclear if the new ruler would remain France's ally, with some fearing that he would enter peace negotiations with the British, in similar vein to the Marathas.

With his capital, Gwalior, under British occupation and the EIC's army advancing towards Poona, in May 1782 Mahadaji Sindhia had seen the writing on the wall and concluded a treaty with Governor-

General Warren Hastings involving the mutual recognition of territories and a Maratha commitment to join the British fight against Mysore. A guarantee was added that France would be prevented from establishing settlements in Maratha territories. In return, the EIC agreed to drop its protégé Raghunath Rao and acknowledge Madhav Rao II as *peshwa*.[63] The anti-British alliance assembled by Nana Fadnavis therefore appeared to be in its final throes, but in Poona the Maratha chief minister delayed ratifying the treaty to which Sindhia had committed. In June, a new agreement was even sketched out with Montigny, who remained present in the Maratha court, to the effect that neither France nor the Marathas would make peace with the British without the other. Plans for a joint campaign against the EIC on the western coast were fleshed out, and the concession of Bombay and Surat to the French envisaged.[64] Studies of these diplomatic manoeuvres usually conclude that Nana was playing a double game: the Maratha leader, they suggest, had decided to sign the treaty with the British but stalled, feigning continued interest in allying with France, to prevent a backlash from Mysore. Nana, after all, had made a commitment to Haidar Ali not to make peace with the British. A second explanation is equally plausible, however: that the chief minister genuinely wanted the alliance with France to bear fruit and was holding out as long as possible for the arrival of Bussy's expeditionary force. In this interpretation, the new draft treaty concluded with Montigny was genuine, and defeating the British still the priority at Poona.

The sequence of events leading to Nana's eventual conclusion of peace with the EIC adds weight to the second explanation. Bussy received a copy of Montigny's new agreement with Nana on arrival at Trincomalee in February 1783. By this point, however, the commander-in-chief, aware of the treaty that Sindhia had signed with the British, had already concluded that the window for joint action with the Marathas was closed. His mind was made up: the expeditionary force would land on the Coromandel Coast and concentrate on the Carnatic, prioritising collaboration with Mysore.[65] When Nana realised this, he signed the treaty with the British. France had failed to deliver its promised support to Poona, forcing the Maratha's hand.[66]

For the British, the conclusion of peace with the Marathas meant the opportunity to divert more resources to the war against Mysore. A new offensive was launched from Bombay that had its desired effect, capturing Mangalore and forcing Tipu to withdraw troops from the Carnatic. Ignoring French pleas to await Bussy's arrival, Tipu chose to return westwards himself to lead the defence of his kingdom. He took with him 600 French soldiers and most of his troops, leaving behind 4,000 sepoys and 8,000 cavalry.[67] A week later, Bussy's force finally arrived at Porto Novo. In light of this timing—with Tipu on his way back to Mysore and peace between the British and the Marathas confirmed—the proclamation announcing his arrival had a strong element of the tragicomic about it. France, it stated, 'having succeeded in redressing the wrongs suffered by the American Colonies from the King of England, and [having] delivered them from the tyranny and oppression to which they had been subjected', would now act to effect 'the complete re-establishment of the ancient government and free independence of the Indians.'[68]

In France, Bussy had requested a force of 9,000 troops and funds of 10 million livres to support them. 'It is infinitely better not to make any attempt at all than to do it in a half-hearted way', he insisted.[69] Versailles had acquiesced to two-thirds of this number of soldiers and provided half of the money, with the other half to be furnished in India by the Dutch. By the time that he landed at Porto Novo, however, Bussy had only 2,500 Europeans with him, with the others dead or still recuperating on the Isle de France. Combined with the French troops already on the Coromandel, this meant a European fighting force of just 3,000, far removed from his original projection, plus a few thousand sepoys. Reinforcements from Bengal meant that the British now had a decided numerical advantage in the Carnatic—a similar number of Europeans plus a well-trained sepoy army of 12,000–15,000.[70] The Dutch, meanwhile, refused to hand over the 5 million livres that their government had promised in Europe, leaving Bussy with sufficient funds to feed and pay his army for five months at most.

From Porto Novo, Bussy's forces marched to Cuddalore, where his headquarters was established. The commander-in-chief refused to go any further, however, before the support of allies was secured.

An appeal to Tipu to reverse his retreat to Mysore produced no results, provoking a diatribe from Bussy about the 'monstrous' ruler and his late father whom all the other courts of India detested.[71] He then reached out to Nizam Ali, evoking the illustrious history of collaboration between France and Hyderabad—by which he meant his own actions in the Deccan in the 1750s—before suggesting that the *nizam* launch an offensive to reclaim all of the Circars from the English.[72] The appeal was far-fetched and fell on deaf ears, with Hyderabad and the EIC at peace, and before long Bussy was despondent. 'I am without allies, without provisions, without means of transport, and in a country devastated beyond imagination', he lamented.[73] For most of the past two decades, France had had allies but no forces at its disposal. Now it had an army, however modest, but its allies had all departed.

In April, the British advanced on Cuddalore. Bussy sent his forces out to engage them on the far bank of the River Ponnaiyar and a bloody battle ensued. British forces then crossed the dried-up riverbed, forcing Bussy's troops to retreat within the walls of Fort St David. As the siege of the fort was prepared, Suffren and his squadron arrived, dispersing the British vessels in the bay, and Cuddalore was relieved. 'Do you need me to beat the enemy on land as well?' an exasperated Suffren asked Bussy.[74] In fact, it was too late for that. A few days later a British frigate arrived on the Coromandel with the news that France and Great Britain had signed an armistice. The war was over, without a serious blow being inflicted on British supremacy in India. 'Little is the advantage which this peace will procure for us', Bussy regretted. 'It will be difficult to preserve the reputation and glory of the nation.'[75]

*

If its overriding objective was to weaken Great Britain by freeing its North American colonies, France's participation in the American War of Independence must be considered a success. Article 1 of the Treaty of Paris, signed in September 1783, recognised the existence of thirteen free, sovereign and independent states in America—the United States—over which all British territorial claims were relinquished. France's direct gains from the war were minimal, however. While Spain was granted Florida and Minorca, Louis XVI's nation regained the Senegal River, lost in 1763, along with the Caribbean islands of Saint Lucia and Tobago, but obtained little more to compensate for its vast expenses in the conflict. In India, control of eighty villages around Pondicherry and eighty-one villages around Karikal—modest territories promising a total annual revenue of just £30,000—was all that could be secured from London, along with the return of Pondicherry, Chandernagore, Karikal, Yanaon and Mahé.[76]

The negotiations preceding the treaty are sufficient evidence to dispel once and for all the notion that France had no interest in re-establishing a territorial empire on the subcontinent. For Foreign Minister Vergennes, like Choiseul before him, the Treaty of Paris of 1763 had been a humiliation. When negotiations with the British government about a new peace began in the spring of 1782, his starting point was that, as far as India was concerned, the December 1754 accord concluded between Godeheu and Saunders in the Carnatic, rather than the peace of 1763, should be the basis of the agreement. In other words, France's losses during the Seven Years' War were to be cancelled, with the territories possessed in southern India just after the recall of Dupleix restored to the nation. The Circars would be divided up between France and Britain, with Masulipatam in French possession, and large swathes of the Carnatic would be returned to the French. The significant sum of 8–10 million livres of annual land revenue was mentioned.[77] Even if, as some scholars have suggested, Vergennes was ready to compromise on these demands from the outset, significant territorial aggrandisement was envisaged, including the recovery of some of the conquests made under Dupleix that had supposedly been disavowed.[78] The reality was, however, that France had not enjoyed the military success on the ground required to justify these claims, making it easy for British negotiators to refuse them. Beyond the concessions mentioned above, all that Vergennes secured was a commitment that French trade on the subcontinent would not be disrupted. Despite the minister's protestations, the humiliating stipulation of 1763 that Chandernagore remain unfortified was reimposed.[79]

As far as the Indian theatre of war was concerned, France's intervention had been a classic case of too little, too late. From 1775, money, equipment and troops had been poured into the conflict in America, but no corresponding investment had been made by the French court in India. When a large expeditionary force was finally dispatched eastwards, its prospects were undermined by negligent planning, and the best chance of defeating the British had already passed. For more than two years, the British had fought simultaneously against Mysore and the Marathas, but at Versailles this glorious opportunity to expel the EIC from southern India was not seized. With little difficulty, these charges of neglect and mismanagement can be extended across the whole two decades from 1763, with insufficient funds and resources preventing plans from being realised and commitments made to allies from being fulfilled. Haidar Ali's invasion of the Carnatic in 1767 and the outbreak of hostilities between the EIC and the Marathas in 1775 stand out as other key moments when more decisive support from Versailles might have produced results, but the French court was consistently slow to respond to developments in India and routinely ignored the advice submitted by its agents on the ground.

While Suffren and his squadron returned to France, Bussy stayed on to oversee the transition to peace, which was complicated by Tipu's refusal to agree a ceasefire with the British. On the Malabar Coast, his army had forced its EIC counterpart to retreat within the walls of Mangalore fort, which the Mysore ruler was now preparing to besiege. During the peace negotiations, however, the British had insisted that the restitution of France's Indian territories would take place only once Mysore and the EIC were at peace, and all Mysore forces withdrawn from the Carnatic—or, failing that, once all French soldiers, including Lallée's unofficial contingent, had been withdrawn from Mysore service.[80] To convince Tipu to accept peace, Bussy argued that the main aim of the conflict—the liberation of America—had been achieved and suggested that the peace agreed by the British and the Marathas made compromise prudent.[81] Tipu, however, viewed the Anglo-French peace as a case of European interests taking precedence over his own and vowed to continue fighting. Only when the French troops in his service were indeed withdrawn, on Bussy's orders, did Tipu reluctantly agree to an armistice and call off the siege. A treaty followed, in which Tipu and the British agreed to return to the pre-war status quo. As we shall see, however, the Mysore ruler was left furious about Bussy's acceptance of peace with the British and subsequent recall of his compatriots, which he considered acts of betrayal.

Arranging the restitution of France's territories was Bussy's last act. In January 1785, a few weeks before the restitution took place, the old commander's heart failed, and with his passing the last significant link between French India and the heady days of imperial expansion and collapse was severed: Dupleix, Bussy and Lally were in their graves, while Law de Lauriston and Gentil—plus Chevalier and Madec—had returned definitively to France. Under British occupation, Pondicherry had this time avoided being razed, but in a further sign that the end of an era was nigh, it and the other French Indian territories were now placed under the administrative responsibility of the governor of the Isle de France, some 5,000 kilometres away, and most of the French soldiers remaining on the Coromandel were removed to the Mascarenes.[82] The war had all but bankrupted the French state, adding a billion livres to its debt, and the retention of a military presence in India was now renounced in favour of spending cuts.[83]

In a final bid to secure profit for the crown from the India trade, the controller-general of Louis XVI's finances, Charles-Alexandre de Calonne, then resolved to launch a new Compagnie des Indes, granting it a seven-year monopoly on French trade with India and China.[84] The company differed from its predecessors in that it was backed by powerful financial interests in Paris and, intriguingly, in London. It envisaged buying Indian commodities not just from local merchants but from the EIC, to the benefit of both the British and French. In a revealing example of how transnational financial interests were able to work above national rivalries, the initial reservations of the EIC's directors, the objections of the British government and the scepticism of some French ministers were overcome. The commercial convention that followed in 1787 saw the British agree to sell fixed quantities of saltpetre and opium to the company, which also benefitted from an exemption from laws prohibiting the import of Indian textiles to France.[85] Within a couple of years, it had begun operations at Pondicherry, Chandernagore and Mahé. The establishment of a trading post at Canton followed.

Private French traders put out by this new monopolising corporation could console themselves that trade in other parts of Asia—just not in India and China—remained open to them. The years immediately following the 1783 peace saw trade between France and the Mascarenes pick up again, along with commerce in the western Indian Ocean between the Mascarenes, Madagascar, East Africa, the Arabian Sea and the Persian Gulf.[86] The trade in slaves was a major part of this activity. Over the preceding decades, the number of slaves imported to the Mascarenes had continued to grow, with the slave population on the islands increasing more than ten-fold to over 70,000 between 1735 and 1787. During the twenty years that followed, this number would almost double again to an estimated 133,000, as the demand for enslaved labour on the islands rose.[87] Though most of these slaves continued to be trafficked from Madagascar and the eastern African coast, approximately 10% were shipped from India, where recurring incidences of war and famine forced many to choose between slavery and starvation. Records confirm that at Karikal, for example, girls were bought for as little as 3–4 pagodas, with boys commanding a slightly higher price, and 12–16 pagodas received for adolescents and young men.[88] In 1789 British authorities at Calcutta and Madras announced bans on the export of slaves from Bengal and the Carnatic respectively, but to the extent that these decrees were enforced, they served only to shift the focus of French slave traders to Mahé and other ports on the Malabar Coast that remained beyond the scope of British influence. The opening of the Mascarenes trade to foreign nationals in 1787 meanwhile encouraged Arab, Persian, Indian and other European merchants to join in the trafficking business. The cross-over between European slave trading in the Indian and Atlantic oceans rarely figures in research, but as one recent study has pointed out, more than 42,000 enslaved people were transported on French ships from the Indian Ocean to the Americas in the final quarter of the eighteenth century, among them hundreds, perhaps thousands, of people of Indian origin.[89]

Regarding the overall geopolitical situation east of the Cape of Good Hope, French hopes of challenging Great Britain had not entirely been extinguished. In November 1785 a secret military alliance was concluded with the Netherlands that offered the French navy the possibility of continuing to benefit from Dutch ports, not least the Cape and Trincomalee, which had been returned to the Netherlands after the war.[90] In spite of the government's perilous finances, voyages to the Persian Gulf, Southeast Asia and China were commissioned by the Ministry of Navy and Colonies under Castries, who refused to accept that France could no longer rival the British. Particular interest was shown in Cochinchina, where military intervention to prop up the Nguyen dynasty clinging to power in the south of the country was envisaged. The expansion of British influence in Southeast Asia represented by their capture of Penang in 1786 was to be countered.[91]

In India, however, the outlook was bleak, with the British secure in their control of Bengal, Bihar, the Circars, the Carnatic and Bombay, and their most serious opponents defeated or pacified. In the north, the brief revival of Shah Alam's power was over, with the emperor incapacitated in Delhi. In July 1788, Madec's old paymasters, the Rohillas, would overrun the capital and blind the emperor, who required Mahadaji Sindhi's intervention a couple of months later to save the city.[92] Further south, Montigny remained at Poona attempting to convince Nana Fadnavis and other ministers of the value of an alliance with France, but the Marathas no longer set much store by French promises and were now interested less in liberating India from the British than in recovering territory lost to Mysore over the preceding decades. Ignoring French pleas to retain a united front against the EIC, Nana and Nizam Ali launched a joint Maratha-Hyderabad offensive against Mysore in December 1785, a conflict which the French, powerless, watched from a distance. A treaty concluded seventeen months later saw Tipu agree to give up a portion of his father's conquests to the Marathas, but the powers at Seringapatam and Poona remained at loggerheads. Soon after, Montigny quit the Maratha capital, realising that his influence there had evaporated.[93]

Perhaps the one encouraging development relating to the Marathas and Hyderabad at this moment came from the inauguration in the service of Mahadaji Sindhia and Nizam Ali of European-trained military units with French or Francophone commanders. While, over the preceding decades, the assistance promised from Pondicherry, the Isle de France and Versailles had consistently failed to materialise, there remained on the subcontinent European figures capable of providing more concrete support to these courts through the training and commanding of bodies of troops, inspired, at least in part, by the example of the French contingent at Mysore.

Benoît de Boigne was a Savoyard with a great military reputation who had served in the Russian army in the Mediterranean, with the French on the Isle de France and with the British at Madras, before entering the service of Sindhia in 1784.[94] For the ruler of Gwalior he raised two highly skilled infantry battalions which, over the next few years, expanded into an impressive force of more than 6,000 with recruits from all over north India. Beyond its discipline and organisation, which included the careful calculation of the number of cows, elephants and camels required to support the troops, what distinguished de Boigne's force was that each soldier was scrupulously paid on time. A medical corps was created to treat the sick and injured, who were even paid during their period of convalescence. Forming a highly effective partnership with the Maratha cavalry, de Boigne's infantry led the recapture of Delhi from the Rohillas in 1788, along with the seizure for Sindhia of the Rajasthani strongholds of Ajmer and Jodhpur. As a Savoyard, de Boigne did not identify as French and, throughout his time in Maratha service, operated independently of the French authorities. As we shall see, however, the army that he established would become a serious worry for the British.[95]

After British pressure had earlier forced him to expel Lallée's contingent from his service, meanwhile, Nizam Ali had come back around to the idea of employing French troops. In 1785 he accepted into his ranks Captain Michel Joachim Marie Raymond, who had learnt his military trade under Lallée at Mysore before serving as Bussy's aide-de-camp on the Coromandel. Made a general, Raymond quickly assembled and trained a force of 700 European-commanded sepoys at Hyderabad and from late 1787 re-established contact with

Pondicherry, pledging to use his position at Nizam Ali's court to advance his country's interests.[96] Though the threat posed by Mysore remained Nizam Ali's main preoccupation, the Hyderabad ruler appears to have been conscious that defeating Tipu might place the British in an unassailable position of dominance in south India.[97] The build-up of Raymond's force was one way to guard against this eventuality and counter British influence on his kingdom.

Beyond these glimmers of hope, the only ally on whom France could still potentially count was Tipu. First, though, the damage done by the abandonment of the Mysore cause in 1783 needed to be undone, a task for which a fresh envoy, Pierre Monneron, was sent to Seringapatam from Pondicherry. The new governor on the Coromandel, David Charpentier de Cossigny, wrote to Tipu to pledge his country's allegiance, and Lallée's troops reintegrated the Mysore army. Tipu did not so much forgive the 1783 betrayal as put it to one side in the interests of his kingdom. France and Mysore, he reasoned, still shared a 'common enemy', and to defeat them French support remained valuable.[98] Continuing the policy of his father, he requested Cossigny to provide 'as many weapons as you can get your hands on' and secured a promise of 8,000 guns.[99] Lallée's force was built up to a total of 5,000 and divided into ten battalions, each under a European commander.[100] The kingdom's foundries were enlarged and its state-of-the-art fortifications strengthened.

As time went on, Tipu revealed himself, like Haidar, to be an intelligent and original ruler who experimented with the modernisation of many aspects of his kingdom. The construction of roads, canals and dams—plus temples and mosques—proceeded at an impressive pace, while water was used to drive machinery in Mysore's own early industrial revolution.[101] In these developments, French technology and engineers were important. New investment was made in the maritime trading company that Haidar had launched, with trading posts established in the Gulf of Oman and the Persian Gulf, and also in the navy, with the ambitious target of assembling a fleet of 100 warships.[102] While trying to compete economically and technologically with the British—as well as militarily—Tipu sought recognition as the legitimate ruler of Mysore, to shed once and for all his family's reputation as usurpers of the Wadiyar dynasty. For this too, he thought that the French might be helpful: Tipu requested their diplomatic intervention at Delhi to secure Shah Alam's blessing for his rule; though the Mughal Emperor no longer controlled his empire, his formal approval of Tipu's reign would have carried a powerful symbolic weight. In parallel, Tipu sent ambassadors to Istanbul to secure recognition from Abdul Hamid I, sultan of the Ottoman Empire and caliph of the Sunni Muslim world, and began to refer to himself as sultan of Mysore.[103]

Tipu struggled, however, to shake the worry that the French in India were unreliable allies, a feeling strengthened when they remained neutral in his 1785–87 conflict with the Marathas and Hyderabad. The sultan therefore resolved to go above the heads of Pondicherry and the Isle de France and send an embassy to Versailles to 'render solid the friendship that has for a long time existed between our two kingdoms.'[104] The groundwork was laid with the exchange of letters between Tipu and Louis XVI. A rifle manufactured in Mysore was gifted to the French king, who agreed to cover the embassy's costs, and by mid-1787 the preparations were complete. Three ambassadors of Tipu would travel to France—Muhammad Osman Khan, Muhammad Dervish Khan and Akbar Ali Khan—accompanied by Monneron, in the first formal embassy of an Indian ruler to Europe.[105]

In June 1788, after a lengthy voyage and stopover on the Isle de France, the ship carrying the party reached Toulon, where fireworks, a trip to the theatre and a tour of the naval station awaited Tipu's delegates.[106] From there they travelled to Marseille and then northwards by horse and coach towards Paris, taking in Grenoble, Lyon, Dijon and Fontainebleau en route. In August, they reached Versailles and their audience with Louis XVI was staged. The great and the good of Louis's court, including Queen Marie Antoinette, watched on as each ambassador presented the king with twenty-one pieces of gold. Louis accepted one piece from each of them before a Persian verse eulogising the monarch was read:

> The universe, O Louis, admires
> Your glory, your grandeur, your immense power;
> To be obeyed, you have only to want it.

> Through your valiant Frenchmen, you support
> The unfortunate people that the English oppress.
> Through your many ships, all the people of India
> Find themselves saved from a destructive war.
> You use all of your care to make of the earth
> A contented family, a prosperous people.
> You have faith, O Louis, that this is your destiny.[107]

Once these formalities were complete, Tipu's specific concerns were presented. 'During the last thirty years', noted the head of the delegation, Muhammad Osman Khan, reading from a script carefully prepared in Mysore:

> the English have taken possession of land worth rupees twenty-six crores in the country of Carnatic, Bengal [and elsewhere] through collusion with the officials of the King of Hindustan, by means of deceit and treachery, and have committed much oppression and tyranny on Muslims and others [...] They have seized Pondicherry two or three times, and made most of the French there their captives and prisoners, and inflicted extreme tyranny and oppression on the French people.[108]

The events of the late war with the British were then recounted, with stress laid on the sacrifices made by Mysore to challenge English power and the limited help received from French parties. The rhetoric of liberation was reversed to present Mysore as the protector and saviour of the French, who were unable to defend themselves from English aggression. Upon succeeding his father, it was claimed, Tipu had delayed negotiating peace with the English 'in consideration of the feelings of the King of France', only to discover a few months later that the French, 'without informing our Government', had agreed peace with the enemy. 'Now we have travelled such a long distance to disclose the breach of promise and acts of disloyalty committed by your servants, since these unreasonable acts have perhaps been committed without your knowledge.'[109]

Tipu's other correspondence from the period suggests that he genuinely thought that Bussy might have made peace with the British in 1783 without the consent of Versailles. The Mysore ruler struggled to accept that a 'statesman and person of nobility' like Louis XVI would have betrayed an ally.[110] The conclusion of Muhammad Osman Khan's speech then challenged the monarch to make up for his country's previous failings. After presenting Tipu's offer to cancel the debts that France had accrued to Mysore during the war, the ambassador outlined his ruler's demands. Foremost was a new offensive and defensive alliance that would see at least 3,000 troops sent out from France. Second was the dispatch to Mysore of a group of expert professionals—among them glassblowers, textile weavers, porcelain artisans, watchmakers, gunsmiths, bombmakers, printers, an engineer and a physician—that would help Mysore develop its industrial and scientific capacities. Finally, in another indication of Tipu's originality and forward thinking, the ambassadors requested that one of Tipu's sons be accepted in France to receive his education.[111]

Louis XVI's response was as non-committal as might have been expected from a court that had never prioritised India and now found itself close to financial ruin. Agreement was forthcoming for the assembling of the group of experts, and a sample offered of plants and seeds from the king's garden, plus a specially designed collection of Sèvres porcelain. The possibility was raised of a commercial treaty involving a French monopoly on trade between Mysore and Europe, but the conclusion of a military alliance was rejected in favour of a vaguely worded accord of friendship.[112] For the contemporary historian Michaud, it was never likely that the embassy's main demand—a military alliance—be taken seriously. His compatriots, he regretted, 'always seduced by the attraction of novelty, welcomed the ambassadors more like objects of curiosity than like the envoys of a powerful ally.'[113]

Muhammad Osman Khan and his colleagues remained in Paris for the next three months, while a group of ninety-eight artisans and experts was assembled to travel with them back to Mysore. During this time, they perhaps enjoyed their status as exotic celebrities too much, running up a hospitality bill that even the court of France found excessive. Eventually, to the relief of Louis's ministers, the 'expensive excellencies' and their recruits were sent on their way, setting sail from Brest in November.[114] During the return voyage, the ambassadors had plenty of time to consider how to break the news that the embassy had achieved very little, but Tipu was not to be placated. When the delegation returned to Seringapatam in May 1789, the Mysore ruler was furious that no military cooperation had been agreed. The ambassadors then reportedly spent so much time at court vaunting the splendours of France that Tipu had them put to death.[115]

As it happened, the agreement of a more concrete alliance with Louis XVI would not have counted for much. As the ambassadors faced Tipu's wrath, the Estates General—an assembly of clergy, aristocracy, nobility and common people—convened at Versailles to present their grievances to Louis and demand far-reaching changes in the country's finances and politics. The events were in motion that would lead to the monarchy's end and signal the curtain call on French imperialism in India.

9

REVOLUTION

Every time an ocean-crossing vessel arrived at Pondicherry it was an event. While a fleet of small boats set off from the beach to help the ship unload, a crowd emerged from the *ville blanche* and the *ville noire* to gather on the seafront, speculating about the cargo and people to be landed, and the news that they would bring from Europe or elsewhere. When the *Bienvenue* approached the colony on 22 February 1790, however, few could have anticipated what a portentous moment it was, because alongside provisions from the Mascarenes, the ship brought news of a major upheaval in France. Not only had a national assembly been formed, marking a major political departure, but in Paris, the Bastille prison—a symbol of royal despotism—had been stormed and its prisoners set free, and a declaration of the rights of man had been issued. In other words, a revolution was underway.

The contribution of events in India over the preceding decades to the outbreak of the Revolution should not be overlooked. Ever since France's catastrophic defeat in the Seven Years' War, the state and its institutions had been under fire, with critics lambasting the corruption, unfairness and basic incompetence of absolutist rule. Instead of compromising, however, the monarchy had persisted in its absolutism and aristocratic privilege, inciting ever-more radical challenges from Enlightenment thinkers who incorporated their nation's failings in India into their critiques of its politics and economy. Military losses exposed the ineptness of the aristocratic officer class, they argued, while commercial setbacks emanated from the failure of ministers to embrace market forces, as the retrograde 1785 relaunch of a monopolising trading company showed.[1] Though the outcome of the American War of Independence had gone some way towards restoring national pride, it had come at too high a cost, adding, as we have seen, a billion livres to the national debt—a significant factor in the general economic downturn of the late 1780s and resulting social unrest.[2] The immediate reaction of French residents of Pondicherry to the news was one of concern: exactly where would this 'great revolution' in the *patrie* lead?[3] Within a few days, however, their hesitation had been replaced by excitement. The French population of the colony had long felt neglected by ministers in France—a sentiment heightened over the previous five years by the arrival in Pondicherry of representatives of the new Compagnie des Indes claiming monopoly rights over trade with Europe, and the equally unpopular decision to place the territories of French India under the control of the Isle de France. Protests against the resulting cuts in civil and military spending and the withdrawal of soldiers to the Mascarenes had ensued, with one petition claiming, perhaps a little melodramatically, that 'the ruin of our establishments, the total annihilation of our commerce in India, the terrible growth of English power, and our servitude in the eyes of Asia, maybe of the whole universe, are the inevitable consequences.'[4] Alongside accounts of the events unfolding in France, the *Bienvenue* carried orders to complete this withdrawal of troops, which, once it became public knowledge, all but guaranteed that the Revolution would be welcomed. 'May God ensure', wrote one inhabitant of Pondicherry, M. de Bury, 'that the nation finally takes care of a portion of its children so cruelly, so unjustly and so impoliticly abandoned.'[5]

Three days after the arrival of the *Bienvenue,* Pondicherry's own revolution began in earnest with a public meeting in front of the government house. The formation of a civilian militia and the occupation of the fort's arsenal were proposed, to ensure that if royal troops departed for the Mascarenes, they did not take the colony's weapons and ammunition with them. A general assembly was then constituted and a committee was elected composed of sixty-five residents of the town, with the popular merchant Jean-François Moracin as president. It was tasked with preparing a set of *mémoires* to be taken back to France and placed before the National Assembly.[6]

Over the weeks that followed, six were drafted. The first was a general lament about the situation of the French in India in light of the neglect and indifference of authorities in the metropole. To redress this problem, the inclusion of two representatives of French India in the National Assembly was requested in the second. *Mémoire* number three reminded the Assembly about the possible advantages to the nation of trade in India, and number four insisted that, to deliver these advantages, free trade was required. The threat posed by the English—'an ambitious people [...] who have never ceased to be our enemy'—was then taken up in *mémoire* five, whose object was to protest against the subservience of the French territories in India to the Isle de France.[7] To this end, it was argued that trade would only be profitable on the subcontinent if backed by political influence and military strength. The contention would, of course, have been familiar to Dupleix, whose recall four decades earlier was described as 'the greatest mistake imaginable' to French interests in India.[8] In the final *mémoire*, the formation of alliances with Indian powers was then discussed, in anticipation of future conflict with the English. 'A cannon shot fired on them by the French would for all of India be the sign for a general uprising in which all people would arm themselves and reunite their efforts to undermine the fragile foundations of their colossal edifice', the committee members asserted.[9] Tipu Sultan, it was added, remained France's most valuable ally on the subcontinent, on account of his implacable hatred of the English.

While three delegates departed for France to place the *mémoires* before the National Assembly, the inauguration of a new political order advanced. The remit of the general assembly was extended to all of French India, with Karikal, Yanaon, Mahé and Chandernagore invited to nominate members to its committee, reduced in size to a more manageable 27. In parallel, a Pondicherry municipality was created, with a mayor and council placed in charge of matters affecting the town only. Camille Charles Le Clerc de Fresne, the royally appointed governor of Pondicherry, had been in post for only four months when the *Bienvenue* arrived, but judiciously agreed to recognise these new institutions while awaiting instructions from France. Significant civil unrest was therefore avoided.

At Karikal, Yanaon and Mahé, the early months of the Revolution followed a similar course. Committees populated by the colonies' most influential French residents were created, and forms of power-sharing were agreed in which committee presidents usually had the upper hand over royal governors. 'The committee decides everything', admitted Governor Le Tellier at Mahé, noting with resignation that finances and justice were no longer in his control.[10] At Chandernagore, however, the Revolution took a far more confrontational turn when its governor, François Emmanuel Dehaies de Montigny, refused to recognise the authority of the revolutionary committee established in his territory. Montigny had been appointed to the governorship of Chandernagore after the failure of his mission at Poona, but quickly proved unpopular among the French in Bengal, suppressing a number of council positions and concentrating power in his own hands, in his view to counter corruption. When the Revolution began, he delayed appearing before the Chandernagore committee before fleeing with his family to the nearby Dutch colony of Chinsurah and from there to Danish Serampore, where an administration-in-exile was established. Chandernagore was now divided, with a minority of residents following Montigny into exile, while others pledged allegiance to the new regime. Montigny and his supporters edged closer to Chandernagore, installing themselves in the governor's country residence, the chateau of Goretty, on the southern edge of the French territory. Fearing attack, the Chandernagore committee then armed its citizens, creating a militia to which 200 sepoys were recruited. 'We would rather perish than return to the chains of despotism', it declared, as tensions rose in the summer of 1790.[11]

To diffuse the situation, the Pondicherry administration realised that it had no choice but to recall Montigny. When the order to this effect reached Bengal, the committee took matters into its own hands, surrounding Goretty and taking Montigny and his supporters prisoner. The hopes that Pondicherry had of re-establishing control over Chandernagore would be dashed, however, when the revolutionary committee refused to treat with Montigny's replacement, Benoît Mottet de La Fontaine, greeting his arrival in the autumn with the declaration that 'we don't need a despot'.[12] In part, the motivations for Chandernagore's assertion of independence were ideological: sharing power with Le Clerc de Fresne, the committee at Pondicherry was not considered revolutionary enough; leaders of the Chandernagore committee like Jean-Baptiste Richemont, a prosecutor in the town court, felt a greater affinity with the Isle de France, where a more radical revolutionary spirit had taken hold.[13] In addition, independence was about financial autonomy: by severing ties with Pondicherry, members of the Chandernagore committee sought to retain for themselves the returns made on the Bengal salt and opium trades, profitable since the Anglo-French commercial convention of three years earlier.

Through 1791 and 1792, the Pondicherry committee muddled on, trying to implement the Revolution's ideas while avoiding a repeat of the 'trouble' at Chandernagore.[14] Developments in France were copied as best as possible—with the unavoidable five- or six-month delay—and improvisations were added. In March 1791, word reached the colony that the National Assembly had granted two seats to French India, as requested, and that the monopoly privileges of the Compagnie des Indes had been abolished in favour of a new era of free trade.[15] Meanwhile, in Paris the writing of a national constitution was ongoing, the news provoking Pondicherry to begin drafting a French Indian constitution. Under its terms, confirmed in August, a very modern separation of powers was codified, with the governor holding executive power, a colonial assembly voting on laws and taxes, and elected judges administering justice. The colonial assembly—the most important institution in the constitution—was in effect the general assembly committee renamed and reduced in size (again) to just twenty-one elected members: fifteen from Pondicherry, three from Chandernagore and one from each of Karikal, Yanaon and Mahé. The principle of religious freedom was also codified.[16]

In August 1791, just after the constitution had been ratified, the *tricolore*—France's new national flag—was hoisted in Pondicherry for the first time. A further outpouring of patriotism followed in the spring when it was learnt that Louis XVI had accepted the constitution in France. Allegiance was sworn to 'the Nation, the King and the Laws!'[17] In line with developments in the metropole, the abolition of all titles of nobility was then declared, and the term 'citizen' adopted. State control over the church was asserted through the introduction of a 'civil constitution for the clergy' involving, among other things, the election of priests, provoking most of Pondicherry's clergymen to take refuge with the Portuguese at San Thomé.[18] Unsurprisingly, Chandernagore refused to accept the constitution that Pondicherry had inaugurated, instead preparing one of its own in which its claim to independence was enshrined. In parallel, the Chandernagore committee addressed an open letter to Pondicherry's citizens and soldiers encouraging them to rise up against their 'reactionary' government and all 'oppressors of humanity'.[19] Dissension among members of the Chandernagore administration saw some imprisoned on the charge of conspiracy to overthrow the Revolution, while Richemont and other powerful figures were accused of adopting the revolutionary cause only to take control of the colony's finances. A descent into anarchy was feared. 'The inhabitants of this *comptoir* have taken advantage of the Revolution not to rejoice in the advantages of a constitution but to free themselves from all laws, new and old', Le Clerc de Fresne regretted.[20]

Concerned about events overseas, the National Assembly then resolved to send officials, labelled commissioners, to each of France's colonies, their declared task to ensure that the colonies were being governed in a manner consistent with the principles of the Revolution.[21] Four commissioners were dispatched to the Indian Ocean, of whom one, Daniel Lescallier, headed directly to Pondicherry. Born into a noble family in Lyon, Lescallier had enjoyed a successful career in the colonies, serving in Saint-Domingue and Grenada before being appointed commissioner-general of French Guyana, yet despite his noble origins, he was a zealous advocate of the Revolution, whose correspondence abounded with references to liberty, equality and justice. On arrival in Pondicherry in September 1792, he found a colony of 'brothers devoured by the thirst for liberty' but, he suggested, in need of a guiding hand to help them quench this thirst.[22] Within weeks he had begun modifying the constitution to ensure its conformity with laws passed in France. The colonial assembly was dissolved and new elections organised. Le Clerc de Fresne was pushed to the margins as Lescallier effectively assumed the role of governor, working with the new legislative.

The philosophical basis of the principles that Lescallier espoused was, of course, a commitment to the rationalism and progress popularised by the *philosophes* and believed to stand in stark contrast to the obscurantism of the past. The supposedly universal applicability of these principles—at least as far as males were concerned—was captured in the first article of the 1789 Declaration of the Rights of Man and of the Citizen that 'Men are born and remain free and equal in rights.'[23] In France, however, the benefits of the Revolution would prove to be far from universal in practice. Not only were the rights of women ignored by the National Assembly—an exclusively male institution until 1945—but in the 1791 constitution the male vote was restricted to property owners, approximately 60% of the total number of adult men. The later adoption of universal male suffrage for men aged 21 or over, in the constitution of 1793, was never implemented.[24]

In India, as in other French colonies, the number of exceptions to the Revolution's universalism proved even more significant, because alongside poorer men there arose the question of what rights and freedoms to accord, if any, to men whose skin colour, culture, customs, religion, language and status as free or enslaved—or the identity of their parents in relation to these criteria—marked them out as different. (The possibility of rights for women was not even discussed.) Of the 30,000 people living in Pondicherry in 1790, some 28,000 were from a Tamil or other Indian background.[25] Just a few days after the formation of the general assembly in February 1790, a group of the highest-ranking Tamils in the colony, among them figures close to the French administration like revenue officer Nayati Mudali and interpreters Rajapa and Maridas, demanded voting rights and representation. When their request was dismissed, they prepared a petition for the National Assembly that read:

> A long period of living under gentle French government has transformed our heart into that of Frenchmen. We consider the King of France our own monarch. The colour of our skin, our dress, our language and some of the civil laws of our caste are the only differences between the French and us. Our heart is so attached and united to this nation that its happiness is ours.[26]

Abbé Grégoire, a radical priest who had already argued for the political rights of free people of colour in the Caribbean, took up the cause in Paris, reading the petition in the Assembly and concluding that 'having French hearts', the petitioners deserved the rights of citizens.[27] In Pondicherry, however, the majority of Frenchmen were opposed to this step. When the Pondicherry municipality was created in the autumn of 1790, the question was reopened. A small number of Frenchmen, led by the Marquis de Culan, argued that the Revolution's fight against 'tyranny' required the recognition that Tamils were 'citizens like us', but their arguments were rejected.[28] Tamils were therefore excluded from the general assembly, its committee and the municipality, while Culan and his supporters were labelled extremists. Some of them were even arrested and deported to France, where the National Assembly would clear them of any wrongdoing.[29]

A second constituency demanding representation were the *topas*—mixed race descendants of liaisons between local women and men of Portuguese extraction—who numbered approximately 1,000 in Pondicherry.[30] Several *topas* had been present at the first meetings of the general assembly in 1790, among them the wealthy merchants Joseph Alfonso, Thomas Flory and Charles Nicolas. When the rules of the assembly were codified, however, they were excluded, and their fledgling political rights taken away. The petition that they submitted to the assembly protesting this decision had little effect, and when the municipality was established, they were denied access to it too. Clearly, most members of Pondicherry's revolutionary institutions had no desire to share their newfound rights.

The ways in which these exclusions were justified merit careful attention, revealing as they are of the limits of Enlightenment universalism among Frenchmen in India at this moment. The starting point was a contention, outlined by the committee of the general assembly, that the universal application of the principle of liberty was inappropriate in Pondicherry in light of the 'big differences between different classes of men'.[31] Indians, in particular, were not yet ready for liberty, because they continued to live according to their own laws and customs. Their system of caste, moreover, meant that the principle of equality needed centuries to 'germinate' and was, for the time being, equally unrealisable among them.[32] In relation to the *topas*, alternative justifications for exclusion were required, because most were Christian and lived in accordance with French civil law. Arguments about bloodline were therefore resorted to: the *topas* were inferior, it was asserted, because they lacked French blood and because they were descended, for the most part, from lower caste women and (former) slaves.[33] It was therefore inappropriate to accord them full rights. This, it should be noted, was not exactly the same thing as an argument based on skin colour, because the rights of individuals born to a French father and an Indian mother (*métis*), whose complexion may have been very similar to that of a *topas*, were not for the most part called into question. It was, though, a race-based argument, in the sense that race was understood at the time in relation to male lineage, and ultimately it was French male lineage that mattered.

If members of the general assembly and committee hoped that Indians and *topas* would accept their inferior status in the new political order quietly, they were disappointed. In March 1791, a large-scale demonstration was organised in Pondicherry to protest against the assembly's continued refusal to change its admission statutes. Martial law was imposed and a house-to-house search conducted to find the instigators. A Tamil representative body imitative of the Pondicherry committee was then formed, and held several meetings.[34]

Tensions continued to mount as the Pondicherry constitution was prepared and then revised, with discussions centring on who exactly should be considered an 'active citizen'. In December 1791, the National Assembly in Paris decreed that in each French colony, local authorities could decide for themselves the rights to be accorded to 'free people of colour' and the 'non-free' in their territories—a concession reflecting the fact that French colonists around the world were generally more conservative on the subject than their compatriots in the Assembly.[35] The colonial assembly in Pondicherry responded by determining that only French men aged 25 and over who owned at least 500 rupees of property or paid at least 5 rupees of rent and had lived in the colony for one year (property owners) or two years (renters) would qualify for active citizenship.[36] Over the preceding months, Indians and *topas* had argued that their long residence in Pondicherry rendered them French. In other words, they suggested that domicile should be the basis for nationality, combining this with arguments about allegiance (e.g. recognition of the French monarch as their own) and assimilation (e.g. that they had learnt to speak French).[37] When the constitution was finalised, these arguments were definitively rejected and the definition of nationality by male bloodline—that only those born to French fathers would be recognised as French—was enshrined in law.

The numbers confirm what a significant decision this was, undermining any chance of the benefits of the Pondicherry Revolution extending beyond a tiny elite. Of the 30,000 residents of the colony, only 214 met the active citizenship criteria—approximately 20% of white people and *métis* and not even 1% of the total population. A small indulgence was offered to *topas*, who, if they were born legitimately to free parents, met the same property and residence criteria as active citizens, and spoke and read French, were permitted to vote in elections to the colonial assembly and the municipality (though not to stand for election themselves). Fourteen of the approximately 1,000 *topas* at Pondicherry were thus added to the electoral register, with a hybrid status somewhere between citizen and subject.[38]

In relation to Indian demands, the only constitutional concession made was that four representatives of the local Tamil community could attend meetings of the colonial assembly where matters affecting them were discussed. An appeal was issued in the *ville noire* for local representatives to be chosen. In parallel, however, the assembly doubled down on the rhetoric that Indians were fundamentally different to Europeans, and ratified this difference by confirming the preservation of separate tribunals for the administration of French and Indian law. What Indians needed, it was argued, was protection rather than liberty. 'The natives living in the colony and its dependencies, of whatever caste, nation or religion, are declared under the protection of the Nation', the assembly announced. 'France will respect their laws, customs and the free exercise of their religion.'[39] Despite the grandeur of the announcement, the rights enjoyed by Indians in Pondicherry hadn't changed in any meaningful way as a result of the constitution: protection in law and freedom of religion had been established much earlier in the century, at least on paper, as we saw in chapter 4. After three years of Revolution, Indians remained subjects rather than citizens, expected to benefit from the protection of French rule without exercising any political agency. Even Lescallier, who had set off from France brimming with revolutionary ideas, now accepted that it would be many years before the Indian population was 'ready' for more rights. Indeed, he rationalised, it was to protect the 'habits, religion and even the prejudices of the Indians' that the granting to them of the rights now enjoyed by (some) Frenchmen had been postponed.[40]

The local population was nonetheless expected to be grateful for the protection that French government provided. The alternative, after all, was 'the despotism that weighs so heavily on natives in the possession of the English and the princes of India', as one member of the colonial assembly put it.[41] Moreover, they were expected to pay for this protection. With trade disrupted, the Pondicherry and Chandernagore administrations were struggling for cash. Taxes were therefore doubled and 'forced loans' extracted from wealthier Indian merchants.[42] A new wave of protests erupted at Pondicherry when the administration refused to recognise the full extent of its debts to one of them, Pooniyar Vinayker Arombatté, whose supporters mobilised the 'whole bazaar' to protest against the injustice in front of the tribunal building. The diary left by one Tamil observer reveals the severity of the repression of these protests, beyond the official euphemisms of 'preventing sedition' and 'restoring order'. After martial law had again been declared, the army took to the streets and aimed two cannons at the protestors, while European residents carrying guns, swords and batons joined them. Locals were struck indiscriminately and several killed, including one stabbed with a bayonet.[43] In parallel, 100 soldiers were sent to suppress a peasant rebellion in the agricultural land around Karikal, where the French-appointed revenue collector Aroquiam was proving unpopular. The peasants were forced back to work after a violent campaign of repression, glossed over in the official account as 'a few examples of severity'.[44]

The divergence, then, between the declared principles of the Revolution—condensed into the slogan 'Liberté, Égalité, Fraternité'—and the experience of the overwhelming majority of residents of French India hardly needs reiterating. Perhaps more noteworthy is the almost systematic way in which, as the 'cult of liberty' advanced among the French in India, new exceptions to it were invented and justified, using arguments based on culture and blood. The course of events, indeed, suggests that, despite its universalist claims, the Revolution ultimately added to prejudices of nationality and race in France's Indian colonies rather than dissolving them.[45] The creation of new legal differences between segments of the population was accompanied by a hardening of social attitudes reflected in new efforts to discourage relationships between French men and non-French women, thereby ensuring that more men legally recognised as French (i.e. having a French father) were white.[46] At times, prejudices of nationality and race threatened to derail the Revolution altogether. The National Guard was supposed to symbolise the new political order's commitment to equality, with men of diverse backgrounds serving together to protect the nation. In Pondicherry, however, the formation of the Guard was delayed for almost two years by the refusal of white French soldiers to serve with either *métis* or *topas*, 'people whose blood is so inferior to ours'. Eventually it was agreed that *métis* 'who carry no obvious sign of mixed blood' would be permitted to join the Guard, while a separate company would be created for the *topas*.[47] In keeping with the hierarchies that the Pondicherry administration had codified, however, the officer of this company would be French.

In other French colonies, it was on the issue of slavery that the exceptions and contradictions of the Revolution reached their apogee. Calls for the abolition of slavery on humanitarian and ethical grounds had grown in France through the 1780s, with the formation of an abolitionist organisation, Les Amis des Noirs, in

February 1788 a landmark moment. When the Revolution began, however, abolitionist voices emboldened by the Declaration of the Rights of Man ran up against powerful slaving interests from cities like Bordeaux and Nantes and a widespread belief that slavery, particularly in the Caribbean, was an essential source of national wealth. The defenders of transatlantic slave trading in France argued that its abolition would lead to national economic collapse, repeating arguments made by slave merchants, plantation owners and other colonists directly benefitting from the trade.[48]

What happened next in the Caribbean is fairly well known. While the new governing committees established in Saint-Domingue, Martinique and other French colonies were dominated by colonial interests intent on maintaining the status quo, popular uprisings erupted demanding abolition and the granting of political rights to free people of colour. France's most valuable Caribbean territory, with over 8,000 plantations and half a million slaves, was Saint-Domingue.[49] The repeated uprisings here would eventually lead the National Assembly to declare all free men equal (April 1792), before abolishing slavery in French colonies in February 1794.[50] As we shall see, however, eight years later the abolition was annulled, as the French government sought to get slave-owning colonists—some of whom had even sided with the British against the Revolution—back on side.

In the Mascarenes, little studied in comparison with the Caribbean, the start of the Revolution was much more radical. When the governor of the Isle de France, Pondicherry veteran Thomas Conway, refused to recognise the assembly established on the island, the government house in Port Louis was stormed. The commander of the French squadron in the port, the Comte de Macnamara, was beaten to death in the street after refusing to sport the revolutionary cockade.[51] In the colony, however, there were now five slaves for every free person; the booming plantation economy relied on slave labour for the production of coffee, sugar and other crops, with slaves imported from Madagascar, East Africa and, in smaller numbers, from India. The institution of slavery was therefore to be defended at all costs, and with it, other existing hierarchies. First, free people of colour, among them sailors of Indian provenance known as *lascars*, were excluded from the assembly, and their request to set up a separate representative body turned down. In the island's 1791 constitution, only propertied French men were enfranchised. The colony then refused to accept the abolition of slavery decreed by the National Assembly in 1794, chasing away the two representatives sent from Paris to enforce the ban. Slaves in the Mascarenes, it was pronounced, had 'not the first idea of liberty or civil equality [...] liberating these savages to look after themselves would reduce them to their original primitive state, the only state that is really theirs.'[52] Moreover, abolition would 'spark a civil war that will not end without the complete destruction of one or the other, or even both parties', it was cautioned.[53] 'The slave liberated today will for one day be our equal and tomorrow our master.'[54] Resisting metropolitan control and largely cut off from France by British domination of the seas, the Mascarenes would effectively govern themselves for the next decade, with the new governor, the Comte de Malartic, forced to act in the interests of the French colonial population. Their slave regimes intensified, with new laws established to prevent insurrections comparable to those in the Caribbean: residents with suspected abolitionist sympathies were deported and the death penalty was introduced for attempts to incite slave resistance. Only once the 1794 abolition had been annulled in 1802, would French colonisers again accept a degree of metropolitan control over the Isle de France and the Isle Bourbon.

In India, at least, the legacy of the Revolution in relation to slavery was more positive. Its impact was not immediate: through most of 1790, 1791 and 1792 French slave merchants continued to export enslaved people to the Mascarenes from the Malabar, Coromandel and Orissan coasts, taking advantage of famine and poverty in southern India. The practice, Le Clerc de Fresne acknowledged from Pondicherry, reflected very badly on his compatriots:

> I admit that it is shameful for the nation that it is the only one to be engaged in this commerce. The quantity of unfortunates who have just been transported to the Isle de France is innumerable. This traffic is prohibited under threat of very severe punishment in Bengal; it is necessary that the same law be applied everywhere.

> It is in vain that we search to excuse the cruelty of this traffic on the pretext that these unfortunates taken or bought from their parents at a very low price would be dead if we had not removed them from the famine that is devastating the country. I think it would be infinitely preferable for those enslaved to have died rather than falling into slavery.[55]

In 1792 the National Assembly decided that it was time to act, instructing its commissioner, Lescallier, to outlaw the export of slaves from French territories in India and to ensure that the ban was enforced. Lescallier was enjoined to 'take the most vigilant precautions to prevent the commerce of Indian children of low caste [...] It is essential to finally put a stop to this shameful trade that the French, and only the French, have openly carried out for so long.'[56] The commissioner agreed, describing the traffic of Indian slaves as a 'degrading trade contrary to the principles of humanity'.[57]

Within a few weeks of his arrival at Pondicherry, he was putting the instructions into effect. In October 1792, a declaration was issued that from 1 November, the trade and trafficking of 'any person from an Asiatic nation or Indian caste' was forbidden in the territories of French India, at risk of fine or imprisonment.[58] Owners of slaves in Pondicherry and the other colonies were ordered to register them with the municipality before the end of the month, after which time any unregistered slaves would be liberated. Those deemed to be mistreating their slaves would have them confiscated and set free. This, of course, was not the same as the abolition of slavery—the possession of slaves remained legal, so long as they were registered and not mistreated. Nor did it prevent residents of French India from buying or selling enslaved Africans, for example. Progress nevertheless had been made, as shown by the liberation of ninety-seven unregistered slaves in Karikal and the efforts of the Yanaon police to ensure the 'humane' treatment of slaves over the next few months.[59] Unlike on the Isle de France, no significant reaction insisting on the unqualified rights of slave owners followed.

The export of slaves from India did not entirely stop—in early 1793, for example, reports were received of more than 700 slaves being covertly loaded onto French ships on the coast of Orissa—

but it was now at least a clandestine activity outlawed by both the British and French authorities.[60] War, meanwhile, was about to break out again between France and Great Britain. The resulting British domination of the Indian Ocean would strike a further blow to the interests of French slave merchants.

*

In the spring of 1790, as the Revolution in Pondicherry began, a new conflict between Mysore and the British was imminent. Its trigger was the decision of Tipu Sultan to invade the territories of the rajah of Travancore, Rama Varma, a British ally whose kingdom extended down the Malabar Coast to the southern tip of the peninsula. The new commander-in-chief of the British forces in India, Charles Cornwallis, welcomed the invasion as a chance to strike a blow against France's main ally in the south and consolidate the British position.[61] Tipu, for his part, had been preparing for a new campaign against the British ever since the peace of 1784, as his embassy to Louis XVI showed. It is, he confided, 'my steady determination to set about the total extirpation and destruction of [these] enemies of the faith'.[62]

As his army amassed on the Mysore-Travancore border, the Sultan requested French help in the pending conflict, writing to Le Clerc de Fresne at Pondicherry and Conway at Port Louis for military assistance.[63] With so few French troops left on the Coromandel, Le Clerc de Fresne was in no position to respond favourably, beyond a few vague words of support, while Conway's attention was elsewhere, as he fought a losing battle to arrest the gathering momentum of the Isle de France's revolution. Tipu therefore had to content himself with the long serving but modest cohort of French troops already in his service under Lallée.

With the Marathas firmly in the anti-Mysore camp, the key question was who Nizam Ali would support in the conflict. Over the preceding two years, signs had emerged that the *nizam* might be open to a rapprochement with Tipu Sultan, on account of their shared religion and mutual concern with preventing the British becoming too powerful.[64] This was music to the ears of Michel

Raymond, whose influence at Hyderabad had swelled since 1785 in line with the expansion of his army in the *nizam*'s service to 3,000 men.[65] As a patriotic Frenchman, Raymond was desperate to avoid another war between Hyderabad and Mysore from which, he surmised, only the British would profit. While trying to convince the *nizam* to side with Mysore, he therefore reached out to Lallée and his French officers, opening up an unofficial channel of communication between the courts of Hyderabad and Seringapatam.[66] Ultimately, however, Raymond's efforts came to nothing. As the British launched their response to Tipu's invasion of Travancore, Nizam Ali joined the Marathas on the EIC's side. Not only were the odds now firmly against Tipu Sultan, but the forces under Raymond and Lallée would inevitably be pressed into action against each other.

For Tipu, the Third Anglo-Mysore War started positively enough. A string of small victories against the British near Coimbatore was followed by an advance into the Carnatic, with Lallée's artillery decisive in breaking the defensive lines. However, the mortal injuries sustained by the Savoyard commander during this offensive were a portent of the reverses to follow. While Tipu's army of 40,000 camped near Pondicherry, and envoys were sent to the town to again request French support, the smaller force that the Sultan had left on the Malabar Coast was defeated by a British contingent from Bombay. Two months later, a surprise British incursion into the Mysore kingdom, led by Cornwallis himself, captured Bangalore, forcing Tipu onto the defensive. Joined by the forces of Nizam Ali, Cornwallis' army then pushed its Mysore counterpart all the way back to Seringapatam before shortages of food and ammunition forced the British commander-in-chief to retreat.[67]

A period of stalemate followed, with the British spending the final months of 1791 in Bangalore and Tipu in his capital. While Raymond wrote to Le Clerc de Fresne requesting Pondicherry to offer its support to Nizam Ali, so that he might rupture his alliance with the British, Le Clerc de Fresne dispatched missives to both Tipu and Cornwallis encouraging them to make peace. The governor was conscious that Mysore would otherwise suffer a heavy defeat, and appears to have convinced Tipu of the same, because before long he too was writing to Cornwallis proposing to send envoys to Bangalore to negotiate peace terms.[68] Cornwallis was not interested in peace, however, and was merely waiting for Maratha reinforcements to arrive before setting out for Seringapatam again. By the end of January 1792, a force of 22,000 sepoys, 15,000 of the *nizam*'s troops and 12,000 Marathas had been assembled, and began its advance on Tipu's capital.[69] After a three-week siege, which saw Raymond's troops facing those formerly under Lallée's command, Tipu capitulated. The punishing treaty that was imposed saw the Mysore ruler stripped of half of his territories and forced to pay 30 million rupees in damages, with his two eldest sons taken into British custody until payment was made. Added to the almost 50,000 men and 800 cannons lost on the Mysore side during the conflict, it was a crushing defeat or, in Le Clerc de Fresne's words, 'a shameful peace for a prince who has all along been attached to our nation and whom we have supported very badly.'[70] While some of the confiscated territories were handed over to the Marathas and the *nizam*, the EIC took possession of most of the Malabar Coast, including the lands surrounding Mahé.

In France, meanwhile, the Revolution was about to enter a new, more radical phase, making further conflict in India very likely. In August 1792, six months on from Tipu's capitulation, Louis XVI was accused of agitating to subvert the constitution and suspended. The following month, the monarchy was abolished and a republic declared, with the National Assembly replaced by an elected Convention. Louis was placed on trial and found guilty of treason. On 21 January 1793, he was executed in the Place de la Révolution. Before long, control of the Convention would be seized by Jacobin and other radical elements whose understanding of liberty and equality translated into the violent persecution of aristocrats, clergymen and others considered 'counterrevolutionaries'—a veritable Reign of Terror.

When news of the suspension of the king and the proclamation of a republic reached Pondicherry, its own revolution also entered a new phase. A 'tree of liberty', symbol of the new monarch-less political order, was planted on the parade ground in the fort to cries of '*Vive la Nation! Vive la République!*' (Long live the nation! Long live the Republic!).[71] The National Guard was finally constituted, its members swearing an oath to sacrifice their lives fighting for the French people and the cause of freedom. The Republican calendar was introduced to mark the beginning of this new era of liberty. Among the colony's citizens, however, divisions began to emerge, with some believing that the Revolution had gone too far. When the *tricolore* flying from a mast in the parade ground was torn down during the night, a group of aristocratic military officers was blamed. Though the ensuing investigation saw them cleared, citizens were warned to be on their guard against 'reactionary' elements in the town.[72]

In parallel, the international ramifications of the abolition of the monarchy played out. First, with the declaration of the Republic, France's attempts to export the Revolution—which had already seen the Duchy of Savoy invaded—began in earnest, and the rhetoric of liberation went into overdrive. Shed of its monarchy and regenerated as a republic, France would defeat tyrants everywhere and spread freedom around the globe. 'The republican revolution will soon deliver, in all the empires of the world, universal liberty', one official of the Convention, Pierre Louis Moline, declared.[73] Where the rhetoric of liberation had earlier meant returning territories to their 'legitimate' rulers by, for example, driving the English out of India and re-establishing Indian princes in their place, liberation now meant conquest and government by France, because French rule meant the rule of the Republic and, ultimately, of the people. 'The sovereignty of the French people', Moline continued, 'is soon going to be recognised by all the people of the earth, and the trumpets of fame will never cease to repeat to them that justice and virtue, the immutable bases of the French constitution, will forever be established among them.'[74] The conquests of French armies—renamed 'armies of liberation'—would ensure not only the 'power, grandeur and immortal glory' of the Republic but 'the happiness of the world'.[75]

The other European powers could not fail to respond to these developments. Before Louis had even been deposed, Austria had threatened to declare war on France in a forlorn effort to save the monarch and his family. France responded by twice attempting to invade the Austrian Netherlands, in April and June 1792, before

Prussian and Austrian troops entered northern France in August. The execution of Louis then provoked the entry of Great Britain into the conflict, along with Spain and the Dutch Republic. For twenty-one of the next twenty-two years, France and Britain would be at war. At stake in the conflict was the future of rival political systems—republicanism and constitutional monarchy—and different ideas about what constituted freedom and progress, as well as the European balance of power and the fate of competing empires.[76]

Among the British in India, the early years of the Revolution had been followed with alarm, with Edmund Burke's influential critique of events in France, published in November 1790, reportedly 'read with universal admiration and approbation' in Calcutta.[77] British authorities had made no attempt to interfere with the events of the Revolution in India, however, except in Bengal, where the revolutionary administration of Chandernagore was financially undermined by Calcutta's refusal to recognise its rights to participate in the province's opium and salt trades.[78] The execution of Louis and the start of a new war with France changed all that, triggering the British to quickly move to occupy the French colonies, in a repeat of events fifteen years earlier. Chandernagore was taken first, on 11 June 1793, its revolutionary government wound up and its leaders imprisoned. A week later, Karikal and Yanaon were occupied, followed in mid-July by Mahé. None of these colonies were in a position to defend themselves when the British forces arrived. When a land and sea force of 24,000 then encircled Pondicherry, the outlook was bleak; the colony had just 800 infantry, 80 artillerymen and 150 volunteers of the National Guard to defend itself.[79] The colonial assembly nevertheless resolved to resist. The fortifications were hastily manned and residents armed. A decree of the assembly announced that, having sworn to defend the cause of liberty, any citizen attempting to leave Pondicherry would be charged with treason and have his citizenship and property confiscated.[80]

The bombardment began at the start of August and lasted three weeks, taking out the French artillery and destroying many houses, yet even more important in Pondicherry's eventual capitulation than this destruction was the news that the British let loose in the colony of the execution of Louis, the first that residents knew of the regicide. Leaflets carrying a picture of the deceased king and the words '*Je meurs innocent*' (I die innocent) were dropped on the town, along with copies of the *Madras Gazette* confirming the details.[81] Those who already harboured doubts about the king's suspension now disavowed the authority of the Convention in Paris and urged negotiation with the British. Shouts of 'Down with the Jacobins! Down with war!' were heard in the street, and when most officers involved in the defence of the colony echoed this sentiment, the die was cast.[82] The articles of capitulation were signed on 23 August, and British forces entered the town. In the days that followed, some residents of Pondicherry wore signs of mourning for the king, and a memorial service was held in the Capuchin church. The tree of liberty was pulled up and the Revolution's most fervent supporters, including Lescallier, were detained.

In their European land campaigns, France's revolutionary armies enjoyed heady successes from the autumn of 1793, with the Austrian Netherlands and the Rhineland captured. Prussia was forced to sue for peace, allowing the territories on the left bank of the Rhine to be incorporated into the Republic, and after French armies crossed the Pyrenees, Spain was also brought to the negotiating table. The Dutch Republic was conquered, with the Prince of Orange, William V, forced into exile in London and a pro-French regime—the Batavian Republic—installed, before attention turned to northern Italy and Austria in 1796. At sea, however, it was a different story, with the nation's Mediterranean fleet surrendering at Toulon, and Corsica captured by the British. In the Caribbean, Martinique, St Lucia and Guadeloupe were also lost (although the latter was recaptured eight months later), and the capital of Saint-Domingue, Port-au-Prince, fell into British hands. The prospective gains in the Indian Ocean occasioned by the establishment of the Batavian Republic were lost as Britain declared war on the new regime and swiftly seized the most important Dutch possessions—the Cape Colony, Malacca, Amboyna and the other Spice Islands, plus the whole sweep of small Dutch colonies on the Indian subcontinent, and Ceylon.

The chances of a French recovery in India may therefore have been slim, but among officials in France, the subcontinent was not forgotten. Vaunting the liberatory potential of his nation's revolutionary armies, Moline reminded his compatriots in the Convention that the English had established a 'frightful tyranny' in India and 'exercised all sorts of cruelties' over its peoples, who required the intervention of the 'courageous' French soldier to set them free.[83] His suggestions were shaped by dispatches sent from the Isle de France by Lescallier, who, after several months of detention in Pondicherry, had been permitted by the British to return to the Mascarenes. While in Pondicherry, Lescallier, like so many compatriots before him, had convinced himself that Indian rulers held a much more favourable view of the French than of the English, and looked to France for liberation from English oppression. 'Their opinion is', he recorded, 'that the French are brave warriors; that 1,000 Frenchmen suffice to defeat 3,000 English. They also have a better opinion of the justice, the generosity and the selflessness of the French, guided by the principles of the regeneration [Revolution].'[84] From the Isle de France he now elaborated on this theme, arguing that his country could reverse the situation in India and 'bring about the fall of the odious colossus of English power in these vast and rich countries' if it made clear to the people of India that it stood for the principles of justice and liberty, rather than domination and conquest. 'Indians of all castes and religions' would then welcome France's return to India as a 'liberator'.[85]

Ceylon, Madagascar and Cochinchina were also identified as sites for the liberatory intervention of French armies—referred to as 'friendly conquests'—but India remained Lescallier's priority. Since the conclusion of the Third Anglo-Mysore War, the triple alliance of Hyderabad, the Marathas and the British had dissolved. This, however, was not really the good news for France that it may have appeared, with the Marathas and Nizam Ali too concerned with fighting each other to turn on the British. Raymond, who continued to serve the *nizam*, had embraced the Revolution's republican turn, and now commanded a force of 10,000 that had taken to manufacturing its own weapons.[86] The French officers in his corps wore revolutionary cockades and carried the *tricolore* into battle. The forces of Mahadaji Sindhia and his successor as ruler of Gwalior, Daulat Sindhia, meanwhile counted on some 18,000 European-trained troops under the Savoyard Benoît de Boigne, who over the preceding years had transformed the district of Aligarh in northern India into his own fiefdom.[87] When these two Francophone-commanded armies met at Kharda, 200 kilometres east of Poona, in March 1795, de Boigne's troops bore the red-and-white crossed flag of the Duchy of Savoy. The far-off upheaval that in September 1792 had seen the armies of the Republic invade and annex the duchy was transported to the green plains of Maharashtra, but this time it was the troops under the Savoyard banner, and therefore the Marathas, who won a decisive victory.[88]

The most promising ally for France consequently remained Tipu Sultan, despite the reduced size and power of his kingdom after his 1792 capitulation. The challenge was to convince the Mysore ruler that an alliance remained in his interest, particularly after the loss of Pondicherry and the other colonies. Moreover, how was the fact that France had deposed and executed its king, who after all was Tipu's ally, to be explained to the absolutist ruler? An official dispatch was sent from Paris to Mysore to report that France was now a republic.[89] Lescallier then entered into contact with Tipu from the Isle de France, recounting the Revolution in a positive light and assuring him that France would recover its position in India.[90]

Biographers of Tipu agree that the defeat of 1792 had a profound impact upon him. From this moment, his court became a more austere and religious place. He began referring to his kingdom as the '*sarkar-i-khudadad*' (God-given realm) and to his struggles against the British as a jihad.[91] Preparations for a new conflict against the arch-enemy began almost immediately after the humiliating peace; the Sultan aimed to recover the territories that he had lost, and dreamed—literally, as we shall see—of driving the British from the subcontinent altogether. The missives that he received from the Isle de France were therefore welcomed. Tipu was not naïve enough to think that France would defeat the British on its own, despite the reports he received of the successes of French revolutionary armies in Europe. Nor, however, did he have any hesitation about collaborating with a nation that had beheaded its king, if its amity was advantageous. While reaching out to other powers like the Afghan ruler Zaman Shah who might be brought into an anti-British coalition, he responded to Lescallier proposing a new alliance against the 'common enemy' that would see Mysore contribute 5,000 soldiers for every 1,000 French soldiers committed. When the next conflict began, the Carnatic would be targeted first, with Madras and Pondicherry wrested from English control, followed by Calcutta and finally Bombay. Once the English had been expelled from India, the Carnatic and Bombay would be shared between Mysore and France, while Bengal became a French possession.[92]

A treaty along these lines was concluded in April 1796 and dispatched to Paris for ratification but, with the attention of France's new Directorate government elsewhere, the approval was still pending when François Ripaud unexpectedly appeared in the Sultan's territories eleven months later.[93] Ripaud had arrived in the Indian Ocean as an officer in Suffren's squadron before settling on the Isle Bourbon, where he earned his living as a merchant and privateer. In early 1797, he landed at Mangalore and travelled on to Seringapatam where, without any official credentials, he presented himself as second-in-command on the Isle de France, come to make good France's commitment to an alliance with Tipu. It is unclear if Ripaud had planned this expedition, with Mysore his intended destination all along; he may have simply been shipwrecked at Mangalore and improvised. What is clear, however, is that he was a patriotic supporter of the Revolution. On the Isle Bourbon he had been a member of the Société des amis de la liberté, a popular revolutionary club, and soon after his arrival in Seringapatam, he established a similar club for the capital's small French population of soldiers and craftsmen.[94] Its members, who numbered just fifty-nine at the outset, were lectured by Ripaud on the constitution and the rights of man; the *tricolore* was hoisted, republican hymns sung and a tree of liberty planted. A new revolutionary code based on the laws of the Reign of Terror was introduced for the French corps in Tipu's service, involving the death sentence for anyone showing 'weakness' in the fight against enemies or weakening the courage of their comrades. Citizens were summoned to swear their 'hatred of all Kings, except Tipu Sultan, the Victorious, and the Ally of the French Republic. War to all tyrants, love for our country and for that of Citizen Tipu.'[95]

What did the 'citizen prince' make of these developments? The only suggestion of Tipu's involvement in the new revolutionary fervour in his capital concerns his reported participation in a parade of the *tricolore* through Seringapatam, accompanied by 500 cannon shots. There is nothing to indicate that he embraced (or indeed was fully aware of) the Revolution's ideas, although he did adeptly incorporate the title 'citizen' into subsequent correspondence with French parties. What interested Tipu most was the encouraging news about military support that Ripaud brought: the Frenchman convinced the Sultan that 10,000 French soldiers and 30,000 Africans were ready on the Isle de France for a new campaign in India.[96] From the Persian notes later discovered in Seringapatam, it is clear that Tipu's ministers doubted the veracity of Ripaud's claims. One warned about the 'disloyalty, bad faith and possible defection of the French' while another reminded Tipu that 'it is the custom of this nation to promise much and deliver little'. A third, blunter still, cautioned that the reported troop numbers in the Mascarenes were false.[97] Tipu, however, allowed himself to be misled and, at Ripaud's suggestion, commissioned a secret embassy to the Isle de France to confirm the terms of alliance for a new war against 'the oppressors of India'.[98]

Two representatives of the state of Mysore, Hussain Ali Khan and Muhammad Ibrahim, accompanied Ripaud back to the Isle de France, setting sail from Mangalore in the final month of 1797 with a cargo of Malabar pepper. If the envoys had doubts about Ripaud before departing, they were heightened during the voyage, as he failed to furnish them with adequate provisions and opened the sealed correspondence from Tipu to the Isle's governor, Malartic. When they reached the Isle in January 1798, Ripaud slipped away, while an audience with the governor was arranged. The envoys outlined Tipu's intention to 'make war against the English until not a single English soldier is left in India', and requested 3,000 cavalry, 3,000 infantry and 200 cannons for the purpose, plus more French artisans skilled in navigation and shipbuilding.[99] Malartic, in response, had no choice but to inform them that they had been misled about the strength of the forces at his disposal, some 700 French soldiers. No troops could be spared for India before reinforcements arrived from France.

It was perhaps in response to Hussain Ali Khan and Muhammad Ibrahim's disappointment at this news that Malartic then went off script. Ignoring concerns about the embassy's secrecy, the governor issued a proclamation declaring that having requested an offensive and defensive alliance with France to 'chase the English from India', Tipu wanted volunteers from the Mascarenes to enlist in his service. 'We invite citizens who may be disposed to enter as volunteers to enrol themselves in their respective municipalities and to serve under the banner of Tipu. The prince also desires to be assisted by free persons of colour.'[100] Despite a ship being sent to the Isle Bourbon to make the request known there too, a meagre eighty volunteers came forward, to which Malartic, after reflection, added sixteen army and five naval officers from his own ranks.[101] The embassy had produced no more concrete assistance than that which had been sent to Paris nine years earlier—and its unintended consequences were grave.

More encouraging news did, at least in the short term, come from the Mediterranean where, a few months later, France invaded Egypt. The idea of conquering Egypt had been entertained in Paris since the 1760s, when Étienne-François de Choiseul considered it. In the following decade, agents had been sent to study the coastline and defences and draw up plans for an invasion. In part, the motivations were economic: the Ottoman province was admired for its rich and fertile soil, which might be used to grow subsistence and cash crops. In addition, its Mamluk rulers were considered unpopular with the local Arab population and therefore deemed sure to support France's arrival. From the outset, however, the conquest of Egypt was also about access to the Indian Ocean and India. With its Mediterranean and Red Sea ports, Egypt offered a shortcut to the Indies for trade and the movement of troops—a vital strategic advantage. Proposals were studied for the re-opening of a canal to connect the two seas—known to have existed many centuries earlier—particularly after a Red Sea trading agreement was struck between France and the Ottoman Empire in 1785.[102]

The advent of the Revolution allowed a strong dose of liberation rhetoric to be added to the justification for the invasion: France would save the Egyptians from their oppressive rulers, replacing Mamluk 'despotism' with republican freedom.[103] The passage to India remained the real focus, however. Via Egypt, India was just sixty days from Europe, a third of the time required on the traditional sea route around the Cape, noted the French consul in Cairo, Charles Magallon, in 1795. 'Once we are masters of the Red Sea, we shall soon control the English and drive them out of India, if an operation of the kind is envisaged by our government.'[104] By early 1798, the mind of Charles Maurice de Talleyrand-Périgord, Minister of Foreign Affairs, was made up. Before the other members of the Directorate, he outlined his plan to occupy Egypt and then send 15,000 troops on to India, where they would join forces with Tipu Sultan. England would be driven from India and thus deprived of 'the sole basis of her grandeur in Europe'.[105]

In March 1798, the formal approval of the Directorate was granted, and Napoleon Bonaparte selected to lead the expedition. The Corsican general had risen to prominence over the previous two years through his successful campaigns in Italy against the Austrians and their allies. The conquest of Egypt and India and 'expulsion of the English from the Orient', as the Directorate's instructions put it, was a project fitting of his ambitions.[106] As his men and fleet assembled at Toulon, Napoleon pored over British maps of India and charts of the Ganges, convinced that 'the nation that controls India controls the world'.[107] In May, the expedition was ready to depart. Thirteen ships of the line, fourteen frigates and some 50,000 men set off from the south coast, capturing Malta before proceeding towards Egypt. As the coast of north Africa came into view, Napoleon addressed his men, hinting at the real object of their campaign, which had hitherto remained secret. 'Soldiers, you are going to undertake a conquest the effects of which on the civilisation and commerce of the world are incalculable. You will deliver to England the strongest and most painful blow, in anticipation of the moment when you can deliver a blow that is fatal.'[108]

On 1 July, the expedition landed at Alexandria, which was quickly taken. Three weeks later, a Mamluk force of about 20,000 was defeated on the west bank of the Nile and Cairo was entered. While Napoleon occupied the capital, a detachment was dispatched to seize Suez, locate its ancient canal and prepare for the arrival of frigates from the Isle de France that would transport troops on to India. Spies were sent into Palestine and Syria to study the viability of an overland campaign to India across the Middle East, Persia and Afghanistan.[109]

While the Ottoman Empire responded by declaring war on France, a very serious setback followed that cut Napoleon's forces off from Europe. At the start of August, the British naval fleet that had been pursuing Napoleon across the Mediterranean located its French counterpart at Aboukir Bay, near the mouth of the Nile. The French fleet was decimated in a surprise British attack, with only two ships of the line and two frigates surviving capture or destruction. As recent scholarship has shown, Napoleon's response was to redouble his efforts to win over the 'hearts and minds' of the Egyptian population by presenting himself not only as a liberator of Arabs from oppressive Mamluk rule but, remarkably, as a protector of Muslims from enemies of the faith and even as a Muslim himself.[110] In parallel, he accelerated plans to advance on India, with the overland route now his focus. 'It is the same distance from Cairo to the Indus as from Bayonne to Moscow', he recorded. 'An army of 60,000 men on 50,000 camels and 10,000 horses, carrying provisions for fifty days and water for six days, would arrive in four months on the Indus, surrounded by Sikhs, Marathas and the peoples of Hindustan impatient to shake off the yoke that oppresses them.'[111] After a further four months securing the reign of the Republic in Egypt—not least through the bloody suppression of a large uprising in Cairo—Napoleon was ready for this campaign to begin. In January 1799, he dispatched a letter to Tipu Sultan announcing that he was 'on the borders of the Red Sea, with an innumerable and invincible army, full of desire to release and relieve you from the iron yoke of England.'[112] A few weeks later, his army marched into Palestine.

What Napoleon didn't know is that for Tipu Sultan it was almost too late. In May 1798, a new British governor-general, Richard Wellesley, had arrived in Calcutta convinced of the need for more military action to consolidate the position of the EIC, ridding the subcontinent once and for all of powers who might pose a threat, and of the French troops supporting them. The aim, shared by the authorities in London, was to ensure that France could never again return to a position of influence on the subcontinent.[113] When news of Tipu's embassy to the Isle de France reached Calcutta the following month, complete with copies of Malartic's proclamation, Wellesley's mind was made up: a new and decisive campaign against Mysore was required. Tipu's request for a military alliance with France constituted an 'unqualified and unambiguous declaration of war', he recorded.[114] The proclamation proved incontrovertibly that Tipu 'entertained the design of calling in the aid of the French, for the extermination of the British power in India.'[115]

Over the next few months, Wellesley maintained regular diplomatic correspondence with Tipu, not letting on that he was aware of the Isle de France embassy, while discreetly preparing for war. As the Madras and Bombay armies readied themselves, the governor-general turned his attention to prospective allies, aiming to reconstruct the triple alliance with Hyderabad and the Marathas that had proven so effective against Mysore six years earlier. Back then, the French corps in the service of Nizam Ali had faithfully (if reluctantly) served Hyderabad and the British against Tipu, but now, with France and Britain at war, a repeat could not be guaranteed. Raymond had unexpectedly passed away in March 1798, probably poisoned by hostile factions in the *nizam*'s court, but in the final years of his life he had again sought a rapprochement between Hyderabad and Mysore, preparing the groundwork, as he saw it, for a French campaign to recapture India.[116] Meanwhile his troops had become even more patriotic, sporting the revolutionary red *bonnet* (cap) and sewing the word *liberté* into their uniforms, while their new commander, Jean-Pierre Piron, instructed them on the rights of man.[117] An essential precursor to the attack on Mysore, reasoned Wellesley, was to remove the threat of this 'French and Jacobin army'.[118]

Exactly why Nizam Ali agreed to enter into a 'treaty of subsidiary alliance' with the British at this moment is open to interpretation. With a new war between the British and Mysore pending, the *nizam* may simply have wanted to see Tipu Sultan defeated, despite the repeated arguments of Raymond and others that the British were the greater long-term menace. The very favourable outcome of the

1790–92 war, when substantial territories had been awarded to Hyderabad, was no doubt in his mind, and he may have felt that the EIC was too powerful a force for his kingdom to resist, particularly with the French extinguished from most parts of the subcontinent. Perhaps the anti-revolutionary propaganda disseminated by the British at the *nizam*'s court had an impact too. Some historians suggest that after the death of Raymond, a trusted partner, the *nizam* began to fear the presence in his capital of a force of 14,000 commanded by officers who swore allegiance to the Revolution.[119]

The terms of the treaty agreed between Wellesley and Nizam Ali saw the latter agree to dismiss all French soldiers from his service. In their place, 6,000 British troops would be stationed at Hyderabad along with an EIC official known as the 'Resident'. The *nizam*'s territories effectively became a British protectorate. A few weeks later, a mutiny of sepoys serving in the French corps was orchestrated; in parallel, British forces encircled the cantonment on the edge of Hyderabad where the corps was based, forcing Piron and his officers to surrender. The 'French army' was neutralised and its huge stores of weapons and ammunition seized. Piron and 124 officers were taken prisoner and shipped back to Europe.[120]

The final preparations for the invasion of Mysore were then made. First, the support of the Marathas was secured, with a promise of 25,000 troops extracted from *peshwa* Baji Rao II.[121] Frenchmen in Pondicherry suspected of leaving the town to volunteer in Tipu's service were detained.[122] As late as 4 November, Wellesley kept up the pretence of amity with Tipu, writing with feigned friendliness to update the Mysore ruler on events in Egypt:

> You have doubtless received information of another excess of that unjustifiable ambition and insatiable rapacity, which have so long marked the conduct of the French Nation. They have invaded Egypt, a country, from which they were in no danger of molestation, and from whose government, they could not even pretend to have received the slightest provocation [...] Nothing can more clearly expose their total disregard of every principle of public faith and honour than this unprovoked and unjustifiable aggression.[123]

Detailing the decimation of the French fleet at Aboukir Bay, he continued:

> It will no doubt afford satisfaction to every friend to justice and good faith, and particularly to every friend of the British Nation, to hear, that by the success of His Majesty's Arms, the French have already suffered for their injustice and temerity [...] Confident from the union and attachment subsisting between us, that this intelligence will afford you sincere satisfaction, I could not deny myself the pleasure of communicating it.[124]

Four days later, however, the governor-general dropped appearances and presented his grounds for war plainly to the Sultan:

> It is impossible that you should suppose me to be ignorant of the intercourse which subsists between you and the French, whom you know to be inveterate enemies of the Company, and to be now engaged in an unjust war with the British Nation. You cannot imagine me to be indifferent to the transactions which have passed between you and the enemies of my Country [...] a connexion which threatens not only to subvert the foundations of friendship between you and the Company, but to introduce into the heart of your kingdom the principles of anarchy and confusion, to shake your own authority, to weaken the obedience of your subjects, and to destroy the religion which you revere.[125]

On this final point, Wellesley was particularly insistent. Perhaps the governor-general genuinely struggled to understand how an absolutist Islamic ruler had ended up in bed with a regicidal republican nation committed to violently anti-religious policies in Europe. British figures who still wanted to avoid the war encouraged Wellesley to use Ottoman Sultan Selim III's declaration of war on France as a means of influencing Tipu. A letter was even extracted from Selim to the Mysore ruler warning that, having invaded both the Papal States and Egypt, the French were clearly 'bent upon the overthrow of all sects and religions' and their replacement by 'a new doctrine, under the name of Liberty'.[126]

In his responses to Wellesley, Tipu refused to admit the charge of 'intercourse' with the French levelled against him. Instead, he repeatedly professed his 'friendship', adding with similar duplicity to Wellesley that 'my friendly heart is to the last degree bent on endeavours to confirm and strengthen the foundations of harmony and union.'[127] The embassy to the Isle de France was explained away as a trading expedition that happened to call on the Mascarenes, while news of the French defeat at Aboukir Bay had, he claimed, 'given me more pleasure than can possibly be conveyed in writing'. 'I possess the firmest hope', he continued:

> that the leaders of the English and the Company Bahadur [the EIC], who ever adhere to the paths of sincerity, friendship and good faith, and are the well-wishers of mankind, will at all times be successful and victorious; and that the French, who are of a crooked disposition, faithless and the enemies of mankind, may ever be depressed and ruined.[128]

Tipu knew that Wellesley was not fooled, however. In December he commissioned one of the naval officers provided by Malartic earlier in the year to return to Paris and make a final appeal to the Directorate for support, while also again writing to the Afghani Zaman Shah about an alliance.[129] The news that France was at war with the Ottoman Empire, followed by the receipt of Selim III's letter, must surely have provoked a moment of reflection: the Sultan was, of course, also caliph, the spiritual leader of Sunni Muslims whose recognition Tipu had sought a decade earlier during the reign of Selim's predecessor. However, by the time Selim's letter arrived at Seringapatam in January 1799, it was in any event too late. More than 20,000 soldiers of the Madras army were amassed at Vellore waiting to invade, while a further 16,000 were on the move from Hyderabad, among them 6,000 of the *nizam*'s cavalry and 4,000 infantrymen from Raymond's disbanded corps.[130]

On 5 March, as Napoleon's forces in Palestine laid siege to the city of Jaffa, these forces, now combined, crossed the border into Mysore from the east, while a further 6,000 troops of the Bombay army invaded from the west. Bangalore was passed without resistance and it was only at Malvalli, fewer than fifty kilometres from Seringapatam, that a serious engagement took place. At some 36,000, Tipu's forces were only slightly outnumbered by the invaders, but by the first week of April they had been forced back to Seringapatam, which was duly besieged.[131] Within the citadel, designed by French military engineers, Tipu had 450 French soldiers—the remnants of Lallée's corps—on his side, commanded by another of the officers freshly arrived from the Isle de France, Brigadier Chapuis. Two weeks into the siege, they led a sortie of 6,000 Mysore troops, and high casualties were sustained.[132] When heavy artillery fire then opened a breach in the fort wall on 3 May, the end was in sight. At 1.30pm the following day, 4,000 British troops poured into the breach and began taking the fort. Tipu, on horseback, joined in the defence, sustaining two bayonet wounds and a shot in the left shoulder. As he lay on the ground bleeding, a British soldier tried to snatch his sword-belt. When he resisted, he was shot in the head and killed. The fighting continued until the evening when the palace was captured and Tipu's body finally identified. At least 10,000 of his soldiers had lost their lives.[133]

Over the days that followed, British officers sorting through the belongings in Tipu's palace made a fascinating discovery—a Persian book in which he had recorded, in his own hand, an account of some of his dreams. Of the thirty-seven dreams captured, roughly three-quarters concern his conflicts with the British and his desire to expel them from India. They range from violent battle scenes, like the burning down of a house in which British soldiers have taken refuge, to more abstract representations, like the depiction of the British as cows and Tipu himself as a tiger ready to pounce. For our purposes, however, one dream in particular stands out. 'It was represented to me', Tipu's account reads,

> that a Frenchman of standing had arrived. I sent for him, and he came. When the Frenchman came, I was absorbed in some business. But as he approached the throne I noticed him and I rose and embraced him. I asked him to take a seat and inquired after his health. The Christian then said: 'I have come with ten thousand Franks to serve the *Sarkar-i-Khudadad* and I have disembarked them all on the shore. They are well-built, stout and young.' I, thereupon, said to him, 'That is fine. Here too all the equipment for war is ready and the followers of Islam are eager, in large numbers, to prosecute Jihad.' At this moment the morning came and I awoke.[134]

Ultimately, serious help from the French had proven nothing more than a dream for Tipu Sultan, as for his father. Meanwhile his attempts to secure their support had been a key factor in his undoing, as the main Persian chronicle of his reign would recognise.[135] Chapuis later claimed that, while some of Tipu's commanders during the siege of Seringapatam were bribed by the British to stand aside, he and his French officers fought alongside the Sultan to the end; yet even if this is true, it was not enough. With the dynasty of Haidar Ali and Tipu Sultan extinguished, the British were another step closer to becoming the 'absolute masters' of India.[136]

*

Two weeks after the fall of Seringapatam, French forces in the Holy Land failed to capture the city of Acre from its Ottoman defenders, sustaining heavy losses in the process. The siege was raised and, with the bubonic plague spreading through his ranks, Napoleon elected for a retreat to Egypt. Three months later, the commander summarily returned to France, convinced that he was needed in the *patrie*. Though his army would remain in Egypt for another two years, they were henceforth on the defensive. The arrival of a British force to support the Ottomans in the spring of 1801 was followed by the surrender of Cairo and Alexandria that summer. In line with the terms of the capitulation, what was left of Napoleon's eastern army was repatriated to Europe on British ships.

Back in France, Napoleon required just a month to organise the coup d'état that saw him installed as the head of a new, more centralised and authoritarian government, the Consulate. After consolidating his power, the First Consul moved to confirm France's territorial gains in Europe, concluding a treaty with Austria that saw French control over the left bank of the Rhine and most of Italy recognised. Negotiations with Great Britain followed about an accord primarily concerning the Mediterranean and extra-European theatres of war. When it was concluded in March 1802, the Peace of Amiens dictated that Britain vacate the Mediterranean, including Egypt, and return all territories gained since 1793 except Trinidad (seized from Spain) and Ceylon (from the Dutch). In exchange,

France would withdraw from the Papal States and the Kingdom of Naples, and respect the independence of Portugal and the Batavian Republic.[137] During the negotiations, France raised the possibility of acquiring new territory in India but, as in 1782–83, this idea was rejected by the British.[138] The final treaty did, at least, commit Britain to return France's five Indian colonies, along with its possessions in the Caribbean. The Cape and former Dutch possessions in India and the Indian Ocean were to be restored to the Batavian Republic.

After eight years of very costly war, amid social tensions at home, both France and Britain had reasons to end hostilities in 1802. The Peace of Amiens was never likely to last long, however. In Britain it was criticised for being too favourable to France, confirming its dominant position in Europe, while for France it was hard to accept British domination of the seas and the shoring up of its maritime empire, the major source of its wealth. On becoming First Consul, Napoleon had made investment in the navy a priority and now turned his attention to the colonies. To get French colonisers in the Caribbean and the Mascarenes back on side, a law was passed confirming the preservation of slavery in colonies where the abolition decree of 1794 had not been enacted. Colonies like Guadeloupe and Saint-Domingue that had abolished slavery were then instructed by Napoleon to re-establish it as soon as possible.[139] In Saint-Domingue, these instructions fuelled a further wave of black resistance to French rule, culminating in the independence of the colony, renamed Haiti, on 1 January 1804.

With respect to India, Napoleon's first step after Amiens was to commission a naval squadron and 1,300 troops to ensure the restitution and reoccupation of Pondicherry and the other colonies. Its commander, Charles Decaen, was a veteran of the Revolutionary Wars renowned for his hostility to the English.[140] The instructions issued by Napoleon told him to act with 'dissimulation' to establish contact with different Indian courts and prepare the ground for a new conflict. If war was again declared on Britain, the commander had 'carte blanche' to acquire 'that glory which keeps alive the memory of men for centuries'.[141] By the time the squadron arrived off Pondicherry in July 1803, rumours were rife that a new war had indeed begun. Two British warships were anchored menacingly just off the coast, and a further seven patrolled the Coromandel. Acting on instructions from Wellesley, the British officials in Pondicherry refused to proceed with the restitution. Fearing attack, Decaen opted to save his fleet and retreat to the Mascarenes, leaving the Union Jack flying over the colony.

Before Decaen reached the Isle de France, confirmation arrived that the peace had been ruptured. France and Great Britain were again at war, and would remain so for the next eleven years, up until 1814. In Europe, the campaigns that followed saw French armies quickly occupy Hannover and Naples before troops amassed at Boulogne in preparation for an invasion—ultimately postponed—of the British Isles. The French Empire was proclaimed in May 1804, with Napoleon crowned emperor in December. The decisions of Russia and Austria to join the new coalition against France then intensified the continental conflict, culminating in the November 1805 French capture of Vienna. In the Caribbean, meanwhile, the Royal Navy started retaking control of France's colonies, beginning with St Lucia and Tobago.

On the Isle de France, Decaen responded to the declaration of war by dissolving the colonial assembly and declaring himself governor. With his squadron needed for the defence of the islands, and the states of Hyderabad and Mysore now firmly under the thumb of the British, his scope for action in India was limited, but some hope was offered by the reports emanating from the subcontinent of conflict between the EIC and the Marathas. His position threatened by rival Maratha chiefs, Baji Rao II had agreed a treaty with the British involving the securing of his position as *peshwa* in return for the permanent stationing of EIC forces at Poona and the guarantee of British input into his foreign policy. Concluded in December 1802, it threatened to turn the Maratha polity, like the Nizam's dominions, into a British dependency, inciting the other Maratha chiefs to rally in opposition.[142]

Among them was Daulat Sindhia of Gwalior who, as we have seen, had an impressive European-trained force at his disposal. By 1803, the size of this army had more than doubled to 40,000.[143] After the departure of Benoît de Boigne for Europe, meanwhile, its command had been taken over by the self-made son of a cloth merchant, Pierre Perron, who appeared determined to advance France's interests in India.[144] Perron, who had also inherited control of de Boigne's vast estates around Aligarh, referred to his troops as the 'French army of Hindustan' and had reached out to Napoleon to offer his services to the *patrie*. From the Isle de France, Decaen's obvious move was therefore to establish contact with Perron and, through him, with Daulat Sindhia, to encourage their defiance of the British and plot a future campaign together. One agent was landed on the Malabar Coast with instructions to head towards Poona, while another disembarked in Bengal with the intention of meeting Perron at Aligarh. In a testament to the reach of British counterintelligence, both were identified and arrested. When Daulat Sindhia, together with the Maratha ruler of Nagpur, Raghuji Bhonsle II, declared war on the British in August 1803, Richard Wellesley's priority was, unsurprisingly, to eliminate the threat posed by Perron's force. EIC forces advanced on Aligarh, where a short battle ensued and part of Perron's fortune was seized. Weakened by the defection of some of his officers to the British side, Perron then negotiated a safe passage out of Aligarh Fort and repatriation to Europe, with his family and remaining riches.

The balance of the Anglo-Maratha war was now distinctly weighted in favour of the British. After capturing Aligarh, they advanced on Delhi, where the remaining French officers in Sindhia's service were stationed under Colonel Louis Bourquien. More than 3,000 Maratha soldiers were killed in battle on the left bank of the Yamuna in a crucial British victory, and the Frenchmen surrendered.[145] The Battle of Delhi was not quite 'the last time British troops faced French officers in South Asia', as one influential recent account of the rise of the EIC suggests, but it did mark their final significant engagement in India during the period of the Revolutionary and Napoleonic Wars and the final battle between Britons and Frenchmen on the subcontinent that had any chance, however slight, of affecting the positions of the two nations in India.[146] In its aftermath, Sindhia too was forced to sign a treaty placing him in a position of dependence on the British, while the Mughal Emperor Shah Alam II was reinstalled in Delhi as a puppet of the EIC. The thrones of Bengal, the Carnatic, Hyderabad, Mysore, Poona, Gwalior and Delhi were all now under some form of British control. Without exception, each had been the object of French aspirations—whether projects of domination or alliance—over the previous six decades.

Back in Europe, Napoleon wasn't ready to throw in the towel just yet, despite these hard realities. In early 1805, he sketched out a plan to send thirty ships and 20,000 troops to India to create a 'diversion' from the continental conflict.[147] In the end, however, French forces in the Caribbean were sent reinforcements instead. The India plan was then dropped when the French navy lost a catastrophic nineteen ships at the Battle of Trafalgar in October. Two years later it was the project of a campaign via Persia that occupied Napoleon's attentions. In May 1807, with his power in Europe close to its peak, the emperor agreed a treaty with the Shah of Persia, Fath-Ali, by which all Brits were expelled from his territories and France permitted to use them as the base for an invasion of India, on land through Afghanistan or by sea across the Persian Gulf. In return, France would supply arms to the Shah, train his army and force Russia out of Georgia, which the Shah considered his territory. General Claude Mathieu de Gardane was dispatched to oversee the development of the Shah's army, training and equipping three battalions during his first few months in Persia, and arranging the construction of new foundries, arsenals and fortifications. In parallel, the island of Kharg, just off the Persian coast, was identified for a French naval base and plans were drawn up for an amphibious invasion of India via the Indus River, echoing René Madec's scheme some thirty years earlier. The treaty between Napoleon and Fath-Ali was flawed almost from the outset, however, because just a month later the emperor reached a peace accord with Alexander I of Russia that rendered impossible the fulfilment of his promises to the Shah concerning Georgia. When Fath-Ali realised that Napoleon's promise was hollow, their agreement was annulled. Gardane and his compatriots were expelled from Persia and the British invited to return.[148]

Having been alarmed by Napoleon's Persian initiative, the British now set about securing the northwest frontier of India, concluding treaties with the rulers of Punjab, Sindh and Afghanistan. In parallel, they started mopping up the remaining Indian Ocean territories still held by the French and their allies. The Cape of Good Hope was recaptured from the Dutch in January 1806, followed over the next few years by Amboyna, the Banda Islands and Java. Tranquebar, on the Coromandel, was seized from the Danish. Attention then turned to the biggest prize of all, the Mascarenes. The small but strategically significant island of Rodrigues, 600 kilometres east of the Isle de France, was seized first, in May 1809. For the next eighteen months it served as the base for an intermittent naval blockade intended to strangle the Mascarenes into submission. In July 1810, the Isle Bourbon was then captured with ease by a British force of 3,500 men and five frigates. Taking the Isle de France promised to be harder, and so, for the purpose, the British assembled one of the largest amphibious forces ever seen in the Indian Ocean, comprised of 6,500 men and no fewer than seventy warships. Decaen tried to organise the Isle's defence but, with just 1,300 men and a few ships at his disposal, it was a lost cause. Four days after the first British soldiers landed, the island capitulated, and with it the 'death blow' was struck to French ambitions in the Indian Ocean.[149]

The years 1809 and 1810 witnessed a similar collapse of the French presence in the Caribbean, with Saint-Domingue, Martinique and Guadeloupe surrendered. When Fort Louis in Senegal was also lost in 1809, France was deprived of its final possession in Africa. In Europe, meanwhile, it was the breakdown of peace with Russia and the ill-fated march to Moscow that saw the tide of the war turn against the French Empire, setting in motion the events that would lead to Napoleon's 1814 abdication. Exiled on the southern Atlantic island of Saint Helena, 7,000 kilometres from Paris, after his short-lived return to power in 1815, Napoleon reflected on the failure of his Indian projects. 'I had long meditated on a decisive expedition to India; but my plans had been constantly frustrated', he recorded in his memoirs. 'The army, when abandoned to itself and placed under the command of a clever and confidential [trustworthy] chief [...] would have renewed the prodigies that were familiar to us, and Europe would have beheld the conquest of India as she had already seen the conquest of Egypt.'[150] 'I have wished only for the glory, the power, the greatness of France', he added, to justify fifteen years of illiberal authoritarianism and devastating warfare.[151] For Napoleon, as for the French in India, the bid for glory had ended in costly and crushing defeat.

10

AFTERLIVES

The Treaty of Paris of May 1814 signalled the end of French imperialism in India. As after the previous two conflicts with Great Britain, in 1763 and 1783, the terms of peace included the restitution of Pondicherry, Karikal, Yanaon, Mahé and Chandernagore to France. In exchange, however, France was forced to recognise British sovereignty over all the territories of India where the EIC had established its control. Moreover, the stipulation of the previous treaties preventing troops from being stationed at Chandernagore and dictating that the town remain unfortified was extended to the other four colonies. France was forbidden from ever again dispatching troops to India, beyond a small number for the preservation of order in its possessions. Elsewhere in the Indian Ocean, the Isle Bourbon was returned to France but not the Isle de France—renamed Mauritius—nor Rodrigues and the Seychelles, all of which would remain in British hands until the final third of the twentieth century. Great Britain now controlled the maritime route to India as well as large parts of the subcontinent.[1] Unlike after the previous two peace settlements, the French authorities this time recognised that their days as an imperial power in India were over. No further challenge was offered to the British domination of India nor any further wars fought on the subcontinent against *la perfide*

Albion (perfidious Albion)—a name accorded to the British from the time of the Revolutionary Wars.[2]

As we will see in this postscript, however, the history of French imperialism on the subcontinent had many afterlives, its legacies felt for a long time after the Napoleonic denouement. First, it must be remembered that the end of French imperialism in India was not the end of French colonialism there. Pondicherry, Karikal, Yanaon, Mahé and Chandernagore were restored to France in 1816 and would remain French possessions for the next century and a half, outlasting even British government in India. Most accounts of French India after 1816 describe the five colonies as 'sleepy little outposts' of France, or words to that effect, suggesting that their economic and strategic value to the *patrie* was very limited.[3] By 1871, however, the population of the five colonies had grown to almost 270,000, of whom all but 2,854 were recorded as Indian.[4] The business of colonial government continued, with power vested in a governor at Pondicherry nominated by ministers in Paris. Revenues from land were annually remitted to France and only a portion re-allocated to French India, a steady drain of the colonies' wealth.[5] The importance of Pondicherry and Karikal to France was greatly enhanced when the conquest and annexation of Vietnam began in 1858. The Coromandel became an important stopping post for French ships headed to Southeast Asia, and Pondicherry and Karikal major procurement stations for labourers, merchants and others needed to support this new imperialist venture.

The Treaty of Paris also included a statement denouncing the slave trade as a practice 'repugnant to the principles of natural justice' and a promise on the part of France to outlaw slave trafficking within five years.[6] An ordinance from the French government condemning slave trading was published in 1817, followed by a law prohibiting it in 1818, but in the Indian Ocean the ban had little impact, at least during the first decade. Research has established that some 107,000 enslaved people were shipped to the Isle Bourbon and British Mauritius between 1810 and the early 1830s to meet the demand of the islands' predominantly French plantation owners. Most of the slaves came from Africa, Madagascar and Southeast Asia, though some continued to be exported from India until at least 1830.[7]

Ultimately, it was the abolition of the institution of slavery (rather than the prohibition of the slave trade) that finally put paid to French slave trafficking in the Indian Ocean—an abolition announced for British colonies in 1833 and French colonies in 1848. Even this, however, constituted qualified progress only, with the slave trade replaced by a system of indentured labour that saw impoverished Indians commit to a minimum of five years of work in British and French colonies now deprived of slaves in return for a free passage and a mediocre wage. Pondicherry and Karikal were key recruitment centres for indentured labourers sent to British Mauritius, the Isle Bourbon, Martinique, Guadeloupe and Guiana over the decades that followed. Almost 194,000 indentured Indians had been shipped to the French colonies when the government of British India, flexing its strength over Pondicherry, finally bowed to the pressure of humanitarian campaigners to prohibit the export of labourers to the French colonies in 1888.[8] However, indentured Indians continued to be sent to Mauritius right up until the abolition of indenture in 1920, with almost half a million arriving on the island in total.[9]

Despite France's reduced circumstances on the subcontinent, India would occupy a large position in the French imagination as the nineteenth century progressed. In popular culture, a consistent flow of novels, travelogues, poems, plays, operas and artworks were produced for public consumption, developing tropes of India as an exotic, spiritual and timeless land peopled with tyrannic sultans, fakirs, snake charmers, alluring women and so forth.[10] In parallel, the serious academic study of India developed, beginning with the creation of a professorship in Indology at the Collège de France in 1815. For the next few decades, Paris was the European centre of Indological studies, the city to which scholars learning Sanskrit flocked. After the failure of its project to control India politically, suggests recent scholarship, France was determined to make sure that it led the European 'intellectual conquest' of India, through the study of manuscripts shipped back from Pondicherry and elsewhere.[11] While tropes about snake charmers and alluring women were (mostly) avoided in this more serious work, the scholarship produced helped construct the idea that India was an ancient but fallen civilisation in need of European intervention to put it on the path towards modernity.

In parallel, the rewriting of the history of French India continued—particularly after the advent of the July Monarchy in 1830. Central to this was the ongoing restoration of the reputation of Joseph François Dupleix, which, as we have seen, began soon after the defeat of 1763. With his policies of imperial expansion, Dupleix was now heralded as a visionary. His recall was a damning indictment of ministers of the *ancien régime* and of the equally dim-witted directors of the long-buried Compagnie. It was because of them that French rule over India had been lost. In part, such writing was an exercise in nostalgia, full of wistful reflections on the glory that could have been. In a more sinister turn, however, historiography about French India was also mobilised to support a new wave of imperial expansion in Algeria, Tahiti, mainland Senegal and Vietnam—the first two under the July Monarch (1830–48) and the latter two during the years of the Second Empire (1852–70). The aim of histories of French India produced in these periods, which invariably focused on the 'glory' years of imperial expansion and the 'betrayal' of Dupleix that followed, was to inspire patriotism in French readers and show that France could be a global power again now that its government was on the right side. France's new colonies would compensate for the lost Indian empire, and ultimately allow British supremacy to be challenged in other parts of the world.[12]

In Pondicherry, the rehabilitation of Dupleix was symbolically completed in 1870 when the statue of the former governor discussed in the opening chapter was raised in the square opposite the government house of French India on a set of ornamental pillars plundered from a temple at Gingee during the Carnatic Wars. The square was renamed the Place Dupleix. A second statue of Dupleix was displayed on the Champs-Elysées in 1887 before taking pride of place in front of the *hôtel de ville* in his hometown of Landrecies, where it still stands today.[13] The context was a further round of imperial conquest—this time under the Third Republic (1870–1940), as Tunisia and Morocco were annexed and territories in Vietnam and West Africa expanded and consolidated before the end of the century. In official discourse and the popular imagination,

Dupleix was now elevated to the status of a national hero, his actions celebrated by the partisans of French imperialism. In 1894, a Comité Dupleix (Dupleix Committee) was even founded to lobby for further overseas expansion. Historians depicted Dupleix as a genius and a martyr, seeking to inspire a new generation of empire builders. They drew conclusions about the failure of French efforts in India designed to prevent the committing of similar mistakes in the colonies of France's new empire.[14] The production of pro-imperial historiography on French India continued into the twentieth century, led by historians who were deeply implicated in the colonial and imperial projects of their day. Indeed, the foremost historian of French India of the 1910s and 1920s, Alfred Martineau, spent six years as governor at Pondicherry (1910–11 and 1913–18)—after a decade serving in French Somaliland, Mayotte and Gabon—before accepting a professorship at the Collège de France. The historical works that he produced centred on the heady days of imperial expansion and collapse, including at least five volumes on Dupleix and one on Bussy.[15]

During the years of the Third Republic, new European ideas about race would also enter historiography on French India: Indian civilisation had fallen into decline because of the mixing of Aryans with people of inferior racial stock; the conquests of Dupleix had been the natural expansion of a superior European race.[16] These racial theories—which also served to justify the new wave of imperial expansion—were mostly expounded by conservatives on the right and far right. Within the Third Republic, they were eclipsed by enthusiasm among 'progressives' for spreading French civilisation among non-European peoples, which became the prime justification for French colonialism around the world after 1870. The influence of the history of French India on the development of this global civilising mission should not be underestimated: from the activities of French missionaries to the notion of exporting the blessings of the Revolution, the idea of improving a colonised land through the importing of aspects of French civilisation had a long genealogy in India. The universalism of the French Enlightenment, on the basis of which the Third Republic's civilising mission was constructed, was partly shaped by the writings of the *philosophes* on India. Furthermore, that *mission civilisatrice* was founded on an assumed contrast between British and French colonialism—the former selfish and exploitative, motivated solely by money, and the latter benevolent and beneficial, motivated by loftier ideals—that had been greatly influenced by events in eighteenth-century India and their subsequent retelling.[17]

The people of the five colonies of French India did not escape from these civilising efforts. A society ridden by caste divisions would be replaced by one of equality, advocates promised. Backward beliefs and superstitions would be eclipsed by the reign of reason. To this end, a more extensive network of schools was created in French India. Control of the schools was gradually taken out of the hands of the Jesuits in favour of direct government control, and the curricula were revised to instil Republican values. A proliferation of new French and dual language (e.g. French-Tamil) newspapers were launched, often with overtly pedagogical intentions. Elections on the basis of universal male suffrage were introduced for the nomination of the representative of French India to the National Assembly and the choosing of members of the Pondicherry and local councils, though the creation of different electoral lists ensured that at least half of the seats in the councils were controlled by Europeans.[18]

The culmination of these initiatives was the introduction of a new law in 1881 giving all male residents of French India the right to acquire French citizenship (which would automatically apply to a man's wife and children as well). The right to citizenship would henceforth be separate from a person's ancestry, skin colour, religion or caste, though gender (and age) determined who got to choose.[19] However, the acquisition of French citizenship was dependent on a person adopting a French name and renouncing their existing personal laws—which recognised distinctions of religion and caste—in favour of the French civil code. In other words, citizenship was conditional on assimilation, with being-French supposed to take precedence over religious and caste identities. Those who chose French citizenship—labelled *renonçants*—were mostly lower caste residents of Pondicherry and Karikal, many of whom had already converted to Catholicism.[20]

In the early twentieth century, Pondicherry and Chandernagore became refuges for nationalists from other parts of India wanted by

British authorities, including Bengali revolutionaries who had taken up arms against the oppressor. The most well-known was Aurobindo Ghose (later Sri Aurobindo), who arrived in Pondicherry in 1910 with an arrest warrant for sedition against his name. In Pondicherry, Ghose would turn to spirituality, founding an ashram dedicated to his philosophy of Integral Yoga that flourishes to this day.[21] For the French authorities, the arrival of freedom fighters from British India was a blessing; granting them asylum was an opportunity to irk the British while claiming a principled commitment to the cause of *liberté*. The rhetoric that France was a 'friend' of India committed to its liberation from oppressive English rule—which, as we have seen, first emerged in the decades after 1763—was recycled and adopted by nationalist leaders too.[22] In the interwar period, Paris would become a centre of Indian nationalist activity as well.

For as long as the focus of Indian nationalists remained British India, the continued French presence on the subcontinent got a free pass. However, the British announcement in 1946 that they would leave India within a year was the cue for liberation movements in the French colonies to be launched, with organisations like the French India National Congress and the National Liberation Front inaugurated.[23] The aim was to deliver India from the last vestiges of European colonialism and 'give a death blow to French imperialism', with the ongoing nationalist struggles in Vietnam and Algeria in mind.[24] After August 1947, the government of independent India also began to demand that the French leave. 'The Indian people cannot accept the continuance of foreign rule over Indian soil', wrote one minister to the French government.[25] 'May I ask your Excellency, in all humility, if he would permit Indian rule over Toulon, Calais or Marseille?' enquired another.[26]

What followed confirms that, although no large-scale conflict erupted comparable to those that would eventually force France out of Vietnam and Algeria, the end of French India was far from a peaceful, consensual process: France would not relinquish control over its Indian colonies without being pushed. First came an announcement in the summer of 1948 that the future of French India would be decided by a referendum in each colony in which all adult residents could vote. Historians have typically heralded this as a 'triumph for democratic ideals' founded on the principle that 'the will of the people must decide', in line with the constitution of France's new Fourth Republic.[27] However, no date was set for the referenda. Promising them was a way for the French authorities to postpone their departure from India while using the language of democracy and distancing themselves from the hard-line stance against decolonisation adopted by the Portuguese in Goa.[28] Moreover, by planning a separate referendum in each colony, France kept open the possibility of retaining some of its Indian possessions while losing others, as an important revisionist work on the decolonisation of French India has recently pointed out.[29]

Political and popular divisions now began to emerge, with nationalist campaigners backed by supporters from independent India facing opposition from those who favoured the preservation of the status quo. Some no doubt had a real affinity with France, among them individuals of mixed French-Indian descent, converts to Catholicism and *renonçants*. Others feared the loss of jobs and pensions linked to service in the French administration, or worried about the economic consequences of the end of French rule. As pro-merger activity intensified, the authorities in Pondicherry banned public gatherings, the dissemination of printed tracts and the spread of 'propaganda' by loudspeaker, parking their commitment to democratic ideals. Nationalist leaders were arrested and faced intimidation by the police.

The first major flashpoint was at Mahé in October 1948 when a protest over voter registration for the colony's forthcoming election escalated. The government house was surrounded and occupied, and the French administrator detained. An Indian flag was hoisted on the building and the integration of Mahé with India announced. A week later, a French warship arrived on the Malabar Coast and unloaded a small body of troops to reoccupy the town, forcing the instigators of this 'October Revolution' to flee.[30] Attention then shifted to Chandernagore, where nationalist sentiment appeared strongest. Recognising that all hope of holding on to the colony was lost, France consented to the staging of the promised referendum in June 1949. Its results were an emphatic rejection of French colonialism and its assimilationist aspirations in Bengal, with 7,417 voters electing for the merger with India and just 112 for continued union with France.[31] The de facto transfer of Chandernagore to the Indian Union took place a year later, in May 1950, though it would be a further four years before this handover was ratified in France.

In Pondicherry, the years 1950 to 1954 saw a worsening spiral of violence: both pro-merger activists and the French authorities were accused of hiring groups of armed men to intimidate their opponents, while the Pondicherry police continued to target nationalist leaders and their sympathisers. Before long, popular protests in favour of union with India had spread to Karikal and Yanaon; in the latter, the French administrator was forced out and the Indian flag raised, in scenes similar to those in Mahé, before French control was reasserted. Hopes that the outcome in Chandernagore would accelerate the holding of the other referenda were therefore disappointed. Their continued deferral was justified by French authorities with the argument that holding free and fair votes was impossible amid the widespread 'agitation'. When France landed more armed police in Pondicherry following a mass pro-merger rally in April 1954, the Government of India protested that such a move contravened the rules prohibiting the build-up of troops in the colony inscribed in the Treaty of Paris of 1814![32]

In the end, the fate of what remained of French India would be decided through diplomacy rather than democratic processes. To force France to the negotiating table, the Indian government withheld electricity and petroleum supplies to Pondicherry and Karikal, restricted cross-border travel and tightened customs regulations, squeezing the colonies economically. Talks in Paris in May 1954 produced no immediate breakthrough, but the fall of the French garrison at Dien Bien Phu in Vietnam in that same month and France's resulting withdrawal from Southeast Asia forced a re-think. France threw in the towel and agreed to the de facto handover of its remaining Indian territories pending the conclusion of a formal treaty. In November 1954, this handover was enacted, with the French flag lowered in Pondicherry, Karikal, Yanaon and Mahé and replaced by the flag of the Indian Union, to jubilant celebrations. The treaty merging Chandernagore with India was finally ratified in the National Assembly.

Under the terms of the Treaty of Cession, signed in May 1956, France recognised Indian sovereignty over Pondicherry, Karikal, Yanaon and Mahé but secured the commitment from the Government of India that they would have a 'special administrative status' and continue to recognise French as an official language until the people or their elected representatives decided otherwise.[33] Residents of the four territories and French nationals living elsewhere in India would have six months from the moment the treaty was ratified to request French nationality, after which they would automatically become citizens of India. More delays ensued, however, with the National Assembly refusing to ratify this treaty—like the earlier Chandernagore treaty—in the years that followed. Again, it was events in another French overseas territory that unblocked the situation. The independence of Algeria in 1962, following eight years of brutal conflict, shattered French aspirations to remain a significant colonial power, and the Treaty of Cession was ratified, six years after it had been signed. Embittered colonialists would denounce the surrender of Vietnam and Algeria and the ratification of the treaties with India by comparing them with the nation's 'betrayal' of Dupleix and the lost Indian empire that resulted.[34]

After six years of waiting and uncertainty, the people of Pondicherry, Karikal, Yanaon and Mahé now had just six months to decide if they wanted to become French. When this time had elapsed, just 7,106 French nationals had been registered (4,944 adults and their children), from a total population of 375,000. The other 368,000 residents of the former French territories became citizens of India.[35] It is tempting to read these figures as another decisive rejection of French colonialism and its civilising mission, but the reality is more complex. The terms of the treaty had made Indian nationality the default, with the demand for French nationality a bureaucratic process involving the need to produce substantial documentation. Research suggests that many residents of the four territories were not aware that the option of French nationality existed, or were discouraged by French authorities from filing for it.[36] After three centuries of colonial occupation, France now worried that too many residents of the former territories of French India might demand citizenship in order to settle in France. Of particular concern were those who were not white, or at least *métis*, and not considered culturally French—'people who are different from us by race, language, religion, customs and traditions', as the French ambassador in India put it.[37] For those who didn't move to France, furthermore, choosing French nationality meant becoming a foreigner in a land that had probably always been home, with an uncertain legal status.

Over subsequent decades, the history of French India has slipped into obscurity, but for those familiar with it, the continuities and legacies are striking, beginning with the demographic inheritance. Of the people accorded French citizenship in 1962, most of those of French or mixed French-Indian ancestry headed to France after obtaining their passports. They were joined by a minority of French nationals of Indian origin, who with their offspring make up close to half of the approximately 100,000 French citizens of South Asian descent living in France today.[38] A small community of approximately 6,000 French nationals of Indian origin meanwhile lives on in India—the vestiges of those who chose French nationality and remained on the subcontinent when the merger took place.[39]

The former territories of French India—and in particular Pondicherry—remain heavily influenced by their imperial and colonial history. In addition to the raft of French institutions still in operation—their presence safeguarded by clauses in the Treaty of Cession—recent years have witnessed significant European settlement in Pondicherry's White Town, not least the arrival of French hoteliers and restaurateurs seeking to profit from the city's popularity with tourists.[40] That tourism involves a large dose of colonial nostalgia, reinforcing the notion that the French presence in India was positive or benign. Given the differences in property prices and in the profile of residents and tourists between different parts of Pondicherry, the designation 'White Town' is more than simply a cartographic hangover on city maps. A persuasive case has been made that the development of Auroville—inaugurated just 10 kilometres from Pondicherry in 1968 as 'a universal town where men and women of all countries are able to live in peace and progressive harmony'—was in fact a neo-colonial project dependent on the appropriation of land, the exclusion of the Tamil population and the exploitation of their labour.[41] The founder of Auroville was the Paris-born Mirra Alfassa—the spiritual partner of Sri Aurobindo—and the support of the French government was crucial to getting the project off the ground.

Within France, it is unlikely that anyone would today evoke the glories of Dupleix—not even the ever more audible coterie of politicians on the far-right—but the legacies of imperialism in India are evident in the built environment and wealth of the country. The headquarters of the Compagnie perpétuelle des Indes, a seventeenth century mansion in central Paris, is today one of the sites of the French national library. The country manor that René Madec had built near Quimper in Brittany after his return from India has been restored as an up-market hotel ('Le Manoir des Indes'), its rooms named after colonial-era locations in the 'East Indies' 'in homage to its historic owner'.[42] Echoes of the history of French India and of the (re)writing of that history are meanwhile discernible in France's obsession with strong male leaders, its problem of police violence and its regular curtailing of the public right to protest—issues that persist in spite or perhaps because of the country's claim to stand for liberty. France's contemporary insistence that minorities must assimilate, and in doing so hide aspects of their identity like their religion from public view, is a direct continuation of the colonial civilising mission. Descendants of formerly colonised people are, of course, the main target of assimilationist policies today, among them people of Indian origin whose ancestors faced similar interventions in French India. The insistence of the French state on not collecting data about ethnicity, religion or national background—itself a legacy of the *mission civilisatrice*—prevents the structural inequalities suffered by these minorities from being recognised and addressed.

In the international sphere, the history of French India is reflected in France's continued penchant for intervention in foreign conflicts, usually framed with reference to freedom, democracy and human rights; in its status as one of the world's largest producers and exporters of arms; and in the neo-colonial activities of French multinationals—not least fossil fuel companies—operating around the world with the support of the French state. Each of these practices is based on a precedent developed and deployed in the service of French imperialism in India. It is widely recognised that Anglophobia—or at least a sense of difference from English-speaking peoples—remains an important characteristic of France's national identity, with clichés about the English as a cold-hearted and commercial people still common.[43] Events in eighteenth-century India, and their retelling, were instrumental in the formation of these ideas.

What about the relationship between France and India today? In January 2024, Emmanuel Macron was received by Narendra Modi in New Delhi on the occasion of Republic Day. Twenty-five years of 'strategic partnership' between the two countries were celebrated, along with their growing 'defence collaboration' (mostly the sale to India of arms and aircraft produced in France). A report of Macron's visit in *India Today* described India and France as 'BFFs' (best friends forever).[44] The two countries seem keen to forget the history of French imperialism on the subcontinent in the interests of geopolitics. France therefore has free reign to promote a positive story of its presence in India in which war, conquest, forced regime change, slave trading and other ugly episodes are left out.[45] This whitewashing matters because it reinforces the notion that France was a 'friendly' coloniser, and in so doing silences the voices of victims that might otherwise be recovered. The violence of imperialism and colonialism are effaced, along with the terms themselves, and efforts to construct a truly postcolonial future are undermined.[46]

As a step towards a more honest reckoning with the country's colonial past, France's 2001 recognition of slave trading as a crime against humanity should be welcomed. Slaving in the Indian Ocean, and the trade in enslaved Indians, were referred to in this official act of recognition.[47] The renovation and reopening of the Musée de la Compagnie des Indes in Lorient in 2007 was also a step in the right direction, although its galleries devote little attention to the consequences for India of the company's actions.[48] More recently, however, as the political centre ground in France has shifted rightwards, conversations about French imperialism and its legacies have become rarer, with those that do take place quickly politicised and shut down. There is, therefore, a vital need for a new wave of Francophone scholarship that moves beyond existing euphemisms and tropes to study the history of French India in all its ugliness. This in turn might lead to new acts of decolonisation, both in France and India, including the removal of statues, the renaming of streets and the teaching of the history of French India in schools. The restitution of objects and archives should be considered, and apologies and reparations might follow. France's policy of maintaining a large cultural presence in Pondicherry, through its schools, colleges and research institutes, should be reviewed. The history of French India might then contribute to necessary conversations in France about the country's wider colonial and imperial past, including the ways in which this past continues to shape the Fifth Republic. The starting point for these efforts must be a recognition that France was an aggressive imperial power in India motivated by its own gain and that of the protagonists involved. The failure of French imperialism does not negate its existence, nor justify its reframing as benevolent. The role of France in India was anything but glorious.

TIMELINE

1664 The Compagnie des Indes is launched, following several earlier aborted French attempts to trade in Asian waters.

1667 A trading post is established at Surat with the permission of Mughal Emperor Aurangzeb. A second trading post is opened at Masulipatam.

1670 For the first time, a French naval fleet is sent to the Indian Ocean. After failing to colonise Madagascar, French settlers are relocated to Reunion Island, which is christened the Isle Bourbon.

1672 The French fleet is driven from Trincomalee by the Dutch after the start of the Franco-Dutch War (1672–78).

1674 The French surrender to the Kingdom of Golconda, allies of the Dutch, after briefly occupying San Thomé. A small party of French refugees from San Thomé settle at Pondicherry with the permission of the local governor, Sher Khan Lodi.

1688 A trading post is established in Bengal at Chandernagore.

1693–97 The Dutch capture and occupy Pondicherry. It is returned to France under the terms of the Treaty of Ryswick, signed at the end of the Nine Years' War (1688–97).

1699 The fortification of Pondicherry begins. Christened Fort Louis, the colony will soon possess the first *fort Vauban* outside of Europe. Pondicherry's governor, François Martin, is recognised as the head of all the Compagnie's establishments in India.

1712	Undermined by financial difficulties, the Compagnie des Indes is stripped of its commercial privileges, which are handed over to an association of merchants from Saint-Malo.
1715	France begins to colonise Mauritius, recently abandoned by the Dutch. The island is renamed the Isle de France. The development of the Isle Bourbon and the Isle de France, collectively known as the Mascarenes, relies on the labour of slaves imported from Africa and India.
1716	In Pondicherry, chief *courtier* Nayiniyappa Pillai is found guilty of 'abuse of power' and 'incitement to sedition'. He is flogged and dies of his injuries in prison. The prosecution of Nayiniyappa by the governor of Pondicherry, Guillaume André Hébert, is widely understood as a result of the Tamil's refusal to convert to Christianity.
1718	Nayiniyappa is posthumously pardoned by the authorities in France and Hébert recalled. The principle of religious tolerance in Pondicherry—first established by a decree in 1708—is reaffirmed.
1719	A new state-backed trading company, the Compagnie perpétuelle des Indes, is launched. It holds a monopoly on trade between France and the Indian Ocean for the next fifty years.
1721	A fortified trading post is established at Mahé on the Malabar Coast, leading to conflict with the British at Tellicherry, just 10 kilometres to the north. A further round of hostilities over Mahé follows in 1739.
1723	A trading post is established at Yanaon on the Godavari River.
1732	The passing away of Nawab Saadatullah Khan ushers in a period of political instability in the Carnatic. Offering their support to Saadatullah Khan's nephew and successor, Dost Ali Khan, the French profit from this instability to begin coining money in Pondicherry and recruit a small army of sepoys.
1739	The Compagnie's alliance with Chanda Sahib, son-in-law of Dost Ali Khan, sees them take possession of the port of Karikal. However, Chanda Sahib is soon taken prisoner by the Marathas.

1742 Joseph François Dupleix is appointed governor of Pondicherry, after a decade as head of the Compagnie's operations in Bengal.

1743 The *nizam* of the Deccan, Asaf Jah I, invades the Carnatic and installs Anwar ud-Din Khan as *nawab*. The Nawayath dynasty of Saadatullah Khan appears to be extinguished.

1746 France sends a naval squadron to India in anticipation of hostilities with Great Britain linked to the War of Austrian Succession (1740–48). A major naval battle takes place off the coast of Negapatam in July. Two months later, French forces besiege and capture Madras. Nawab Anwar ud-Din intervenes in the conflict on the British side but his army is routed by the French at the Battle of Adyar.

1747 French forces try and fail to expel the British from the Coromandel by also capturing Fort St David in Cuddalore.

1748 Pondicherry withstands a British siege. Madras is returned to Britain almost entirely razed after the Treaty of Aix-la-Chapelle is signed in October 1748. Chanda Sahib is released from his imprisonment at the hands of the Marathas. The death of Asaf Jah I launches a succession struggle in the Deccan, with his nephew Muzaffar Jang challenging his son Nasir Jang for the throne. Muzaffar Jang and Chanda Sahib ally to make bids for the thrones of the Deccan and Carnatic respectively. Dupleix decides to lend them French support.

1749 Muzaffar Jang and Chanda Sahib's joint army invades the Carnatic, supported by a French corps. Anwar ud-Din is killed in battle and Chanda Sahib crowned *nawab*. The Compagnie and its officials are rewarded by Chanda Sahib with money and *jagirs* (land grants). Anwar ud-Din's second son, Muhammad Ali, resolves to resist Chanda Sahib and appeals for help from Nasir Jang. The British begin assisting Muhammad Ali.

1750 Nasir Jang invades the Carnatic. In December, however, he is assassinated by a group of his own commanders. Muzaffar Jang is crowned *nizam* and visits Pondicherry to bestow rewards on the French, including more *jagirs*. Dupleix is awarded the title of deputy *nizam*.

1751 Muzaffar Jang sets off for Hyderabad to secure control of his new throne, accompanied by a French corps under Charles Joseph Patissier de Bussy. En route he is killed in an ambush. Bussy replaces him with one of his brothers, Salabat Jang. Additional territorial concessions are extracted from the new *nizam*. Fighting continues in the Carnatic, with the French supporting Chanda Sahib and the British backing Muhammad Ali. Chanda Sahib and the French fail to capture Muhammad Ali's stronghold of Trichinopoly. Chanda Sahib's capital, Arcot, is taken by the British in a surprise attack.

1752 French forces surrender at Srirangam. Chanda Sahib is captured and beheaded. The directors of the Compagnie in Paris become aware of these reverses and warn Dupleix against further war-making. In the Deccan, Bussy struggles to secure Salabat Jang's position in the face of internal opposition and Maratha aggression.

1753 Salabat Jang grants the Compagnie control of the Circars. However, attempts to collect revenue from this territory are defeated. The debts of Dupleix and the Compagnie mount. Peace talks with the British break down.

1754 The directors of the Compagnie decide to recall Dupleix, who sets sail for France in October. A ceasefire is agreed with the British by his interim successor, Charles Godeheu, followed by a peace treaty.

1756 The French adopt a position of neutrality as conflict begins in Bengal between the British and Nawab Siraj ud-Daula.

1757 The British capture Chandernagore after news of the start of the Seven Years' War (1756–63) reaches India. A small French contingent fights with Siraj ud-Daula against the British at Plassey. Bussy captures Visakhapatnam from the EIC. Fighting resumes in the Carnatic as reinforcements arrive from France.

1758 Further reinforcements arrive from France, with control of the French army in India taken over by Thomas Arthur de Lally-Tollendal. Fort St David is captured from the British. A disastrous expedition is undertaken to extract revenue from the rajah of Tanjore. Major naval battles take place against the British off the coasts of Cuddalore and Negapatam.

1759 Madras is besieged but not captured. The French navy sustains heavy losses on its return to the Coromandel from the Mascarenes. The British divert forces from Bengal to expel the French from the Circars, capturing Yanaon and Masulipatam. After Lally-Tollendal's recall of Bussy from Hyderabad, Salabat Jang abandons his French protectors and signs a treaty with the British recognising their possession of the Circars.

1760 The British gain a decisive victory at Vandavasi and take control of the Carnatic. Karikal is surrendered in April. The siege of Pondicherry begins in September. Jean Law de Lauriston forms an alliance with Emperor Shah Alam II to recapture Bihar and Bengal from the British.

1761 Pondicherry falls to the British in January, followed by Mahé in February. The collapse of France's nascent Indian empire is complete. Lally-Tollendal is taken back to Europe as a British prisoner. On his return to France he is imprisoned, tried for treason and finally executed in 1766. Law de Lauriston is captured by the British near Patna.

1763 The Treaty of Paris confirms the stripping back of French possessions in India to the five small colonies of Pondicherry, Karikal, Yanaon, Mahé and Chandernagore. The treaty stipulates that Chandernagore cannot be re-fortified nor troops stationed there.

1765 Jean Law de Lauriston returns to India as governor of the French territories. Before long, he and the governor of Chandernagore, Jean-Baptiste Chevalier, are planning a new war to recover France's position and 'liberate' the subcontinent from the British.

1766 France's chief minister Étienne-François de Choiseul orders the discrete build-up of forces in the Mascarenes in preparation for a surprise attack on the British possessions in India. The plan is labelled 'Operation Hindustan'.

1768 The publication of Voltaire's *Précis du siècle de Louis XV* draws attention in France to the future of the French presence in India. It is followed by the influential, collaboratively written *Histoire philosophique et politique des établissemens et du commerce des Européens dans les deux Indes* (1770).

1769 The monopoly of the Compagnie perpétuelle des Indes is suspended, inaugurating a period of free trade between France and the Indian Ocean. The following year, the Compagnie is wound up and its territories become colonies of the crown.

1770 A small contingent of French officers is sent to the kingdom of Mysore to serve in the ranks of Haidar Ali, who has recently been at war with the British (1767–69). France begins to train and equip the Mysore army. Jean-Baptiste Chevalier tries to form a coalition of north Indian rulers to expel the British from Bengal, among them Mir Qasim, Shuja ud-Daula and Shah Alam II.

1771–72 Treaties are concluded with *peshwa* Madhav Rao I and the Maratha leader of Gwalior, Mahadaji Sindhia, promising French-Maratha military collaboration against the British and their allies. However, the French government fails to ratify the treaties and dispatch the requisite troops.

1772 Mercenary René Madec enters the service of Shah Alam II with a view to preparing the emperor's army for an invasion of Bengal. A plan is soon after developed, in negotiation with the emperor, for the French occupation of the province of Tatta on the Sindh coast.

1775 The American War of Independence (1775–83) sees ministers in France devote new attention to a campaign against Great Britain in India. Joseph Alexis Pallebot de Saint-Lubin is sent from Paris to the Maratha court at Poona.

1778 After two years of covertly supporting the American patriots, France declares war on Great Britain. British forces occupy the five French colonies in India.

1779 A coalition of the three most powerful kingdoms of southern India—Mysore, the Marathas and Hyderabad—is formed against the British. With its attention focused on America, France offers the coalition little concrete support.

1780 Haidar Ali invades the Carnatic, with a small French mercenary force on his side. The British suffer a serious defeat at Pollilur.

1781 Six French warships arrive on the Coromandel from the Isle de France. Reinforcements are dispatched from France under celebrated naval commander Pierre André de Suffren. Bussy is convinced out of retirement to lead a large expeditionary force to India.

1782 Suffren arrives on the Coromandel and opens negotiations with Haidar Ali about joint military action in the Carnatic. Bussy's expeditionary force is delayed on the Isle de France by a serious outbreak of scurvy. Haidar Ali passes away in December and is succeeded by his son Tipu Sultan.

1783 The expeditionary force finally arrives on the Coromandel, but only after Tipu Sultan has withdrawn from the Carnatic. Peace is concluded between the Marathas and the British. News of an armistice between France and Great Britain then reaches India. The peace treaty that follows means the return of Pondicherry, Karikal, Yanaon, Mahé and Chandernagore to France, plus the recognition by Great Britain of French possession of eighty villages around Pondicherry and eighty-one villages around Karikal. French demands for much larger territorial concessions are rejected by British negotiators.

1785 The French Indian territories are placed under the administrative responsibility of the Isle de France, and most French troops withdrawn from the subcontinent. A new Compagnie des Indes is launched with a seven-year monopoly on French trade with India and China. A small French mercenary corps enters the service of Nizam Ali under the command of Michel Joachim Marie Raymond.

1788 Tipu Sultan sends an embassy to Versailles to request more significant military and economic collaboration between Mysore and France. Louis XVI and his ministers are non-committal.

1790 News reaches India of the beginning of the French Revolution. Pondicherry and the other colonies establish new governing committees. The governor of Chandernagore, François Emmanuel Dehaies de Montigny, is recalled after refusing to share power with the committee in his colony. Delegates are sent to represent French India in the National Assembly in Paris. The privileges of the new Compagnie are suspended and free trade resumed.

1791 A constitution for the territories of French India is prepared in Pondicherry. However, only a tiny portion of residents are recognised as citizens and granted political rights.

1792 Regulations are passed to outlaw the trade and trafficking of Indian slaves in the French colonies, though the illicit exporting of enslaved Indians from the subcontinent on French ships continues until at least 1830. The Third Anglo-Mysore War (1790–92) ends in a serious defeat for Tipu Sultan, whose request for French support is unanswered. Louis XVI is suspended and a republic declared. In Europe, the Revolutionary Wars (1792–1802) begin.

1793 The execution of Louis XVI in January is followed by the declaration of war on Great Britain. The British occupy Pondicherry and the other French Indian colonies again.

1797 François Ripaud arrives unexpectedly in Mysore and presents himself to Tipu Sultan as an ambassador sent from the Isle de France. A revolutionary club is established at Seringapatam. Two Mysore ambassadors return with Ripaud to the Mascarenes to confirm the terms of a new military alliance against the British.

1798 Napoleon invades Egypt, with India as his target. The British resolve to declare war on Tipu Sultan. A treaty of alliance between the British and Nizam Ali sees the expulsion of French troops from Hyderabad.

1799 Tipu Sultan is killed as Seringapatam falls to the British. Napoleon abandons Egypt to return to France.

1802–03 Napoleon, now First Consul, concludes the Peace of Amiens. A squadron is sent to India under Charles Decaen to ensure the restitution of France's colonies. By the time that it arrives, France and Britain are again at war. The British occupation of the colonies is therefore prolonged.

1803 From the Isle de France, Decaen tries to establish contact with Maratha leader Daulat Sindhia and the French commander in his service, Pierre Perron. However, during the Second Anglo-Maratha War (1803–05), Sindhia is defeated and Perron repatriated to France.

1805	Napoleon develops new plans for a maritime campaign to India. They are abandoned after the Battle of Trafalgar.
1807	The Treaty of Finckenstein, concluded with the Shah of Persia, Fath-Ali, opens the way for an overland campaign to India. The agreement collapses in 1809 after France fails to force Russia to recognise Persian sovereignty over Georgia.
1810	Great Britain captures France's remaining Indian Ocean possessions, the Isle Bourbon and the Isle de France. Any last French hopes of a revival in India are extinguished.
1816	Pondicherry, Karikal, Yanaon, Mahé and Chandernagore are restored to France under the terms of the Treaty of Paris (1814). However, the fortification of the colonies and the stationing of troops in them are forbidden. France's days as an imperialist power on the subcontinent are over.
1950	Possession of Chandernagore is relinquished after a referendum the previous year shows that residents are overwhelmingly in favour of joining India. The handover of the colony is ratified in France four years later.
1956	France signs the Treaty of Cession ceding Pondicherry, Karikal, Yanaon and Mahé to India. It is finally ratified in 1962 after the collapse of French rule in Algeria.
2001	France recognises slave trading as a crime against humanity. The Indian Ocean and the trade in enslaved Indians are referred to in this official act of recognition.

GLOSSARY

cartaz	Permits for maritime trade issued by the Portuguese in the Indian Ocean.
casus belli	An act or event that justifies or is used to justify a war.
circar	A district in the Mughal Empire, from the Persian word *sarkar*. The Circars were a large area of fertile land on the east coast of India around Masulipatam, made up of five *circars*.
compagnie	A trading company, like the Compagnie des Indes and its successor, the Compagnie perpétuelle des Indes.
comptoir	A trading post. The term was often used to describe the five main colonies of French India: Pondicherry, Karikal, Yanaon, Chandernagore and Mahé.
courtier	A broker or intermediary, particularly in commercial transactions. In Pondicherry, the French appointed a chief *courtier* from within the Tamil community to work closely with the governor as a broker, translator, diplomat and advisor.
diwan	A revenue officer or first minister in the Mughal administrative structure.
firman	A formal edict issued by the Mughal Emperor.

fort Vauban	A fort constructed in line with the principles of renowned military engineer, the Marquis de Vauban (1633–1707). Fort Louis in Pondicherry was the first *fort Vauban* outside of Europe.
gentiles	Term used by the French to describe inhabitants of India considered indigenous to the subcontinent, who would later be termed 'Hindu'.
gloire	Glory. From the outset, the French presence in India was intended to enhance the glory of the country and its monarch.
jagir	A land grant conferring revenue collection rights on the holder. *Jagirs* were traditionally temporary, and could be withdrawn by Mughal authorities, though French grantees like Dupleix appear to have considered them permanent territorial concessions.
jizya	A tax levied on non-Muslim people in the Mughal Empire, particularly during the reign of Aurangzeb (r. 1658–1707).
libération	Liberation. In French discourse, the liberation of India from British rule was one of the main reasons advanced for France's continued presence on the subcontinent after 1763.
liberté, égalité, fraternité	The iconic slogan of the French Revolution: liberty, equality, fraternity. During the Revolutionary Wars, France was committed to the spreading of these principles beyond its borders, including to India.
malabars	A generic term denoting the people of southern India, among them the predominantly Tamil population of the Coromandel Coast.
mansadbar	A Mughal officer. The title of *mansadbar* conferred on its holder a ranking specifying the number of horses and elephants that he should maintain.
mémoire	A text written to draw attention to or explain a topic. The plural *mémoires* is used in the historical and biographical sense of a person's memoirs.

métis	Mixed race. In the colonies of French India, this typically meant a person with an Indian mother and a white father or more distant male ancestor from France.
mission civilisatrice	The French mission to spread its civilisation among non-European peoples, a major justification for French colonialism in India after 1870.
nawab	The governor of a Mughal region like Bengal or the Carnatic. *Nawabs* were at least nominally appointed by the Mughal Emperor or, in the case of the Carnatic, by the *nizam* of Hyderabad, who was himself officially named by the emperor.
nizam	The title of the rulers of the state of Hyderabad, also referred to as the Deccan, who recognised the supreme authority of the Mughal Emperor.
noirs	Literally 'blacks', a catch-all term for non-white people around the world, including in India. Often derogatory.
palais des Indes	The Palace of the Indies, the name given by Joseph François Dupleix to the grandiose government house completed in Pondicherry in 1751 and destroyed a decade later after the British capture of the city.
patrie	The homeland, France.
peshwa	The chief minister of the Maratha confederation. After 1749 the position of *peshwa* was hereditary and the incumbent the de facto supreme Maratha authority.
philosophes	Philosophers and writers of the French Enlightenment. Among them were figures like Voltaire and Denis Diderot who wrote at length about India.
rajah	A king, prince or local ruler, usually Hindu.

renonçants	Residents of French India who, in line with a law passed in 1881, chose French citizenship on the condition of assimilation, adopting French names and renouncing their existing personal laws in favour of the French civil code.
revanche	Revenge. Exacting revenge on Great Britain for defeat in the Seven Years' War (1756–63) was a cornerstone of France's foreign policy in the decades that followed.
sarkar-i-khudadad	The God-given realm, the name given by Tipu Sultan to his Mysore kingdom after 1792.
sepoy	An Indian soldier in the service of the French or British, commanded by a European officer.
système	The complex financial arrangements put in place in France by Scottish economist John Law between 1716 and 1720, involving the launch of the Compagnie perpétuelle des Indes, its merging with the national bank and the attempted demonetisation of the economy.
topas	People of Indo-Portuguese descent, usually issued from relationships between local women and men of Portuguese extraction.
tricolore	The blue, white and red ensign adopted as France's national flag during the Revolution. Its design was fixed in 1794 under the First Republic.
ville blanche	The 'White Town'. Each colony of French India had a *ville blanche* where most French and other European residents lived.
ville noire	The 'Black Town', in which most non-European residents of the French colonies lived, though the cartographic division of the colonies into 'white' and 'black' parts did not mean complete social segregation.

NOTES

1. GLORIOUS FAILURE

1. As many readers will recognise, this speech is adapted from Jawaharlal Nehru's address to the constituent assembly on 14 August 1947. It has been translated into French by the author. For the text and audio recording of the original speech, see 'A tryst with destiny', https://www.cam.ac.uk/files/a-tryst-with-destiny (accessed 15.11.24).
2. 'Puducherry Population 2024', https://www.census2011.co.in/census/city/495-puducherry.html (accessed 15.11.24). The figures refer to the Pondicherry municipality rather than the larger Union Territory of Puducherry, which includes the surrounding area and three other former French colonies in India—Karikal, Yanaon and Mahé.
3. A significant proportion of existing studies are confined to the lifespan of a particular iteration of the French East India Company (Compagnie des Indes), which, as we will see, was wound up and relaunched several times in the eighteenth century. On the period of the first Compagnie (1664–1714), see especially Ames, *Colbert*; and Ménard-Jacob, *La Première Compagnie*. On the interregnum that followed and the period of the second Compagnie (1719–70), see Haudrère, *La Compagnie*; Manning, *Fortunes à faire*; and Vigié, *Dupleix*. Ray, *The Merchant*, considers the first company and the first two decades of its successor but stops abruptly in 1739. On the period 1763–1815, including the short-lived final company (1785–93), see Cross, *Company Politics*; Das, *Myths and Realities*; Sen, *The French in India*; and Sinha, *The Politics of Trade*. The first volume of Jacques

Weber's recent oeuvre, *La France et l'Inde*, is one exception that does cover the whole period of this study, synthesising more narrowly focused works. In addition to the titles written by Ames and Cross mentioned above, important recent studies of aspects of French colonialism in India emanating from British and American universities include Agmon, *A Colonial Affair*; Marsh, *India*; Mohan, *Claiming India*; Namakkal, *Unsettling Utopia*; and Shovlin, *Trading*. Other existing works are referenced in the course of this book.

4. On the doctrine of mercantilism, see chapter 2.
5. The figure is adapted from a similar calculation in Mikaberidze, *The Napoleonic Wars*, p. 6.
6. The Portuguese, whose presence in India dated to the late sixteenth century, were more often allies of France in the wars of the period. When they found themselves on opposite sides of a conflict in Europe, for example during most of the War of Spanish Succession (1701–14), hostilities in India were avoided.
7. For example, Vincent (ed.), *L'aventure*; Weber (ed.), *Les relations*; and Weber, *La France et l'Inde*, vol. 1, the subtitle of which refers simply to France 'meeting' India ('*l'Inde entrevue*'). In 2024, the Bibliothèque nationale de France launched a new online platform, the France–South Asia digital library, to host resources relating to the 'shared heritage' of France and South Asian countries. Here too the terms 'colonialism' and 'imperialism' are avoided in favour of 'the relations forged between France and this region of the world', despite almost all of the resources on the site dating and relating to the imperial–colonial period. See 'France-Asie du Sud: des patrimoines partagés en ligne', https://heritage.bnf.fr/france-southasia (accessed 15.11.24).
8. See, among other studies, Agmon, *A Colonial Affair*; Geller, 'Towards'; Smith, 'The Failed Empire'; and Vaghi, *La France et l'Inde*.
9. See the opening section of chapter 7 for a discussion of France's approach to India after 1763 and of how my interpretation of French motivations in this later period departs from existing scholarship.
10. On the different treatment of European and non-European prisoners of war, see Thompson, *Dupleix*, p. 882; and Pillai, *The Diary*, vol. 11, p. 151. French and British accounts of the two nations' wars in India abound with references to the value of 'European blood' and how its 'spilling' was regrettable. See, for example, Lawrence, 'Narrative', p. 8. No such regrets appear to have existed about the spilling of non-European blood.
11. Namakkal, *Unsettling Utopia*, pp. 143–4. The idea that France was a 'good' coloniser has its origins in French discourses about India dating

to the years immediately after 1763 (see below). The reasons for its perseverance to this day are discussed in the final chapter.

12. In additional to Namakkal's study of the violent end of French India in the twentieth century, on which more in the final chapter, other recent works shedding light on the damaging consequences of French colonialism include Agmon, *A Colonial Affair*; Ames, *Colbert*; and Mohan, *Claiming India*.
13. On the EIC and its close links to the English and later the British state, see Stern, *The Company-State*. On the organisation of the different European companies, see Prakash, *European Commercial Enterprise*, pp. 72–81.
14. To cite just one example of each: David, *Military Blunders*; Schiffer, *Spectacular Flops*; and Mandelbaum, *Mission Failure*.
15. Agmon, *A Colonial Affair*, p. 172, n. 12. On the commercial successes, see Manning, *Fortunes à faire*, pp. 27–45; Haudrère, *La Compagnie,* pp. 261–330; and Sinha, *The Politics of Trade*, pp. 74–118.
16. Agmon, *A Colonial Affair*, p. 5.
17. Jones, *The Great Nation*, p. 20.
18. On the sense of '*l'Inde perdue*' after 1763, see Marsh, *India*, pp. 78–84. Given that France did establish, briefly hold and then lose control over large territories in southern and central India, I would not describe this discourse as a 'myth', as Marsh does, but I recognise that it grew rapidly and was influential in the shaping of later French plans for India. I agree, furthermore, that the discourse often implied that French supremacy in India under Dupleix had a stability which in fact it did not. By suggesting that France had lost its Indian empire through the negligence of authorities in Paris and Versailles, discourses of '*l'Inde perdue*' overlooked the main reasons why France's dominant position in India did not last. These are considered in chapter 6.
19. See for example Moline, *Mémoire*, p. 35, a text considered in chapter 9.
20. Pillai, *The Diary.* This English translation was published in twelve volumes over a period of twenty-four years from 1904 to 1928. The first entry dates to September 1736 and the last to September 1760, a few months before Ananda passed away.
21. For a discussion of French national identity in the early modern period, see Bell, 'Recent works'. As Linda Colley has shown, British identity was similarly in the process of formation during this period, with conflict against France one of the key factors shaping it. See Colley, *Britons*. In this book, the terms 'English' and 'England' are used for the period before the foundation of the Kingdom of Great

Britain in 1707. 'British' and 'Great Britain' are used for the period after the Acts of Union, and as a convenient shorthand when both the pre- and post-1707 periods are concerned. French sources refer throughout the timespan of the book to '*les Anglais*' (the English). The terms 'English' and 'England' are therefore used when these sources are quoted or paraphrased.

22. Among the important figures considered in the book who were naturalised as French were François Caron, from a Protestant family in Brussels, who was appointed the first director-general of the Compagnie des Indes after previously serving for the VOC; and Thomas Arthur, the Comte de Lally, a general of Irish Jacobite ancestry who would be held responsible for France's capitulation in India in 1761. Approximately a quarter of soldiers in the French army at this time were foreign-born, with Irish-, Swiss-, Savoyard- and German-born peoples particularly present. On this final point, see Lafont, 'Observations', p. 149.
23. Maya Jasanoff's important work *Edge of Empire* reminds us that even among French speakers in eighteenth-century India there were individuals who did not identify as French. Some identified with states like Savoy that had not yet been incorporated into France, while others considered themselves 'cosmopolitan' rather than identifying with a single nation. Their biographies—for example the different countries in which they lived and the different armies that they served—confirm this cosmopolitanism. The extent to which French-speaking mercenaries in the service of different Indian powers acted patriotically, in the interests of France, is considered in chapters 7, 8 and 9.
24. For a brief discussion, see Agmon, *A Colonial Affair*, p. 172, n. 7.

2. THE PROMISE OF INDIA

1. The narrative that follows is based on Pyrard's account of his travels: Pyrard, *The Voyage*.
2. Pyrard, *The Voyage*, vol. 1, p. 429.
3. Martin, *Description*.
4. A third edition followed during Pyrard's lifetime in 1619 and a fourth in 1679. The English translation referred to in this chapter is of the third edition.
5. Pyrard, *The Voyage*, vol. 2, pp. 250–1.
6. Pyrard, *The Voyage*, vol. 1, p. 408.
7. Pyrard, *The Voyage*, vol. 1, p. 359.

8. Pyrard, *The Voyage*, vol. 2, pp. 248–9.
9. Pyrard, *The Voyage*, vol. 1, p. 366.
10. Pyrard, *The Voyage*, vol. 1, p. 327.
11. Pyrard, *The Voyage*, vol. 1, p. 359.
12. Pyrard, *The Voyage*, vol. 1, p. 404.
13. Pyrard, *The Voyage*, vol. 2, pp. 141–3.
14. Pyrard, *The Voyage*, vol. 2, p. 372.
15. Pyrard, *The Voyage*, vol. 2, p. 346.
16. Ray, *The Merchant*, vol. 1, p. 2.
17. On these attempts, see Malleson, *History*, pp. 5–6; and Ray, *The Merchant*, vol. 1, pp. 3–5.
18. An excellent introduction is Subrahmanyam, *The Portuguese Empire*.
19. Useful introductions to the Dutch presence in Asia include Boxer, *The Dutch*; Gaastra, *The Dutch*; and Parthesius, *Dutch Ships*.
20. On the early years of the English company in the Indian Ocean, see Keay, *The Honourable Company*; Chaudhuri, *The Trading World*; and Veevers, *The Origins*.
21. Pyrard, *The Voyage*, vol. 2, p. 178.
22. Pyrard, *The Voyage*, vol. 2, p. 200.
23. Pyrard, *The Voyage*, vol. 2, p. 65.
24. Pyrard, *The Voyage*, vol. 2, p. 222.
25. Pyrard, *The Voyage*, vol. 2, p. 147.
26. Pyrard, *The Voyage*, vol. 2, p. 203.
27. Malleson, *History*, pp. 6–8.
28. A good introductory survey is Eccles, *The French*.
29. Ray, *The Merchant*, vol. 1, p. 8; Kaeppelin, *La Compagnie*, p. 3.
30. Ray, *The Merchant*, vol. 1, pp. 8–10; and for Flacourt's side of the story, Flacourt, *Histoire*.
31. See Rothrock, 'Seventeenth-Century India' and Oaten, *European Travellers*, pp. 184–213 for an overview of these authors and their travels.
32. Tavernier, *Les six voyages*. See also Rothrock, 'Seventeenth-Century India', p. 172.
33. Ménard-Jacob, *La Première Compagnie*, p. 92.
34. La Boullaye-Le Gouz, *Les voyages*, p. 123. On La Boullaye-Le Gouz's travels, see also Castonnet des Fosses, *La Boullaye Le Gouz*.
35. La Boullaye-Le Gouz, *Les voyages*, p. 197.
36. Bernier, *Travels*, p. 199.
37. Bernier, *Travels*, p. 286.
38. The most recent notable example is Mansel, *King of the World*.

Other important studies include Chaline, *Le règne de Louis XIV* and Hautecœur, *Louis XIV.*

39. Mansel, *King of the World*, p. 104.
40. Malleson, *History*, pp. 10–11; Ames, *Colbert*, pp. 13–17. Ames's work is the leading study on the Compagnie's foundation and first ten years of operation (1664–74).
41. Ames, *Colbert,* pp. 6, 14. For a more detailed study of Colbert's economic ideas and policies, see Cole, *Colbert*.
42. Ames, *Colbert*, p. 7.
43. 'Articles et conditions', Dernis (ed.), *Recueil ou collection*, vol. 1, pp. 37–49.
44. Ames, *Colbert*, pp. 18–21.
45. Cited in Lespagnol, 'La Compagnie', p. 42.

3. ESTABLISHING A FOOTHOLD

1. Charpentier, *Discours*, pp. 4–6.
2. Charpentier, *Discours*, pp. 7–8.
3. Charpentier, *Discours*, p. 30.
4. Charpentier, *Discours*, p. 29.
5. Charpentier, *Discours*, p. 31.
6. Charpentier, *Discours*, p. 32.
7. Charpentier, *Discours*, p. 41.
8. Charpentier, *Discours*, pp. 59–60.
9. On this subscription campaign see Ames, *Colbert*, pp. 24–5.
10. Ames, *Colbert*, p. 25.
11. Ménard-Jacob, *La Première Compagnie*, p. 9. See also Agmon, *A Colonial Affair*, p. 7.
12. Ames, *Colbert*, p. 39.
13. Estienne, 'Le port de Lorient'.
14. Malleson, *History*, pp. 12–13; Kaeppelin, *La Compagnie*, pp. 9–10.
15. Ames, *Colbert*, pp. 30–1.
16. Malleson, *History*, p. 16.
17. Martin, *Mémoires*, vol. 2, p. 434.
18. Cited in Ames, *Colbert*, p. 107.
19. Bernier, *Travels*, p. 202.
20. Malleson, *History*, pp. 15–16; Ménard-Jacob, *La Première Compagnie*, pp. 100–1.
21. An excellent introduction to south India in this period is provided in Asher and Talbot, *India before Europe*, esp. pp. 163–85.
22. Ménard-Jacob, *La Première Compagnie*, pp. 98–100.

23. Ménard-Jacob, *La Première Compagnie*, pp. 36–7; Ames, *Colbert*, p. 105.
24. Martin, *Mémoires*, vol. 1, p. 494.
25. La Haye refers to himself in the third person as 'Monsieur le Viceroy' throughout his partial and self-justifying account of the events that followed: La Haye, *Journal*. Historians are fortunate to have several first-hand French accounts of events in India during the years of this first naval mission to Asia (1670–74), in addition to La Haye's journal, namely: L'Estra, *Relation*; Carré, *The Travels*; Bellanger de Lespinay, *Mémoires*; and Martin, *Mémoires*, vols 1 and 2. These sources are drawn upon in the narration that follows.
26. Ames, *Colbert*, pp. 91–5.
27. Carré, *The Travels*, vol. 2, p. 389.
28. Ames, *Colbert*, p. 91.
29. Ivermee, *Hooghly*, pp. 72–3.
30. Ames, *Colbert*, pp. 123–5.
31. Cited in Ames, *Colbert*, p. 157.
32. Ménard-Jacob, *La Première Compagnie*, p. 241; Ames, *Colbert*, p. 154.
33. Carré, *The Travels*, vol. 2, p. 360.
34. Carré, *The Travels*, vol. 2, p. 379.
35. Ames, *Colbert*, p. 178.
36. Martin, *Mémoires*, vol. 1, pp. 472–8.
37. See Lynn, *The Wars*, for an account of the Franco-Dutch War (1672–78) in Europe and an introduction to the other key conflicts of Louis XIV's reign, including the Nine Years' War (1688–97) and the War of Spanish Succession (1701–14).
38. See La Haye, *Journal*, part 2, pp. 189–99 for the articles of the capitulation.
39. On the advantages and disadvantages of Pondicherry's natural location, see Labernadie, *Le Vieux Pondichéry*, pp. 12–13; Ménard-Jacob, *La Première Compagnie*, pp. 97–8; and Malleson, *History*, p. 33.
40. Martin, *Mémoires*, vol. 2, pp. 55–62.
41. Labernadie, *Le Vieux Pondichéry*, pp. 22–4.
42. Martin, *Mémoires*, vol. 2, p. 106.
43. Labernadie, *Le Vieux Pondichéry*, pp. 27–8.
44. Ray, *The Merchant*, vol. 1, p. 358.
45. L'Estra, *Relation*, p. 190.
46. Ivermee, *Hooghly*, pp. 94–6.
47. Ménard-Jacob, *La Première Compagnie*, p. 108.
48. Mantienne, 'Le commerce', pp. 48–60; Ménard-Jacob, *La Première Compagnie*, pp. 108–9, 148; Mansel, *King of the World*, pp. 287–90.
49. Mansel, *King of the World*, pp. 287–9.

50. See Ménard-Jacob, *La Première Compagnie*, p. 68 for year-by-year figures of ships leaving for and returning to France from India during this period.
51. Martin, *Mémoires*, vol. 2, p. 171–2.
52. Martin, *Mémoires*, vol. 2, p. 269.
53. Ménard-Jacob, *La Première Compagnie*, p. 252.
54. Martin, *Mémoires*, vol. 2, p. 346.
55. Ménard-Jacob, *La Première Compagnie*, p. 109.
56. Ray, *The Merchant*, vol. 1, pp. 185–6, 347–9; and for an extensive analysis of the consequences of these restrictions, Gottmann, *Global Trade*.
57. Ménard-Jacob, *La Première Compagnie*, p. 68.
58. Martin, *Mémoires*, vol. 2, p. 329.
59. Ménard-Jacob, *La Première Compagnie*, p. 69.
60. Ray, *The Merchant*, vol. 1, p. 128.
61. Ames, *Colbert,* p. 189; Association des amis du SHD Lorient, 'La vie à bord', p. 136.
62. Ménard-Jacob, *La Première Compagnie*, p. 60.
63. Martin, *Mémoires*, vol. 1, pp. 551–2.
64. Ray, *The Merchant*, vol. 1, p. 268.
65. Cited in Ménard-Jacob, *La Première Compagnie*, p. 286.
66. Martin, *Mémoires*, vol. 1, p. 197.
67. Carré, *The Travels*, vol. 3, p. 679.
68. 'Arrest du Conseil d'état', Dernis (ed.), *Recueil ou collection*, vol. 1, pp. 355–8.
69. Ray, *The Merchant*, vol. 1, pp. 182–3; Ménard-Jacob, *La Première Compagnie*, p. 68.
70. The similarities between Louis XIV and Aurangzeb were not lost on some French observers. See Ménard-Jacob, *La Première Compagnie*, pp. 191–4 for a discussion.
71. Martin, *Mémoires*, vol. 3, pp. 51–3.
72. Labernadie, *Le Vieux Pondichéry*, p. 31.
73. Martin, *Mémoires*, vol. 3, pp. 101–3.
74. Martin, *Mémoires*, vol. 3, pp. 322–6.
75. See Challe, *Journal*, for an account of this squadron.
76. Malleson, *History*, pp. 26–7.
77. Martin, *Mémoires*, vol. 3, p. 341.
78. Martin, *Mémoires*, vol. 3, pp. 355–7.
79. Martin, *Mémoires*, vol. 3, p. 336.
80. For a summary of the terms of the treaty, see Lynn, *The Wars*, p. 261.
81. Malleson, *History*, pp. 33–4.

82. 'It is indispensable for the commerce and business of the company to preserve good relations with the princes and governors of the country', recorded the Pondicherry council to justify this payment. Délibérations du Conseil Supérieur, 1 February 1701, INDE/A/1, p. 1.
83. Labernadie, *Le Vieux Pondichéry*, pp. 61–4; Ménard-Jacob, *La Première Compagnie*, pp. 121–6.
84. Délibérations du Conseil Supérieur, 29 January 1705, INDE/A/1, p. 27.

4. LIFE AND DEBT

1. Haudrère, *La Compagnie*, vol. 1, p. 35.
2. Ray, *The Merchant*, vol. 1, pp. 442–53; and for a detailed study of the Saint-Malo association, Lespagnol, *Messieurs*.
3. Ames, *Colbert*, p. 22.
4. Agmon, *A Colonial Affair*, p. 12; Weber, 'La mosaïque', p. 144.
5. On the diversity of the population of Pondicherry at this time, see Agmon, *A Colonial Affair*, pp. 12–13; Weber, 'La mosaïque'; and Labernadie, *Le Vieux Pondichéry*, p. 121.
6. For a discussion, see Malangin, 'On the topic'.
7. Ménard-Jacob, *La Première Compagnie*, pp. 155–61.
8. As Agmon notes, the line between Pondicherry's *ville blanche* and *ville noire* was 'porous' not impermeable. Agmon, *A Colonial Affair*, p. 13.
9. On the role of *courtier*, Haudrère, 'La Compagnie', pp. 52–4; Agmon, *A Colonial Affair*, pp. 23–7; Ménard-Jacob, *La Première Compagnie*, pp. 181–4; and Stephen, *Pondicherry*, pp. 185–203.
10. Ames, *Colbert,* p. 41.
11. Haudrère, 'La Compagnie', pp. 52–4.
12. Agmon, *A Colonial Affair*, pp. 52–6.
13. Ray, *The Merchant*, vol. 2, pp. 616–17.
14. Martin, *Mémoires*, vol. 2, pp. 493–4; Stephen, *Pondicherry*, pp. 125–7.
15. Challe, *Journal*, vol. 2, p. 190.
16. Ivermee, *Hooghly*, p. 32.
17. Cited in Labernadie, *Le Vieux Pondichéry*, p. 32.
18. Cited in Weber, 'La mosaïque', p. 147.
19. Martin, *Mémoires*, vol. 3, p. 533. On these shortages and attempts to organise the import of rice to Pondicherry, see for example: Delibérations du Conseil Supérieur, 11 February 1709, INDE/A/1, pp. 108–9.
20. Ray, *The Merchant*, vol. 1, p. 454.

21. Agmon, *A Colonial Affair*, pp. 97–101. A copy of the edict of Louis XIV establishing the council and authorising it to administer justice can be found in the Archives d'outre-mer. Édit de Louis XIV portant création d'un conseil souverain, February 1701, INDE/B/3.
22. Cited in Haudrère, 'La Compagnie', p. 59. The Frenchman in question was Bertrand-François Mahé de La Bourdonnais, on whom more below and in the next chapter.
23. Haudrère, 'La Compagnie', pp. 58–62. On this trade, see also Manning, *Fortunes à faire*, pp. 71–88.
24. 'Déclaration du Roy', Dernis (ed.), *Recueil ou collection*, vol. 1, pp. 50–69.
25. Ménard-Jacob, *La Première Compagnie*, pp. 162–5.
26. Olagnier, *Les Jésuites*, p. 12.
27. [Anon. (ed.)], *The Travels*, pp. 55, 105.
28. [Anon. (ed.)], *The Travels*, p. 113.
29. Cited in Olagnier, *Les Jésuites*, p. 110.
30. The 'Malabar Rites' controversy has been written about extensively. In relation to the Pondicherry mission, see especially Mathew, 'Missionaries', pp. 355–71; Haudrère, 'Des chrétiens', pp. 88–94.
31. [Anon. (ed.)], *The Travels*, pp. 3–4.
32. [Anon. (ed.)], *The Travels*, p. 110.
33. Agmon, *A Colonial Affair*, p. 77.
34. [Anon. (ed.)], *The Travels*, p. 106.
35. Weber, 'La mosaïque', p. 162.
36. [Anon. (ed.)], *The Travels*, p. 131.
37. Challe, *Journal*, vol. 2, p. 159.
38. Pillai, *The Diary*, vol. 4, p. 462.
39. Ménard-Jacob, *La Première Compagnie*, pp. 165–8.
40. Agmon, *A Colonial Affair*, p. 13; Haudrère, 'Des chrétiens', p. 97.
41. Haudrère, 'Des chrétiens', pp. 96–7.
42. Ménard-Jacob, *La Première Compagnie*, p. 172.
43. Olagnier, *Les Jésuites*, pp. 22–3.
44. Cited in Agmon, *A Colonial Affair*, p. 29.
45. Olagnier, *Les Jésuites*, pp. 26–8; Haudrère, 'Des chrétiens', pp. 97–8.
46. For narratives of the events that followed, see Olagnier, *Les Jésuites* and Ray, *The Merchant*, vol. 1, pp. 463–83; and for an absorbing exploration of their context and significance, Agmon, *A Colonial Affair*.
47. M. le Chevalier to Fr Tachard, 20 October 1708, MF/8971, pp. 17–20.
48. Cited in Olagnier, *Les Jésuites*, p. 16.
49. This was in fact Hébert's second spell as governor, after a first from

1708 to 1712, either side of which Pierre Dulivier was in charge at Pondicherry. During his first spell as governor, Hébert had appointed Nayiniyappa as chief courtier and shown himself far more prepared to oppose Jesuit demands. Critics of Hébert's conduct after his return to Pondicherry in 1715 have argued that he struck a deal with the Jesuits during his time in Paris: that in return for Jesuit support for his reappointment as governor, he agreed to remove Nayiniyappa from office and perhaps even to prosecute him. For brevity, these details are omitted from the body of the chapter. See Agmon, *A Colonial Affair*, pp. 3–4.

50. Olagnier, *Les Jésuites*, pp. 54–7. As Agmon notes, Hébert's debts to Nayiniyappa and others may also explain why he was so keen to prosecute his former colleague. Agmon, *A Colonial Affair*, p. 182.
51. Ménard-Jacob, *La Première Compagnie*, pp. 164–5.
52. Cited in Olagnier, *Les Jésuites*, p. 107.
53. Haudrère, *La Compagnie*, vol. 1, p. 34.
54. Cited in Haudrère, *La Compagnie*, vol. 1, p. 34.
55. Jones, *The Great Nation*, p. 55.
56. Jones, *The Great Nation*, pp. 61–2.
57. Haudrère, *La Compagnie*, vol. 1, pp. 37–8.
58. Claeys, 'La grande crise', p. 57. See Shovlin, *Trading*, pp. 115–45 for a recent analysis of Law's financial ideas and their influence.
59. Jones, *The Great Nation*, pp. 61–4; Haudrère, *La Compagnie*, vol. 1, p. 39.
60. Claeys, 'La grande crise', pp. 58–9; Haudrère, *La Compagnie*, vol. 1, pp. 48–51.
61. Manning, *Fortunes à faire*, p. 221.
62. [Anon.], *Arrest du Conseil d'Estat*.
63. Claeys, 'La grande crise', p. 60.
64. Jones, *The Great Nation*, p. 62.
65. Claeys, 'La grande crise', p. 60; Jones, *The Great Nation*, pp. 68–9.
66. Claeys, 'La grande crise', p. 61.
67. Haudrère, *La Compagnie*, vol. 1, pp. 85–6.
68. Frémont, 'Un comptoir', p. 81.
69. Ray, *The Merchant*, vol. 2, pp. 651–81.
70. Haudrère, *La Compagnie*, vol. 1, pp. 273–85.
71. Haudrère, *La Compagnie*, vol. 1, p. 281.
72. Haudrère, *La Compagnie*, vol. 1, pp. 287–94.
73. Haudrère, *La Compagnie*, vol. 1, pp. 313–15. On the Compagnie's fluctuating commercial fortunes in this period, see also Manning, *Fortunes à faire*, pp. 27–45.

74. An important recent exception is Allen, *European Slave Trading*; and on aspects of French slave trading in the Indian Ocean, Vaughan, *Creating*; Alpers, 'The French Slave Trade'; Stephen, *Pondicherry*, pp. 121–32; and Haudrère, *Les Français*, pp. 229–47.
75. On this multidimensionality, see Allen, *European Slave Trading*, pp. 24–6.
76. Cited in Allen, *European Slave Trading*, p. 8.
77. Pyrard, *The Voyage*, vol. 2, p. 66.
78. Allen, *European Slave Trading*, p. 9.
79. Ivermee, *Hooghly*, p. 32.
80. Allen, *European Slave Trading*, p. 9.
81. Allen, *European Slave Trading*, p. 9.
82. Allen, *European Slave Trading*, p. 114.
83. Pettigrew, *Freedom's Debt*, p. 11.
84. Allen, *European Slave Trading*, pp. 10–14.
85. See Peabody, *'There are no slaves'*, for an extensive enquiry into this principle.
86. Mansel, *King of the World*, p. 126.
87. 'Articles et conditions', Dernis (ed.), *Recueil ou collection*, vol. 1, pp. 37–49.
88. [Anon.], *Le Code Noir.*
89. [Bernier], 'Nouvelle division de la terre'. For a discussion, see Rubiés, 'Race'.
90. Vaughan, *Creating*, p. 39.
91. Mansel, *King of the World*, p. 286.
92. On Crozat's life and career, see Ménard, *Le Français.*
93. Haudrère, *La Compagnie*, vol. 1, pp. 229–30.
94. Allen, *European Slave Trading*, p. 72.
95. On the French colonisation of Mauritius and the institution of slavery on the island, see Vaughan, *Creating.*
96. Haudrère, *La Compagnie*, vol. 1, p. 274.
97. For example, the extensive trade in slaves of Bertrand-François Mahé de La Bourdonnais, governor of the Mascarenes from 1735 to 1747, on whom more in the chapters that follow.
98. Alpers, 'The French Slave Trade', p. 87.
99. Martin, *Mémoires*, vol. 2, p. 494.
100. Allen, *European Slave Trading*, p. 117.
101. Allen, *European Slave Trading*, pp. 10, 117.
102. Stephen, *Pondicherry*, pp. 123–4.
103. Allen, *European Slave Trading*, pp. 76–7.
104. Ray, *The Merchant*, vol. 2, p. 617; Stephen, *Pondicherry*, p. 130.

105. [Anon.], *Le Code Noir*, p. 7.
106. Vaughan, *Creating*, p. 42.
107. [Anon.], *Le Code Noir*, pp. 8–9.
108. Vaughan, *Creating*, p. 53.
109. Thank you to Jeanne Constans for this observation and other invaluable comments on the draft.
110. See Labernadie, *Le Vieux Pondichéry*, pp. 88–90, for a typical example of this older historiography.
111. Challe, *Journal*, vol. 2, p. 189.

5. IMPERIAL EXPANSION

1. Bayly, *Indian Society*, pp. 7–44.
2. Manning, *Fortunes à faire*, pp. 208–9.
3. Délibérations du Conseil Supérieur, 10 September 1736, INDE/A/3, pp. 343–9; Labernadie, *Le Vieux Pondichéry*, pp. 148–54. See Olagnier, *Un grand colonial inconnu*, for a biography of Dumas.
4. 'Traité avec l'Emir Elmas et le Cady Mehemed Ebenzeid', 8 March 1737, INDE/B/10.
5. 'Traité fait avec le Roi de Tanjore', [July 1738], Martineau (ed.), *Lettres*, pp. 60–1. On the events that followed, see the correspondence in this volume of archive material up to p. 96.
6. Délibérations du Conseil Supérieur, 22 February 1739, INDE/A/3, pp. 454–5; Vigié, *Dupleix*, pp. 169–71.
7. On the Compagnie's relationship with the Marathas, major protagonists in events to follow, see Hatalkar, *Relations*. The Maratha polity was a federation, with the courts at Tangore and Nagpur—plus Gwalior, which we will encounter later—recognising the authority of the supreme Maratha leader, the *peshwa*, at Poona.
8. Vigié, *Dupleix*, p. 175.
9. The best biography of Dupleix of the last thirty years is Vigié, *Dupleix*. The large number of older studies includes Cultru, *Dupleix*; Clarin de La Rive, *Dupleix*; Dodwell, *Dupleix and Clive*; Hamont, *Un essai d'empire*; Malleson, *Dupleix*; Martineau, *Dupleix et l'Inde*; Martineau, *Dupleix*; and Thompson, *Dupleix*.
10. Vigié, *Dupleix*, p. 103.
11. A near-contemporary description of the colony can be found in 'Voyage de M. le chevalier d'Albert dans les Indes', MF/9090, pp. 145–6. See also Ivermee, *Hooghly*, pp. 95–6.
12. Vigié, *Dupleix*, pp. 127–8.

13. On Dupleix's trade at Chandernagore, see Ray, *The French*, pp. 90–111.
14. Vigié, *Dupleix*, pp. 28–9.
15. Cited in Vigié, *Dupleix*, p. 123 and Thompson, *Dupleix*, p. 697.
16. Cited in Weber, 'La mosaïque', p. 148.
17. Vigié, *Dupleix*, p. 122.
18. Cited in Vigié, *Dupleix*, p. 124.
19. Haudrère, *La Compagnie*, vol. 2, pp. 716–17.
20. Pillai, *The Diary*, vol. 1, pp. 186–90.
21. Pillai, *The Diary*, vol. 1, p. 244.
22. Pillai, *The Diary*, vol. 1, p. vii–xix.
23. Dupleix had convinced the Vincent family to join him in Bengal from Pondicherry. With Dupleix's encouragement, Jacques then undertook a series of long-distance voyages to Arabia, Persia and elsewhere, expeditions which ultimately undermined his health and led to his early death. Perhaps unsurprisingly, some suggest that the relationship between Jeanne and Dupleix started before Jacques's demise and that the last of the eleven children born during Jeanne and Jacques's marriage was in fact Dupleix's. See for example Rose Vincent's *Le temps d'un royaume*, a semi-fictionalised account of Jeanne's life in novel form.
24. See especially Guët, *Origines*. This biography is scathing about Jeanne's role at Pondicherry, taking after Ananda's criticisms of her (see below).
25. See Gaebelé, *Créole*, a much more positive biography offering a corrective to the accusations made by Guët; and on the contracts in Jeanne's name, Cultru, *Dupleix*, pp. 323–31. As Agmon points out, it is no doubt not coincidental that the later biography restoring Jeanne's reputation was written by a woman, Yvonne Gaebelé, wife of one of the mayors of Pondicherry in the 1930s. Agmon, 'Failure on display', pp. 870–1.
26. To cite just one example: 'As the master of Pondicherry does not know how to govern properly, and will hear no advice, the town is going to ruin [...] As he listens to his wife, he tells me not to interfere, and says, "Let us see what Madame advises."' Pillai, *The Diary*, vol. 4, pp. 32–4.
27. Cited in Thompson, *Dupleix*, p. 122.
28. Cited in Thompson, *Dupleix*, p. 103.
29. Hatalkar, *Relations*, p. 71.
30. Pillai, *The Diary*, vol. 1, p. 212.
31. Pillai, *The Diary*, vol. 1, p. 210.

32. Cited in Vigié, *Dupleix*, p. 189.
33. Vincent, 'Relations'.
34. Cited in Dodwell, *Dupleix and Clive*, p. 3.
35. Manning, *Fortunes à faire*, pp. 197–9.
36. On La Bourdonnais, see Crepin, *Mahé* and Haudrère, *La Bourdonnais*.
37. Haudrère, *La Bourdonnais*, pp. 114–16.
38. Haudrère, *La Bourdonnais*, p. 118.
39. Martineau, *Dupleix*, pp. 88–91.
40. Cited in Thompson, *Dupleix*, p. 121.
41. Cited in Vigié, *Dupleix*, p. 208.
42. Vigié, *Dupleix*, pp. 216–17.
43. Pillai, *The Diary*, vol. 2, p. 25.
44. Pillai, *The Diary*, vol. 2, p. 279.
45. Dodwell, *Dupleix and Clive*, p. 42.
46. Haudrère, *La Bourdonnais*, pp. 130–3. La Bourdonnais's 'journal' is an important though partial account of the campaign that followed. 'Journal de la campagne de La Bourdonnais', MAR/B/4/59, ff. 271–92.
47. Pillai, *The Diary*, vol. 1, p. 299 and vol. 2, p. 127.
48. Pillai, *The Diary*, vol. 1, p. 301.
49. Dupleix and La Bourdonnais were just two years apart in age and since the 1720s had been rivals for promotion in the Compagnie and in private Indian Ocean trade. Dupleix had been unhappy about La Bourdonnais's nomination as governor of the Mascarenes in 1735; La Bourdonnais for his part had designs on the governorship of Pondicherry. While Dupleix had arrived at his position with the help of his education and family connections, La Bourdonnais claimed to be a self-made man. This too was a source of friction between the pair. See Haudrère, *La Bourdonnais*, pp. 42, 120, 156.
50. 'Capitulation de Fort St George et de la ville de Madras', 21 September 1746, 8MD/6, ff. 79–87.
51. Pillai, *The Diary*, vol. 2, p. 345.
52. Cited in Thompson, *Dupleix*, p. 141.
53. Cited in Crepin, *Mahé*, p. 342.
54. Cited in Thompson, *Dupleix*, p. 159.
55. Cited in Thompson, *Dupleix*, p. 163.
56. Vigié, *Dupleix*, p. 246.
57. Cited in Love, *Vestiges*, vol. 2, p. 377.
58. Cited in Pillai, *The Diary*, vol. 3, pp. 63–4.
59. Cited in Cultru, *Dupleix*, p. 225.
60. Malleson, *Dupleix*, p. 41; Dalrymple, *The Anarchy*, p. 52.

61. Pillai, *The Diary*, vol. 2, p. 279.
62. Pillai, *The Diary*, vol. 3, p. 143.
63. Keay, *The Honourable Company*, pp. 284–5; Dodwell, *Dupleix and Clive*, p. 28.
64. Pillai, *The Diary*, vol. 5, p. 237.
65. Pillai, *The Diary*, vol. 5, p. 290.
66. See Dupleix, 'Relation du siège de Pondichéry', [1748], COL/C2/82, ff. 63–117.
67. Pillai, *The Diary*, vol. 5, p. 362.
68. Cited in Clarin de La Rive, *Dupleix*, p. 37.
69. Cited in Nazelle, *Dupleix*, pp. 335–6.
70. In Dupleix's view, Anwar ud-Din was 'set against the French', as his support for the British siege of Pondicherry had shown. 'It was essential for the nation to impose itself on an Indian sovereign capable of such a treason', he later explained, 'while also procuring the Compagnie considerable advantages.' Dupleix, 'Relation des faits principaux concernant le rétablissement de la famille de Chandasaëb sur le trône d'Arcatte', [1749], COL/C2/82, ff. 231–5.
71. Cited in Thompson, *Dupleix*, p. 217.
72. Vigié, *Dupleix*, pp. 298–9.
73. Cited in Thompson, *Dupleix*, p. 212.
74. Dupleix, 'Relation des faits principaux concernant le rétablissement de la famille de Chandasaëb sur le trône d'Arcatte', [1749], COL/C2/82, ff. 231–5. See also Cultru, *Dupleix*, pp. 234–6; Clarin de La Rive, *Dupleix*, pp. 82–5.
75. Cited in Thompson, *Dupleix*, p. 215.
76. Baugh, *The Global*, pp. 66–7.
77. Vigié, *Dupleix*, p. 307.
78. Dodwell, *Dupleix and Clive*, p. 41.
79. Vigié, *Dupleix*, p. 309.
80. Pillai, *The Diary*, vol. 8, p. 2.
81. Vigié, *Dupleix*, p. 312.
82. Cited in Thompson, *Dupleix*, pp. 255, 279.
83. Pillai, *The Diary*, vol. 6, pp. 393–4.
84. Lawrence, 'Narrative', p. 14.
85. See for example Malleson, *Dupleix*, pp. 88–9.
86. The details of the killing are glossed over in Dupleix's report of events, which notes simply that the *nizam* was killed by gunshot. See Dupleix, 'Relation abrégée de la victoire remportée près de Pondicheri sur Naser Zingue', 20 December 1750, COL/C2/82, f. 365.
87. Vigié, *Dupleix*, pp. 325–6; Dodwell, *Dupleix and Clive*, p. 53.

88. Gentil, *Mémoires*, p. 50.
89. Vigié, *Dupleix*, p. 324.
90. Dupleix, 'Journal de ce qui s'est passé depuis la mort de Nazerjingue et pendant le séjour du seigneur Mouzaferingue dans la ville de Pondichéry', [1751], COL/C2/82, ff. 355–64. For Muzaffar Jang's decree naming Dupleix as deputy *nizam*, see 'Paravana', December 1750, INDE/B/40.
91. Vigié, *Dupleix*, p. 327.
92. Labernadie, *Le Vieux Pondichéry*, pp. 196–200.
93. Pillai, *The Diary*, vol. 7, p. 6.
94. Vigié, *Dupleix*, p. 329.
95. On Bussy's career in India, see Martineau, *Bussy*; Chassaigne, *Bussy*; and Pousse, *Le marquis*. Pousse's recent study, published in 2017, is typical of another alarming tendency in Francophone scholarship on French India that perseveres to this day—an uncritical, almost hagiographical focus on the 'great men' of empire. The book begins with a lament that not a single street or square is named after Bussy in Paris, while Pondicherry has had the temerity to rename its Rue de Bussy after Lal Bahadur Shastri, the second prime minister of independent India (pp. 13–14).
96. Cited in Thompson, *Dupleix*, pp. 473–4.
97. Cited in Martineau, *Bussy*, p. 30.
98. Cited in Thompson, *Dupleix*, p. 478.
99. Cited in Martineau, *Bussy*, p. 30.
100. Cited in Martineau, *Bussy*, p. 38.
101. Cited in Clarin de La Rive, *Dupleix*, p. 124.
102. Cited in Thompson, *Dupleix*, p. 493.
103. Cited in Vigié, *Dupleix*, p. 397.
104. On these plans, see Cultru, *Dupleix*, pp. 274–5.

6. IMPERIAL COLLAPSE

1. Cited in Vigié, *Dupleix*, p. 350.
2. Cited in Cultru, *Dupleix*, p. 294.
3. Lawrence, 'Narrative', p. 6.
4. Vigié, *Dupleix*, p. 356.
5. Pillai, *The Diary*, vol. 8, p. 41.
6. Pillai, *The Diary*, vol. 7, p. 438.
7. Pillai, *The Diary*, vol. 7, p. 439.
8. Cited in Cultru, *Dupleix*, p. 273.
9. Pillai, *The Diary*, vol. 7, p. 435.

10. Pillai, *The Diary*, vol. 8, p. 52.
11. Vigié, *Dupleix*, p. 361.
12. Pillai, *The Diary*, vol. 8, p. 65.
13. Pillai, *The Diary*, vol. 8, p. 95.
14. Jacques Law was the nephew of Scottish wizard John Law, encountered in the previous chapter, and the younger brother of Jean Law de Lauriston, on whom more shortly.
15. Pillai, *The Diary*, vol. 8, p. 114.
16. Dodwell, *Dupleix and Clive*, p. 67.
17. Lawrence, 'Narrative', pp. 14–15.
18. Dupleix to Saunders, 18 February 1752, in Martineau, (ed.), *La politique*, pp. 1–98, on pp. 96–7.
19. Cited in Thompson, *Dupleix*, p. 223.
20. Cited in Thompson, *Dupleix*, p. 260.
21. Lafont, 'Observations', pp. 121–2.
22. Bussy to Dupleix, 15 September 1751, COL/C2/83, ff. 22–3.
23. Cited in Thompson, *Dupleix*, p. 525.
24. Cited in Martineau, *Bussy*, p. 80.
25. Cited in Thompson, *Dupleix*, p. 570.
26. Cited in Cultru, *Dupleix*, p. 338.
27. Cited in Cultru, *Dupleix*, p. 341.
28. Cited in Clarin de La Rive, *Dupleix*, p. 128.
29. Cited in Clarin de La Rive, *Dupleix*, pp. 143–4.
30. 'Traduction de la relation de la levée du siège de Trichinopoly publiée dans la Gazette de Londres', [1752], COL/C2/84, ff. 64–6.
31. See for example the anonymous *mémoire* written on 14 July 1753, COL/C2/84, ff. 38–48.
32. Cited in Vigié, *Dupleix*, p. 422.
33. Cited in Thompson, *Dupleix*, p. 793.
34. Cited in Martineau, *Bussy*, p. 83.
35. Pillai, *The Diary*, vol. 8, p. 149.
36. A first approach to the viceroy had been made after the British occupation of San Thomé in 1748 but the Portuguese had shown little enthusiasm for an alliance, preferring to remain neutral as Anglo-French hostilities played out.
37. Dodwell, *Dupleix and Clive*, p. 69.
38. Cited in Thompson, *Dupleix*, p. 400.
39. Pillai, *The Diary*, vol. 8, p. 442.
40. Pillai, *The Diary*, vol. 8, p. 308.
41. 'Mémoire du 16 octobre 1753', Martineau (ed.), *La politique*, pp. 99–135, on p. 129.

42. 'Mémoire du 16 octobre 1753', Martineau (ed.), *La politique*, pp. 99–135, on p. 99.
43. The acceptance of Dupleix's land-for-revenue argument at face value is common to recent and older scholarship. See for example Haudrère, *La Compagnie*, vol. 2, pp. 731–2; and Martineau, *Dupleix*, p. 236. Even Vigié appears to accept its sincerity, focusing his analysis on the accuracy of the argument—was the acquisition of land really a viable alternative to the export of bullion?—rather than the reasons why it was made. See Vigié, *Dupleix*, pp. 427–38. An exception recognising that Dupleix's *mémoire* 'played skilfully on the preconceptions and prejudices of the Company and the court' is Manning, *Fortunes à faire*, pp. 214–15.
44. Dodwell, *Dupleix and Clive*, p. 73.
45. Cited in Thompson, *Dupleix*, p. 447.
46. Cited in Thompson, *Dupleix*, p. 428.
47. Each of these districts was known individually as a *circar*, a corruption of the Persian term *sarkar* used in Mughal administration.
48. Cited in Thompson, *Dupleix*, p. 655.
49. Cited in Martineau, *Bussy*, p. 115.
50. Dodwell, *Dupleix and Clive*, p. 93.
51. 'Observations', MF/8971, pp. 69–75r, on p. 72r.
52. Martineau, *Dupleix et l'Inde*, vol. 3, p. 26.
53. Pillai, *The Diary*, vol. 8, p. 365.
54. Vigié, *Dupleix*, pp. 398, 483.
55. Vincent, 'Dupleix', p. 143. An important factor in Ananda's loss of confidence in Dupleix was the extent of his own personal indebtedness, which he blamed on the governor. See Pillai, *The Diary*, vol. 9, pp. 54–7.
56. Silhouette wanted Bussy recalled as well, insisting that his actions were 'dangerous and odious in their tyranny'. Cited in Cultru, *Dupleix*, pp. 363–4.
57. Cited in Clarin de La Rive, *Dupleix*, pp. 163–4. On the slow progress of the negotiations, see the report of the Duc de Mirepoix, French ambassador in London, 17 January 1754, 8CP/437, ff. 25–7, and other correspondence in this volume.
58. Godeheu left a detailed journal of his voyage and time at Pondicherry. See 'Journal de mon voyage', MF/8993, pp. 5–110r.
59. Godeheu, 'Mémoire justificatif', MF/8993, pp. 140–52; Pillai, *The Diary*, vol. 9, p. 148.
60. See the collection of correspondence between Dupleix and Godeheu, July–October 1754, in COL/C2/84, ff. 171–315.

61. Vigié, *Dupleix*, p. 506.
62. Pillai, *The Diary*, vol. 9, pp. 53–4.
63. Cultru, *Dupleix*, p. 283. The quote comes directly from Dupleix's October 1753 *mémoire*. See Martineau (ed.), *La politique*, pp. 99–135, on p. 131. Repeated by many historians, it is another example of Dupleix's own justifications for events being accepted without question.
64. Cultru, *Dupleix*, p. 243; Dodwell, *Dupleix and Clive*, p. 45; Manning, *Fortunes à faire*, p. 202.
65. Thompson, *Dupleix*, p. 258.
66. As Vigié notes, Chanda Sahib retained the 'fiction of power'. Vigié, *Dupleix*, p. 364.
67. Cited in Vigié, *Dupleix*, p. 397.
68. For details and estimations of the value of the *jagirs*, see Cultru, *Dupleix*, pp. 344–8.
69. Labernadie, *Le Vieux Pondichéry*, pp. 257–9. See 'Lettres patentes du 10 décembre 1751', INDE/B/36, for a directive forbidding Compagnie officials from accepting presents in their own name.
70. Cited in Martineau, *Bussy*, p. 83.
71. For example, Cultru, *Dupleix*, pp. 289–336; Martineau, *Dupleix*, pp. 353–62.
72. Dalrymple, 'The East India Company'; Dalrymple, *The Anarchy*, p. xxxi.
73. One contemporary even used this term. See Vigié, *Dupleix*, p. 398.
74. On Dupleix's supposed 'optimism', see for example Martineau, *Dupleix*, p. 242.
75. Cultru, *Dupleix*, p. 350.
76. Cited in Vigié, *Dupleix*, pp. 398–9.
77. On these tensions and the events leading to the start of the Seven Years' War, see Baugh, *The Global*, pp. 1–168.
78. 'Articles du traitté conditionnel', 31 December 1854, 8MD/6, ff. 358–64.
79. Keay, *The Honourable Company*, p. 293.
80. Cambridge, *An Account*, p. 132.
81. Dodwell, *Dupleix and Clive*, pp. 94–5.
82. Hall, *Europe and Burma*, pp. 60–73.
83. Ivermee, *Hooghly*, p. 77; Dodwell, *Dupleix and Clive*, p. 118.
84. Chandernagore council to Masulipatam council, 26 April 1756, in Hill (ed.), *Bengal*, vol. 1, p. 1.
85. Law de Lauriston, *Mémoire*, p. 56.

86. Chandernagore council to de la Bretesche, 9 June 1756, in Hill (ed.), *Bengal*, vol. 1, pp. 15–16, on p. 16.
87. [Anon.] to Demontorcin, 1 August 1756, in Hill (ed.), *Bengal*, vol. 1, pp. 173–84, on p. 173.
88. Furnier to Dupleix, 24 August 1756, in Hill (ed.), *Bengal*, vol. 1, pp. 204–6, on p. 205; Bausset to Dupleix, 8 October 1756, in Hill (ed.), *Bengal*, vol. 1, pp. 229–32, on p. 231.
89. [Anon.] to Demontorcin, 1 August 1756, in Hill (ed.), *Bengal*, vol. 1, pp. 173–84, on p. 184.
90. Cited in Hill, *Three Frenchmen*, p. 18.
91. Baugh, *The Global*, p. 291.
92. Keay, *The Honourable Company*, pp. 311–12.
93. William Watts, the British representative at Siraj's court, claimed to have obtained the *nawab*'s permission for the attack in a letter stating that 'the enemies of the English are my enemies, whether they be Indians or Europeans'. Jean Law de Lauriston was adamant, however, that this letter was a forgery and that no such permission had been given. See Gopal, *How the British Occupied Bengal*, p. 167; and for Law de Lauriston's response, Law de Lauriston, *Mémoire*, p. 122.
94. Renault to Leyrit, 28 March 1757, in Hill (ed.), *Bengal*, vol. 2, p. 298.
95. Law de Lauriston's *Mémoire* is an important first-hand account of this escape and what followed. An English language overview can be found in Hill, *Three Frenchmen*, pp. 64–131.
96. Keay, *The Honourable Company*, pp. 319–27; Ivermee, *Hooghly*, p. 83.
97. Martineau, *Bussy*, p. 218.
98. Cited in Martineau, *Bussy*, p. 187.
99. Pillai, *The Diary*, vol. 10, p. 397 and vol. 11, p. 49.
100. Dodwell, *Dupleix and Clive*, p. 160; Baugh, *The Global*, p. 464.
101. On Lally, see Hamont, *La fin d'un empire*; and Owen, 'Count Lally'.
102. Cited in Owen, 'Count Lally', p. 502.
103. Baugh, *The Global*, p. 464.
104. Pillai, *The Diary*, vol. 11, p. 151.
105. Cambridge, *An Account*, p. 175.
106. Baugh, *The Global*, pp. 465–6; Perrod, 'La fin du rêve', p. 224.
107. Cited in Labernadie, *Le Vieux Pondichéry*, p. 299.
108. Lally to Bussy, 13 June 1758, in Bussy, *Mémoire*, 'Lettres' section, pp. 2–7, on p. 3.
109. Dodwell, *Dupleix and Clive*, pp. 165–6; Baugh, *The Global*, p. 468.
110. Pillai, *The Diary*, vol. 11, p. 253.
111. Pillai, *The Diary*, vol. 11, p. 255.
112. Cited in Dodwell, *Dupleix and Clive*, p. 167.

113. The most extensive account of the siege is that of the British Company's military historian Robert Orme. See Orme, *A History*, vol. 2, part 2, pp. 385–459.
114. Dodwell, *Dupleix and Clive*, p. 170.
115. Pillai, *The Diary*, vol. 11, p. 298.
116. Law de Lauriston, *Mémoire*, p. 177.
117. Baugh, *The Global*, p. 473.
118. Cambridge, *An Account*, p. 276.
119. After the defeat at Chendurthi, Lally considered dispatching Bussy to the Circars to save the day, but weeks were lost in negotiations between the pair, as Bussy sought assurances that he could lead the campaign as he wished, notably by re-establishing links with Salabat Jang. After much delay, Lally finally decided to send a different commander, Moracin, in Bussy's place. He arrived too late, a week after Masulipatam had fallen.
120. Cited in Martineau, *Bussy*, p. 177.
121. Cited in Thompson, *Dupleix*, p. 479.
122. Baugh, *The Global*, p. 476.
123. Labernadie, *Le Vieux Pondichéry*, pp. 303–4.
124. Pillai, *The Diary*, vol. 11, p. 402.
125. Cited in Pillai, *The Diary*, vol. 11, p. 440.
126. Délibérations du Conseil Supérieur, 26 June 1759, INDE/A/3, pp. 551–67.
127. Martineau, *Bussy*, pp. 269–75; Baugh, *The Global*, p. 478.
128. Baugh, *The Global*, p. 478; Perrod, 'La fin du rêve', p. 231.
129. Dodwell, *Dupleix and Clive*, pp. 185–6.
130. Délibérations du Conseil Supérieur, 18 August 1760, INDE/A/3, pp. 629–31.
131. Pillai, *Diary*, vol. 11, pp. 76, 205.
132. Pillai, *Diary*, vol. 11, p. 236.
133. Pillai, *Diary*, vol. 11, pp. 290–1.
134. Baugh, *The Global*, pp. 481–2.
135. On this final year of Law de Lauriston's efforts, see Law de Lauriston, *Mémoire*, pp. 425–77.
136. Cited in Love, *Vestiges*, vol. 2, pp. 584–5.

7. REANIMATION

1. On the global course of the Seven Years War, see Baugh, *The Global*.
2. For the terms of the Treaty of Paris, Baugh, *The Global*, pp. 639–650; and Jones, *The Great Nation*, pp. 244–5.

3. Jones, *The Great Nation*, pp. 244–5.
4. Dupleix's demands for the reimbursement of expenses incurred while governor at Pondicherry remained unanswered by the directors right up to his death. Beyond disagreement over amounts spent and received, the key question was whether the governor had acted with the directors' authorisation in his wars of imperial expansion, which they continued to deny. As we have seen, the reality was more complex, given that Dupleix's early successes were welcomed by the directors—a fact which, as Vigié notes, the directors belatedly recognised in 1763. See Vigié, *Dupleix*, p. 482.
5. Cited in Vigié, *Dupleix*, p. 521.
6. Jeanne Dupleix had died in December 1756, within 18 months of her arrival in France.
7. Jones, *The Great Nation*, pp. 219–20. The most influential writer on the degenerating effects of the climate of India was Montesquieu in *De l'esprit des loix* (1748).
8. Voltaire, *Précis*, vol. 2, p. 161.
9. Voltaire, *Précis*, vol. 2, pp. 76–7.
10. Cited in Vincent, 'L'apogée', p. 94.
11. On the trial, see Perrod, *L'affaire*. Perhaps surprisingly, given his parallel criticisms of Dupleix, Voltaire was among Lally's defenders and labelled his execution 'one of those murders committed with the sword of justice' (Voltaire, *Fragments*, p. 156). In Voltaire's view, Lally had been made a scapegoat for the wider failings of the French monarchy and military during the war.
12. Law de Lauriston to the chargé des affaires des Indes, 10 May 1765, NAF/9365, ff. 39–44.
13. Labernadie, *Le Vieux Pondichéry*, p. 335.
14. Kennedy, 'Anglo-French rivalry', pp. 266–7.
15. Haudrère, *La Compagnie*, vol. 2, p. 755.
16. On this debate, see Haudrère, *La Compagnie*, vol. 2, pp. 789–801.
17. 'Ordonnance du Roi', 30 December 1772, INDE/B/172; Malangin, 'La crise', p. 85.
18. Law de Lauriston to [illegible], 18 August 1770, NAF/9365, ff. 289–98.
19. Chevalier, 'Mémoire sur l'Inde', 1768, NAF/9365, ff. 130–43.
20. Law de Lauriston to the Duc de Choiseul, 10 May 1765, NAF/9365, f. 45. Recent research questions the idea that Muhammad Ali was simply a puppet of the British, noting that he retained responsibility for revenue collection and judicial administration in the Carnatic through most of his long reign, which lasted until 1795. See Marshall,

The Making, pp. 234–5. However, this was certainly not the impression of French observers at the time.

21. Shah Alam also consented to the separation of the Carnatic from the Deccan in the Mughal administrative structure, so that Muhammad Ali was no longer a vassal of the *nizam* of Hyderabad.
22. Deloche, *Jean-Baptiste Chevalier*, pp. 80–94; Kennedy, 'Anglo-French rivalry', pp. 128–48.
23. Chevalier to Hastings, 2 July 1775, NAF/23329, ff. 137–56. On Chevalier, see Deloche, *Jean-Baptiste Chevalier* and Chevalier, *Les aventures*.
24. Chevalier to the Duc de Praslin, 10 January 1769, NAF/9366, ff. 1–9.
25. Chevalier to Terray, 6 January 1771, NAF/9366, ff. 77–104.
26. Sen, *The French in India*, pp. 82–3.
27. [Law de Lauriston], 'Mémoire sur les diverses nations européennes établies dans l'Inde', [1767], INDE/B/100. For a summary of this *mémoire*, see Sen, *The French in India*, pp. 154–6.
28. Chevalier, 'Plan d'attaque dans l'Inde', 15 March 1769, NAF/9366, ff. 10–24.
29. Law de Lauriston to [anon.], 9 February 1758, Hill (ed.), *Bengal*, vol. 3, pp. 263–5, on p. 263.
30. See chapter 6. My understanding differs in this respect from that of Kate Marsh, who suggests that the discourse of liberating India from English rule took off in France in about 1780. I suggest, in contrast, that it began two decades earlier, during the Seven Years' War, among Frenchmen in India, and was then adopted in France from about 1765. See Marsh, *India*, p. 82.
31. Chevalier, 'Plan d'attaque dans l'Inde', 15 March 1769, NAF/9366, ff. 10–24.
32. Chevalier to the Duc de Praslin, 10 January 1769, NAF/9366, ff. 1–9.
33. Roubaud, *Le politique indien*, p. 85.
34. Voltaire, *Fragments*, p. 162.
35. On the text and its influence, see Israel, *Democratic Enlightenment*, pp. 413–42.
36. [Raynal, (ed.)], *Histoire*, vol. 1, p. 376.
37. [Raynal, (ed.)], *Histoire*, vol. 2, p. 128.
38. [Raynal, (ed.)], *Histoire*, vol. 2, p. 98.
39. Roubaud, *Le politique indien*, p. 122.
40. Roubaud, *Le politique indien*, p. 86.
41. [Raynal, (ed.)], *Histoire*, vol. 2, p. 137.

42. [Raynal, (ed.)], *Histoire*, vol. 1, p. 384.
43. Choiseul, *Mémoire*, p. 8.
44. Choiseul, *Mémoire*, pp. 16–19.
45. Choiseul, *Mémoire*, p. 8.
46. On the build-up of forces on the Isle de France, see Das, *Myths and Realities*, pp. 133–7.
47. Das, *Myths and Realities*, p. 284. Lafont concurs that 'there was a rejection of any colonial domination in India by the French government' during this period, although he does note instances of divergence between official policy and events on the ground. See Lafont, *Indika*, pp. 150–2. In recent years, other scholars have re-examined the French approach to India after 1763. They recognise that France continued to pursue 'political' ambitions on the subcontinent but, in stressing that France's priority was to contest Great Britain's ascendancy, tend to overlook the extent of France's own continued territorial ambitions. See Margerison, 'French Visions'; Vaghi, *La France et l'Inde*, pp. 52–123; Malangin, 'Renoncer à l'Inde?', pp. 411–33; and Platania, 'L'originalité'.
48. Das, *Myths and Realities*, pp. 285, 292. Das contends that 'the emerging role of the nation as a liberating force for the oppressed Indians took the character of a bona fide commitment' (p. 285).
49. See for example 'Projets de lettres à Ayder Aly Khan', 14 December 1775, NAF/9368, ff. 136–41. My emphasis.
50. Law de Lauriston to [illegible], 20 October 1767, NAF/9365, ff. 105–12.
51. Law de Lauriston to the chargé des affaires des Indes, 10 May 1765, NAF/9365, ff. 39–44.
52. Law de Lauriston, *État politique*, p. 168. This text was written in 1777 but reflects Law de Lauriston's views from 1765 onwards.
53. Lafont, 'Observations', pp. 128–32.
54. Dalrymple, *The Anarchy*, p. 242.
55. On Haidar Ali as ruler of the Mysore kingdom, see especially Sinha, *Haidar Ali*; Bowring, *Haidar Ali*, pp. 11–116; and Habib (ed), *Resistance*.
56. Marshall, *The Making*, pp. 230–1.
57. Law de Lauriston to [illegible], 23 February 1769, NAF/9365, ff. 214–23.
58. An important first-hand account of the conflict was left by one French solider involved, Maistre de la Tour, in his *Histoire*. See also Bowring, *Haidar Ali*, pp. 49–58; and Sinha, *Haidar Ali*, pp. 70–94.
59. [La Tour], *Histoire*, vol. 2, p. 3.
60. Dalrymple, *The Anarchy*, p. 243.

61. 'Mémoire sommaire des motifs de l'envoy du S. Hügel dans L'Inde', [1772], COL/C2/123, ff. 4–5r.
62. Hugau, *Le Voyage*, p. 13.
63. Chevalier, 'Plan d'attaque dans l'Inde', 15 March 1769, NAF/9366, ff. 10–24.
64. Chevalier to Terray, 6 January 1771, NAF/9366, ff. 77–104. Chevalier's efforts to form alliances with different Indian courts are also discussed in Deloche, *Jean-Baptiste Chevalier*, pp. 107–36; and Sen, *The French in India*, pp. 112–53.
65. Gentil, *Mémoires*, is an important account of these events.
66. Untitled memo on relations with Shuja ud-Daula, 17 March 1771, COL/C2/246, ff. 42–5r.
67. Shuja ud-Daula to the Duc de Choiseul, [undated], COL/C2/246, ff. 47–47r.
68. On the troop numbers on the Isle de France, see Das p. 134.
69. Cited in Kennedy, 'Anglo-French rivalry', p. 212. See also 'Extract of General Letter to Bengal', 25 March 1770, IOR/I/1/4.
70. One of the officers involved, Captain Hugau, left an important account of the secret expedition, later published as *Le Voyage*.
71. 'Mémoire sommaire des motifs de l'envoy du S. Hügel dans L'Inde', [1772], COL/C2/123, ff. 4–5r.
72. Hugau, *Le Voyage*, pp. 68–71.
73. Lafont, 'Les mémoires', p. 161.
74. Law de Lauriston to de Ternay, 21 April 1773, NAF/9365, ff. 385–90.
75. Russel to Law de Lauriston, 5 September 1772, NAF/9365, ff. 366–7.
76. Lafont, 'Observations', p. 131.
77. Lafont, 'Les mémoires', p. 176.
78. 'Tableau de la situation politique de nos affaires en Inde', 1 March 1776, NAF/9368, ff. 148–51.
79. Haidar Ali Khan to Baudouin, 2 June 1775, COL/C2/139, ff. 339–339r.
80. 'Rapport de M. Russel', 2 August 1773, COL/C2/128, ff. 247–247r.
81. Sen, *The French in India*, pp. 97–100.
82. Law de Lauriston, *État politique*, pp. 23–4.
83. Law de Lauriston, *État politique*, p. 93.
84. Law de Lauriston, *État politique*, pp. 82–3.
85. Duprat, *Voyage*, p. 21.
86. Duprat, *Voyage*, p. 24.
87. On these events, see Dalrymple, *The Anarchy*, pp. 259–82.
88. Chevalier to Terray, 6 January 1771, NAF/9366, ff. 77–104.

89. 'Traduction de l'accord', 29 January 1773, COL/C2/128, ff. 261–261r.
90. Hatalkar, *Relations*, pp. 173–5.
91. Law de Lauriston to Terray, 13 October 1771, COL/C2/118, ff. 252–77.
92. Cited in Madec, *Mémoire*, p. 152.
93. Hatalkar, *Relations*, pp. 173, 176.
94. Modave, *Voyage en Inde*, p. 181. On Madec, see Barbé, *Le nabab*; Besson, *Les aventuriers*, pp. 51–87; and Sen, *The French in India*, pp. 128–49; plus Madec's *Mémoire*.
95. Madec, *Mémoire*, p. 116.
96. Cited in Madec, *Mémoire*, p. 118.
97. Cited in Madec, *Mémoire*, p. 123.
98. Characteristically, Chevalier manipulated the truth, implying that the government in Versailles had instigated the alliance with Shah Alam and stating, incorrectly, that 10,000 troops were amassed on the Isle de France ready to invade India. See Madec, *Mémoire*, p. 124.
99. Madec, *Mémoire*, p. 139.
100. Cited in Barbé, *Le nabab*, p. 147.
101. Madec, *Mémoire*, p. 161.
102. Besson, *Les aventuriers*, p. 76.
103. Cited in Madec, *Mémoire*, pp. 133–4.
104. Cited in Barbé, *Le nabab*, p. 146.
105. On the famine and British culpability, see Ivermee, *Hooghly*, pp. 88–91.
106. Modave was a friend of Voltaire and the Duc de Choiseul, who had arrived in India after a failed attempt as a plantation owner on the Isle de France. His *Voyage en Inde* is an important resource on events at different Indian courts between 1773 and 1776, whereafter he died at Masulipatam.
107. Cited in Barbé, *Le nabab*, p. 143.
108. Cited in Barbé, *Le nabab*, p. 163.
109. Sen, *The French in India*, pp. 137–8.
110. Modave, *Voyage en Inde*, pp. 158–9.
111. Chevalier to Sartine, 11 August 1776, NAF/9366, ff. 275–9.
112. Modave, *Voyage en Inde*, pp. 455–6.
113. Cited in Barbé, *Le nabab*, p. 135.

8. RECKONING

1. Cited in Das, *Myths and Realities*, p. 55.

2. Jones, *The Great Nation*, p. 305.
3. Beaumarchais, *Le vœu*, p. 8.
4. Panon, a French agent at Patna, put the figure at 85–87 million francs (Panon to Bellecombe, 21 April 1777, NAF/9368, ff. 219–26). Chevalier did not offer a precise figure but warned that 'if the English control India, they will before long control the four corners of the world.' (Chevalier to Castries, 21 October 1777, NAF/9366, ff. 281–5).
5. 'Mémoire de l'Abbé de l'Estevan', 1775, COL/C2/164, no. 42.
6. A new edition of the *Histoire philosophique et politique* was at this point in preparation. When it appeared in 1780, it too held the EIC responsible for the Bengal famine and concluded: 'Who would have imagined that this company, changing all of a sudden its conduct and system, would make the people of Bengal regret the despotism of their former masters? [...] A methodical tyranny has succeeded the exercise of arbitrary authority. The extractions have been general and regular; the oppression has been continual and absolute. The art of destructive monopoly has been perfected.' Raynal (ed.), *Histoire*, vol. 1, p. 380.
7. Bussy, *Journal,* p. 154.
8. Cited in Weber, *La France et l'Inde*, vol. 1, p. 415.
9. Cited in Weber, *La France et l'Inde*, vol. 1, p. 402.
10. Cited in Barbé, *Le nabab*, p. 153.
11. Bussy, *Journal,* p. 5. In a telling sign of the new mood in Versailles, Dupleix's debts were now posthumously liquidated and his reputation in official circles restored. Two years later, Lally was posthumously pardoned of his conviction for treason during the Seven Years' War.
12. 'Projets de lettres à Ayder Aly Khan', 14 December 1775, NAF/9368, ff. 136–41.
13. Das, *Myths and Realities*, pp. 83–4.
14. Law de Lauriston estimated that 800 French soldiers were employed in Indian courts in 1776. He was sceptical about how many would be induced back to serve their country, noting that their pay and conditions were usually far better as mercenaries. Law de Lauriston, *État politique* , pp. 142, 150. Modave meanwhile thought that most of the mercenaries were 'dishonourable and stupid drunkards'. Modave, *Voyage en Inde*, pp. 419–20.
15. 'Mémoire du roi pour servir d'instructions particulières au Sr. de Bellecombe', 10 February 1776, AN COL A/20, ff. 94–111. On the instructions received by Bellecombe, see also Das, *Myths and Realities*,

pp. 150–2. The quote comes from a slightly later *mémoire* written at Versailles, cited in Barbé, *Le nabab*, p. 133.

16. 'Projets de lettres à Ayder Aly Khan', 14 December 1775, NAF/9368, ff. 136–41.
17. Bellecombe to [illegible], January 1777, NAF/9368, ff. 202–6.
18. Das, *Myths and Realities*, pp. 219–20.
19. On these developments in the Maratha polity, see Hatalkar, *Relations*, pp. 177–80; and Das, *Myths and Realities*, pp. 178–82.
20. Saint-Lubin first went to India as a medical assistant during the Seven Years' War, and during this conflict was trusted by Lally with a secret mission to Calcutta. He returned for a second spell in India in 1766, taking service with Haidar Ali, before quitting Mysore for Madras, raising questions about his loyalty. See Sen, *The French in India*, pp. 181–2.
21. For Bellecombe's views on Saint-Lubin, see 'Observations sur les sipayes', 24 January 1778, INDE/B/290.
22. Hatalkar, *Relations*, p. 189; Das, *Myths and Realities*, p. 185. Records relating to Saint-Lubin's embassy can be found in the French diplomatic archives. See 8MD/4, ff. 164–245.
23. 'Tableau de la situation politique de nos affaires en Inde', 1 March 1776, NAF/9368, ff. 148–51.
24. Deloche, *Jean-Baptiste Chevalier*, pp. 122–4.
25. 'I judged from your silence that the project did not interest you and therefore abandoned it', wrote Madec to Chevalier to explain his departure. Madec, *Mémoire*, p. 207.
26. Deloche, *Jean-Baptiste Chevalier*, pp. 139–47; Ivermee, *Hooghly*, pp. 115–7.
27. See Bellecombe's account of the siege, reproduced in Bellecombe, *Essai biographique*, pp. 39–73.
28. Cited in Sen, *The French in India*, p. 194.
29. Important accounts of this and subsequent British campaigns against the Marathas can be found in Keay, *The Honourable Company*, esp. pp. 401–8; and Dalrymple, *The Anarchy*, esp. pp. 244–6.
30. Cited in Dalrymple, *The Anarchy*, p. 246.
31. Sen, *The French in India*, p. 22.
32. Sen, *The French in India*, p. 18.
33. Hatalkar, *Relations*, pp. 204–5.
34. Jones, *The Great Nation*, p. 305.
35. Dalrymple, *The Anarchy*, p. 246; Sinha, *Haidar Ali*, p. 186.
36. See Sarkar, 'Haidar Ali's invasion', pp. 26–7. This chapter is in fact the translation of a first-hand account of the war in the Carnatic from 28

May to 4 November 1780, written by one of the officers in Lallée's corps.

37. Keay, *The Honourable Company*, p. 412.
38. Cited in Sarkar, 'Haidar Ali's invasion', p. 31.
39. [La Tour], *Histoire*, vol. 2, p. 200.
40. Sen, *The French in India*, p. 222; Labernadie, *Le Vieux Pondichéry*, pp. 365–6.
41. Chevalier to Castries, 18 February 1782, NAF/9366, ff. 312–18.
42. Bussy, *Journal,* p. 231.
43. Sen, *The French in India*, pp. 199–200.
44. Lafont, 'Les mémoires', p. 168.
45. On Suffren's campaign in the Indian Ocean, see his *Journal*, and for a biography, Bertrand, *Suffren*.
46. Hatalkar, *Relations*, pp. 207–8.
47. Sen, *The French in India*, p. 202; Hatalkar, *Relations*, p. 210.
48. Piveron de Morlat's *Mémoire* is an important resource on these negotiations and what followed. The Frenchman would remain in the Mysore camp until 1785.
49. Sen, *The French in India*, p. 222.
50. Piveron de Morlat, *Mémoire*, pp. 116, 134.
51. The term 'black' was used here to refer to Haidar's own soldiers and more widely, in keeping with contemporary usage, to all non-Europeans.
52. Sen, *The French in India*, pp. 276–7; Das, *Myths and Realities*, pp. 212–13.
53. 'Extracts from Draft Statement', appendix D in Brittlebank, *Tiger*, pp. 129–32, on p. 132.
54. Suffren's highly original tactics were one of the key reasons for this. Instead of organising his ships in the traditional fashion to fight in a line, he attempted to outflank opponents and attack enemy ships from the rear, picking them off one-by-one. After Suffren, these tactics became commonplace and were notably adopted in the Royal Navy by Horatio Nelson. See Sen, *The French in India*, pp. 228–9.
55. Piveron de Morlat, *Mémoire*, pp. 155–61; Bertrand, *Suffren*, pp. 262–8.
56. Bussy, *Journal,* p. 143.
57. Piveron de Morlat, *Mémoire*, p. 157.
58. Bussy, *Journal,* p. 132; Bussy to Suffren, 19 June 1782, INDE/A/19, pp. 289–92.
59. Hatalkar, *Relations*, pp. 275–6.
60. Motais de Narbonne to Castries, 19 October 1782, NAF/9372, ff. 48–53.

61. Denis-Launay to Bussy, 9 October 1782, NAF/9372, ff. 46–8.
62. Michaud, *Histoire*, vol. 1, p. 82. As Hasan points out, there is no evidence to corroborate this account, which does not reflect Haidar's waning confidence in the reliability of the French towards the end of his life, and was probably imagined by Michaud. See Hasan, *History*, p. 22.
63. Keay, *The Honourable Company*, pp. 415–6.
64. Hatalkar, *Relations*, pp. 212–13; Sen, *The French in India*, pp. 334–5.
65. Bussy, *Journal,* p. 321.
66. The vague and non-committal letter that Bussy then wrote to Nana Fadnavis from Porto Novo the following month (March 1783) confirmed that the Maratha chief minister was right to give up on concrete help from the French. Hatalkar, *Relations*, pp. 220–1.
67. Bussy, *Journal,* p. 326.
68. Cited in Kennedy, 'Anglo-French rivalry', p. 238.
69. Bussy, *Journal,* pp. 6, 169.
70. For these figures, see Sen, *The French in India*, p. 345.
71. Bussy, *Journal,* p. 339. See also Bussy to Castries, 31 March 1783, INDE/B/399.
72. Das, *Myths and Realities*, pp. 221–2.
73. Cited in Martineau, *Bussy*, p. 343.
74. Cited in Labernadie, *Le Vieux Pondichéry*, p. 369.
75. Cited in Hasan, 'The French', p. 43.
76. For the peace terms relating to France and Britain, see 'The definitive treaty of peace' in [Anon. (ed.)], *A Collection of all the Treaties*, vol. 3, pp. 334–74.
77. 'Re-establish France in India on the footing of 1754' reads a confidential memo on the topic. 'Note confidentielle sur les moyens d'acheminer les préliminaires de la paix', 8CP/538, ff. 197–8, on f. 197. On the negotiations, see Kennedy, 'Anglo-French rivalry', pp. 150–8; and Stockley, *Britain and France*, pp. 107–10.
78. Stockley, *Britain and France*, p. 108.
79. On the British rejection of the proposed peace terms, see 'Observations sur la réponse de la Cour de Londres', 8CP/538, ff. 309–27.
80. Hasan, *History*, p. 53. The negotiators also insisted that France secure the release of British prisoners of war from Tipu's custody.
81. Martineau, *Bussy*, p. 389; Piveron de Morlat to Tipu Sultan, September 1785, COL/C2/169, ff. 149–51.
82. Labernadie, *Le Vieux Pondichéry*, pp. 382–3. The governor of Pondicherry was from this moment onwards answerable to the governor of the Isle de France.

83. On the astronomical state debt, see Jones, *The Great Nation*, p. 318.
84. 'Arrêt du Conseil d'État du Roi portant établissement d'une nouvelle Compagnie des Indes', 14 April 1785, INDE/B/831. On the new company and this period of commercial collaboration between French and British interests, see Nussbaum, 'The Formation'; Sinha, *The Politics of Trade,* pp. 122–32; Cross, *Company Politics*; and Shovlin, *Trading*, pp. 228–72.
85. Nussbaum, 'The Formation', p. 497.
86. For the data, see Haudrère, *Les Français*, p. 94.
87. Allen, *European Slave Trading*, p. 73.
88. Sinha, *The Politics of Trade,* p. 108.
89. Allen, *European Slave Trading*, p. 104. The total number of slaves transported across the Atlantic on French ships is estimated at 1.38 million, of which 433,061 are known to have been embarked during this same period (1776–1800). See the Slave Voyages database, https://www.slavevoyages.org/assessment/estimates (accessed 20.6.23).
90. Kennedy, 'Anglo-French rivalry', p. 329.
91. For a discussion, see Kennedy, 'Anglo-French rivalry', pp. 284–303. Intervention in Cochinchina had earlier been advocated by Chevalier. See Deloche, *Jean-Baptiste Chevalier*, pp. 129–30.
92. Dalrymple, *The Anarchy*, pp. 294–305.
93. Hatalkar, *Relations*, pp. 262–3; Conway, 'Résumé de la position française en Inde', 6 February 1788, COL/C2/184, ff. 10–39.
94. On de Boigne and his time in Sindhia's service, see Besson, *Les aventuriers*, pp. 162–93; Lafont, *Indika*, pp. 177–204; Compton, *A particular account*, pp. 15–108; Malleson, *Final French Struggles*, pp. 159–229; and Jasanoff, *Edge of Empire*, pp. 90–101.
95. For a discussion of de Boigne's identity and loyalties, see Jasanoff, *Edge of Empire*, pp. 90–101. De Boigne arrived in India in 1777 and served in the Madras army until 1782, during which time he saw action against the French. After leaving India in 1796, he settled in England and was naturalised as a British subject. Savoy was invaded by France during the Revolutionary Wars but only definitively annexed in 1860.
96. On Raymond at Hyderabad, see Besson, *Les aventuriers*, pp. 214–27; Malleson, *Final French Struggles*, pp. 238–45; McClay, 'Monsieur Raymond'; and Lafont, 'Observations', pp. 136–40. A selection of Raymond's letters from Hyderabad was collected together by Jadunath Sarkar and published as Sarkar, 'General Raymond'.
97. See the anonymous *mémoire* written at Pondicherry, 1788, NAF/9373, ff. 189–90.

98. Tipu Sultan to Piveron de Morlat, 24 September 1785, COL/C2/169, ff. 154–5.
99. Tipu Sultan to de Cossigny, [undated], COL/C2/172, f. 32.
100. Lafont, 'Observations', p. 129.
101. On Tipu Sultan as ruler of Mysore, see especially Hasan, *History*; Brittlebank, *Tiger*; Forrest, *Tiger of Mysore*; and Bowring, *Haidar Ali*, pp. 117–227.
102. MacDougall, 'In support', p. 83.
103. For a discussion of Tipu's efforts to establish his 'legitimacy', see Brittlebank, *Tipu Sultan's Search*.
104. Tipu Sultan to Souillac, 3 August 1785, COL/C2/169, ff. 63–4r.
105. As we saw in chapter 3, the Siamese ruler Ramathibodi III had sent an embassy to Versailles a century earlier (1686). Representatives of the *nawab* of the Carnatic, Muhammad Ali, and the rajah of Tanjore, Thuljaji Bhonsle, travelled to London in the 1770s, but their visits did not have the status of embassies.
106. A contemporary account is provided by Gentil, who was present to receive the ambassadors at Versailles. Gentil, *Mémoires*, pp. 316–38. See also Hasan, *History*, pp. 118–24.
107. Gentil, *Mémoires*, pp. 327–8.
108. 'Extracts from Draft Statement', appendix D in Brittlebank, *Tiger*, pp. 129–32, on pp. 129–30.
109. 'Extracts from Draft Statement', appendix D in Brittlebank, *Tiger*, pp. 129–32, on pp. 131–2.
110. See for example Tipu Sultan to the King of France, 6 October 1785, COL/C2/169, ff. 161–2r.
111. 'Traduction du document présenté au Roi', 30 July 1788, COL/C2/172, ff. 251–6.
112. Hasan, *History*, pp. 121–2.
113. Michaud, *Histoire*, vol. 1, p. 138.
114. Cited in Hasan, *History*, p. 122.
115. Gentil, *Mémoires*, pp. 336–8, also noted in Jasanoff, *Edge of Empire*, pp. 161, 359.

9. REVOLUTION

1. For a discussion of the French state's failure to embrace market forces and a less privilege-ridden society in the years preceding the Revolution, see Jones, *The Great Nation*, pp. 322–35. On the critical economic situation in 1789, see pp. 395–410 of the same work.
2. On the eve of the Revolution, 310 million livres, more than half of

the annual state budget, was spent paying the interest on previous borrowing, including the 1 billion livres borrowed during the American War of Independence. Mikaberidze, *The Napoleonic Wars*, pp. 6–7. Mikaberidze's study is an extremely thorough recent history of the Revolutionary and Napoleonic Wars around the world and a key source of background information for this chapter.

3. Cited in Labernadie, *La Révolution*, p. 22.
4. Mémoire sur l'évacuation de Pondichéry, [1789], NAF/9373, ff. 200–17. The petition continued with a lament about the former 'days of glory' of the French in India under the '*grand homme*' (great man) Dupleix.
5. Cited in Labernadie, *La Révolution*, p. 30.
6. The most detailed account of the Revolution in French India is Labernadie, *La Révolution*. See also Castonnet des Fosses, *La Révolution*; Gobalakichenane, 'La Révolution'; Weber, *La France et l'Inde*, vol. 1, pp. 435–78; and Sen, *The French in India*, pp. 426–92, plus the articles referenced below.
7. Cited in Labernadie, *La Révolution*, p. 32. Extracts of the *mémoires* are on pp. 31–7. The original texts, complete with the signatures of members of the committee, can be found in INDE/A/50, pp. 1–68.
8. Cited in Labernadie, *La Révolution*, p. 33.
9. Cited in Labernadie, *La Révolution*, p. 34.
10. Cited in Labernadie, *La Révolution*, p. 319.
11. Cited in Sen, *The French in India*, p. 461. On the revolution at Chandernagore, see also Ivermee, *Hooghly*, pp. 117–22.
12. Cited in Labernadie, *La Révolution*, p. 243. It didn't help that Mottet, a naval officer, was also Montigny's predecessor, having had a short and unsuccessful spell as governor of Chandernagore before Montigny's arrival in 1788.
13. The animosity between Richemont and Montigny was a key factor in the Chandernagore Revolution's confrontational turn in 1790. Richemont was among the officials dismissed from office by Montigny before the Revolution began. He returned to Chandernagore after having his dismissal overturned, determined to bring about Montigny's downfall, just as the Revolution was beginning. See Ivermee, *Hooghly*, pp. 119–22.
14. Le Clerc de Fresne to [illegible], 29 June 1792, NAF/9373, ff. 393–5.
15. The abolition of the Compagnie's monopoly had in fact been voted for in the Assemblée Nationale in March 1790, as part of the Revolution's more general movement towards the liberalisation of trade in France,

before the Pondicherry committee's *mémoire* on the subject had even been written. The Compagnie traded between France and India for three more years before being liquidated in 1793.

16. Labernadie, *La Révolution*, pp. 78–85.
17. Cited in Castonnet des Fosses, *La Révolution*, p. 14.
18. Sen, *The French in India*, p. 442.
19. The letter is reproduced in full in Labernadie, *La Révolution*, pp. 257–61.
20. Le Clerc de Fresne to [illegible], 29 June 1792, NAF/9373, ff. 393–5.
21. The other motivation for the dispatch of the commissioners was to re-assert a degree of central control over the colonies, guarding against the 'separatist tendencies' that some were feared to be displaying. Labernadie, *La Révolution*, p. 117.
22. Cited in Labernadie, *Le Vieux Pondichéry*, p. 397.
23. 'The Declaration of the Rights of Man of the Citizen', https://www.elysee.fr/en/french-presidency/the-declaration-of-the-rights-of-man-and-of-the-citizen (accessed 1.3.24).
24. Jones, *The Great Nation*, pp. 427–8. For a detailed analysis, see Crook, *Elections*.
25. Gobalakichenane, 'La Révolution', p. 11.
26. Cited in Weber, *La France et l'Inde*, vol. 1, p. 466.
27. Cited in Smith, 'Révolution(s)', p. 74.
28. Cited in Labernadie, *La Révolution*, p. 50.
29. Culan, who escaped deportation by fleeing Pondicherry, was accused of supporting the Tamil cause only to claim control of the general assembly and its committee. Labernadie, *La Révolution*, pp. 50–4.
30. Taffin, 'Citoyens', p. 237.
31. Cited in Labernadie, *La Révolution*, p. 66.
32. Cited in Weber, *La France et l'Inde*, vol. 1, p. 473.
33. Taffin, 'Citoyens', p. 237.
34. Gobalakichenane, 'La Révolution', pp. 51–2.
35. Cited in Weber, *La France et l'Inde*, vol. 1, p. 468.
36. Labernadie, *La Révolution*, pp. 125–6.
37. For a discussion, see Carton, 'Shades of Fraternity'.
38. To this total was added seventeen active citizens from Karikal and fifteen from Yanaon. Chandernagore, as we have seen, refused to recognise the validity of the constitution prepared at Pondicherry, while Mahé was slow in finalising its list of active citizens. See Labernadie, *La Révolution*, pp. 126, 168 and for the list, appendix 1, pp. i–xvii.

39. 'Articles de l'Assemblée coloniale de Pondichéry', appendix 2 in Labernadie, *La Révolution*, pp. xix–xviii, on pp. xx–xxi.
40. Cited in Taffin, 'Citoyens', p. 245.
41. Cited in Smith, 'Révolution(s)', p. 75.
42. Cited in Labernadie, *La Révolution*, p. 241.
43. 'Extraits du journal de Vîrânaïcker II', annex 1, Gobalakichenane, 'La Révolution', pp. 82–145, on pp. 129–33.
44. 'Correspondance relative au retour d'un détachement envoyé à Karikal', October 1791, COL/C2/295, ff. 5–10.
45. The phrase 'cult of liberty' is used by Susan Peabody in her study of the tension between the proliferation of ideas of liberty in France and the reality of slavery in French colonies in the second half of the eighteenth century. She suggests that the 'rigidification of racial ideology' in France at this time was the result of this tension; racism was a means of justifying exceptions to the 'abstract notion of freedom'. See Peabody, *'There are no slaves'*, pp. 68–71.
46. Smith, 'Révolution(s)', p. 75; Taffin, 'Citoyens', p. 240.
47. Cited in Smith, 'Révolution(s)', p. 73.
48. The argument, although morally reprehensible, had a basis in fact. By 1790 there were 650,000 slaves in French colonies in the Caribbean. Their labour was used in the production of sugar, indigo, tobacco, coffee and other crops whose value to France had grown significantly since 1770. See Israel, *Revolutionary Ideas*, p. 398; and Mikaberidze, *The Napoleonic Wars*, p. 41.
49. Mikaberidze, *The Napoleonic Wars*, p. 41.
50. The latter decision was made only after Great Britain had seized control of Saint-Domingue and most other French Caribbean possessions, rendering the decree largely symbolic as far as the Caribbean was concerned.
51. On the events of the Revolution in the Mascarenes, see Prentout, *L'Île de France*, pp. 73–93; Wanquet, *Histoire*; Sivasundaram, *Waves*, pp. 97–103.
52. Cited in Wanquet, *Histoire*, vol 2, p. 486.
53. Cited in Sivasundaram, *Waves*, p. 101.
54. Cited in Wanquet, *Histoire*, vol 2, p. 487.
55. Cited in Labernadie, *La Révolution*, p. 122. Details of several voyages during these years are provided in Allen, *European Slave Trading*, pp. 98, 118–20.
56. Cited in Labernadie, *La Révolution*, p. 122.
57. Cited in Weber, *La France et l'Inde*, vol. 1, p. 471.
58. Cited in Weber, *La France et l'Inde*, vol. 1, p. 472.

59. Labernadie, *La Révolution*, p. 173.
60. Allen, *European Slave Trading*, p. 98.
61. Cornwallis was a veteran of the Seven Years' War and the American War of Independence. As the general of the British army who had surrendered at Yorktown in October 1781, he was widely held responsible in Britain for the loss of the American colonies. He arrived in India determined to restore his reputation and make sure that no similar fate befell the British possessions on the subcontinent. What is more, he was highly suspicious of the intentions of the French in India. 'The French Nation has long seen with jealous impatience the extensive power and influence which we possess in this part of the world, and their attempts to subvert it have been manifest in a variety of secret machinations and unavowed intrigues', he recorded. Cited in Kennedy, 'Anglo-French rivalry', p. 185. See also Dalrymple, *The Anarchy*, pp. 314, 323–4; Hasan, *History*, pp. 147–52.
62. Cited in Bowring, *Haidar Ali*, p. 216.
63. Sen, *The French in India*, pp. 523–4.
64. Hasan, *History*, pp. 179–82.
65. Sarkar, 'General Raymond', p. 134.
66. Dalrymple, *The Anarchy*, p. 341.
67. Narratives of the Third Anglo-Mysore War include Hasan, *History*, pp. 186–270; Forrest, *Tiger of Mysore*, pp. 126–202; and Dalrymple, *The Anarchy*, pp. 323–7.
68. Sen, *The French in India*, p. 525; Hasan, *History*, p. 248.
69. Dalrymple, *The Anarchy*, p. 324.
70. Untitled note written at Pondicherry, 9 March 1792, NAF/9373 ff. 379–82. Le Clerc de Fresne also blamed Tipu's tactics, noting that he had 'shown in this war more energy than conduct. If he had made earlier and better use of his means, his enemies would never have been able to enter his country.' For the figures, see Michaud, *Histoire*, vol. 1, p. 150.
71. Cited in Labernadie, *La Révolution*, p. 137. For a fuller account, see the proceedings of the General Assembly, 1 April 1793, INDE/A/52, pp. 368–75.
72. Castonnet des Fosses, *La Révolution*, p. 23.
73. Moline, *Mémoire*, p. 4.
74. Moline, *Mémoire*, p. 25.
75. Moline, *Mémoire*, p. 35; Jasanoff, *Edge of Empire*, p. 120.
76. Jasanoff notes that the Revolutionary and Napoleonic Wars differed from previous conflicts between France and Britain in that 'the clash was no longer between two different models of crown, church and

state; it was between two drastically opposing visions of society' and therefore 'fervently ideological'. See Jasanoff, *Edge of Empire*, pp. 117–18.

77. Cited in Kennedy, 'Anglo-French rivalry', p. 242.
78. The British authorities in Calcutta also prevented the deportation of Montigny and his supporters to France and granted them asylum in the EIC's territories. See Ivermee, *Hooghly*, p. 121.
79. Sen, *The French in India*, p. 446.
80. Labernadie, *La Révolution*, p. 149. The siege is recounted in the 'Précis historique de ce qui s'est passé au siège de Pondichéry en 1793', NAF/9373, ff. 418–34.
81. Labernadie, *Le Vieux Pondichéry*, pp. 405–6.
82. Castonnet des Fosses, *La Révolution*, p. 31.
83. Moline, *Mémoire*, p. 16.
84. Cited in Besson, *Les aventuriers*, p. 220.
85. For Lescallier's report to the Convention, dated 16 October 1794, see COL/C2/304, ff. 68–78. Summaries are provided in Sen, *The French in India*, pp. 530–2; and Labernadie, *La Révolution*, pp. 339–42.
86. Sarkar, 'General Raymond', p. 126.
87. Jasanoff, *Edge of Empire*, p. 92.
88. Weber, *La France et l'Inde*, vol. 1, pp. 500–1; Batbedat, 'Au service', pp. 162–3.
89. Smith, 'Révolution(s)', pp. 71–2.
90. 'Exposé de nos liaisons avec Tipou Sultan', 1794, NAF/9373, ff. 435–6.
91. Brittlebank, *Tiger*, pp. 67–8; Michaud, *Histoire*, vol. 1, p. 151.
92. 'Écrit de la part de Tipou Sultan', 17 April 1796, COL/C2/304, ff 138–9r.
93. On Ripaud, see Michaud, *Histoire*, vol. 1, p. 172–84; Sen, *The French in India*, pp. 549–55; and Sivasundaram, *Waves*, pp. 104–9.
94. Weber, *La France et l'Inde*, vol. 1, p. 489. Given Ripaud's enthusiasm for the ideas of the revolution, the club was more than a mere 'publicity stunt' (Sivasundaram, *Waves*, p. 108).
95. On these events, see the 'Procès-verbal des séances du club des jacobins formé à Seringapatam', annex 3, Michaud, *Histoire*, vol. 1, pp. 251–76. The quote comes from p. 271.
96. Sen, *The French in India*, p. 550.
97. 'Traduction des papiers persans trouvés dans le palais de Tippoo-Sultan', annex 5, Michaud, *Histoire*, vol. 1, pp. 340–76, on pp. 344, 352 and 354.
98. Cited in Weber, *La France et l'Inde*, vol. 1, p. 511.

99. Cited in Hasan, *History*, p. 288.
100. 'Proclamation', 30 January 1798, [Anon. (ed.)], *Official Documents*, p. 160.
101. Michaud, *Histoire*, vol. 1, p. 183.
102. For details, see Jasanoff, *Edge of Empire*, pp. 129–31.
103. Michaud, *Histoire*, vol. 1, p. 158.
104. Cited in Mikaberidze, *The Napoleonic Wars*, p. 90.
105. Cited in Weber, *La France et l'Inde*, vol. 1, p. 511. See also Charles-Roux, *L'Angleterre*, pp. 178–9.
106. Cited in Mikaberidze, *The Napoleonic Wars*, p. 74.
107. Cited in Weber, *La France et l'Inde*, vol. 1, p. 506. See also Gaffarel, *La politique*, pp. 351–2.
108. Cited in Weber, *La France et l'Inde*, vol. 1, p. 507.
109. Charles-Roux, *L'Angleterre* pp. 246–56.
110. Jasanoff, *Edge of Empire*, pp. 137–48.
111. Charles-Roux, *L'Angleterre*, p. 175.
112. Bonaparte to Tipu Sultan, 26 January 1799, annex 6, Michaud, *Histoire*, vol. 1, p. 377. The letter was intercepted by the British off the coast of Jeddah the following month and never reached Seringapatam.
113. Historians disagree about whether Wellesley's fears of a French revival in India were genuine or instrumentalised to justify a new policy of 'offensive militarism' (Jasanoff, *Edge of Empire*, p. 123). The truth no doubt lies somewhere between the two. Given the success of France's revolutionary armies elsewhere, fears of the French 'menace' were real, although Wellesley's policies were also informed by strategic calculation. On Wellesley, see Dalrymple, *The Anarchy*, pp. 337–40.
114. Cited in Sen, *The French in India*, p. 553.
115. [Anon. (ed.)], 'Extract from a letter', *Official Documents*, pp. ix–xx, on p. x.
116. Ripaud to Tipu Sultan, 23 May 1797, annex 6, Michaud, *Histoire*, vol. 1, pp. 336–9.
117. Batbedat, 'Au service', pp. 165–6.
118. Cited in Batbedat, 'Au service', pp. 165–6. See also Dalrymple, *The Anarchy*, pp. 339–40.
119. Batbedat, 'Au service', p. 166.
120. Hasan, *History*, p. 291. For a description of this coup, see Dalrymple, *The Anarchy*, pp. 341–3.
121. Dalrymple, *The Anarchy*, p. 345.
122. Labernadie, *Le Vieux Pondichéry*, p. 409.
123. Wellesley to Tipu Sultan, 4 November 1798, [Anon. (ed.)], *Official Documents*, pp. 150–1, on p. 150.

124. Wellesley to Tipu Sultan, 4 November 1798, [Anon. (ed.)], *Official Documents*, pp. 150–1, on pp. 150–1.
125. Wellesley to Tipu Sultan, 8 November 1798, [Anon. (ed.)], *Official Documents*, pp. 151–3, on p. 152.
126. Selim III to Tipu Sultan, 20 September 1798, [Anon. (ed.)], *Official Documents*, pp. 163–5, on pp. 164–5.
127. Tipu Sultan to Wellesley, 20 November 1798, [Anon. (ed.)], *Official Documents*, pp. 153–4, on p. 153.
128. Tipu Sultan to Wellesley, 18 December 1798, [Anon. (ed.)], *Official Documents*, pp. 154–5, on p. 154.
129. Four Mysore officials travelled with the officer, Dubuc. The party made it as far as the Seychelles before being taken into British custody, by which time Tipu was dead. Dubuc did later make it back to Paris to inform Napoleon of Tipu's demise. See Hasan, *History*, pp. 300–1.
130. For these troop numbers, see Hasan, *History*, p. 306; and Forrest, *Tiger of Mysore*, pp. 377–8. The promised Maratha troops did not arrive in time for the fighting (Dalrymple, *The Anarchy*, p. 345).
131. Forrest, *Tiger of Mysore*, p. 285; Dalrymple, *The Anarchy*, p. 348.
132. Lafont, *Indika*, p. 156.
133. Hasan, *History*, p. 317.
134. 'French troops', Husain (ed.), *The Dreams*, pp. 81–2; also cited in Jasanoff, *Edge of Empire,* p. 162.
135. Kirmani, *The History*, p. 252.
136. 'Rapport officiel du Chef de Brigade Chapuis', 30 April 1801, COL/C2/305, ff. 3–9. After the war, most of Tipu's remaining territories were divided up between the EIC and Hyderabad. The Wadiyar dynasty deposed by Haidar Ali was then reinstated at Mysore, with the five-year-old Krishnaraja Wadiyar III placed on the throne under British supervision.
137. For a summary and discussion of the terms, see Mikaberidze, *The Napoleonic Wars*, pp. 125–7.
138. Sen, *The French in India*, pp. 560–1.
139. Mikaberidze, *The Napoleonic Wars*, p. 135.
140. Mikaberidze, *The Napoleonic Wars*, p. 129.
141. Cited in Prentout, *L'Île de France*, p. 27.
142. On the terms of the treaty, see Dalrymple, *The Anarchy*, pp. 358–9; and Hatalkar, *Relations*, p. 265.
143. Lafont, 'Observations', p. 146.
144. On Perron, who is not to be confused with Piron at Hyderabad, see Martineau, *Le Général Perron*; Besson, *Les aventuriers*, pp. 194–213;

Compton, *A particular account*, pp. 221–336; and Brantes, 'A Glimpse of France'.

145. Compton, *A particular account*, p. 312.
146. Dalrymple, *The Anarchy*, p. 380. A number of French officers served in the Sikh kingdom in the Punjab between 1822 and 1846. At least one took part in the First Anglo-Sikh War (1845–46). See Lafont, *Indika*, pp. 205–14; and Weber, *La France et l'Inde*, vol. 1, pp. 565–84.
147. Prentout, *L'Île de France*, pp. 401–12; Gaffarel, *La politique*, pp. 378–9.
148. Gaffarel, *La politique*, pp. 386–416; Mikaberidze, *The Napoleonic Wars*, pp. 430–40; Sen, *The French in India,* pp. 580–6.
149. Cited in Sivasundaram, *Waves*, p. 119. On the British capture of the Masacarenes, including the figures mentioned above, see Mikaberidze, *The Napoleonic Wars*, pp. 496–8; and Malleson, *Final French Struggles*, pp. 124–57.
150. Cited in Las Cases, *Mémorial*, vol. 2, part 3, pp. 248–9.
151. Cited in Las Cases, *Mémorial*, vol. 2, part 4, p. 132. The Revolutionary and Napoleonic Wars cost an estimated 6 million lives around the world. Mikaberidze, *The Napoleonic Wars*, p. 628.

10. AFTERLIVES

1. Other terms of the peace included the surrender by France of all its territorial gains in Europe subsequent to 1792, and the relinquishing of French control over Tobago and Saint Lucia to the British, though Martinique, Guadeloupe and Guiana were recognised as French. The Cape of Good Hope—also vital for the maritime route to India—remained in British hands after the war. See Mikaberidze, *The Napoleonic Wars*, pp. 484–5.
2. As Mikaberidze notes, the Revolutionary and Napoleonic Wars also marked the end of the great age of European trading companies in the Indian Ocean (Mikaberidze, *The Napoleonic Wars*, p. 632). The final Compagnie des Indes was wound up in 1793, as we saw in the previous chapter, and the VOC dissolved in 1799. The EIC lost its trading monopoly in 1813 and, with colonial government henceforth its main focus, was closely regulated by the state, which then took over the territories of the company in India in 1858. These changes confirmed the dawn of a new age in which free trade was the prevailing economic orthodoxy.
3. Mohan, *Claiming India*, p. 348.
4. Weber, *La France et l'Inde*, vol. 1, p. 849. 133,588 lived in Pondicherry; 96,520 in Karikal; 24,266 in Chandernagore; 8,084 in Mahé; and

5,728 in Yanaon. Most of the European and 'mixed' population lived in Pondicherry: 2,161 out of the total of 2,854.

5. Weber, *La France et l'Inde*, vol. 1, p. 691.
6. Cited in Mikaberidze, *The Napoleonic Wars*, p. 632.
7. Allen, *European Slave Trading*, pp. 10, 118; Weber, *La France et l'Inde*, vol. 1, p. 792. Clearly, the bans on the export of slaves announced by British and French authorities in India in the 1790s (see the previous chapter) did not eradicate the practice.
8. Weber, *La France et l'Inde*, vol. 1, p. 830; Northrup, 'Indentured Indians', p. 259. The export of indentured labourers from French India and their shipping to French colonies, which also took place from British India, were governed by an Anglo-French convention signed in 1861 that was supposed to set minimum standards for the treatment of labourers. Alleged French abuses of the terms of the convention was the main reason for suspending it.
9. Northrup, *Indentured Labor*, p. 21.
10. For an overview, see Mohan, *Claiming India*, pp. xxviii–xxxiii.
11. An important recent study of this 'intellectual conquest' is Mohan, *Claiming India*, although the phrase itself comes from Marsh, who has also considered the topic (Marsh, *India*, p.140). Mohan writes that this was a matter of 'national pride'; the public view, which also shaped the motivations of the scholars involved, was that 'having irrevocably lost India to the British the French could at least claim a superior understanding of India' (pp. xxvi–xxvii).
12. On historiography on French India in the nineteenth and twentieth centuries and the link with new colonial and imperial projects, see Vigié, *Dupleix*, pp. 538–58; Weber, *La France et l'Inde*, vol. 2, pp. 304–27; Agmon, 'Failure on Display'; and Marsh, 'Territorial Loss', pp. 2–6.
13. Vigié, *Dupleix*, p. 548.
14. British authors of the nineteenth and early twentieth century also studied Dupleix with admiration and tried to draw lessons from France's mistakes that could be applied to the preservation of British rule in India. See for example Malleson, *History*, pp. 333–7.
15. On Martineau and 'the role of historical thinking and the production of historiography by and for colonial administrators', see Agmon, 'Failure on Display'. The volumes written by Martineau are listed in the bibliography.
16. Mohan, *Claiming India,* pp. 345–6; Vigié, *Dupleix*, p. 542.
17. This understanding of British colonialism was reinforced among French observers by the Indian Rebellion of 1857–58 and its brutal

suppression, which appeared to confirm the tyrannical nature of British rule. See Frith, *The French*. The French, in contrast, were in India to 'serve the interests of humanity', as one writer of the Third Republic put it (Labernadie, *Le Vieux Pondichéry*, p. 424).

18. On the policies of the Third Republic in French India, see Weber, *Pondichéry*, pp. 213–322; Weber, *La France et l'Inde*, vol. 2, pp. 233–310; and Raffin, *Republican Citizenship*.
19. Namakkal, *Unsettling Utopia*, p. 80.
20. On the reaction of upper caste Hindus against this assimilationist approach, including their alliance with French conservatives equally opposed to the policies of the Third Republic, see Weber, 'Chanemougam'.
21. Ghose had already spent one year in prison in Calcutta accused of being involved in the Alipore Bomb Plot—an attempt to assassinate a British magistrate that had seen two British women killed. He was acquitted of this charge and released in May 1909. A number of biographies of Ghose recount these events, including Chaturvedi, *Mystic Fire*.
22. Even Mahatma Gandhi would later speak in praise of France and its commitment to liberty, overlooking the realities of life in France's colonial empire in the interwar period. See Marsh, 'Pondichéry', p. 21.
23. On the decolonisation of French India, see Neogy, *Decolonization*; Namakkal, *Unsettling Utopia*; More, *Freedom movement*; Sen, *Chandernagore*; and Miles, *Imperial Burdens*, pp. 57–82.
24. Cited in Sen, *Chandernagore*, p. 139.
25. Cited in Sen, *Chandernagore*, p. 309.
26. Cited in Sen, *Chandernagore*, p. 151.
27. Neogy, *Decolonization*, p. 93.
28. Namakkal, *Unsettling Utopia*, pp. 70–6.
29. Namakkal, *Unsettling Utopia*, p. 116.
30. More, *Freedom movement*, is dedicated to these events at Mahé.
31. Sen, *Chandernagore*, is focused on the campaign for independence at Chandernagore. For the referendum results, see p. 145.
32. Neogy, *Decolonization*, p. 260.
33. The terms of the treaty are reproduced as an appendix in Namakkal, *Unsettling Utopia*, pp. 209–22.
34. 'The feeling of betrayal that our combatants in Indochina or Algeria feel today, their predecessors experienced before them', wrote Roger Glachant in his *Histoire de l'Inde des Français* (1965). Cited in Vigié, *Dupleix*, p. 558.

35. Weber, *La France et l'Inde*, vol. 2, pp. 746–8.
36. Rai, *The Legacy*, p. 111; Weber, *La France et l'Inde*, vol. 2, p. 746.
37. Cited in Namakkal, *Unsettling Utopia*, p. 147.
38. Namakkal, *Unsettling Utopia*, p. 165. As Namakkal notes, the French state does not collect data on the ethnicity or national background of its citizens, which makes the exact figures impossible to ascertain. Among the other French nationals of South Asian descent living in France today are a significant number of Tamil refugees from the civil war in Sri Lanka, and their descendants.
39. Namakkal, *Unsettling Utopia*, p. 168.
40. Namakkal, *Unsettling Utopia*, pp. 202–3.
41. The study in question is Namakkal, *Unsettling Utopia*. See especially pp. 173–200. The quote is from a speech made by Mirra Alfassa in 1965, taken from the Auroville website, https://auroville.org (accessed 9.3.24).
42. 'Manoir des Indes', https://fr.gaultmillau.com/hotels/manoir-des-indes (accessed 9.3.24).
43. A good discussion of enduring French stereotypes about British and American people can be found in E. Chabal, 'Les Anglo-Saxons'.
44. Anshul, 'Why Emmanuel Macron'.
45. Blake Smith points out that in 2017 France launched a programme of cultural diplomacy called 'Bonjour India' that promised to tell Indian people 'the story of how and when we met'. The programme 'discreetly avoid[ed] many topics of the Franco-Indian past'. Smith, 'The Failed Empire'.
46. Namakkal reminds us that official accounts of decolonisation, claiming that it was peaceful and consensual, similarly efface people's lived experience of the process. For many who experienced it, decolonisation was a painful and violent 'rupture'. She recounts that the term 'French colonisation' was removed from a talk given at a conference in Auroville in 2012 to mark the fiftieth anniversary of the Treaty of Cession and replaced by the term 'French presence' at the suggestion of the French ambassador. See Namakkal, *Unsettling Utopia*, pp. 143–4, 203–4.
47. Loi n° 2001-434 du 21 mai 2001 tendant à la reconnaissance de la traite et de l'esclavage en tant que crime contre l'humanité, *Légifrance*, https://www.legifrance.gouv.fr/loda/id/JORFTEXT000000405369/ (accessed 9.3.24).
48. In an interesting essay on the museum, Marsh notes that the curating of its permanent collection falls into certain traps common to

historiography on French India, including a nostalgic focus on the eighteenth century, and the treatment of the company's slave trading and presence in India as if they were unrelated. Marsh, 'Les paradoxes'.

BIBLIOGRAPHY

Archival sources

Archives nationales, Paris

Fonds de la Marine, Service général, Campagnes (MAR/B/4)
Fonds des colonies, Inde (COL/C2)

Archives nationales d'outre-mer, Aix-en-Provence

Dépôt des fortifications des colonies (DFC)
Fonds territoriaux, Établissements français de l'Inde (INDE)

Bibliothèque nationale de France, Paris

Manuscrits français (MF)
Nouvelles acquisitions françaises (NAF)

British Library, London

India Office Records, The French in India Series (IOR/I/1)

Centre des Archives diplomatiques, La Courneuve

Correspondance politique, Angleterre (8CP)
Mémoires et documents, Asie (8MD)

Published collections of archival sources

[Anon. (ed.)], *A Collection of All the Treaties of Peace, Alliance, and Commerce, between Great-Britain and Other Powers, from the Treaty Signed at Munster in 1648 to the Treaties Signed at Paris in 1783*. Three volumes (London: J. Debrett, 1785).

— (ed.), *Official Documents, Relative to the Negotiations Carried on by Tippoo Sultaun, with the French Nation and Other Foreign States* (Calcutta: The Honorable Company's Press, 1799).

Dernis (ed.), *Recueil ou collection des titres, édits, déclarations, arrêts, règlemens et autres pièces concernant la Compagnie des Indes orientales établie au mois d'août 1664*. Four volumes (Paris: Antoine Boudet, 1755–56).

Hatalkar, V. G. (ed.), *French Records (Relating to the History of the Marathas)*. Nine volumes (Bombay: Maharashtra State Board for Literature and Culture, 1980).

Hill, S. C. (ed.), *Bengal in 1756–1757: A Selection of Public and Private Papers Dealing with the Affairs of the British in Bengal During the Reign of Siraj-Uddaula*. Three volumes (London: John Murray, 1905).

Husain, M. (ed.), *The Dreams of Tipu Sultan* ([Unknown]: Pakistan Historical Society, 1957).

Martineau, A. (ed.), *Lettres et conventions des gouverneurs de Pondichéry avec différents princes hindous, 1666–1793* (Pondicherry: Société de l'histoire de l'Inde française, 1911–14).

— (ed.), *Correspondance du conseil supérieur de Pondichéry et de la Compagnie*. Six volumes (Pondicherry: Société de l'histoire de l'Inde française, 1920–30).

— (ed.), *La politique de Dupleix: d'après sa lettre à Saunders du 18 février 1752 et son mémoire du 16 octobre 1753* (Pondicherry: Société de l'histoire de l'Inde française, 1927).

Contemporary publications

[Anon.], *Le Code Noir ou édit du Roy* (Paris: Saugrain, 1685).

— (ed.), *The Travels of Several Learned Missioners of the Society of Jesus, into Diverse Parts of the Archipelago, India, China and America* (London: R. Gosling, 1714 [1713]).

— , *Arrest du Conseil d'Estat du Roy, concernant la Banque et la Compagnie des Indes. Du 23. fevrier 1720* (Paris: Imprimerie royale, 1720).

Beaumarchais, P. A. C. de, *Le vœu de toutes les nations, et l'intérêt de toutes les puissances, dans l'abaissement et l'humiliation de la Grande-Bretagne* ([Unknown]: [Unknown], 1778).

Bellanger de Lespinay, L. A., *Mémoires de L. A. Bellanger de Lespinay sur son voyage en Indes Orientales (1670–75)* (Vendome: Charles Huet, 1895).

Bellecombe, H. de, *Essai biographique sur Guillaume-Léonard de Bellecombe (1728–1792), suivi de la relation du siège de Pondichéry en 1778* (Agen: Vve Lamy, 1896).

Bernier, F., *Travels in the Mogul Empire, AD 1656–1668* (Westminster: Archibald Constable and Co., 1891 [1671]).

[—], 'Nouvelle division de la terre par les différentes espèces ou races d'homme qui l'habitent', *Le Journal des Sçavans pour l'année M. DC. LXXXIV* (Paris: Florentin Lambert et Jean Cusson, 1684), pp. 133–40.

Bussy, C. J. P. de, *Mémoire à consulter et consultation pour le sieur de Bussy, maréchal des camps & armées du roi, au sujet du mémoire que le sieur de Lally, lieutenant général, vient de répandre dans le public* (Paris: 1766).

—, *Journal de Bussy, commandant général des forces de terre et de mer dans l'Inde, 13 novembre 1781–31 mars 1783*. Edited by A. Martineau (Pondicherry: Société de l'histoire de l'Inde française, 1932).

Cambridge, R. O., *An Account of the War in India, Between the English and French, on the Coast of Coromandel, from the Year 1750 to the Year 1761* (London: T. Jefferys, 1762).

Carré, B., *The Travels of the Abbé Carré in India and the Near East 1672–74*. Three volumes (New Delhi: AES, 1990).

Challe, R., *Journal d'un voyage fait aux Indes orientales*. Three volumes (Rouen: J.B. Machuel le jeune, 1721).

Charpentier, F. *Discours d'un fidèle sujet du roi touchant l'établissement d'une compagnie françoise pour le commerce des Indes orientales* (Paris: [Unknown], 1665).

—, *Relation de l'établissement de la Compagnie française pour le commerce des Indes orientales* (Paris: Cramoisy, 1665).

Chevalier, J. B., *Les aventures de Jean-Baptiste Chevalier dans l'Inde orientale (1752–1765): mémoire historique et journal de voyage à Assem*. Edited by J. Deloche (Paris: École française d'Extrême-Orient, 1984).

Choiseul, E. F. de, *Mémoire de Monsieur de Choiseul remis au roi en 1765*. Edited by C. Giraud (Paris: Imp. Nationale, 1881).

Duprat, P. A., *Voyage du Comte Duprat dans l'Inde* (London: [Unknown], 1780).

Flacourt, E. de, *Histoire de la grande isle Madagascar [...] avec une relation de ce qui s'est passé ès années 1655, 1656 et 1657*. Two volumes (Paris: G. Clouzier, 1661).

Gentil, J. B. J., *Mémoires sur l'Indoustan, ou Empire mogol* (Paris: Petit, 1822).

Hugau, C., *Le voyage extraordinaire d'un capitaine de dragons chez Hyder Ali*

Khan: 1769–1772. Edited by F. de Valence (Paris: Maisonneuve & Larose, 2001).

Kirmani, H. A. K., *The History of the Reign of Tipu Sultan, Being a Translation of the Neshani Hyduri* (London: Oriental Translation Fund of Great Britain and Ireland, 1864).

La Boullaye-Le Gouz, F. de, *Les voyages et observations du sieur de La Boullaye Le Gouz* (Paris: Gervais Clovsier, 1653).

La Bourdonnais, B. F. de, *Mémoire pour le sieur de La Bourdonnais, avec les pièces justificatives* (Paris: Delaguette, 1750).

La Haye, J. B. de, *Journal du voyage des grandes Indes*. Two volumes (Paris: Robert et Nicolas Pepie, 1698).

[La Tour, M. de]., *Histoire d'Ayder-Ali-Khan, ou nouveaux mémoires sur l'Inde*. Two volumes (Paris: Cailleau, 1783).

Las Cases, E. de, *Mémorial de Sainte Hélène: Journal of the Private Life and Conversations of the Emperor Napoleon at St. Helena*. Four volumes (London: Henry Colburn, 1823).

Law de Lauriston, J., *État politique de l'Inde en 1777* . Edited by A. Martineau (Paris: H. Champion, 1913).

—, *Mémoire sur quelques affaires de l'Empire mogol 1756–61*. Edited by A. Martineau (Paris: Société de l'histoire des colonies françaises, 1913).

Lawrence, S., 'Narrative of the war on the coast of Coromandel, from the beginning of the troubles to the year 1754' in R. O. Cambridge (ed.), *An Account of the War in India, Between the English and French, on the Coast of Coromandel, from the Year 1750 to the Year 1761* (London: T. Jefferys, 1762), pp. 1–100.

L'Estra, F., *Relation ou journal d'un voyage fait aux Indes orientales* (Paris: Estienne Michallet, 1677).

Madec, R., *Mémoire de René Madec. Nabab dans l'Empire mogol—commandant d'un parti français au service de l'empereur (1736–1784)*. Edited by M. Vignes and J. Deloche (Pondicherry: Alliance Française, 1983).

Martin, F., *Description du premier voyage fait aux Indes orientales par les françois en l'an 1603* (Paris: Laurens Sonnius, 1604).

—, *Mémoires de François Martin, fondateur de Pondichéry (1665–1696)*. Three volumes. Edited by A. Martineau (Paris: Société d'Éditions Géographiques, Maritimes et Coloniales, 1931–33).

Michaud, J. F., *Histoire des progrès et de la chute de l'empire de Mysore, sous les règnes d'Hyder-Aly et Tippoo-Saïb*. Two volumes (Paris: Giguet, 1801).

Modave, L. L. de, *Voyage en Inde du Comte de Modave, 1773–1776. Nouveaux mémoires sur l'état actuel du Bengale et de l'Indoustan*. Edited by J. Deloche (Paris: École française d'Extrême-Orient, 1971).

Moline, P. L., *Mémoire historique et politique sur les Indes Orientales* (Paris: Maret, 1795).

Montesquieu, *De l'esprit des loix*. Two volumes (Geneva: Barrillot et fils, 1748).

Orme, R., *A History of the Military Transactions of the British Nation in Indostan, from the Year MDCCXLV*. Two volumes (London: F. Wingrave, 1803).

Pillai, A. R., *The Diary of Ananda Ranga Pillai*. Twelve volumes (Madras: Government Press, 1904–28).

Piveron de Morlat, A., *Mémoire sur l'Inde (1786): les opérations diplomatiques et militaires françaises aux Indes pendant la guerre d'indépendance américaine*. Edited by J. M. Lafont (Paris: Riveneuve, 2012).

Pyrard, F., *The Voyage of François Pyrard of Laval to the East Indies, the Maldives, the Moluccas and Brazil*. Two volumes (London: Hakluyt Society, 1887 [1619]).

[Raynal, G. T. (ed.)], *Histoire philosophique et politique des établissemens & du commerce des Européens dans les deux Indes*. Six volumes (Amsterdam: [Unknown], 1770).

— (ed.), *Histoire philosophique et politique des établissemens & du commerce des Européens dans les deux Indes*. Ten volumes (Geneva: Jean-Leonard Pellet, 1780).

Roubaud, P. J. A, *Le politique indien, ou considérations sur les colonies des Indes orientales* (Amsterdam: [Unknown], 1768).

Suffren, P. A., *Journal de bord du bailli de Suffren dans l'Inde: 1781–1784*. Edited by H. Moris (Paris: Challamel, 1888).

Tavernier, J. B., *Les six voyages de Jean-Baptiste Tavernier*. Two volumes (Paris: Gervais Clouzier et Claude Barbin, 1676).

Voltaire, *Précis du siècle de Louis XV*. Two volumes (Geneva: [Unknown], 1769).

—, *Fragments sur l'Inde, sur le général Lalli et sur le comte de Morangiès* ([Unknown]: [Unknown], 1773).

Secondary works

Agmon, D., *A Colonial Affair: Commerce, Conversion, and Scandal in French India* (Ithaca: Cornell University Press, 2017).

—, 'Failure on Display: The Meaning of Eighteenth-Century French India in Twentieth-Century Colonial Administration and Historiography', *The Journal of Modern History*, vol. 91 (2019), pp. 848–82.

Allen, R. B., *European Slave Trading in the Indian Ocean, 1500–1850* (Athens, Ohio: Ohio University Press, 2014).

Alpers, E. A., 'The French Slave Trade in East Africa (1721–1810)', *Cahiers d'Études africaines*, vol. 37 (1970), pp. 80–124.

Ames, G. J., *Colbert, Mercantilism and the French Quest for Asian Trade* (DeKalb: Northern Illinois University Press, 2016).

Annoussamy, D., 'The Merger of French India' in K.S. Mathew and S. J. Stephen (eds.), *Indo-French Relations* (Delhi: Pragati, 1999), pp. 64–76.

—, *L'intermède français en Inde: secousses politiques et mutations juridiques* (Pondicherry: Institut français de Pondichéry, 2005).

—, *Pondicherry: A Social and Political History* (Pondicherry: Institut français de Pondichéry, 2020).

Anshul, G. K., 'Why Emmanuel Macron and the French are India's closest "mitron"', *India Today*, 25 January 2024, https://www.indiatoday.in/india/story/emanuel-macron-pm-narendra-modi-75-republic-day-chief-guest-26-january-indo-french-strategic-partnership (accessed 26.1.24).

Asher, C. B. and C. Talbot, *India before Europe* (Cambridge: Cambridge University Press, 2006).

Association des amis du SHD Lorient, 'La vie à bord' in R. Estienne (ed.), *Les Compagnies des Indes* (Paris: Gallimard, 2013), pp. 132–9.

Barbé, E., *Le nabab René Madec: histoire diplomatique des projets de la France sur le Bangale et le Pendjab (1772–1808)* (Paris: Felix Alcan, 1894).

Batbedat, J., 'Au service des princes indiens' in R. Vincent (ed.), *L'aventure des Français en Inde, du XVIIe au XXe siècle* (Pondicherry: Kailash, 2011), pp. 141–74.

Baugh, D., *The Global Seven Years War, 1754–1763* (London and New York: Routledge, 2011).

Bayly, C. A., *Indian Society and the Making of the British Empire: The New Cambridge History of India II.1* (Cambridge: Cambridge University Press, 1988).

Bell, D., 'Recent Works on Early Modern French National Identity', *The Journal of Modern History*, vol. 68, no. 1 (1996), pp. 84–113.

Bertrand, M., *Suffren de Saint-Tropez aux Indes* (Paris: Perrin, 1991).

Besson, M., *Les aventuriers français aux Indes (1775–1820)* (Paris: Payot, 1932).

Bowring, L. B., *Haidar Ali and Tipu Sultan and the Struggle with the Musalman Powers of the South* (Dehra Dun: EBD Publishing, n.d.).

Boxer, C. R., *The Dutch Seaborne Empire 1600–1800* (London: Pelican, 1973).

Brantes, Charles-H. de, 'A Glimpse of France in the Hughly Belt: Perron in Chinsurah' in Lipi Ghosh and Rila Mukherjee (eds), *Rethinking*

Connectivity: Region, Place, and Space in Asia (Delhi: Primus Books, 2016), pp. 96–103.

Brittlebank, K., *Tipu Sultan's Search for Legitimacy: Islam and Kingship in a Hindu Domain* (New Delhi: Oxford University Press India, 1998).

—, *Tiger: The Life of Tipu Sultan* (Swansea: Claritas, 2020).

Carton, A. 'Shades of Fraternity: Creolization and the Making of Citizenship in French India, 1790–1792', *French Historical Studies*, vol. 31, no. 4 (2008), pp. 581–607.

Castonnet des Fosses, H., *La Révolution et les clubs dans l'Inde française* (Nantes: V. Forest et E. Grimaud, 1885).

—, *La Boullaye Le Gouz, sa vie et ses voyages* (Angers: Germain et G. Grassin, 1891).

Chabal, E., 'Les Anglo-Saxons', Aeon, 18 September 2017, https://aeon.co/essays/the-anglo-saxon-is-not-american-or-british-but-a-french-alter-ego (accessed 9.3.24)

Chaline, O., *Le règne de Louis XIV* (Paris: Flammarion, 2010).

Charles-Roux, F., *L'Angleterre et l'expédition française en Égypte* (Cairo: Société royale de géographie d'Égypte, 1925).

Chassaigne, M., *Bussy en Inde* (Paris: R. Clavreuil, 1976).

Chaturvedi, A. N., *Mystic Fire: The Life of Sri Aurobindo* (Bengaluru: Rupa, 2022).

Chaudhuri, K. N., *The Trading World of Asia and the English East India Company, 1660–1760* (Cambridge: Cambridge University Press, 1978).

Claeys, T., 'La grande crise financière de la fin du règne de Louis XIV' in R. Estienne (ed.), *Les Compagnies des Indes* (Paris: Gallimard, 2013), pp. 56–61.

Clarin de La Rive, A., *Dupleix ou les Français aux Indes orientales* (Lille: Desclée de Brouwer, 1888).

Cole, C. W., *Colbert and a Century of French Mercantilism*. Two volumes (New York: Columbia University Press, 1939).

Colley, L., *Britons: Forging the Nation 1707–1837* (New Haven, Connecticut: Yale University Press, 2008).

Crepin, P., *Mahé de La Bourdonnais, gouverneur général des îles de France et de Bourbon (1699–1753)* (Paris: Société de l'histoire des colonies françaises, 1922).

Crook, M., *Elections in the French Revolution: An Apprenticeship in Democracy, 1789–1799* (Cambridge: Cambridge University Press, 1996).

Cross, E., *Company Politics: Commerce, Scandal, and French Visions of Indian Empire in the Revolutionary Era* (New York: Oxford University Press, 2023).

Cultru, P., *Dupleix. Ses plans politiques. Sa disgrâce* (Paris: Hachette, 1901).

Dalrymple, W., 'The East India Company: The Original Corporate Raiders', *The Guardian*, 4 March 2015, https://www.theguardian.com/world/2015/mar/04/east-india-company-original-corporate-raiders (accessed 7.4.22).

—, *The Anarchy: The Relentless Rise of the East India Company* (London: Bloomsbury, 2020).

Das, S., *Myths and Realities of French Imperialism in India, 1763–1783* (New York: Peter Lang, 1992).

David, S., *Military Blunders* (London: Constable, 2012).

Deloche, J., *Jean-Baptiste Chevalier (1729–1789): le dernier champion de la cause française en Inde* (Paris: Ecole française d'Extrême Orient et Les Indes savants, 2003).

Dodwell, H., *Dupleix and Clive: The Beginning of Empire* (London: Methuen & Co., 1920).

Eccles, W. J., *The French in North America, 1500–1765* (Michigan: Michigan State University Press, 1998).

Estienne, R., 'Le port de Lorient, comptoir industrieux des Indes' in R. Estienne (ed.), *Les Compagnies des Indes* (Paris: Gallimard, 2013), pp. 96–109.

Farrère, C., *L'Inde perdue* (Paris: Ernest Flammarion, 1935).

Forrest, D. M., *Tiger of Mysore: The Life and Death of Tipu Sultan* (Bombay: Allied Publishers, 1970).

Frémont, G., 'Un comptoir en plein essor' in R. Vincent (ed.), *Pondichéry, 1671–1761: l'échec d'un rêve d'empire* (Paris: Éditions Autrement, 1993), pp. 67–87.

Frith, N., *The French Colonial Imagination: Writing the Indian Uprisings, 1857–1858, from Second Empire to Third Republic* (Lanham, MD: Lexington, 2010).

Gaastra, F. *The Dutch East India Company: Expansion and Decline* (Zutphen: Walburg Pers, 2003).

Gaebelé, Y. R., *Créole et grande dame: Johanna Bégum, marquise Dupleix, 1706–1756* (Pondicherry: Bibliothèque colonial, 1934).

Gaffarel, P., *La politique coloniale en France de 1789 à 1830* (Paris: Félix Alcan, 1908).

Geller, J. H., 'Towards a New Imperialism in Eighteenth-Century India: Dupleix, La Bourdonnais and the French Compagnie des Indes', *Portuguese Studies*, vol. 16 (2000), pp. 240–55.

Glachant, R., *Histoire de l'Inde des Français* (Paris: Plon, 1965).

Gobalakichenane, M., 'La Révolution française des Tamouls de Pondichéry' (PhD thesis, Université de Nantes, 1997).

Gottmann, F., *Global Trade, Smuggling, and the Making of Economic Liberalism:*

Asian Textiles in France 1680–1760 (Basingstoke: Palgrave Macmillan, 2016).

Guët, I. M., *Origines de l'Inde française: Jân Begum (Mme Dupleix) 1706–1756* (Paris: Librarie Militaire de L. Baudoin, 1892).

Habib, I. (ed.), *Resistance and Modernization under Haidar Ali and Tipu Sultan* (New Delhi: Tulika, 1999).

Hall, D. G. E., *Europe and Burma: A Study of European Relations with Burma until the Annexation of Thibaw's Kingdom 1886* (London: Oxford University Press, 1945).

Hamont, T., *Un essai d'empire français au XVIIIe siècle: Dupleix d'après sa correspondance inédite* (Paris: E. Plon, 1881).

—, *La fin d'un empire français aux Indes sous Louis XV. Lally-Tollendal, d'après des documents inédits* (Paris: E. Plon, 1887).

Hasan, M., *History of Tipu Sultan* (Calcutta: World Press, 1971).

—, 'The French in the Second Anglo-Mysore War' in I. Habib (ed.), *Resistance and Modernization under Haidar Ali and Tipu Sultan* (New Delhi: Tulika, 1999), pp. 35–48.

Hatalkar, V. G., *Relations between the French and the Marathas (1688–1815)* (Bombay: University of Bombay, 1958).

Haudrère, P., *La Bourdonnais. Marin et aventurier* (Paris: Desjonquères, 1992).

—, 'La Compagnie des Indes' in R. Vincent (ed.), *Pondichéry, 1671–1761: l'échec d'un rêve d'empire* (Paris: Éditions Autrement, 1993), pp. 44–66.

—, 'Des chrétiens chez les hindous' in R. Vincent (ed.), *Pondichéry, 1671–1761: l'échec d'un rêve d'empire* (Paris: Éditions Autrement, 1993), pp. 88–106.

—, *La Compagnie française des Indes au XVIIIe siècle*. Two volumes (Paris: Les Indes Savantes, 2005).

—, *Les Français dans l'océan Indien (XVIIe–XIXe siècle)* (Rennes: Presses Universitaires de Rennes, 2014).

Hautecœur, L., *Louis XIV, Roi Soleil* (Paris: Librairie Plon, 1953).

Hill, S. C., *Three Frenchmen in Bengal, or the Commercial Ruin of the French Settlements in 1757* (London: Longmans, Green & Co., 1903).

Israel, J., *Democratic Enlightenment: Philosophy, Revolution and Human Rights* (Oxford: Oxford University Press, 2013).

—, *Revolutionary Ideas: An Intellectual History of the French Revolution from The Rights of Man to Robespierre* (Princeton: Princeton University Press, 2014).

Ivermee, R., *Hooghly: The Global History of a River* (London: Hurst, 2020).

Jasanoff, M., *Edge of Empire: Conquest and Collecting in the East* (London: Harper Perennial, 2006).

Jones, C., *The Great Nation: France from Louis XIV to Napoleon* (London: Penguin, 2003).

Kaeppelin, P., *La Compagnie des Indes orientales et François Martin* (Paris: Augustin Challamel, 1908).

Keay, J., *The Honourable Company: A History of the English East India Company* (London: HarperCollins, 1993).

Kennedy, B. E., 'Anglo-French Rivalry in India and the Eastern Seas, 1763–1793: A Study of Anglo-French Tensions, and of their Impact on the Consolidation of British Power in the Region' (PhD thesis, Australian National University Canberra, 1969).

Labernadie, M. V., *La Révolution et les établissements français dans l'Inde, 1790–1793, d'après les archives de Pondichéry, des notes et des correspondances inédites* (Paris: Ernest Leroux, 1930).

—, *Le Vieux Pondichéry 1673–1815: histoire d'une ville coloniale française* (Pondicherry: Bibliothèque Publique, 1936).

Lafont, J. M., *Indika: Essays in Indo-French Relations* (New Delhi: Manohar, 2000).

—, 'Observations sur la présence militaire française dans les États indiens 1750–1849' in J. Weber (ed.), *Les relations entre la France et l'Inde de 1673 à nos jours* (Paris: Les Indes Savantes, 2002), pp. 119–54.

—, 'Les mémoires du lieutenant-colonel Russel au sujet de Mysore' in J. Weber (ed.), *Les relations entre la France et l'Inde de 1673 à nos jours* (Paris: Les Indes Savantes, 2002), pp. 155–77.

Lespagnol, A., *Messieurs de Saint-Malo: une élite négociante au temps de Louis XIV* (Saint Malo: l'Ancre de Marine, 1991).

—, 'La Compagnie des Indes Orientales' in R. Estienne (ed.), *Les Compagnies des Indes* (Paris: Gallimard, 2013), pp. 42–55.

Love, H. D., *Vestiges of Old Madras 1640–1800*. Three volumes (London: John Murray, 1913).

Lynn, J. A., *The Wars of Louis XIV 1667–1714* (Abingdon: Routledge, 2013).

MacDougall, P., 'In Support of Napoleon's Great Adventure—the Navy of Tipu Sultan' in A. Coats (ed.), *Where Empires Collide: Dockyards and Naval Bases around the Indian Ocean* (Portsmouth: Naval Dockyards Society, 2022), pp. 81–7.

Malangin, R., 'On the Topic of the Topas: the Porous Fringes of the French Colonial Society in India during the Eighteenth Century', *Revue historique de Pondichéry*, vol. 25 (2013–14), pp. 69–80.

—, 'La crise des établissements français des Indes (1768–1773)', *Annales historiques de la Révolution française*, vol. 375 (2014), pp. 69–88.

—, 'Renoncer à l'Inde? Comptoirs, agents et aventuriers aux Indes orientales à la fin du XVIIIe siècle (1761–1785)' (PhD thesis, Université de Nantes, 2017).

Malleson, G. B., *History of the French in India: From the Founding of Pondicherry in 1674 to the Capture of that Place in 1761* (London: Longmans, Green, & Co., 1868).

—, *Final French Struggles in India and on the Indian Seas* (London: Wm. H. Allen & Co., 1878).

—, *Dupleix (Rulers of India Series)* (Oxford: Clarendon Press, 1890).

Mandelbaum, M., *Mission Failure: America and the World in the Post-Cold War Era* (Oxford: Oxford University Press, 2016).

Manning, C., *Fortunes à faire: The French in Asian Trade* (London and New York: Routledge, 1996).

Mansel, P., *King of the World: The Life of Louis XIV* (London: Allen Lane, 2019).

Mantienne, F., 'Le commerce intra-asiatique français aux XVIIe et XVIIIe siècles' in J. Weber (ed.), *Les relations entre la France et l'Inde de 1673 à nos jours* (Paris: Les Indes Savantes, 2002), pp. 49–72.

Margerison, K., 'French Visions of Empire: Contesting British Power in India after the Seven Years War', *English Historical Review*, vol. 130, no. 544 (2015), pp. 583–612.

Marsh, K., 'Territorial Loss and the Construction of French Colonial Identities, 1763–1962' in K. Marsh and N. Frith (eds), *France's Lost Empires: Fragmentation, Nostalgia, and* la fracture coloniale (Lanham, MD: Lexington, 2010), pp. 1–13.

—, 'Pondichéry: Archive of "French" India', *Francosphères*, vol. 3, no. 1 (2014), pp. 9–23.

—, 'Les paradoxes de la commémoration de l'Inde française', *Outre-Mers*, nos. 388–9 (2015), pp. 117–34.

—, *India in the French Imagination: Peripheral Voices, 1754–1815* (London: Routledge, 2016).

Marshall, P. J., *The Making and Unmaking of Empires: Britain, India, and America c. 1750–1783* (Oxford: Oxford University Press, 2007).

Martineau, A., *Dupleix et l'Inde française*. Four volumes (Paris: Société d'éditions géographiques, maritimes et coloniales, 1920–28).

—, *Dupleix: sa vie et son oeuvre* (Paris: Société d'éditions géographiques, maritimes et coloniales, 1931).

—, *Le Général Perron, généralissime des Armées de Seindia et du Grand Mogol* (Paris: Société d'éditions géographiques, maritimes et coloniales, 1931).

—, *Bussy et l'Inde française* (Paris: Société de l'histoire des colonies françaises, 1935).

Mathew, K. S., 'Missionaries from the Atlantic Regions and the Social

Change in the French Pondicherry from the Seventeenth to Nineteenth Centuries' in J. Weber (ed.), *Les relations entre la France et l'Inde de 1673 à nos jours* (Paris: Les Indes Savantes, 2002), pp. 349–72.

Ménard, P., *Le Français qui possédait l'Amérique: la vie extraordinaire d'Antoine Crozat, escroc millionnaire sous Louis XIV* (Paris: Le Cherche Midi, 2017).

Ménard-Jacob, M., *La première Compagnie des Indes (1664–1704): apprentissages, échecs et héritage* (Rennes: Presses Universitaires de Rennes, 2016).

Mikaberidze, A. *The Napoleonic Wars: A Global History* (Oxford: Oxford University Press, 2020).

Miles, W. F. S., *Imperial Burdens: Countercolonialism in Former French India* (Boulder, Colorado: L. Rienner, 1995).

Mohan, J., *Claiming India: French Scholars and the Preoccupation with India in the Nineteenth Century* (London: Sage, 2018).

More, J. B. P., *Freedom Movement in French India: the Mahe Revolt of 1948* (Tellicherry: IRISH, 2001).

Namakkal, J., *Unsettling Utopia: The Making and Unmaking of French India* (New York: Columbia University Press, 2021).

Nazelle, H. H., *Dupleix et la défense de Pondichéry* (Paris: Librairie Honoré Champion, 1908).

Neogy, A. K., *Decolonization of French India: Liberation Movement and Indo-French Relations 1947–1954* (Pondicherry: Institut Francais de Pondichéry, 1997).

Nicolas, B. and P. Combes, *Musée de la Compagnie des Indes, Musée d'art et d'histoire de la Ville de Lorient: Un cheminement à travers l'histoire et les collections* (Lorient: Musée de la Compagnie des Indes, 2020).

Northrup, D., *Indentured Labor in the Age of Imperialism, 1834–1922* (Cambridge: Cambridge University Press, 1995).

—, 'Indentured Indians in the French Antilles. Les immigrants indiens engagés aux Antilles françaises', *Revue française d'histoire d'outre-mer*, vol. 87, nos. 326–7 (2000), pp. 245–71.

Nussbaum, F. L., 'The Formation of the New East India Company of Calonne', *The American Historical Review*, vol. 38, no. 3 (1933), pp. 475–97.

Oaten, E. F., *European Travellers in India During the Fifteenth, Sixteenth, and Seventeenth Centuries* (London: Kegan Paul Trench Trübner and Co., 1909).

Olagnier, P., *Les Jésuites à Pondichéry et l'affaire Naniapa (1705 à 1720)* (Paris: Société de l'histoire des colonies françaises, 1932).

—, *Un grand colonial inconnu: le gouverneur Benoist Dumas* (Paris: Société de l'histoire des colonies françaises, 1936).

Owen, S. J., 'Count Lally', *The English Historical Review*, vol. 6, no. 23 (1891), pp. 495–534.

Parthesius, R., *Dutch Ships in Tropical Waters: the Development of the Dutch East India Company (VOC) Shipping Network in Asia 1595–1660* (Amsterdam: Amsterdam University Press, 2009).

Peabody, S., *'There Are No Slaves in France': The Political Culture of Race and Slavery in the Ancien Régime* (Oxford: Oxford University Press, 1997).

Perrod, P. A., *L'affaire Lally-Tolendal: le journal d'un juge* (Paris: C. Klincksieck, 1976).

—, 'La fin du rêve d'empire' in R. Vincent (ed.), *Pondichéry, 1671–1761: l'échec d'un rêve d'empire* (Paris: Éditions Autrement, 1993), pp. 221–31.

Pettigrew, W. A., *Freedom's Debt: The Royal African Company and the Politics of the Atlantic Slave Trade, 1672–1752* (Chapel Hill: University of North Carolina Press, 2013).

Platania, M. 'L'originalité de la politique française en Inde, 1750–1783. Grands établissements ou commerce?', *Bulletin de l'Institut Pierre Renouvin*, no. 34 (2011/2), pp. 91–102.

Pousse, M., *Le marquis de Bussy: l'Inde offerte à la France* (Paris: L'Harmattan, 2017).

Prakash, O., *European Commercial Enterprise in Pre-Colonial India: The New Cambridge History of India II.5* (Cambridge: Cambridge University Press, 1998).

Prentout, H., *L'Île de France sous Decaen, 1803–1810: essai sur la politique coloniale du premier Empire et la rivalité de la France et de l'Angleterre dans les Indes orientales* (Paris: Hachette, 1901).

Raffin, A., *Republican Citizenship in French Colonial Pondicherry, 1870–1914* (Amsterdam: Amsterdam University Press, 2022).

Rai, A., *The Legacy of French Rule in India (1674–1954): An Investigation of a Process of Creolization* (Pondicherry: Institut Français de Pondichéry, 2008).

Rao, V. N., D. Shulman and S. Subrahmanyam, *Textures of Time: Writing History in South India, 1600–1800* (Delhi: Permanent Black, 2006).

Ray, A., *The Merchant and the State: The French in India, 1666–1739*. Two volumes (New Delhi: Munshiram Manoharlal, 2004).

Ray, I., *The French East India Company and the Trade of the Indian Ocean: A Collection of Essays by Indrani Ray*. Edited by L. Subramanian (New Delhi: Munshiram Manoharlal, 1999).

Richards, J. F., *The Mughal Empire: The New Cambridge History of India I.5* (Cambridge, Cambridge University Press, 1993).

Rothrock, G. A., 'Seventeenth-Century India through French Eyes', *The Historian*, vol. 22, no. 2 (1960), pp. 163–84.

Rubiés, J. P., 'Race, Climate and Civilization in the Works of François Bernier' in M. Fourcade and I. G. Županov (eds.), *L'Inde des Lumières: discours, histoire, savoirs (XVIIe–XIXe siècle)* (Paris: École des hautes études en sciences sociales, 2013), pp. 53–78.

Sarkar, J., 'Haidar Ali's Invasion of the Eastern Carnatic, 1780' in I. Habib (ed.), *Resistance and Modernization under Haidar Ali and Tipu Sultan* (New Delhi: Tulika, 1999), pp. 21–34.

Schiffer, M. B., *Spectacular Flops: Game-Changing Technologies that Failed* (New York: Eliot Werner, 2019).

Seeley, J. R., *The Expansion of England: Two Courses of Lectures* (London: Macmillan & Co., 1883).

Sen, S. N., *Chandernagore: From Bondage to Freedom 1900–1955* (New Delhi: Primus Books, 2012).

Sen, S. P., *The French in India, 1763–1816* (New Delhi: Munshiram Manoharlal, 1971).

Sherwani, H. K., *History of the Qutb Shahi Dynasty* (New Delhi: Munshiram Manoharlal, 1974).

Shovlin, J., *Trading with the Enemy: Britain, France, and the 18th-Century Quest for a Peaceful World Order* (New Haven and London: Yale University Press, 2021).

Sinha, A., *The Politics of Trade, Anglo-French Commerce on the Coromandel Coast, 1763–1793* (New Delhi: Manohar, 2002).

Sinha, N. K., *Haidar Ali* (Calcutta: A. Mukherjee & Co., 1941).

Sivasundaram, S., *Waves Across the South: A New History of Revolution and Empire* (London: William Collins, 2020).

Smith, B., 'Révolution(s) en Inde: dimensions coloniales, diplomatiques et culturelles, 1789–1799', *Outre-Mers*, vol. 103, nos 388–9 (2015), pp. 65–77.

—, 'The Failed Empire: France's Troubled Obsession with India', *The Caravan*, 1 March 2018, https://caravanmagazine.in/reviews-essays/france-troubled-obsession-with-india (accessed 9.3.24)

Stephen, S. J., *Pondicherry Under the French: Illuminating the Urban Landscape, 1674–1793* (Delhi: Primus Books, 2018).

Stern, P. J., *The Company-State: Corporate Sovereignty and the Early Modern Foundations of the British Empire in India* (Oxford: Oxford University Press, 2011).

Stockley, A., *Britain and France at the Birth of America: The European Powers and the Peace Negotiations of 1782–1783* (Exeter: University of Exeter Press, 2001).

Subrahmanyam, S., *The Portuguese Empire in Asia, 1500–1700: A Political and Economic History* (Chichester: Wiley-Blackwell, 2012).

Taffin, D. 'Citoyens et Malabars à Pondichéry pendant la Révolution française' in C. Wanquet (ed.), *Révolution française et océan Indien: prémices, paroxysmes, héritages et déviances* (Paris: L'Harmattan, 1996), pp. 235–48.

Thompson, V. M., *Dupleix and His Letters (1742–1754)* (New York: Robert O. Ballou, 1933).

Vaghi, M., *La France et l'Inde: commerces et politique impériale au XVIIIe siècle* (Sesto San Giovanni: Mimesis, 2016).

Vaughan, M., *Creating the Creole Island: Slavery in Eighteenth Century Mauritius* (Durham and London: Duke University Press, 2005).

Veevers, D., *The Origins of the British Empire in Asia, 1600–1750* (Cambridge: Cambridge University Press, 2020).

Vincent, R., 'Dupleix: une ambitieuse politique' in R. Vincent (ed.), *Pondichéry, 1671–1761: l'échec d'un rêve d'empire* (Paris: Éditions Autrement, 1993), pp. 121–43.

—, 'Relations franco-anglaises avant 1754 de l'amitié à l'affrontement' in J. Weber (ed.), *Les relations entre la France et l'Inde de 1673 à nos jours* (Paris: Les Indes Savantes, 2002), pp. 73–82.

— (ed.), *L'aventure des Français en Inde, du XVIIe au XXe siècle* (Pondicherry: Kailash, 2011).

—, 'L'apogée de Pondichéry' in R. Vincent (ed.), *L'aventure des Français en Inde, du XVIIe au XXe siècle* (Pondicherry: Kailash, 2011), pp. 62–95.

Vigié, M., *Dupleix* (Paris: Fayard, 1993).

Wanquet, C., *Histoire d'une révolution, La Réunion (1789–1803)*. Three volumes (Marseille: J. Laffitte, 1981–84).

—, 'Les îles Mascareignes, l'Inde et les Indiens pendant la Révolution française', *Revue française d'histoire d'outre-mer*, vol. 78, no. 290 (1991), pp. 29–57.

Weber, H., *La Compagnie française des Indes (1604–1875)* (Paris: A. Rousseau, 1904).

Weber, J., *Les établissements français en Inde au XIXe siècle (1816–1914)*. Five volumes (Paris: Librairie de l'Inde, 1988)

—, 'Chanemougam, "King of French India": Social and Political Foundations of an Absolute Power under the Third Republic', *Economic and Political Weekly*, vol. 26, no. 6 (1991), pp. 291–302.

—, 'La mosaïque pondichérienne' in R. Vincent (ed.), *Pondichéry, 1671–1761: l'échec d'un rêve d'empire* (Paris: Éditions Autrement, 1993), pp. 144–63.

—, *Pondichéry et les comptoirs de l'Inde après Dupleix: la démocratie au pays des castes* (Paris: Denöel, 1996).

— (ed.), *Les relations entre la France et l'Inde de 1673 à nos jours* (Paris: Les Indes Savantes, 2002), pp. 73–82.

—, *La France et l'Inde des origines à nos jours*. Four volumes (Paris: Les Indes Savantes, 2019–22).

Wilson, J., *India Conquered: Britain's Raj and the Chaos of Empire* (London: Simon & Schuster, 2016).

INDEX